For David K ✓ Y0-CAR-595

for the admiration
and affection —

Jan. 2, 2014

THE EMBATTLED CONSTITUTION

The Embattled Constitution

Edited by Norman Dorsen

With Catharine DeJulio

NEW YORK UNIVERSITY PRESS

New York and London

NEW YORK UNIVERSITY PRESS
New York and London
www.nyupress.org

References to Internet websites (URLs) were accurate at the time of writing.
Neither the author nor New York University Press is responsible for URLs that
may have expired or changed since the manuscript was prepared.

LIBRARY OF CONGRESS CATALOGING-IN-PUBLICATION DATA
The embattled constitution / edited by Norman Dorsen with Catharine DeJulio.
pages cm
"Fourth volume of the James Madison lectures."
Includes bibliographical references and index.
ISBN 978-0-8147-7012-2 (cloth : alk. paper)
1. Constitutional law—United States. I. Dorsen, Norman, editor of compilation.
II. DeJulio, Catharine, editor of compilation.
KF4550.A2E65   2013
342.73—dc23   2012049427

New York University Press books are printed on acid-free paper, and their binding materials
are chosen for strength and durability. We strive to use environmentally responsible suppliers
and materials to the greatest extent possible in publishing our books.

Manufactured in the United States of America

10 9 8 7 6 5 4 3 2 1

This Book Is Dedicated To

M. BLANE MICHAEL '68
Late Judge of the U.S. Court of Appeals for the Fourth Circuit
James Madison Lecturer 2009

CONTENTS

Acknowledgments   ix

Introduction   1
  Norman Dorsen

1 Our Democratic Constitution   7
  Stephen Breyer

2 Federal and State Courts: Restoring a Workable Balance   37
  Guido Calabresi

3 Judicial Methodology, Southern School Desegregation,   55
  and the Rule of Law
  David S. Tatel

4 Our Eighteenth-Century Constitution   107
  in the Twenty-First-Century World
  Diane P. Wood

5 Judging under the Constitution: Dicta about Dictum   139
  Pierre N. Leval

6 Judge Henry Friendly and the Mirror of Constitutional Law   169
  Michael Boudin

7 Toward One America: A Vision in Law   193
  J. Harvie Wilkinson III

8 Securing Fragile Foundations: Affirmative   207
  Constitutional Adjudication in Federal Courts
  Marsha S. Berzon

9 Reading the Fourth Amendment: Guidance   245
   from the Mischief That Gave It Birth
   M. Blane Michael

10 Living Our Traditions   273
    Robert H. Henry

11 Statutes   297
    Robert A. Katzmann

   About the Contributors   357

   About the Editors   359

   Index   361

ACKNOWLEDGMENTS

My principal thanks are to Cate DeJulio, '11, who worked closely with me from the beginning in editing this book and did so intelligently, efficiently, and with unfailing good humor.

Dean Richard Revesz has supported the James Madison lectures with enthusiasm and wisdom.

Linda Anderson of the Law School's Development Office conscientiously handled countless administrative details in organizing the lecture programs and bringing them to fruition.

Along with her many other duties, my assistant Gail Thomas worked constructively on many aspects of these lectures.

INTRODUCTION

NORMAN DORSEN

The publication of *The Embattled Constitution*, the fourth volume of the James Madison lectures, which were founded in 1959, marks a new phase of constitutional law and civil liberties.[1] The lectures published here appear at a time when the Supreme Court is sharply polarized, with seemingly intractable political forces sustaining, indeed encouraging, its ideological divisions.

The Supreme Court has always been split. In the 1920s and 1930s three Justices—Holmes, Brandeis, and Stone—sought to overthrow the Court's constitutional formalism that invalidated legislative attempts to soften the rigors of laissez-faire capitalism while simultaneously rejecting most civil liberties claims. In 1937 they succeeded.[2] A brief period of near unanimity among the Justices unraveled in the early 1940s, when the Court was closely divided on many issues, often with five conservatives facing four liberals. In the middle and late 1950s, a similar 5–4 conservative majority tended to dominate.[3]

But by the time the first four James Madison lectures were published in 1963, in *The Great Rights*, the Court had begun to fashion remarkable changes in constitutional law. The years 1962–1969 was the only period in American history when a majority of Justices were determined to expand civil liberties in many spheres, including free speech, religious liberty, racial justice, privacy, and criminal justice. The Madison lectures contributed to the intellectual climate that nurtured a broader judicial conception of the Constitution. In 1960, in the first lecture, Justice Black publicly presented his theory of an "absolute" constitutional protection for free expression. The next year Chief Justice Warren discussed principles for weighing government claims of military necessity against individual freedoms. In 1962, Justice Douglas presented the thesis that the people of the United States needed even broader protections than are provided by the Bill of Rights; he hoped that this approach would lead to a "renaissance in liberty." Finally, Justice Brennan plowed a subject that is as old as the country—the relationship between the states and the Bill of Rights.

Civil libertarians at the time could be pardoned for exuding an unaccustomed optimism, reflected in Edmond Cahn's preface to *The Great Rights*. He said, "Year by year, save only its mottled performance in the field of national security, the Court seems to bring deeper understanding, wider sympathy, and more intelligent analysis to the moral aspects of legal problems," by which he meant the sort of views contained in the first Madison lectures. But such attitudes proved, at best, to be premature.

The Evolving Constitution, the second volume of James Madison lectures, was published in 1987, its title aptly summarizing developments after 1963. As noted above, the remainder of the 1960s constituted the high water mark of civil liberties. The ensuing period was one of increasingly conservative doctrine, generated mainly by new Supreme Court Justices, concerning the rights of poor people, the right to travel, and the death penalty, among other issues.

Nevertheless, during this period the Court provided greater (but far from complete) protection for racial minorities, protection against sex discrimination, some free-expression and religious-freedom victories, and the sexual-privacy decisions in *Griswold v. Connecticut* and *Roe v. Wade*, which went beyond constitutional text (as Justice Douglas's James Madison lecture had urged) to protect rights to contraceptives and abortion as part of family planning. The Court's failure in 1985 to recognize the sexual privacy of homosexuals in *Bowers v. Hardwick* was a bitter pill. But it illustrates how the Constitution "evolves"; the case was overruled in 2003.

The lectures published in *The Evolving Constitution* included articles on equality and free speech that built on the jurisprudence of the 1960s; there were articles that looked forward to the judicial protections eventually accorded women and, much later, homosexuals; and there was analysis of statutory rights accorded the elderly and physically disabled. Other articles focused on the administration of justice and the importance of precedent.

The third volume of Madison lectures, aptly titled *The Unpredictable Constitution*, appeared in 2002. While the book was being prepared for publication, the Supreme Court decided *Bush v. Gore*, which determined the 2000 presidential election in a scenario that was almost unthinkable to those familiar with the Court's history and practices. The ruling was "political" not only in the sense that it decisively affected the political direction of the country, and not merely in that the Court's ruling had no judicial precedent. Even more striking, the two rationales provided by the five-person majority—one involving the asserted requirements of the Electoral College and the other an equality theory—were so lacking in constitutional backing that critics believed the justices in the majority were driven by a fixed desire to reach a foreordained result.

There were other unexpected decisions during this period, including the worrying possibilities offered by two cases in the mid-1990s that departed from sixty years of precedent to impose limits on Congress's power to legislate under the Commerce Clause. A few years later the Court seemed to return to its longstanding consensus that counseled deference to congressional judgments concerning the commerce power. The recent Supreme Court decision upholding the individual insurance mandate of the Affordable Care Act ("Obamacare") under Congress's taxing power rather than the commerce power leaves this important constitutional area still unsettled despite Chief Justice Roberts's dicta, if adopted, that would narrow the scope of the Commerce Clause.

The Unpredictable Constitution addressed other difficult and uncertain issues. Two creative lectures analyzed the "reasonable doubt" standard for criminal convictions and the "harmless error" rule, questions that arise regularly in constitutional cases. Other lectures addressed the scope of habeas corpus; denounced a Supreme Court decision that affirmed a death penalty despite substantial doubts of the prisoner's guilt; criticized a series of rulings, including one upholding sex segregation at the Virginia Military Institute, because they allegedly disguised normative goals with vague and unworkable interpretive principles; and bemoaned the apparent inconsistency in the way that states allocate benefits under government assistance programs.[4]

The current collection of lectures in *The Embattled Constitution* appears at a time when the two wings of the Supreme Court have become more intensely divided, with the four Justices in each camp locked in on certain types of cases. Very often, decisions are determined by the "swing" Justice, earlier Sandra Day O'Connor and now Anthony Kennedy. Although the Justices have issued a considerable number of unanimous or near-unanimous decisions, such agreement is rare in major constitutional cases. Indeed, lawyers tend to direct their arguments to the Court principally to the Justice who seems to hold the deciding vote.

Pending before the Court, or decided after this volume went to press, are issues that, when the dust settles, will clarify what kind of country we are. Among these are abortion, racial affirmative action, criminal justice, the status of homosexuals, the scope of congressional legislative authority, the wartime power of the President, and the many-sided relationship between religion and government. Some of these matters were once thought to be settled, or at least confined to narrow points of difference, but that is not the case now. The Constitution is truly embattled.

The lectures in this book span a wide area. Four of them concern intertwined methodological and substantive questions. Judge Pierre Leval discusses the implications of dicta, a frequent issue for judges in all courts. Judge Robert Katzmann, making extensive use of legislative materials, probes a range of approaches to statutory interpretation. Judge Guido Calabresi, seeking a workable balance between federal and state courts, evaluates aspects of federal jurisdiction, including diversity cases and the gnawing problems of state action. And Judge Diane Wood convincingly exposes the deficiencies of originalism as a guide to constitutional and statutory interpretation.

Two lecturers look to leading jurists of an earlier generation as models. Former Judge Robert Henry describes Justice John Marshall Harlan as the quintessential principled conservative, striving to preserve traditional constitutional values while being willing to adapt the Constitution to new circumstances and insights. Judge Michael Boudin celebrates Judge Henry Friendly, a judge of the U.S. Court of Appeals for the Second Circuit, for whom he clerked. Friendly was virtually unmatched for his intellect, learning, and creativity, and he has been lionized as a leading judge of his era.[5] Coincidentally, Justice Harlan and Judge Friendly practiced law together for many years and were close friends.

Other lecturers criticize certain Supreme Court decisions. Judge Marsha Berzon focuses on "Bivens actions," that is, private suits for damages against federal officials who violate an individual's constitutional rights. The Constitution does not mention such actions, but the Court in 1971 held that they could be implied as an appropriate remedy to enforce constitutional rights. Judge Berzon's lecture recounts how the Court has recently narrowed the scope of these implied remedies at a great cost to civil liberties.

Judge David Tatel traces the path of school desegregation following the Supreme Court's iconic 1954 ruling in *Brown v. Board of Education* that "in the field of public education the doctrine of 'separate but equal' has no place," and its 1968 decision holding that states have an affirmative duty to eliminate racial segregation "root and branch." After an exhaustive review, Judge Tatel shows how the Court, sometimes in disingenuous opinions, has retreated from these principles.

Judge M. Blane Michael turns to history to provide a guide to the substantive content of the Fourth Amendment. In many cases the Supreme Court has rejected individual claims of privacy, for example, to deposit slips or financial statements that had been provided to a bank, while in other disputes, such as those over computer files stored online, the lower courts are still wrestling with the issue. Michael avoids broad prescriptions. He emphasizes that the issues present at the country's founding still exist in altered form, and argues that appropriate solutions can be facilitated by astute application of longstanding principles.[6]

All the lectures in the book cast an eye toward the future as well as the past. But Judge J. Harvie Wilkinson and Justice Stephen Breyer, in particular, propose solutions for the current divisions. Judge Wilkinson condemns the "sheer magnitude of mutual hate," and he urges a turn to national unity, not as a form of superficial patriotism but as a way of reconciling the extraordinary diversity of American society. To achieve this end, Judge Wilkinson asserts that law is indispensable and process is the key to making law work.

Justice Breyer takes another tack. His lecture was delivered in 2001, before the polarization of either the Supreme Court or the body politic reached its current level. Resting on the work of Benjamin Constant, a French political philosopher, Breyer discusses the liberty of the "ancients," that is, the Greeks and Romans, who encouraged increased participation by the people in public affairs. To this he contrasts the "modern liberty" of the eighteenth and nineteenth centuries, which focused on individual independence from government restriction. Breyer considers both to be important ingredients of liberty, but he argues that judges, by placing "greater emphasis" on ancient liberty, will encourage a more flourishing democracy as well as governmental actions "consistent with individual dignity and community need."

We cannot know, if their ideas are adopted, whether Judge Wilkinson's or Justice Breyer's approach might mitigate harsh differences within the Court. Nor can we know whether the proposals of the other Madison lecturers represented in this book would improve the rationality and justness of the law. What we do know is that neither a system of judicial review nor a fair system of government can exist without the sort of informed and disinterested analysis that these lectures provide.

NOTES

1. The James Madison lectures are a project of the Arthur Garfield Hays Civil Liberties Program at New York University School of Law.

2. The transformative cases were West Coast Hotel v. Parrish, 300 U.S. 309 (1937) (Fourteenth Amendment due process) and NLRB v. Jones and Laughlin Steel Corp., 301 U.S. 1 (1937) (Commerce Clause).

3. During the 1940s, the liberal Justices were Hugo Black, William O. Douglas, Frank Murphy, and Wiley Rutledge. In the late 1950s they were Black, Douglas, Earl Warren, and William Brennan. The majorities during these periods were shifting, and there were many cases in which the liberal faction prevailed.

4. The founders of the Madison lectures stipulated that they be delivered by an appellate federal judge, that is, a Justice of the U.S. Supreme Court or a judge of a U.S. court of appeals. The only departure from this pattern occurred in 2000, when the Lord Chancellor of Great Britain, the Rt. Honorable Lord Irvine of Lairg, was invited to commemorate the fortieth anniversary of the series and to celebrate the Law School's Hauser Global Law School Program.

5. My brother, David M. Dorsen, has written a biography of Judge Friendly, published in March 2012, entitled *Judge Henry Friendly: Greatest Judge of His Era.*

6. Judge Michael, to whom this book is dedicated, was a 1968 graduate of New York University School of Law. He was devoted to the public interest throughout his career and was an outstanding federal judge. He died in 2010.

1

Our Democratic Constitution

STEPHEN BREYER

The United States is a nation built on principles of human liberty—a liberty that embraces concepts of democracy. The French political philosopher Benjamin Constant understood the connection. He distinguished between liberty as practiced by the ancient Greeks and Romans and the "liberty" of the eighteenth- and nineteenth-century "moderns."[1] Writing thirty years after the French Revolution and not long after the adoption of our American Constitution, Constant said that the "liberty of the ancients" consisted of an "active and constant participation in collective power."[2] The ancient world, he added, believed that liberty consisted of "submitting to all the citizens, without exception, the care and assessment of their most sacred interests."[3] Liberty thereby "ennobles their thoughts, and establishes among them a kind of intellectual equality which forms the glory and power of a people."[4]

Constant distinguished that "liberty of the ancients" from the more "modern liberty" consisting of "individual independence" from governmental restriction.[5] Having seen the Terror, he argued that this "liberty of the moderns" was necessary to protect the individual from the excesses of democratic majorities and those acting in their name. But, he said, we must not renounce "either of the two sorts of freedom[;] . . . it is necessary . . . to learn to combine the two together."[6]

This lecture was delivered on October 22, 2001, and appeared in *77 N.Y.U. L. Rev.* 245 (2002). Justice Breyer expanded upon his lecture in Stephen Breyer, *Active Liberty* (2005).

The ideas that underlie these concepts, including the importance of citizen participation in government, were in the minds of those who helped to create America's government. Jefferson, for example, spoke directly of the rights of the citizen as "a participator in the government of affairs,"[7] and Adams referred to the importance of ensuring that all citizens have a "positive Passion for the public good."[8] My discussion concerns the role that this more "ancient," participatory, active liberty might play when courts interpret the Constitution, including its more "modern" individual liberty-protecting provisions.[9]

I shall focus upon several contemporary problems that call for governmental action and potential judicial reaction. In each instance I shall argue that, when judges interpret the Constitution, they should place greater emphasis upon the "ancient liberty," i.e., the people's right to "an active and constant participation in collective power."[10] I believe that increased emphasis upon this active liberty will lead to better constitutional law—law that will promote governmental solutions consistent with individual dignity and community need.

At the same time, my discussion will illustrate an approach to constitutional interpretation that places considerable weight upon consequences—consequences valued by basic constitutional purposes. It disavows a contrary constitutional approach, a more "legalistic" approach that places too much weight upon language, history, tradition, and precedent alone while understating the importance of consequences. If the discussion helps to convince you that the more "consequential" approach has virtue, so much the better.

I.
A.

Three important views underlie my discussion. First, the Constitution, considered as a whole, creates a framework for a certain kind of government. Its general objectives can be described abstractly as including: (1) democratic self-government; (2) dispersion of power (avoiding concentration of too much power in too few hands); (3) individual dignity (through protection of individual liberties); (4) equality before the law (through equal protection of the law); and (5) the rule of law itself.[11]

The Constitution embodies these general objectives in particular provisions. In respect to self-government, for example, Article IV guarantees a "Republican Form of Government";[12] Article I insists that Congress meet at least once a year,[13] that elections take place every two[14] (or six)[15] years, and that a census take place every decade;[16] the Fifteenth,[17] Nineteenth,[18] Twenty-fourth,[19] and Twenty-sixth[20] Amendments secure virtually universal adult suffrage. But a general constitutional objective such as self-government plays a constitutional role beyond the interpretation of an individual provision that refers to it directly. That is because constitutional courts must consider the relation of one provision to another. They must consider the document as a whole.[21] And consequently, the document's handful of general purposes will inform judicial interpretation of many clauses that do not refer directly to the general objective in question. My examples seek to show how that is so. And, as I have said, they will suggest a need for judges to pay greater attention to one of those general objectives, namely participatory democratic self-government.

Second, the Court, while always respecting language, tradition, and precedent, nonetheless has emphasized different constitutional objectives at different periods in its history. Thus, one can characterize the early nineteenth century as a period during which the Court helped to establish the authority of the federal government, including the federal judiciary.[22] During the late nineteenth and early twentieth centuries, the Court underemphasized the Constitution's efforts to secure participation by African American citizens in representative government—efforts related to the participatory "active liberty" of the ancients.[23] At the same time, it overemphasized protection of property rights, such as an individual's freedom to contract without government interference,[24] to the point where President Franklin Roosevelt commented that the Court's *Lochner*-era decisions had created a legal "no-man's land" that neither state nor federal regulatory authority had the power to enter.[25]

The New Deal Court and the Warren Court emphasized "active liberty." The former did so by dismantling various *Lochner*-era distinctions, thereby expanding the scope of democratic self-government.[26] The latter did so by interpreting the Civil War Amendments in light of their purposes to mean what they say, thereby helping African Americans become members of the nation's community of self-governing citizens—a community that the Court expanded further in its "one person, one vote" decisions.[27]

More recently, in my view, the Court has again underemphasized the importance of the citizen's active liberty. I will argue for a contemporary emphasis that better combines "the liberty of the ancients" with that "freedom of governmental restraint" that Constant called "modern."

Third, the real-world consequences of a particular interpretive decision, valued in terms of basic constitutional purposes, play an important
role in constitutional decision making. To that extent, my approach differs from that of judges who would place nearly exclusive interpretive
weight upon language, history, tradition, and precedent. In truth, the difference is one of degree. Virtually all judges, when interpreting a constitution or a statute, refer at one time or another to language, to history, to
tradition, to precedent, to purpose, and to consequences. Even those who
take a more literal approach to constitutional interpretation sometimes
find consequences and general purposes relevant. But the more "literalist" judge tends to ask those who cannot find an interpretive answer in
language, history, tradition, and precedent alone to rethink the problem
several times before making consequences determinative. The more literal judges may hope to find, in language, history, tradition, and precedent objective interpretive standards; they may seek to avoid an interpretive subjectivity that could confuse a judge's personal idea of what is
good for that which the Constitution demands; and they may believe that
these "original" sources more readily will yield rules that can guide other
institutions, including lower courts. These objectives are desirable, but I
do not think the literal approach will achieve them, and, in any event,
the constitutional price is too high. I hope that my examples will help
to show why that is so, as well as to persuade you that it is important to
place greater weight upon constitutionally valued consequences, my consequential focus in this lecture being the effect of a court's decisions upon
active liberty.

B.

To recall the fate of Socrates is to understand that the "liberty of the
ancients" is not a sufficient condition for human liberty. Nor can we rep-
licate today the ideal represented by the Athenian agora or the New England town meeting. Nonetheless, today's citizen does participate in democratic self-governing processes. And the "active liberty" to which I refer
consists of the Constitution's efforts to secure the citizen's right to do so.

To focus upon that active liberty, to understand it as one of the Constitution's handful of general objectives, will lead judges to consider the constitutionality of statutes with a certain modesty. That modesty embodies
an understanding of the judges' own expertise compared, for example,
with that of a legislature. It reflects the concern that a judiciary too ready

to "correct" legislative error may deprive "the people" of "the political experience, and the moral education and stimulus that come from . . . correcting their own errors."[28] It encompasses that doubt, caution, prudence, and concern—that state of not being "too sure" of oneself—that Learned Hand described as the "spirit of liberty."[29] In a word, it argues for traditional "judicial restraint."

But active liberty argues for more than that. I shall suggest that increased recognition of the Constitution's general democratic participatory objectives can help courts deal more effectively with a range of specific constitutional issues. I shall use examples drawn from the areas of free speech, federalism, privacy, equal protection, and statutory interpretation. In each instance, I shall refer to an important modern problem of government that calls for a democratic response. I shall then describe related constitutional implications. I want to draw a picture of some of the different ways that increased judicial focus upon the Constitution's participatory objectives can have a positive effect.

In emphasizing active liberty, I do not intend to understate the great importance of securing other basic constitutional objectives, such as personal liberty—what Constant called "modern liberty"—and equal protection. Obviously courts must offer protection against governmental infringement of those rights, including infringement by democratic majorities. What could be more important? Yet modern (or "negative") liberty is not the primary subject of this lecture.

II.
A.

I begin with free speech and campaign finance reform. The campaign finance problem arises out of the recent explosion in campaign costs along with a vast disparity among potential givers. A typical contested House seat in the 2000 election, for example, led to campaign expenditures of $308,000 per candidate (an open contested seat averaged about $522,000 per candidate); a typical contested Senate seat led to expenditures of $2.7 million per candidate (an open seat averaged about $6.1 million per candidate); and the two major-party presidential candidates spent approximately $306 million.[30] In 1999, congressional candidates together spent over $1 billion.[31] Only nine years earlier, the comparable costs were about a third of that—$340 million.[32] Comparable figures from abroad show far lower expenditures, with a British or Canadian

Parliamentary candidature leading to direct campaign expenditure of about $13,000 and $43,000, respectively.[33] A major cause of the difference seems to be the cost of television advertising time, which now approximates $10,000 per minute in a major city; in the 2000 election parties and candidates spent between $770 million and $1 billion on television ads.[34]

A very small number of individuals underwrite a very large share of these enormous costs. The *New York Times* reports that the major parties collected $137 million dollars in soft money (money that avoids most current legal restrictions) during the 2000 campaign.[35] And 739 contributors provided two-thirds of this sum—making an average contribution of about $100,000 each.[36] That is 739 citizens out of the 200 million or more citizens eligible to vote—a minuscule percentage.[37] Indeed, only four percent of those 200 million citizens contributed anything at all.[38] The upshot is a concern by some that the matter is out of hand—that too few individuals contribute too much money and that, even though money is not the only way to obtain influence, those who give large amounts of money do obtain, or appear to obtain, too much influence. The end result is a marked inequality of participation. That is one important reason why legislatures have sought to regulate the size of campaign contributions.

The basic constitutional question is not the desirability of reform legislation but whether, how, or to what extent the First Amendment permits the legislature to impose limitations or ceilings on the amounts individuals, organizations, or parties can contribute to a campaign or on the kinds of contributions they can make. The Court has considered this kind of question several times; I have written opinions in some of those cases;[39] and here I shall not go beyond what I previously have written.

One cannot (or, at least, I cannot) find an easy answer to the constitutional questions in language, history, or tradition. The First Amendment's language says that Congress shall not abridge "the freedom of speech."[40] But it does not define "the freedom of speech" in any detail. The nation's founders did not speak directly about campaign contributions. Madison, who decried faction, thought that members of Congress would fairly represent all their constituents, in part because the "electors" would not be the "rich" any "more than the poor."[41] But this kind of statement, while modestly helpful to the campaign reform cause, is hardly determinative.

Neither can I find answers in purely conceptual arguments. Some argue, for example, that "money is speech"; others say "money is not speech." But neither contention helps much. Money is not speech, it is money. But the expenditure of money enables speech; and that expenditure is often necessary to communicate a message, particularly in a political context. A law that forbids the expenditure of money to convey a message could effectively suppress that communication.

Nor does it resolve the matter simply to point out that campaign contribution limits inhibit the political "speech opportunities" of those who wish to contribute more. Indeed, that is so. But the question is whether, in context, such a limitation abridges "the freedom of speech." And to announce that this kind of harm could never prove justified in a political context is simply to state an ultimate constitutional conclusion; it is not to explain the underlying reasons.

To refer to the Constitution's general participatory self-government objective, its protection of "active liberty," is far more helpful. That is because that constitutional goal indicates that the First Amendment's constitutional role is not simply one of protecting the individual's "negative" freedom from governmental restraint. The Amendment in context also forms a necessary part of a constitutional system designed to sustain that democratic self-government. The Amendment helps to sustain the democratic process both by encouraging the exchange of ideas needed to make sound electoral decisions and by encouraging an exchange of views among ordinary citizens necessary to their informed participation in the electoral process. It thereby helps to maintain a form of government open to participation (in Constant's words, by "all the citizens, without exception").[42] The relevance of this conceptual view lies in the fact that the campaign finance laws also seek to further the latter objective. They hope to democratize the influence that money can bring to bear upon the electoral process, thereby building public confidence in that process, broadening the base of a candidate's meaningful financial support, and encouraging greater public participation. They consequently seek to maintain the integrity of the political process—a process that itself translates political speech into governmental action. Seen in this way, campaign finance laws, despite the limits they impose, help to further the kind of open public political discussion that the First Amendment also seeks to encourage, not simply as an end, but also as a means to achieve a workable democracy.

For this reason, I have argued that a court should approach most campaign finance questions with the understanding that important First Amendment–related interests lie on both sides of the constitutional equation and that a First Amendment presumption hostile to government regulation, such as "strict scrutiny," is consequently out of place.[43] Rather, the court considering the matter without the benefit of presumptions must look realistically at the legislation's impact, both its negative impact on the ability of some to engage in as much communication as they wish and the positive impact upon the public's confidence and consequent ability to communicate through (and participate in) the electoral process.

The basic question the Court should ask is one of proportionality. Do the statutes strike a reasonable balance between their electoral speech-restricting and speech-enhancing consequences? Or do they instead impose restrictions on that speech that are disproportionate when measured against their corresponding electoral and speech-related benefits, taking into account the kind, the importance, and the extent of those benefits, as well as the need for the restrictions in order to secure them?

The judicial modesty discussed earlier suggests that, in answering these questions, courts should defer to the legislature's own answers insofar as those answers reflect empirical matters about which the legislature is comparatively expert, for example, the extent of the campaign finance problem, a matter that directly concerns the realities of political life. But courts cannot defer when evaluating the risk that reform legislation will defeat the very objective of participatory self-government itself—for example, where laws would set limits so low as to elevate the reputation-related or media-related advantages of incumbency to the point where they would insulate incumbents from effective challenge.

I am not saying that focus upon active liberty will automatically answer the constitutional question in particular campaign finance cases. I argue only that such focus will help courts find a proper route for arriving at an answer. The positive constitutional goal implies a systemic role for the First Amendment; and that role, in turn, suggests a legal framework, i.e., a more particular set of questions for the Court to ask. Modesty suggests where, and how, courts should defer to legislatures in doing so. The suggested inquiry is complex. But courts both here and abroad have engaged in similarly complex inquiries where the constitutionality of electoral laws is at issue. That complexity is demanded by a Constitution that provides for judicial review of the constitutionality of electoral rules while granting Congress the effective power to secure a fair electoral system.

Focus upon participatory self-government also helps where other kinds of First Amendment problems are at issue. Our Court recently reviewed, for example, a federal law that required every mushroom grower to contribute to a common mushroom grower advertising fund.[44]

The Court, believing that the law amounted to pure regulation of speech unmixed with other forms of regulation, applied certain First Amendment antiregulation presumptions and agreed with the objecting mushroom grower that the law was unconstitutional. I disagreed, primarily because I did not find the pure-speech/mixed-speech distinction persuasive.[45]

The problem that the case reflects is more important than its subject, mushrooms, initially implies. It asks when courts should distinguish among different speech-related activities for the purpose of applying a strict, or moderately strict, presumption of unconstitutionality. And that is an important and difficult question to answer.

There are those who argue for limiting distinctions on the ground that the Constitution does not distinguish among kinds of speech.[46] The Constitution protects "the freedom of speech" from government restriction. "Speech is speech and that is the end of the matter." But to limit distinctions to the point where First Amendment law embodies the slogan "speech is speech" cannot work. That is because the Constitution, including the First Amendment, seeks more than an individual's "negative" freedom from government restriction. It also seeks democratic government. And citizens use speech to conduct virtually all the activities they would have government regulate.

Today's workers manipulate information, not wood or metal. Yet the modern, information-based workplace, no less than its more materially based predecessors, requires the application of community standards seeking to assure, for example, the absence of anticompetitive restraints, the accuracy of information, the absence of discrimination, the protection of health, safety, the environment, the consumer, and so forth.

Laws that embody these standards affect speech. Warranty laws require private firms to include on labels statements of a specified content. Securities laws and consumer protection laws insist upon the disclosure of information that businesses might prefer to keep private. For example, health laws forbid tobacco advertising to children. Agriculture laws, like the mushroom law, require farmers to pay for common product advertising. Antidiscrimination laws insist that employers prevent employees from making certain kinds of statements. Communications laws require cable broadcasters to provide network access. Campaign finance laws, as mentioned, restrict citizen contributions to candidates.

To treat all these instances alike, to scrutinize them all as if they all represented a similar kind of legislative effort to restrain a citizen's negative liberty to speak, would both lump together many different kinds of activities and seriously interfere with democratic self-government—unless, of course, the First Amendment were to be watered down to the point where it offered little meaningful protection. The kind of strong speech protection needed to guarantee a free democratic governing process, if applied to all governmental efforts to control speech without distinction (e.g., securities or warranties), would limit the public's economic and social choices well beyond any point that a liberty-protecting framework for democratic government could demand. That, along with a singular lack of modesty, was the failing of *Lochner*.[47] No one wants to replay that discredited history in modern First Amendment guise. Rather, virtually everyone, including "speech is speech" advocates, sees a need for distinctions. The question is, which ones?

At this point, reference back to the Constitution's more general objectives, including active liberty, helps in two ways. First, "active liberty" is particularly at risk when law restricts speech that takes place in areas related to politics and policymaking by elected officials. That special risk justifies special, strong pro-speech judicial presumptions in these areas.[48]

Second, where ordinary commercial or economic regulation is at issue, this special risk is absent. But there is more to consider. Here strong pro-speech presumptions themselves risk imposing what is, from the perspective of positive liberty, too severe a restriction upon the legislature—a restriction that would dramatically limit the size of the legislative arena that the Constitution opens for public action. That risk cautions against use of those special, strong pro-speech judicial presumptions.

This is not to say that in these latter areas, such as commercial speech or speech related to economic regulation, Congress, in legislating, is home free. Traditional, "modern," negative liberty—the individual's freedom from government restriction—remains critically important. Irrespective of context, a particular rule affecting speech could, in a particular instance, require individuals to act against conscience, inhibit public debate, threaten artistic expression, censor views in ways unrelated to a program's basic objectives, or create other risks of abuse. These possibilities themselves form the raw material out of which courts will create different presumptions applicable in different speech contexts. Even in the absence of presumptions, courts still will examine individual instances with the possibilities of such harm in mind.

What I am saying is that, in applying First Amendment presumptions, we must distinguish among areas, contexts, and forms of speech.

Reference to basic general constitutional purposes can help generate the relevant distinctions. And reference back to at least one general purpose, "active liberty," will help generate distinctions needed if the law is to deal effectively with such modern problems as campaign finance and workplace regulation.

B.

I turn next to federalism. My example below suggests a need to examine consequences valued in terms of active liberty.

The Court's recent federalism cases fall into three categories. First, the Court has held that Congress may not write laws that "commandeer" a state's legislative or executive officials, say by requiring a state legislature to write a particular kind of law (for example, a nuclear waste storage law)[49] or by requiring a local official to spend time enforcing a federal policy (for example, requiring a local sheriff to see whether a potential gun buyer has a criminal record).[50] Second, the Court has limited Congress's power (under the Commerce Clause or the Fourteenth Amendment) to force a state to waive its Eleventh Amendment immunity from suit by private citizens.[51] Third, the Court has limited the scope of Congress's Commerce Clause powers, finding that gun possession near local schools and violence against women in local communities did not sufficiently "affect" interstate commerce.[52]

Although I dissented in each case, I recognize that each holding protects liberty in its negative form—to some degree. Each of them, in one respect or another, makes it more difficult for the federal government to tell state and local governments what they must do. To that extent they free citizens from certain restraints that a more distant central government might otherwise impose. But constitutional principles of federalism involve active as well as negative freedom. They impose limitations upon the distant central government's decision making not simply as an antirestrictive end but also as a democracy-facilitating means.

Justice Sandra Day O'Connor has set forth many of the basic connections. By guaranteeing state and local governments broad decision-making authority, federalist principles facilitate "novel social and economic experiments,"[53] secure decisions that rest on knowledge of local circumstances,[54] and help to develop a sense of shared purposes among local citizens. Through increased transparency, they make it easier for citizens to hold government officials accountable. And by bringing government closer to home, they help maintain a sense of local community. In all these ways they facilitate and encourage citizen participation in governmental decision making—Constant's classical ideal. We must evaluate the Court's federalism decisions in terms of both forms of liberty. When we do so, we shall find that a cooperative federalism, allocating specific problem-related roles among national and state governments, will protect both forms of liberty, including the active liberty that the Court's decisions overlook.

A concrete example drawn from toxic chemical regulation exemplifies the kind of technologically based problem modern governments are asked to solve. Important parts of toxic substance regulation must take place at the national level. Chemical substances ignore state boundaries as they travel through air, water, or soil, and consequently they may affect the environment in more than one state. Their regulation demands a high level of scientific and technical expertise to which the federal government might have ready access, at least initially. A federal regulator might be better able than state regulators to create, for example, a uniform risk discourse designed to help ordinary citizens better understand the nature of risk. And only a federal regulator could set minimum substantive standards designed to avoid a race to the bottom among states hoping to attract industry.

At the same time, certain aspects of the problem seem better suited for decentralized regulation by state or local governments. The same amounts of the same chemical may produce different toxic effects depending upon local air, water, or soil conditions. The same standard will have different economic effects in different communities. And affected citizens in different communities may value the same level of toxic-substance cleanup quite differently. To what point should we clean up the local waste dump and at what cost?

Modern efforts to create more efficient regulation recognize the importance of that local involvement. They seek a kind of cooperative federalism that would, for example, permit federal officials to make expertise available to state and local officials while seeking to separate expert and fact-related matters from more locally based questions of value. They would also diminish reliance upon classical command-and-control regulation, supplementing that regulation with incentive-based, less restrictive regulatory methods, such as taxes and marketable rights. Such efforts, by placing greater power to participate and to decide in the hands of individuals and localities, can further both the negative and active liberty interests that underlie federalist principles. But will the Court's recent federalism decisions encourage or discourage those cooperative, or incentive-based, regulatory methods?

In my view, the "commandeering" decisions, such as *United States v. Printz*, might well hinder a cooperative program, for they could prevent Congress from enlisting local officials to check compliance with federal minimum standards.[55] Rather, Congress would have to create a federal enforcement bureaucracy (or, perhaps, create unnecessary federal spending programs). Given ordinary bureaucratic tendencies, that fact, other things being equal, will make it harder, not easier, to shift regulatory power to state and local governments. It will make it more difficult, not easier, to experiment with incentive-based regulatory methods. And while some argue that Congress can bypass the "commandeering" decisions through selective and aggressive exercise of its spending power (at least as that doctrine currently exists),[56] there is little evidence that Congress has taken this path.

I can make the same point with another example underlined by the tragic events of September 11. In a dissenting opinion, Justice Stevens wrote that the "threat of an international terrorist, may require a national response before federal personnel can be made available to respond . . . . Is there anything [in the Constitution] . . . that forbids the enlistment of state officers to make that response effective?"[57] That enlistment, by facilitating the participation of local and state officials, would help both the cause of effective security coordination and the cause of federalism.

The Eleventh Amendment decisions could hinder the adoption of certain kinds of "less restrictive" regulatory methods. Suppose, for example, that Congress, reluctant to expand the federal regulatory bureaucracy, wished to encourage citizen suits as a device for ensuring state-owned (as well as privately owned) toxic waste dump compliance. Or suppose that Congress, in order to encourage state or local governments to impose environmental taxes, provided for suits by citizens seeking to protest a particular tax assessment or to obtain a tax refund.

Decisions in the third category—the Court's recent Commerce Clause power decisions—would neither prohibit nor facilitate citizen participation in "cooperative" or "incentive-based" regulatory programs. Still, the Court's determination to reweigh congressional evidence of "interstate effects" creates uncertainty about how much evidence is needed to find the constitutionally requisite effect. And certain portions of the Court's reasoning, such as its refusal to aggregate "noneconomic" causes of interstate effects, create considerable doctrinal complexity.[58] Both may leave Congress uncertain about its ability to legislate the details of a cooperative federal, state, local, and regulatory framework. This uncertainty makes it less likely that Congress will enact those complex laws—laws necessarily of national scope. To that extent, one can see these decisions as unhelpful to the cause of active liberty.

I do not claim that these consequences alone can prove the majority's holding wrong. I suggest only that courts ask certain consequence-related questions and not rely entirely upon logical deduction from text or precedent. I ask why the Court should not at least consider the practical effects on local democratic self-government when it elaborates the Constitution's principles of federalism—principles that seek to further that kind of government.

The toxic substance example (and the current national crisis) also suggests a need for federal legislative flexibility. And that need, in turn, argues for a more flexible judicial approach. In this respect one might contrast the well-established judge-made doctrine applying the "dormant Commerce Clause."[59] That doctrine, also reflecting basic principles of federalism, focuses on local economic protectionism, another serious modern problem in a globalized economy. It requires courts to examine state laws that, for example, might prohibit importing peaches grown with certain pesticides, insist on the use of special steel for elevator cables, or prevent interstate trucks from transporting dynamite during daylight hours. Courts ask whether such laws reasonably protect a state's citizens from dangerous pesticides, faulty elevators, and risks of explosion, or whether, instead, they unreasonably protect the state's peach growers, steelmakers, and contractors from out-of-state competition.[60]

The relevant point here is that the Court's dormant Commerce Clause decisions are not final. Congress can overturn them by statute. It can also delegate the initial power to decide to an expert agency, such as the Federal Department of Transportation, which will, after opportunity for public comment, decide subject to judicial review for reasonableness. Compared to the more recent decisions, dormant Commerce Clause doctrine is flexible, permitting greater use of experts while permitting consideration of the Constitution's democratic objectives. It leaves the last word to the public acting through its elected representatives. It is a classic example of democracy-induced judicial modesty embodied in constitutional principle.

The dormant Commerce Clause, of course, is a different constitutional principle, and its history differs from the principles that underlie the Court's recent federalism decisions. But dormant Commerce Clause decisions raise a relevant question. Could courts find sets of presumptions that would work in similar ways, for example, "clear statement"[61] or "hard look"[62] requirements, which focus upon the thoroughness of the legislature's consideration of a matter and the explicit nature of its conclusion? My object here is not to answer this question. But, in light of the Constitution's democratic objectives, it must be asked.

C.

I next turn to a different kind of example. It focuses upon current threats to the protection of privacy, defined for this purpose as the power to "control information about oneself."[63] It seeks to illustrate what active liberty is like in modern America when we seek to arrive democratically at solutions to important technologically based problems. And it suggests a need for judicial caution and humility when certain privacy matters, such as the balance between free speech and privacy, are at issue.

The "privacy" problem is unusually complex. It clearly has become more so since the terrorist attacks. For one thing, those who agree that privacy is important disagree about why. Some emphasize the need to be left alone, not bothered by others. Some say that privacy is important because it prevents people from being judged out of context. Others emphasize the way in which relationships of love and friendship depend upon trust, which implies a sharing of information not available to all. Still others find connections between privacy and individualism, in that privacy encourages nonconformity. A final group finds connections between privacy and equality, in that limitations upon the availability of individualized information leads private businesses to treat all customers alike. For some, or all, of these reasons, legal rules protecting privacy help to ensure an individual's dignity.

The law may protect privacy only because of the way in which technology interacts with different laws. Some laws, such as trespass, wiretapping, eavesdropping, and search-and-seizure laws, protect particular places or sites, such as homes or telephones, from searches and monitoring.[64] Other laws protect not places, but kinds of information, for example, laws that forbid the publication of certain personal information even by a person who obtained that information legally.[65] Taken together, these laws protect privacy to different degrees depending upon place, individual status, kind of intrusion, and type of information.

Further, technological advances have changed the extent to which present laws can protect privacy. Video cameras now monitor shopping malls, schools, parks, office buildings, city streets, and other places that present law leaves unprotected. Scanners and interceptors can overhear virtually any electronic conversation. Thermal imaging devices detect activities taking place within the home. Computers record and collate information obtained in any of these ways and others. This technology means an ability to observe, collate, and permanently record a vast amount of information about individuals that the law previously may have made available for collection but that, in practice, could not easily have been recorded and collected. The nature of the current or future privacy threat depends upon how this fact will affect differently situated individuals.

These circumstances mean that efforts to revise privacy law to take account of the new technology will involve, in different areas of human activity, the balancing of values in light of predictions about the technological future. If, for example, businesses obtain detailed consumer purchasing information, they may create individualized customer profiles. Those profiles may invade the customer's privacy. But they also may help firms provide desired products at lower cost. If, for example, medical records are placed online, patient privacy may be compromised. But the ready availability of those records may lower insurance costs or help a patient carried unconscious into an operating room. Or if all information about an individual's genetic makeup is completely confidential, that individual's privacy is protected—but suppose a close relative, a nephew or cousin, needs the information to assess his own cancer risk?

Nor does a "consent" requirement automatically answer the dilemmas suggested, for consent forms may be signed without understanding, and, in any event, a decision by one individual to release or to deny information can affect others as well.

Legal solutions to these problems will be shaped by what is technologically possible. Should video cameras be programmed to turn off? Recorded images to self-destruct? Computers instructed to delete certain kinds of information? Should cell phones be encrypted? Should web technology, making use of an individual's privacy preferences, automatically negotiate privacy rules with distant web sites as a condition of access?

The complex nature of these problems calls for resolution through a form of participatory democracy. Ideally, that participatory process does not involve legislators, administrators, or judges imposing law from above. Rather, it involves law revision that bubbles up from below. Serious complex changes in law are often made in the context of a national conversation involving, among others, scientists, engineers, people in business, and the media, along with legislators, judges, and many ordinary citizens whose lives the new technology will affect. That conversation takes place through many meetings, symposia, and discussions, through journal articles and media reports, through legislative hearings and court cases. Lawyers participate fully in this discussion, translating specialized knowledge into ordinary English, defining issues, creating consensus. Typically, administrators and legislators then make decisions, with courts later resolving any constitutional issues that those decisions raise. This "conversation" is participatory democratic process itself.

The presence of this kind of problem and this kind of process helps to explain, because it suggests a need for, judicial caution or modesty. That is why, for example, the Court's decisions so far have hesitated to preempt that process. In one recent case the Court considered a cell phone conversation that an unknown private individual had intercepted with a scanner and delivered to a radio station.[66] A statute forbade the broadcast of that conversation, even though the radio station itself had not planned or participated in the intercept.[67] The Court had to determine the scope of the station's First Amendment right to broadcast given the privacy interests that the statute sought to protect. The Court held that the First Amendment trumped the statute, permitting the radio station to broadcast the information.[68] But the holding was narrow. It focused upon the particular circumstances present, explicitly leaving open broadcaster liability in other, less innocent, circumstances.[69]

The narrowness of the holding itself serves a constitutional purpose. The privacy "conversation" is ongoing. Congress could well rewrite the statute, tailoring it more finely to current technological facts, such as the widespread availability of scanners and the possibility of protecting conversations through encryption. A broader constitutional rule might itself limit legislative options in ways now unforeseeable. And doing so is particularly dangerous where *statutory* protection of an important personal liberty is at issue.

By way of contrast, the Court held unconstitutional police efforts to use, without a warrant, a thermal imaging device placed on a public sidewalk.[70] The device permitted police to identify activities taking place within a private house. The case required the Court simply to ask whether the residents had a reasonable expectation that their activities within the house would not be disclosed to the public in this way—a well-established Fourth Amendment principle. Hence the case asked the Court to pour new technological wine into old bottles; it did not suggest that doing so would significantly interfere with an ongoing democratic policy conversation.

The privacy example suggests more by way of caution. It warns against adopting an overly rigid method of interpreting the Constitution—placing weight upon eighteenth-century details to the point where it becomes difficult for a twenty-first-century court to apply the document's underlying values. At a minimum it suggests that courts, in determining the breadth of a constitutional holding, should look to the effect of a holding on the ongoing policy process, distinguishing, as I have suggested, between the "eavesdropping" and the "thermal heat" types of cases. And it makes clear that judicial caution in such matters does not reflect the fact that judges are qualifying their legal concerns with practical considerations. The Constitution itself is a practical document; it authorizes the Court to proceed pragmatically when it examines new laws in light of the Constitution's values.

D.

My fourth example concerns equal protection and voting rights, an area that has led to considerable constitutional controversy. Some believe that the Constitution prohibits virtually any legislative effort to use race as a basis for drawing electoral-district boundaries unless, for example, the effort seeks to undo earlier invidious race-based discrimination.[71] Others believe that the Constitution does not so severely limit the instances in which a legislature can use race to create majority-minority districts.[72] Without describing the details of the two positions, I will point out the relevance of the Constitution's democratic objective.

That objective suggests a simple, but potentially important, constitutional difference in the electoral area between invidious discrimination, penalizing members of a racial minority, and positive discrimination, assisting members of racial minorities. The Constitution's Fifteenth Amendment prohibits the former, not simply because it violates a basic Fourteenth Amendment principle, namely that the government must treat all citizens with equal respect, but also because it denies minority citizens the opportunity to participate in the self-governing democracy that the Constitution creates. By way of contrast, affirmative discrimination ordinarily seeks to enlarge minority participation in that self-governing democracy. To that extent it is consistent with, and indeed furthers, the Constitution's democratic objective.[73] That consistency, along with its more benign purposes, helps to mitigate whatever lack of equal respect any such discrimination might show to a disadvantaged member of a majority group.

I am not saying that the mitigation will automatically render any particular discriminatory scheme constitutional. But the presence of this mitigating difference supports the view that courts should not apply the strong presumptions of unconstitutionality that are appropriate where invidious discrimination is at issue. My purpose, again, is to suggest that reference to the Constitution's "democratic" objective can help us apply a different objective here, equal protection. And in the electoral context, the reference suggests increased legislative authority to deal with multiracial issues.

E.

My last example focuses upon statutory interpretation and a potential relationship between active liberty and statutory drafting. Students of modern government complain that contemporary political circumstances too often lead Congress to ignore its own committees and to draft legislation, through amendments, on the House or Senate floor. This tendency may reflect a membership that is closely divided between the parties, single-interest pressure groups that (along with overly simplified media reporting) discourage compromise, or an election system in which voters tend to hold individuals rather than parties responsible. The consequence is legislation that is often silent, ambiguous, or even contradictory in respect to key interpretive questions. In such cases the true answer as to what Congress intended about such issues as the creation of a private right of action, the time limits governing an action, the judicial deference due an agency's interpretation of the statute, or other technical questions of application may well be that few in Congress thought about the matter.

How are courts, which must find answers, to interpret these silences? Of course, courts first will look to a statute's language, structure, and history to help determine the statute's purpose, and then use that purpose, along with its determining factors, to help find the answer. But suppose that these factors, while limiting the universe of possible answers, do not themselves prove determinative. What then?

At this point, courts are typically pulled in one of two directions. The first is linguistic. The judge may try to tease further meaning from language and structure, followed by application of language-based canons of interpretation designed to limit subjective judicial decision making.[74] The second is purposive. Instead of deriving an artificial meaning through the use of general canons, the judge will ask instead how a (hypothetical) reasonable member of Congress, given the statutory language, structure, history, and purpose, *would have* answered the question had it been presented. The second approach has a theoretical advantage. It reminds the judge of the law's democratic source, i.e., that it is in Congress, not the courts, where the Constitution places the authority to enact a statute. And it has certain practical advantages sufficient in my view to overcome any risk of subjectivity.

The Court recently considered the matter in an administrative law case. The question was whether a court should defer to a customs inspector's on-the-spot ad hoc interpretation of a customs statute.[75] A well-known administrative law case, *Chevron v. Natural Resources Defense Council,*[76] sets forth an interpretive canon stating that, when an agency-administered statute is ambiguous, courts should defer to a reasonable agency interpretation. But how absolute is *Chevron's* canon? Does it mean that courts should *normally* defer or *always* defer? The Court held that *Chevron* was not absolute.[77] It required deference only where Congress would have wanted deference. And the Court suggested criteria for deciding what Congress would have wanted where Congress provided no indication and perhaps did not think about the matter.[78]

Why refer to a hypothetical congressional desire? Why produce the complex and fictional statement, "It seems unlikely *Congress* would have wanted courts to defer here?" The reason is that the fiction provides guidance of a kind roughly similar to that offered by Professor Corbin's "reasonable contracting party" in contract cases.[79] It focuses the judge's attention on the fact that democratically elected individuals wrote the statute in order to satisfy certain human purposes. And it consequently increases the likelihood that courts will ask what those individuals would have wanted in light of those purposes. In this instance, I believe the approach favored reading exceptions into *Chevron*'s canon where necessary to further those statutory purposes.

That flexibility is important. Dozens of different agencies apply thousands of different statutes containing untold numbers of lacunae in untold numbers of different circumstances. In many circumstances, as *Chevron* suggests, deference makes sense; but in some circumstances deference does not make sense. The metaphor—focusing on what a reasonable person likely would have wanted—helps bring courts to that conclusion. To treat *Chevron*'s rule purely as a judicial canon is less likely to do so.

In a different case, the Court focused on an ambiguity in the habeas corpus statute.[80] That statute limits the period of time during which a state prisoner may file a federal habeas corpus petition to one year after a state court conviction becomes final.[81] A subsection tolls the one-year period while "a properly filed application for State postconviction or *other collateral review*" is pending.[82] Do the italicized words, "other collateral review," include federal habeas review? I.e., is the one-year period tolled in the case of a prisoner who mistakenly files for federal habeas in federal court before he exhausts all state collateral remedies? The question is important (almost half of all federal habeas petitions fall into this category); but it is highly technical, and it is unlikely that anyone in Congress thought about it.

Again, to imagine a hypothetical reasonable member of Congress helps. That is because an interpretation that denies tolling also would close the doors of federal habeas courts to many state prisoners and it would do so *randomly*. Would a reasonable member of Congress—even a member who feared that state prisoners too often took advantage of federal habeas proceedings—want to deny access to the Great Writ *at random*? Given our traditions, I believe the answer to this question must be "no." And I suspect the majority reached a different result, not because it would have answered the question I just posed differently, but, rather, because it did not pose the question at all. Instead, the majority simply teased an answer out of language-based canons.[83]

In the customs case, then, the fictional member of Congress helped bring about an administrative law rule that would tie a statute's interpretation to the human needs that led Congress to enact a particular statute. In the habeas corpus case, the fiction would have helped produce an interpretation more consistent with our human rights tradition. In both cases the metaphor helped avoid the more rigid interpretations that follow from relying solely on canons. To that extent it helps to harmonize a court's daily work of interpreting statutes with the Constitution's democratic and liberty-protecting objectives.

III.

The instances I have discussed encompass different areas of law—speech, federalism, privacy, equal protection, and statutory interpretation. In each instance, the discussion has focused upon a contemporary social problem—campaign finance, workplace regulation, environmental regulation, information-based technological change, race-based electoral districting, and legislative politics. In each instance, the discussion illustrates how increased focus upon the Constitution's basic democratic objective might make a difference—in refining doctrinal rules, in evaluating consequences, in applying practical cautionary principles, in interacting with other constitutional objectives, and in explicating statutory silences. In each instance, the discussion suggests how that increased focus might mean better law. And "better" in this context means both (1) better able to satisfy the Constitution's purposes, and (2) better able to cope with contemporary problems. The discussion, while not proving its point purely through logic or empirical demonstration, uses examples to create a pattern. The pattern suggests a need for increased judicial emphasis upon the Constitution's democratic objective.

My discussion emphasizes values underlying specific constitutional phrases, sees the Constitution itself as a single document with certain basic related objectives, and assumes that the latter can inform a judge's understanding of the former. Might that discussion persuade those who prefer to believe that the keys to constitutional interpretation instead lie in specific language, history, tradition, and precedent and who fear that a contrary approach would permit judges too often to act subjectively?

Perhaps so, for several reasons. First, the area of interpretive disagreement is more limited than many believe. Judges can, and should, decide most cases, including constitutional cases, through the use of language, history, tradition, and precedent. Judges will often agree as to how these factors determine a provision's basic purpose and the result in a particular case. And where they differ, their differences are often differences of modest degree. Only a handful of constitutional issues—though an important handful—are as open in respect to language, history, and basic purpose as those that I have described. And even in respect to those issues, judges must find answers within the limits set by the Constitution's language. Moreover, history, tradition, and precedent remain helpful, even if not determinative.

Second, the judges who emphasize language, history, tradition, and precedent cannot justify their practices by claiming that is what the Framers wanted, for the Framers did not say what factors judges should emphasize when seeking to interpret the Constitution's open language.[84] Nor is it plausible to believe that those who argued about the Bill of Rights, and made clear that it did not contain an exclusive detailed list, had agreed about what school of interpretive thought should prove dominant in the centuries to come. Indeed, the Constitution itself says that the "enumeration" in the Constitution of some rights "shall not be construed to deny or disparage others retained by the people."[85] Professor Bailyn concludes that the Framers added this language to make clear that "rights, like law itself, should never be fixed, frozen, that new dangers and needs will emerge, and that to respond to these dangers and needs, rights must be newly specified to protect the individual's integrity and inherent dignity."[86] Instead, justification for the literalist's practice itself tends to rest upon consequences. Literalist arguments often seek to show that such an approach will have favorable results, for example, controlling judicial subjectivity.

Third, judges who reject a literalist approach deny that their decisions are subjective and point to important safeguards of objectivity. A decision that emphasizes values, no less than any other, is open to criticism based upon (1) the decision's relation to the other legal principles (precedents, rules, standards, practices, institutional understandings) that it modifies or reinforces; and (2) the decision's consequences, i.e., the way in which the entire bloc of decision-affected legal principles subsequently affects the world. The relevant values, by limiting interpretive possibilities and guiding interpretation, themselves constrain subjectivity; indeed, the democratic values that I have emphasized themselves suggest the importance of judicial restraint. A constitutional judge's need for consistency over time also constrains subjectivity. That is why Justice O'Connor has explained the need in terms of a constitutional judge's initial decisions creating "footprints" that later decisions almost inevitably will follow.[87]

Fourth, the literalist does not escape subjectivity, for his tools—language, history, and tradition—can provide little objective guidance in the comparatively small set of cases about which I have spoken. In such cases,

the Constitution's language is almost always nonspecific. History and tradition are open to competing claims and rival interpretations.[88] Nor does
an emphasis upon rules embodied in precedent necessarily produce clarity, particularly in borderline areas or where rules are stated abstractly.
Indeed, an emphasis upon language, history, tradition, or prior rules in
such cases may simply channel subjectivity into a choice about: Which
history? Which tradition? Which rules? The literalist approach will then
produce a decision that is no less subjective but that is far less transpar-
ent than a decision that directly addresses consequences in constitutional
terms.

Finally, my examples point to offsetting consequences—at least if "literalism" tends to produce the legal doctrines (related to the First Amendment, to federalism, to statutory interpretation, to equal protection) that
I have criticized. Those doctrines lead to consequences at least as harmful, from a constitutional perspective, as any increased risk of subjectivity. In the ways that I have set out, they undermine the Constitution's
efforts to create a framework for democratic government—a government
that, while protecting individual liberties, permits individual citizens to
govern themselves.

IV.

To reemphasize the constitutional importance of democratic self-government may carry with it a practical bonus. We are all aware of figures that
show that the public knows ever less about, and is ever less interested in,
the processes of government. Foundation reports criticize the lack of high
school civics education.[89] Comedians claim that more students know the
names of the Three Stooges than the three branches of government. Even
law school graduates are ever less inclined to work for government—with
the percentage of those entering government (or nongovernment public
interest) work declining dramatically over the last generation.[90] Indeed,
polls show that, over the same period of time, the percentage of the public trusting the government declined at a similar rate.[91]

This trend, however, is not irreversible. Indeed, trust in government
has shown a remarkable rebound in response to last month's terrible trag-
edy.[92] Courts cannot maintain this upward momentum by themselves.
But courts, as highly trusted government institutions,[93] can help, in part
by explaining in terms the public can understand just what the Constitution is about. It is important that the public, trying to cope with the

problems of national, state, and local community, understands that the Constitution does not resolve, and was not intended to resolve, society's problems. Rather, the Constitution provides a framework for the creation of democratically determined solutions, which protect each individual's basic liberties and assure that individual equal respect by government, while securing a democratic form of government. We judges cannot insist that Americans participate in that government, but we can make clear that our Constitution depends upon their participation. Indeed, participation reinforces that "positive passion for the public good" that John Adams, like so many others, considered a necessary condition for "Republican Government" and any "real Liberty."[94]

That is the democratic ideal. It is as relevant today as it was two hundred or two thousand years ago. Today it is embodied in our Constitution. Two thousand years ago, Thucydides, quoting Pericles, set forth a related ideal—relevant in his own time and, with some modifications, still appropriate to recall today. We Athenians, said Pericles, do not say that the man who fails to participate in politics is a man who minds his own business. We say that he is a man who has no business here.[95]

NOTES

1. BENJAMIN CONSTANT, *The Liberty of the Ancients Compared with That of the Moderns (1819)*, *in* POLITICAL WRITINGS 309, 309-28 (Biancamaria Fontana trans. & ed., 1988).
2. *Id.* at 316.
3. *Id.* at 327.
4. *Id.*
5. *Id.* at 325-26.
6. *Id.* at 327.
7. Letter from Thomas Jefferson to Joseph C. Cabell (Feb. 2, 1816), *in* 1 THE FOUNDERS' CONSTITUTION 142 (Philip B. Kurland & Ralph Lerner eds., 1987).
8. Letter from John Adams to Mercy Warren (Apr. 16, 1776), *in* 1 THE FOUNDERS' CONSTITUTION, *supra* note 7, at 670.
9. The term "active liberty" is not quite the same as Isaiah Berlin's concept of "positive liberty," but there are obvious similarities. *See* Isaiah Berlin, Two Concepts of Liberty, Inaugural Lecture Before the University of Oxford (Oct. 31, 1958), *in* FOUR ESSAYS ON LIBERTY 118, 118-72 (1969).
10. CONSTANT, *supra* note 1, at 316.
11. For a nuanced discussion of the principles underlying the third and fourth objectives, see generally RONALD DWORKIN, FREEDOM'S LAW: THE MORAL READING OF THE AMERICAN CONSTITUTION 15-35 (1996); RONALD DWORKIN, LAW'S EMPIRE 176-265 (1986).

12. U.S. CONST. art. IV.

13. *Id.* art. I, § 4, cl. 2.

14. *Id.* art. I, § 2, cl. 1.

15. *Id.* art. I, § 3, cl. 1.

16. *Id.* art. I, § 2, cl. 3.

17. *Id.* amend. XV.

18. *Id.* amend. XIX.

19. *Id.* amend. XXIV.

20. *Id.* amend. XXVI.

21. *See* JACK N. RAKOVE, ORIGINAL MEANINGS: POLITICS AND IDEAS IN THE MAKING OF THE CONSTITUTION 11 (1996) (using historical context surrounding framing and ratification of Constitution to illuminate debate about role originalism should play in constitutional interpretation).

22. *See, e.g.,* McCulloch v. Maryland, 17 U.S. (4 Wheat.) 316 (1819) (upholding Congress's power to charter national bank); Marbury v. Madison, 5 U.S. (1 Cranch) 137 (1803) (establishing federal courts' power to review constitutionality of congressional legislation).

23. *See, e.g.,* Giles v. Harris, 189 U.S. 475 (1903) (refusing to enforce voting rights); The Civil Rights Cases, 109 U.S. 3 (1883) (interpreting Civil War Amendments narrowly).

24. *See, e.g.,* Lochner v. New York, 198 U.S. 45 (1905) (striking down workplace health regulations on substantive due process grounds).

25. WILLIAM E. LEUCHTENBURG, THE SUPREME COURT REBORN 133 (1995).

26. *See, e.g.,* Wickard v. Filburn, 317 U.S. 111, 125 (1942) (rejecting distinction between "direct" and "indirect" effects on interstate commerce); NLRB v. Jones & Laughlin Steel Corp., 301 U.S. 1 (1937) (upholding constitutionality of National Labor Relations Act and abandoning "indirect effects" test of validity of Commerce Clause legislation); W. Coast Hotel Co. v. Parrish, 300 U.S. 379 (1937) (rejecting argument that minimum-wage law for women violated constitutional right to freedom of contract).

27. *See, e.g.,* Reynolds v. Sims, 377 U.S. 533 (1964) (requiring application of "one person, one vote" principle to state legislatures); Baker v. Carr, 369 U.S. 186 (1962) (finding that Equal Protection Clause justified federal court intervention to review voter apportionment); Gomillion v. Lightfoot, 364 U.S. 339 (1960) (striking down racial gerrymandering on Fifteenth Amendment grounds).

28. JAMES BRADLEY THAYER, JOHN MARSHALL 106 (Da Capo Press 1974) (1901).

29. LEARNED HAND, THE SPIRIT OF LIBERTY 190 (2d ed. 1952); *cf. id.* at 109 ("If [a judge] is in doubt, he must stop, for he cannot tell that the conflicting interests in the society for which he speaks would have come to a just result. . . .").

30. CTR. FOR RESPONSIVE POLITICS, ELECTION OVERVIEW, 2000 CYCLE: STATS AT A GLANCE, *at* http://www.opensecrets.org/overview/index.asp?Cycle=2000 (last visited Mar. 8, 2002) (aggregating totals using Federal Election Commission (FEC) data).

31. FED. ELECTION COMM'N, FEC REPORTS ON CONGRESSIONAL FINAN-
    CIAL ACTIVITY FOR 2000, http://www.fec.gov/press/051501congfinact/0515
    01congfinact.html (May 15, 2001).

32. *Id.*

33. *See* Antony Barnett & Andy McSmith, *Four More MPs in Expense Ploy*,
    OBSERVER (U.K.), Apr. 11, 1999, at 1; Patrick Basham, *U.S. Doesn't Want This
    Canadian Import*, DAYTON DAILY NEWS, Dec. 11, 2000, at 8A.

34. ALLIANCE FOR BETTER CAMPAIGNS, DOLLARS V. DISCOURSE: CAM-
    PAIGNS & TELEVISION, *at* http://www.bettercampaigns.org/Doldisc/camptv.
    htm (last visited Mar. 18, 2002); Lorraine Woellert & Tom Lowry, *A Political
    Nightmare: Not Enough Airtime*, BUSINESSWEEK ONLINE (Oct. 23, 2000), *at*
    http://www.businessweek.com/2000/00 43/b3704204.htm.

35. Don Van Natta Jr. & John M. Broder, *The Republicans: The Few, the Rich, the
    Rewarded Donate the Bulk of G.O.P. Gifts*, N.Y. TIMES, Aug. 2, 2000, at A1.

36. *Id.*

37. *See* U.S. CENSUS BUREAU, U.S. DEP'T OF COMMERCE, STATISTICAL
    ABSTRACT OF THE UNITED STATES: 2000, at tbls.477, 478 & 480 (120th
    ed. 2000).

38. *Cf.* JEFFREY H. BIRNBAUM, THE MONEY MEN 7 (2000) (discussing 1992
    data, which also showed four percent of adult population contributed that cycle).

39. *See, e.g.*, Nixon v. Shrink Mo. Gov't PAC, 528 U.S. 377, 399-405 (2000) (Breyer,
    J., concurring).

40. U.S. CONST. amend. I.

41. THE FEDERALIST NO. 57 (James Madison).

42. CONSTANT, *supra* note 1, at 327.

43. *See Nixon*, 528 U.S. at 399-400 (Breyer, J., concurring).

44. United States v. United Foods, Inc., 533 U.S. 405 (2001).

45. *Id.* at 2345 (Breyer, J., dissenting) ("Nearly every human action that the law
    affects, and virtually all governmental activity, involves speech.").

46. *See, e.g.*, 44 Liquormart, Inc. v. Rhode Island, 517 U.S. 484, 522 (1996) (Thomas,
    J., concurring in part and concurring in the judgment).

47. Lochner v. New York, 198 U.S. 45 (1905).

48. *But see supra* notes 40-44 and accompanying text.

49. New York v. United States, 505 U.S. 144 (1992).

50. Printz v. United States, 521 U.S. 898, 921 (1997).

51. *E.g.*, Bd. of Trs. of Univ. of Ala. v. Garrett, 531 U.S. 356 (2001) (holding that suits
    under Americans with Disabilities Act for money damages against states are barred
    by Eleventh Amendment); Seminole Tribe v. Florida, 517 U.S. 44 (1996) (holding
    that Congress cannot abrogate state's sovereign immunity under Article I).

52. United States v. Morrison, 529 U.S. 598 (2000) (Violence Against Women Act);
    United States v. Lopez, 514 U.S. 549 (1995) (Gun-Free School Zones Act).

53. New State Ice Co. v. Liebman, 285 U.S. 262, 311 (1932) (Brandeis, J., dissenting).

54. *See, e.g.*, County of Riverside v. McLaughlin, 500 U.S. 44, 53-54 (1991).

55. *See Printz*, 521 U.S. at 921 n.11, 976-77 (1997) (Breyer, J., dissenting).

56. *See* Michael Dorf & Barry Friedman, *Shared Constitutional Interpretation*, 2000 SUP. CT. REV. 61, 100 n.154; *see also Printz*, 521 U.S. at 917-18.

57. *Printz*, 521 U.S. at 940 (Stevens, J., dissenting).

58. *See* United States v. Lopez, 514 U.S. 549, 625-31 (1995) (Breyer, J., dissenting) (detailing shortcomings of Court's approach).

59. *See, e.g.*, C & A Carbone, Inc. v. Clarkstown, 511 U.S. 383, 401-02 (1994) (O'Connor, J., concurring).

60. *See, e.g.*, Wyoming v. Oklahoma, 502 U.S. 437 (1992) (striking down Oklahoma law that discriminated against out-of-state coal).

61. *See, e.g.*, Gregory v. Ashcroft, 501 U.S. 452 (1991) (requiring "clear statement" by Congress when it legislates in area traditionally regulated by states).

62. *See, e.g.*, United States v. Virginia, 518 U.S. 515, 541 (1996) (noting that reviewing courts should take "hard look" at state laws that provide for dissimilar treatment for men and women).

63. M. ETHAN KATSH, LAW IN A DIGITAL WORLD 228 (1995).

64. *E.g.*, 18 U.S.C. § 2511 (1994 & Supp. II 1997) (regulating electronic surveillance).

65. *E.g.*, 15 U.S.C. § 6802 (Supp. V 2000) (regulating disclosure of personal information by financial institutions).

66. Bartnicki v. Vopper, 532 U.S. 514, 518-19 (2001).

67. 18 U.S.C. § 2511(1)(c) (1994); *see also Bartnicki*, 532 U.S. at 523-24.

68. *Bartnicki*, 532 U.S. at 532-35.

69. *Id.* at 533.

70. Kyllo v. United States, 536 U.S. 27, 40 (2001).

71. *See, e.g.*, Hunt v. Cromartie, 526 U.S. 541 (1999) (overturning district court's grant of summary judgment in racial gerrymandering case because state legislature's motivation was in dispute).

72. *See, e.g.*, Shaw v. Reno, 509 U.S. 630, 658 (1993) (White, J., dissenting).

73. *Cf.* JOHN HART ELY, DEMOCRACY AND DISTRUST 135-79 (1980) (discussing representation-reinforcing theory of judicial review and constitutional interpretation).

74. *See, e.g.*, ANTONIN SCALIA, COMMON-LAW COURTS IN A CIVIL-LAW SYSTEM: THE ROLE OF UNITED STATES FEDERAL COURTS IN INTERPRETING THE CONSTITUTION AND LAWS, IN A MATTER OF INTERPRETATION: FEDERAL COURTS AND THE LAW 26-27 (Amy Gutmann ed., 1997).

75. United States v. Mead Corp., 533 U.S. 218, 221 (2001).

76. Chevron U.S.A. Inc. v. Natural Res. Def. Council, Inc., 467 U.S. 837 (1984).

77. *Mead Corp.*, 533 U.S. at 227-37 (recognizing that Court has applied varieties "of judicial deference").

78. *Id.* at 271-72.

79. *See* JOHN D. CALAMARI & JOSEPH M. PERILLO, THE LAW OF CONTRACTS 3.10 (2d ed. 1977).

80. Duncan v. Walker, 533 U.S. 167 (2001).

81. 28 U.S.C. § 2244(d)(1) (Supp. II 1997).

82. § 2244(d)(2) (emphasis added).

83. *See Duncan*, 533 U.S. at 172-75.

84. RAKOVE, *supra* note 21, at 339-65.

85. U.S. CONST. amend. IX.

86. Bernard Bailyn, The Living Past—Commitments for the Future, Remarks at the First Millennium Evening at the White House (Feb. 11, 1998), http://clinton4. nara.gov/Initiatives/Millennium/bbailyn.html.

87. *See* Stephen Breyer, *Judicial Review: A Practicing Judge's Perspective*, 78 TEX. L. REV. 761, 769 (2000) (relating Justice O'Connor's analogy).

88. *Compare, e.g.*, Alden v. Maine, 527 U.S. 706, 715-27 (1999) (using historical analysis to support Court's holding), *with id.* at 764-98 (Souter, J., dissenting) (using historical analysis to support opposite conclusion).

89. *See, e.g.*, NAT'L CTR. FOR EDUC. STATISTICS, U.S. DEP'T. OF EDUC., THE NAEP 1998 CIVICS REPORT CARD (1999).

90. Harry T. Edwards, *A Lawyer's Duty To Serve the Public Good*, 65 N.Y.U. L. REV. 1148, 1152-53 (1990) (noting that during the 1980s, "the number of graduates entering public interest law dropped by nearly fifty percent, with less than two percent of the graduates of the nation's top schools going directly into public interest work during the mid-1980s").

91. Lydia Saad, *Americans' Faith in Government Shaken but Not Shattered by Water-gate*, http://www.gallup.com/poll/releases/pr970619.asp (June 19, 1997) (sub-scriber content) (on file with the *New York University Law Review*).

92. Tom Shoop, *Trust in Government Up Dramatically, Polls Show, at* http:/www. govexec.com/dailyfed/1001/100101ts1.htm (Oct. 1, 2001).

93. *See* Saad, *supra* note 91 (explaining that, in 1997, public trust in judicial branch exceeded trust in executive and legislative branches).

94. Adams, *supra* note 8, at 670.

95. THUCYDIDES, THE PELOPONNESIAN WAR 108-15 (Thomas Hobbes trans., Univ. of Chi. Press 1989) (1629) (quoting The Funeral Oration of Pericles).

2

Federal and State Courts

Restoring a Workable Balance

GUIDO CALABRESI

We take the role of the inferior federal courts in this country for granted. It seems to us perfectly natural to have independent and inferior federal courts below the Supreme Court, and a separate system of state courts. But in fact, our system of parallel state and federal courts is unusual in a federalism, to put it mildly. In Canada, for instance, the provincial supreme courts are named by the central government.[1] It's as if the judges of the New York Court of Appeals or the justices of the Connecticut Supreme Court were named by the President of the United States. In Europe, there are virtually no inferior European courts. One goes from the national courts of France, Italy, Germany, and so on, directly to a European High Court, without (with the possible exception of antitrust) having any lower European courts.[2] In other words, it's as if we had *just* the courts of Connecticut, New York, California, and the rest, for *all* cases, and then went to our High Court in Washington, D.C.

In the United States, the strange parallel structure of state and federal courts was first considered at the time our Constitution was created. Its source, as with so much else, was James Madison. The idea of separate lower federal courts was Madison's, and Madison originally wanted the Constitution itself to provide for and grant jurisdiction to lower federal courts, just as it did for the Supreme Court.[3] He lost. But Madison, that pesky little man with such a great mind, didn't give up easily. And so he suggested that if—*someday*—it might be too much work for the Supreme

This lecture was delivered on October 15, 2002, and appeared in *78 N.Y.U. L. Rev.* 1293 (2003).

Court to deal with all of the federal issues that might arise, wouldn't it be useful if, under those circumstances (should they *ever* come about), Congress could create lower federal courts and give them jurisdiction . . . if that should ever happen. And that proposal got through.[4] So the Convention that had rejected the idea of lower federal courts endowed in the Constitution with a particular jurisdiction, nevertheless allowed Congress to establish them.[5] Congress did so almost immediately, in 1789, with the Judiciary Act,[6] at the behest of Oliver Ellsworth of Connecticut.[7] Whether he was put up to it by Madison or not I do not know, but I would not be surprised if he were. Thus were the lower federal courts created.

Over time, the balance between them and the state courts has changed greatly, but it has always rested on three or four pillars. The balance—one that is currently in crisis—is the balance that I grew up with in law school. It is the balance of some sixty years ago, the balance, if you will, since *Erie*,[8] and since the coming of Supreme Court certiorari jurisdiction.[9] It is the balance of the mid-twentieth century.

What was that balance, why is it in crisis today, and what can we do about the crisis? I will focus on four aspects of the balance. First, federal violations—federal actors violating federal rights—were tried in the lower federal courts. When the federal government allegedly did something that violated a federal right, constitutional or otherwise, federal courts were usually involved from the beginning. Second, criminal law; this was generally local and arose in state courts. Third, most private law in traditional common law areas—torts, contracts, and so on—was also in state courts. The exceptions were relatively few diversity cases and, even as to these, after *Erie*, substantive local law ruled.[10] And last, there were state violations—state actors allegedly violating federal rights. In this area, regardless of what had been the case earlier, starting about sixty years ago, such cases were often tried first, or reviewed de novo, in federal courts. One didn't count on the Supreme Court reviewing state court decisions on these issues: federal courts were able to find the facts and decide questions of law, preparing them for the Supreme Court should that court wish to hear them.

Of these four pillars of federal-state court relations, I will argue that three—those involving criminal law, private law, and state violations—are currently in crisis, if not crumbling, and I will make some rather radical, and some less radical, suggestions for reasserting or reconstructing them.

I. The First Pillar in Crisis: Criminal Law

We all know that, increasingly in the last sixty years, criminal law of the ordinary sort has become federalized. Every time Congress meets, it passes a new law, or new laws, or many new laws, declaring actions that are already state crimes—acts parallel to those already prohibited by the states and punished by the states—to be federal crimes as well.[11] Why is that so? Because it is politically successful. When people are upset by some behavior, it is easy for Congress to say, "We will make it a federal crime." And Congress uses the Commerce Clause or some other clause to do so.[12]

This has been happening again and again, even in the face of some resistance. For instance, the Supreme Court has tried to limit this tendency in the *Lopez* line of cases.[13] But that approach hasn't really stopped the trend. And I don't think it *will* in the future.

My colleague, Dennis Jacobs, recently dissented in a case involving the Hobbs Act,[14] saying, in effect, "It can't go *that* far, for heaven's sake, or we can make everything a Hobbs Act crime."[15] But the majority, said, "No. That's what Congress can do. It's a Commerce Clause thing and there it is."[16] In the end, *Lopez*-type approaches, whether by courts of appeals or by the Supreme Court, cannot solve the problem because any solutions that would prohibit the federal government from making some of these things federal crimes either don't go far enough to keep the federalization of criminal law from overwhelming us, or go so far as to restrain the federal government from taking actions in areas where only the federal government can act effectively.

It's a game attempt, but it simply does not work. That people—even those who push for it—don't believe that it can work can be readily seen. Thus, some legislators who hailed the Supreme Court's restriction on criminalizing, as a federal matter, certain types of behavior—violence against women,[17] for example—are the very ones who proposed that Congress pass a law prohibiting what they call partial-birth abortions.[18] Now one can feel however one wants about these abortions—about whether they are good or bad—but if one believes that there is no constitutionally valid federal interest in prohibiting violence against women under the Commerce Clause, it is very hard to understand what the valid federal interest is in banning this type of abortion. It is hard to understand because, in fact, people want contradictory things. They want the federal government to make criminal those things they believe to be deeply wrong, and (at the same time) they worry about the federalization of criminal law.

Apart from the dramatic change that such federalization effects in our federal system, making criminal law national rather than local causes great problems for the lower federal courts. I would guess that cases that involve federal criminal law, where there is already a state criminal statute that would cover the same thing, total somewhere between thirty and fifty percent of the Second Circuit's appellate docket, depending on how you define that docket and those cases. Most of the drug cases, of course, fall into that category. If the federal courts are overwhelmed—with the result that they become ever larger, and inevitably of lower quality, all of the problems that Judge Newman spoke of in his review of the situation of federal courts several years ago[19]—it is preeminently due to this. What, then, can we do?

Well, here's a possible solution.[20] Suppose Congress were to pass a law that said that whenever a federal crime parallels a state crime, both crimes will be tried, together, in state courts. Federal prosecutors are available, the FBI can investigate, but the power to *try* the case in the first instance—the jurisdiction—will lie not in federal courts, but in state courts. Some of you will say "Brady"[21] and say that it is unconstitutional to assign federal duties to the state courts, and so on. But Brady *doesn't apply* to courts: It applies to everything else *but* courts, as various Supreme Court decisions during the Second World War, as well as postwar Office of Price Administration cases, have made clear.[22]

Since Congress *can* assign criminal cases under federal law to state courts, suppose that Congress were to say: *State* courts are where such cases will be tried. The federal government could continue to make all sorts of things federal crimes. And it could, if it wanted, demand that the penalties be more severe than those mandated by state laws. But, as a practical matter, the power to try such federal crimes would revert to local government.

Of course there might be some cases where such an approach wouldn't work. I would want to allow either party to petition the federal court (maybe the district court, maybe the court of appeals) to have such a special case be tried in a federal court. The petition would presumably be granted only if there was some reason to think the state court couldn't handle the case. And I would also want to have a system of certification so that if, in the course of trying out a case that seemingly could be heard as well in the state court, some unsettled question of complicated federal law arose, the state court could certify that issue to the federal court of appeals. And the court of appeals could accept "the question" and give back an answer as to the applicable federal law.[23]

If Congress were to pass such a law, then thirty to fifty percent of the Second Circuit's appellate docket would disappear. And the trial of matters that are basically local—even though Congress wanted to impose a higher or a different penalty—would return to the way that they were treated from Madison's time until a few years ago.[24] Incidentally, this might also mean that federal judges—who are generally not picked for their knowledge of criminal law, while state judges much more often are—could return to the solemn duty of dealing with securities cases, which we handled so well in Learned Hand's time.

II. The Second Pillar in Crisis: Private Law

In a national economy, the existence of diversity and pendent jurisdiction has meant that more and more cases are being tried in federal courts, even though the issue is one of local law. There are whole areas of law—certain aspects of intellectual property law, for example—that are not governed directly by federal law, but that are in federal courts because they are pendent to federal laws. In such areas, federal courts are supposed to state what the law of, say, New York is. As a result, in these areas, the law of New York is the law made by Second Circuit judges like Jon Newman and Pierre Leval. It is made spectacularly well, perhaps. But this is supposed to be *local* law, articulated by state judges, not by federal courts. The same is even more true in diversity cases dealing with torts and contracts, for the presence of national companies frequently leads to federal jurisdiction.

The problem here is that federal courts often get state law wrong because federal judges don't know state law and are not the ultimate decision makers on it. Inevitably, this leads to considerable forum shopping of just the sort that *Erie* sought to avoid.[25] One party or the other tries to get into federal courts because it *hopes* that the federal courts will get the law wrong.[26] I could give you any number of examples. For instance, the concept of duty in the tort law of New York is virtually unique to New York and is very complicated. As a result, federal judges who deal with the concept of duty in a New York tort case frequently get it wrong.

One answer to this problem is the one favored by quite a few federal judges: Simply get *rid* of diversity jurisdiction. Judge Feinberg, among others, has argued for that.[27] I'm against it for several reasons. First, I do not believe that the problem of the level playing field, which was the original reason for the creation of diversity jurisdiction, has ceased to exist. I think that it *matters*, if you are a citizen of New York, whether your case will be tried in a Texas state court or in a federal court, or, if you are a citizen of Texas, whether your case will be tried in a New York state court or in a federal court. If you're not a citizen of the forum state, I think, especially at the lower court level, that it makes a difference what the court is.[28] If you think of France and Germany it's perfectly obvious, but I think that it is true in this country as well. And I believe it would matter even more if there weren't the "out" of diversity. The fact that people *can* go into a federal court, and avoid potential prejudice, makes the state courts a little more careful.

But there's another reason to keep diversity jurisdiction, and that is that diversity has an important unifying effect on the law. Federal courts tend to look to national law in these areas. When, on state law issues, judges like Newman or Leval focus on what the law is or should be, they are guided by the law all over the country, and that is a useful thing. National law shouldn't be the last word as to the state law, but having courts that are keenly aware of national law speak about state law does have a unifying effect, which it would be too bad to lose.

Well, what's the answer? My long-suffering colleagues know what *my* answer is, and that is certify, certify, certify.[29] In other words, I believe that whenever there is a question of state law that is even possibly in doubt, the federal courts should send the question to the highest court of the state, and let the highest court of the state decide the issue as it wishes. Federal judges don't like to certify because we think we know, better than the states, what state law ought to be. But that isn't the point. We should be humble. We should realize that it is state law, and hence that it is up to the states. Moreover, we should recognize that the parties have a right to have state, rather than federal, judges decide issues of state law. If we are unwilling to certify frequently—indeed to certify almost all the time—then a more radical solution would be to have Congress pass a law allowing a party to petition the highest court of the state to review, if it chooses, a decision on state law made by the federal courts of appeals. I don't think that that should be necessary, if we would just do our job of certifying. But it is a solution if we don't.

Where does that put federal appellate courts? I think that in cases of this sort, the intermediate federal courts should be no more than the

"Appellate Division for Diversity Cases." We should think of ourselves as an intermediate state court whose function it is to decide *provisionally*, and let the highest court of the state ultimately determine state law. When I say that, I talk about a kind of certification that is quite different from the one that we are used to. What federal judges should do, if state law is uncertain, is write an opinion that says what we think that law ought to be. We should write an opinion of the same sort that the state's appellate division would write. And then we should certify, so that the New York Court of Appeals is able to decide (1) not to take the case, if it thinks that we are right, or if it is not ready to take the issue up, or if it just doesn't want to bother to take it at that time; or (2) to take it, if it likes, in exactly the same way it does cases brought up (on certiorari, essentially) from the appellate division.

If federal judges did that, if we had that structural view of our role, then we would not be *insulted* when the New York Court of Appeals declines certification. Now, when the New York Court of Appeals declines certification, some federal judges walk around saying, "What did they *do* to us? After all, *we* are the Second Circuit, they should listen to us!" My view is exactly the opposite. We have indicated how we would decide something, or simply explicated our doubts on the issue. If the state's highest court doesn't want to take it, great! That gives us authority to impose *our* view of state law, *provisionally*, until the highest court of the state decides to resolve the question.

Such an approach would also avoid the problem of delay, which is one reason why many federal judges don't like to certify. The only cases that *would* be delayed are the ones that the New York Court of Appeals decided were worth taking: in other words, those that it deemed important for a state court to decide. The others, it would simply decline to take. And, since it doesn't take more than a month or two for the New York Court of Appeals to say, "Thank you, we decline" (as it does frequently with the appellate division), no significant delay would occur. Such a view of certification would, moreover, preserve the unifying function of diversity jurisdiction. We on the Second Circuit would still be in a position to speak to national law, and could put before the New York Court of Appeals, or the Connecticut or Vermont Supreme Courts, what we think the law ought to be, given the more national vision that our court likely has. But the state high court could then accept our view or not, as it wishes.

Frequent certification would also have another advantage, which is very important in terms of the third pillar of the federal-state court balance now in crisis. It would have us act humbly in our relationship to the New York, Vermont, or Connecticut courts—to the state courts. These courts would realize that where it is their responsibility, and their law, we understand that we have no special expertise at all—that we are an intermediate court in their system, subject to them.[30] And that would be extremely useful for the last point that I want to make.

III. The Third Pillar in Crisis: State Action

Some sixty or seventy years ago, cases involving state action that (allegedly or possibly) violated federal rights, instead of being tried out primarily in the states, with a review of the federal claim only at the Supreme Court, increasingly came to be tried in the lower federal courts. Some people thought that this occurred in reaction to massive resistance in the South, when some southern states attempted not to follow the Supreme Court's desegregation orders.[31] And this was certainly one of the circumstances behind the popularity of that approach, but massive resistance was only a contingent reason for it. The *real* reason why it became essential for lower federal courts to hear these cases was that the Supreme Court had decided to take fewer cases after the advent of certiorari jurisdiction.[32] As a practical matter, it was *impossible* for the Supreme Court adequately to police state courts to see whether state actions violated federal rights, and that made it essential for lower federal courts to hear such cases.[33] A hundred cases a year cannot test whether what the states are doing adequately protects federal rights.

The need for such *federal* fact and law finding increased for another, related reason: The same thing that had happened with review from state high courts to the U.S. Supreme Court was also happening *within* the states. The New York Court of Appeals and the Connecticut Supreme Court, for example, were now hearing a very small proportion of the appeals from the decisions of the lower state courts.[34] And many of the appeals that the state high courts took, understandably, involved state issues that these courts felt they had to deal with. So, if there weren't a way—in lower federal courts—of protecting federal rights from state action, it would be the lowest courts of the state, or perhaps the appellate divisions, that would be charged with the awesome task of protecting federal constitutional rights. That did not, and cannot, work.

The intermediate courts of any state have other things that they must be more concerned with. They are not experts on federal law and, with great respect to them, many are not good at it. Moreover, they are not all that interested in federal law, nor should they be. The result was that for some sixty years, through section 1983 actions, through declaratory judgment actions, through habeas petitions, through any number of other devices, lower federal courts got into the business of deciding these cases either in the first instance or essentially de novo.[35]

Recently that's all changed. We now have any number of rules, judicial and statutory, that make it difficult for lower federal courts seriously to review state actions allegedly in violation of federal rights.[36] There are three reasons for the change. First, the state courts started feeling insulted by the fact that the federal courts were deciding these issues and telling state courts they were wrong. State judges got mad and hurt and in effect said, "Who are *they* to tell us how to do our job?" Notice that this is the other side of federal judges' lack of humility with respect to state law. It would be very different if federal judges said, "We are federal judges, we have more knowledge of federal law. You are state judges, you have more knowledge of state law. Let each of us do our job and not be insulted."

The second reason for the change is the converse of the role southern states played in bringing about first-instance consideration of these cases in federal courts. Today, rather than criticizing southern resistance and implying that there is a need for greater federal court oversight, commentators talk about how the Ninth Circuit and other federal courts are "running wild" and "going too far" in protecting federal rights.[37] But that is the same kind of contingent argument, intimately connected to the political climate of a particular era, and it is no more fundamental or generalizable than was the opposite argument based on southern resistance.

The third reason for criticizing the heavy involvement of lower federal courts in such civil rights cases is a more serious one. In acting in these cases, federal courts were in an unusual role. They were dealing with federal law issues, of course, but often they were dealing with naked federal issues. That is, a federal constitutional right was involved, but it came up starkly, rather than arising in the course of a total litigation. For example, a case in federal court might involve the interpretation of a *state* statute that might, or might not, violate a federal law, depending on how it was construed. Was public nude photography permitted in New York?[38] What kinds of restrictions on assisting suicide did New York provide?[39] These were state statutes, the constitutionality of which, on the basis of a hypothetical interpretation of the statute's meaning, federal courts were called on to decide. In this respect, federal courts were in a position more akin to European constitutional courts, which are regularly called on collaterally to decide "neat" constitutional questions.

Contrast those cases with what federal courts do when an analogous issue comes up under a *federal* statute. Any number of delaying, avoiding, Bickelian passive-virtue tactics[40] are then available. The federal court can, for example, interpret the federal statute to avoid the constitutional issue. It has full control of the case and can slow down the constitutional question, the question of the fundamental right, until it is mature and ready for decision. Federal courts do this almost without thinking about it in fully federal cases; it is second nature. When federal courts get similar cases from a state, however, it is hard for them to do the same thing.[41]

I believe that federal judges have to learn how to deal with state laws and state actions in the same prudent fashion they use for federal ones. Otherwise, they will be too aggressive, and states will properly get angry. Again, there are ways, and certification is one. The Supreme Court told the lower federal courts, in *Arizonans for Official English v. Arizona*,[42] that they should ask the state's highest court to interpret the relevant statute before deciding on its constitutionality. Suppose, in the assisted suicide case,[43] that instead of deciding the case, and instead of having the Supreme Court decide the case, the Second Circuit had certified to the New York Court of Appeals the question of whether the New York law prohibiting assisted suicide (a) meant assisted suicide of somebody who was already dying, and (b) applied to *doctors* assisting suicide. Do we know what the New York Court of Appeals would have done? It is quite possible that the New York Court of Appeals would have interpreted the New York statute in a way that would have caused the whole issue of federal rights over state action to disappear. If that had been a *federal* statute, I do not doubt that a federal court of appeals would have done an awful lot of statutory interpretation before reaching any constitutional issue.

Once again, the state court might decline certification. But then the federal court would be free to interpret the state statute itself to avoid or delay the constitutional issue. Indeed, that is, desirably I think, what can be said to have happened in the nude photography case.[44]

Certification is not the only technique for slowing down such cases. Federal courts should read the decisions of European constitutional courts, which have developed many methods for handling, with nuance and care, overly stark constitutional questions.[45] I would like federal courts to learn from these European courts that, when the question is one of a state statute or of state behavior, there exist any number of ways in addition to certification that can make plenary federal review less brittle. If our courts did this, it would become more acceptable to return to a system in which issues of federal rights are tried out first in federal courts, even when they involve state action.

Such a return is as necessary now as it was sixty years ago, because it remains the case that the Supreme Court of the United States is not in a position adequately to protect those rights, and neither are the highest courts of the states. All of these courts can only take very few cases. And if such alleged rights are to be adequately examined and, where appropriate, protected, plenary consideration in lower federal courts is essential.

IV. Restoring the Balance

What, then, is the new and workable balance that I propose? I could give many details, but a short summary is enough:

1. Federal claims: Jurisdiction in cases asserting federal rights against federal actors need not be changed. Such suits are properly in federal court and remain there currently, as do civil claims under federal statutes.
2. Criminal law: These cases usually belong in state courts, even if they involve federal crimes, so long as the crime is parallel to one that exists in the state. Reverse certification to federal courts is encouraged if a separate and undecided federal question arises.
3. Private law: Federal courts are the "appellate division" for diversity cases and other cases involving state laws. Certification to the states is, therefore, called for, but after the federal court has indicated how it would decide the case if certification is refused. The state courts are then free to accept certification or not as they choose.
4. Federal rights against state actors: De novo or original consideration in federal courts is appropriate, with certification to states for state law interpretation and with frequent use of European-style passive virtues applied to such "collateral" constitutional reviews. (I am here incorporating by reference the many devices by which the European constitutional courts avoid deciding constitutional questions too soon.)[46]

The effect of these changes would be that each set of courts would do what it knows and does best; that local dominance in traditionally local areas would be reestablished, and that federal dominance, when issues of federal rights are involved, would also be reestablished; and that each set of courts would learn that it is not a matter of "who is better than whom," but rather that each should be humble about acknowledging the existence of areas as to which it knows less than other courts. Moreover, if we did these things, there would be what economists, with their usual infelicity of phrase, would term significant "external benefits." Federal dockets would be reduced, and this would reinforce the unique position of the federal courts of appeals—the position that makes being a judge on a federal court of appeals such a wonderful job.

It would make courts such as mine the court of last resort in all sorts of cases involving federal issues. (This is so whenever we can be confident that the Supreme Court is not interested, and hence that what we say governs.) In such situations, which is most of the time, we would write the kind of opinion that is suitable to a court of last resort. At other times, we are an intermediate federal court.[47] This occurs in situations in which we believe that the Supreme Court will take the case. It is then our job to write a menu for that Court—to write not as final decision makers, but instead to canvass all the possible ways in which the case should come out—so that the Supreme Court, when it takes the case, gets not only a result from us, but different approaches among which it might choose. Finally, in many cases involving local law, we are an intermediate state court. We then must readily yield to the state courts on state law. But we can give our opinion of what that law is, based both on local law precedents and on what other states do in like cases. We can in such situations speak to what we think state law ought to be, but always adding, "On this, we are a lower court, and it is up to you, higher state courts, to decide."

Three different hats, in one court. What a challenge. What fun. Madison would smile, I think.

NOTES

1. British North America Act, 30 & 31 Vict., c. 7, 96 (1867) (Eng.) (establishing structure of Canadian government).
2. *See* Treaty on European Union, Dec. 24, 2002, art. 35, http://europa.eu.int/eur-lex/en/treaties/dat/EC consol.html#000501 (establishing court of justice and conferring jurisdiction).
3. RECORDS OF THE FEDERAL CONVENTION OF 1787, at 21-22 (Max Farrand ed., 1911).
4. *Id.* at 125, 127.
5. U.S. CONST. art. III, § 1.
6. Judiciary Act of 1789, § 11, 1 Stat. 73, 78 (codified as amended at 28 U.S.C. § 41 (2000)).

7. *See* WILLIAM R. CASTO, THE SUPREME COURT IN THE EARLY REPUB-
LIC: THE CHIEF JUSTICESHIPS OF JOHN JAY AND OLIVER ELLS-
WORTH 27-53 (1995).

8. Erie R.R. Co. v. Tompkins, 304 U.S. 64 (1938).

9. Certiorari jurisdiction was established in the Judiciary Act of 1925, Pub. L. No.
68-415, 43 Stat. 936 (codified as amended in scattered sections of 28 U.S.C.).

10. *Erie*, 304 U.S. at 79-80.

11. *See, e.g.*, 18 U.S.C. § 844(i) (2000) (arson); § 1951 (robbery, extortion).

12. *See, e.g.*, United States v. Nelson, 277 F.3d 164, 190-91 (2d Cir. 2002) (holding
that statute prohibiting private violence motivated by victim's race, religion,
or other discriminatory reason is constitutional exercise of Congress's power
under section two of Thirteenth Amendment because of victim's use of public
facility); *see also* Yakus v. United States, 321 U.S. 414, 422, 444 (1944) (noting
that War Powers Clause, U.S. Const. art. 1, § 8, gives Congress constitutional
authority to prescribe commodity prices and to criminalize sale of commodi-
ties at higher prices as war emergency measure). *See generally* Edward D. Re,
*Federal-State Relations: The Allocation and Distribution of Powers of Government
in the United States*, 15 ST. THOMAS L. REV. 265, 276-83 (2002) (discussing
Congress's power to legislate using Commerce Clause).

13. *See, e.g.*, Jones v. United States, 529 U.S. 848, 850-51 (2000) (holding that federal
arson statute, 18 U.S.C. § 844(i) (2000), if applied to arson of owner-occupied
residence not used for any commercial purposes, would exceed Congress's Commerce Clause powers); United States v. Morrison, 529 U.S. 598, 601-02 (2000)
(holding that Violence Against Women Act's regulation of intrastate noneconomic activity exceeds Congress's Commerce Clause powers); Printz v. United
States, 521 U.S. 898, 936-40 (1997) (Thomas, J., concurring) (noting that Congress
lacks power under Commerce Clause to regulate "wholly intrastate, point-of-sale
transactions"); United States v. Lopez, 514 U.S. 549, 551 (1995) (holding that Gun-
Free School Zones Act exceeds Congress's Commerce Clause powers).

14. 18 U.S.C. § 1951 (2000).

15. *See* United States v. Jamison, 299 F.3d 114, 121-23 (2d Cir. 2002) (Jacobs, J.,
dissenting).

16. *See id.* at 118-19 (majority opinion by Leval, J., with which McLaughlin, J., concurred) (noting Second Circuit's conclusion that Supreme Court's decision in
Lopez does "not raise the de minimis threshold for satisfying the jurisdictional
element of the Hobbs Act" (citing United States v. Arena, 180 F.3d 380, 389-90
(2d Cir. 1999); United States v. Farrish, 122 F.3d 146, 148 (2d Cir. 1997))).

17. *See Morrison*, 529 U.S. 598.

18. *See, e.g.*, Partial-Birth Abortion Ban Act of 2003, S. 3, 108th Cong. (2003) (passed);
Partial-Birth Abortion Ban Act of 2003, H.R. 760, 108th Cong. (2003) (passed).

19. *See* Jon O. Newman, Remarks Given at a Panel Discussion on "Legal Issues in
the 21st Century" at the Fifty-Seventh Judicial Conference of the Third Circuit
in Philadelphia, Pa. (May, 15, 1997), *in* 70 TEMP. L. REV. 1125, 1128-29 (1997).

20. It is one that might also do away with such small abominations as dual
sovereignty-double jeopardy, which become ever more possible when there are

ever more things that are both federal crimes and state crimes. I mention this because that was the abomination that Justice Black was particularly concerned with in the 1958 Term when I was clerking for him. As he predicted, correctly, *see* Bartkus v. Illinois, 359 U.S. 121, 163-64 (Black, J., dissenting), dual sovereignty-double jeopardy is used especially in cases that are politically hot—when the person who had been acquitted is politically unpopular—whether from the right or the left. *See, e.g.*, United States v. Nelson, 277 F.3d 164 (2d Cir. 2002) (involving federal civil rights conviction of African American youth who had been acquitted in state court of murder charges arising from death of Orthodox Jewish man during racially motivated riot); United States v. Koon, 833 F. Supp. 769 (C.D. Cal. 1993) (involving federal civil rights conviction of officers who had been acquitted in state court of charges arising from their beating of Rodney King).

21. *See* Printz v. United States, 521 U.S. 898 (1997) (holding that Brady Act violates Tenth Amendment by imposing obligation on state officers to execute federal laws).

22. *See, e.g.*, Testa v. Katt, 330 U.S. 386, 394 (1947) (holding that Rhode Island courts cannot decline jurisdiction over claim under Emergency Price Control Act where courts otherwise "have jurisdiction adequate and appropriate under established local law to adjudicate this action"); Miles v. Ill. Cent. R.R., 315 U.S. 698, 703-04 (1942) (stating that where Congress conferred concurrent jurisdiction on state courts to enforce Federal Employers' Liability Act (FELA) and prohibited removal of actions brought in state courts, "opportunity to present causes of action arising under the F.E.L.A. in the state courts came . . . from [] federal" law, and therefore, "the courts of the several states must remain open to such litigants on the same basis that they are open to litigants with causes of action springing from a different source" because "the Federal Constitution makes the laws of the United States the supreme law of the land, binding on every citizen and every court and enforceable wherever jurisdiction is adequate for the purpose"); *see also* Mondou v. N.Y., New Haven & Hartford R.R. Co., 223 U.S. 1, 59 (1912) ("Rights arising under [FELA] may be enforced, as of right, in the courts of the states when their jurisdiction, as prescribed by local laws, is adequate to the occasion.").

23. Naturally, such certification would have to be structured so that the federal courts would decide only cases and controversies and not give advisory opinions. But that should be readily doable.

24. Obviously, if Congress were to pass such a law, it would be wise to grant states the funds to take on the additional cases. But given the relative costs of federal and state courts, it could easily do so in ways that would be financially advantageous both to the federal and local fiscs, and especially to the state courts.

25. Erie R.R. Co. v. Tompkins, 304 U.S. 64, 74-75 (1938).

26. Charles E. Clark, a predecessor of mine both as Yale Law School dean and on the Second Circuit, predicted this in an article he wrote soon after Erie. Charles E. Clark, *State Law in the Federal Courts: The Brooding Omnipresence of Erie v. Tompkins*, 55 YALE L.J. 267, 290-94 (1946). What Clark was most worried

about was the forum shopping that would occur if federal courts were required to follow old or dubious state court precedents. Because certification was not around at the time he wrote, and because he, correctly, viewed abstention as too cumbersome, Clark urged federal courts to be more flexible in their reading of state law. Absent certification, this seemed to him the best way to avoid having federal courts get state law wrong. For an example of a federal court addressing such an issue, see *Mason v. The American Emery Wheel Works*, 241 F.2d 906 (1st Cir. 1957).

27. *See* Wilfred Feinberg, *Is Diversity Jurisdiction an Idea Whose Time Has Passed?* N.Y. ST. B.J., July 1989, at 14.

28. *See, e.g.*, Pappas v. Middle Earth Condo. Ass'n, 963 F.2d 534, 539-41 (2d Cir. 1992) (holding that allowing defense counsel's statements designed to appeal to jury's regional bias in negligence action was reversible error and noting that original rationale for diversity jurisdiction—"fear that state courts would be prejudiced against out-of-state litigants"—"retains validity").

29. *See, e.g.*, Mark A. Varrichio & Assocs. v. Chi. Ins. Co., 312 F.3d 544, 548-50 (2d Cir. 2002) (certifying uncertain question of state law to New York Court of Appeals); Tri-State Employment Servs., Inc. v. Mountbatten Sur. Co., 295 F.3d 256, 269 (2d Cir. 2002) (same); Allstate Ins. Co. v. Serio, 261 F.3d 143, 149-54 (2d Cir. 2001) (same); Henderson v. INS, 157 F.3d 106, 123-24 (2d Cir. 1998) (same).

30. Done this way, with the understanding that state courts can readily decline certification, the volume of such cases would not be overly burdensome. Distinguished members of the New York Court of Appeals have made this point to me and others on my court.

31. Commentators have argued that the Supreme Court's decision in *Monroe v. Pape*, 365 U.S. 167 (1961), reinterpreting the phrase "under color of state law" and thereby opening lower federal courts to many more lawsuits under 42 U.S.C. § 1983 (2000), "rested upon a fundamental distrust of state courts to protect federal rights." Barry Friedman, *A Revisionist Theory of Abstention*, 88 MICH. L. REV. 530, 539 (1989).

32. *See* Edward A. Hartnett, *Questioning Certiorari: Some Reflections Seventy-Five Years After the Judges' Bill*, 100 COLUM. L. REV. 1643, 1646 & n.12 (2000) (collecting citations showing that, prior to passage of Judiciary Act of 1925, Court heard more than 300 cases per year).

33. *See, e.g.*, Barry Friedman, *A Tale of Two Habeas*, 73 MINN. L. REV. 247, 253-54 (1988) ("The Court expanded the scope of the writ of habeas corpus . . . because the Court recognized that it no longer could shoulder the burden on direct review of scrutinizing constitutional claims arising in state criminal proceedings.").

34. *See* CONN. GEN. STAT. § 51-197f (2003) (giving Connecticut Supreme Court discretionary review in general); CONN. GEN. STAT. § 51-199 (2003) (enumerating small class of cases that Connecticut Supreme Court must hear); N.Y. C.P.L.R. § 5602 (McKinney 2003) (giving New York Court of Appeals discretionary review in general).

35. *See* 28 U.S.C. §§ 2201-2202 (2000) (declaratory judgments); 28 U.S.C. § 2254 (1994) (amended 1996) (habeas corpus); 42 U.S.C. 1983 (2000); *see, e.g.*, Douglas v. Green, 363 U.S. 192 (1960) (reversing district court's denial of writ of habeas corpus); *see also supra* notes 30 and 32 and accompanying text.

36. *See, e.g.*, Antiterrorism and Effective Death Penalty Act of 1996, Pub. L. No. 104-132, 110 Stat. 1214 (1996) (codified as amended in scattered sections of 28 U.S.C.); Prison Litigation Reform Act of 1995, Pub. L. No. 104-134, 110 Stat. 1321 (1996) (codified as amended in scattered sections of 18, 28 & 42 U.S.C.); Teague v. Lane, 489 U.S. 288, 310 (1989).

37. *See, e.g.*, Editorial, *One Nation, Under Zeus*, WALL ST. J., June 27, 2002, at A20 (deploring Ninth Circuit's ruling that recitation of Pledge of Allegiance in public schools violates Establishment Clause of First Amendment); George F. Will, *Court of Silliness Strikes Again*, SEATTLE POST-INTELLIGENCER, Nov. 8, 2001, at B6.

38. *See* Tunick v. Safir, 209 F.3d 67, 68 (2d Cir. 2000) (certifying to New York Court of Appeals question of whether photographic shoot involving 75 to 100 nude models arranged in abstract formation on public street qualifies under exemptions to statutory ban on public nudity for entertainment or performance in "play, exhibition, show or entertainment"; whether such exemptions are limited to indoor activities; and, if exemptions do not apply to such activity or apply only to such activity conducted indoors, whether statutes banning public nudity so interpreted violate New York Constitution).

39. *See* Quill v. Vacco, 80 F.3d 716, 732 (2d Cir. 1996) (Calabresi, J., concurring) (noting that New York Court of Appeals had never clarified, and legislative history cast some doubt upon, question of whether New York ban on assisted suicide, first enacted in 1828, was "ever meant to apply to a treating physician"), *rev'd*, 521 U.S. 793.

40. *See* Alexander M. Bickel, *The Supreme Court, 1960 Term—Foreword: The Passive Virtues*, 75 HARV. L. REV. 40, 49 (1961) (advocating judicial restraint through use of such tactics as interpreting statutes so as to avoid constitutional issues).

41. It is hard at least in part because it seems grabby for the federal court to say what the state statute means. Grabby and to some extent academic, since the state court can later on give the same statute a totally different reading.

42. 520 U.S. 43, 76-79 (1997).

43. *See Quill*, 80 F.3d 716.

44. *See* Tunick v. Safir, 228 F.3d 135, 136-37 (2d Cir. 2000). *But see id.* at 137 (Sack, J., concurring); Tunick v. Safir, 209 F.3d 67, 90-100 (2d Cir. 2000) (Sack, J., concurring).

45. *See* United States v. Then, 56 F.3d 464, 468-69 (2d Cir. 1995) (Calabresi, J., concurring) (describing German and Italian courts' practice of announcing when laws are "heading toward unconstitutionality" and citing sources).

46. I have noted some of these devices in *Then*:

> Both the Constitutional Courts of Germany and Italy have addressed the problem of laws that were rational when enacted, but which, over time, have become increasingly dubious. Rather than jumping in and

striking the laws down, or leaving them undisturbed and thereby allowing legislative inertia to dominate, these Courts have found a middle
ground. They have, in a few cases, announced that laws, because of
changed circumstances, were heading toward unconstitutionality.

Id.; see also DONALD P. KOMMERS, THE CONSTITUTIONAL JURISPRU-
DENCE OF THE FEDERAL REPUBLIC OF GERMANY 60-61 & n.118 (1989)
(chronicling cases and explaining that Constitutional Court of Germany utilizes
this technique most often for "equal-protection claims . . . to give the legislature
time to adjust to changing conditions"); CHRISTIAN BECK PESTALOZZA,
VERFASSUNGSPROZESSRECHT: DIE VERFASSUNGSGERICHTSBARKEIT
DES BUNDES UND DER LÄNDER: MIT EINEM ANHANG ZUM INTER-
NATIONALEN RECHTSSCHUTZ 20, at 337 & n.313 (3d ed. 1991) (describing
German practice and citing cases).

47. For a sophisticated analysis, see Calvert Magruder, *The Trials and Tribulations of
an Intermediate Appellate Court*, 44 CORNELL L.Q. 33 (1968).

3

Judicial Methodology, Southern School
Desegregation, and the Rule of Law

DAVID S. TATEL

Americans have fiercely debated the proper role of Article III courts in our constitutional system ever since Chief Justice John Marshall declared in *Marbury v. Madison* that it is "emphatically the province and duty of the judicial department to say what the law is."[1] This debate often has focused on Supreme Court decisions involving some of our nation's most historic events: the Court's 1873 evisceration of the Fourteenth Amendment's Privileges or Immunities Clause,[2] its use of substantive due process to strike down progressive legislation at the turn of the century,[3] its invalidation of key New Deal programs,[4] and its opinion in *Roe v. Wade*[5] are but a few of the decisions that have reignited the controversy over the meaning and risks of "judicial activism."

This paper focuses on one of the more recent chapters in this centuries-old debate. Reacting to what they perceived to be judicial activism under Chief Justice Earl Warren's leadership, Presidents Richard Nixon, Ronald Reagan, and George H. W. Bush all promised to appoint "strict constructionists" to the Supreme Court rather than "activists" who would pursue personal policy agendas.[6] Those three Presidents appointed the five Justices who, led by Chief Justice William Rehnquist, now make up the Supreme Court's most frequent majority. Have these Justices fulfilled their appointing Presidents' promises? Those who answer "yes" point to decisions involving the Commerce Clause, federalism, criminal law, and church-state relations, and argue that the Rehnquist Court has

This lecture was delivered on October 27, 2003, and appeared in *79 N.Y.U. L. Rev.* 1071 (2004).

refrained from the expansive constitutional jurisprudence that characterized the Warren Court, adhered to the text and original understanding
of the Constitution, and restored the proper balance between states and
the federal government.[7] Those who answer "no" cite many of the same
cases and, of course, *Bush v. Gore*,[8] arguing that the Rehnquist Court has
become one of the most activist Courts in history.[9]

To explore the debate about judicial activism, I have looked back at
the Rehnquist Court's opinions in two school desegregation cases, *Board
of Education v. Dowell*[10] and *Missouri v. Jenkins*.[11] I did not choose these
cases only because I know them well from my work before joining the
D.C. Circuit.[12] Rather, I chose them because of their relationship to *Brown
v. Board of Education*[13] and its progeny, decisions that perhaps best exem-
plify the Warren Court's view of the Constitution and of federal court
power. Given the Rehnquist Court's very different views of constitutional
interpretation and the role of the federal courts, and given that a crucial
test for any court is its ability to follow precedent with which it may disagree, I thought it would be interesting to examine how the Rehnquist
Court dealt with Warren Court precedents. There is another reason for
focusing on these two decisions: 2004 is the fiftieth anniversary of *Brown
v. Board of Education,* and this paper is my contribution to the *Brown*
retrospective.

Let me begin with the entirely misleading label "judicial activist." The
term is usually used by a politician or commentator who, unhappy with
a decision's outcome, accuses the judge of pursuing a personal agenda,
often adding, as though it proves the point, that the judge is an appointee
of President X or President Y. Such results-focused criticism may advance
the critic's rhetorical or political cause, but whether a decision is a legitimate act of judging turns on far more than its outcome. It turns primarily
on whether its outcome evolved from those principles of judicial methodology that distinguish judging from policymaking. For example, is the
decision consistent with principles of stare decisis—that is, does the decision follow precedent, or, if not, does it either explain why otherwise controlling case law does not apply or forthrightly overrule that case law on
principled grounds? Is the decision faithful to constitutional and statutory text and to the intent of the drafters? Does it appropriately defer to
the policy judgments of Congress and administrative agencies? Does it
apply the proper standard of review to lower-court fact findings? Are the
issues it resolves generally limited to those raised by the parties? Does it
avoid unnecessary dicta? And finally, are its results openly and rationally

explained? As the Supreme Court has stated, "a decision without principled justification would be no judicial act at all."[14]

Of course, such principles, even if assiduously applied, will never standardize decisionmaking completely, for interpreting precedent, as well as constitutional and statutory text, requires judgment, and reasonable judges can disagree. By following these and other rules of judging, however, life-tenured judges from across the political spectrum maximize the extent to which their decisions are driven not by personal policy agendas but by the application of law to established fact. Critical to the principle of judicial restraint, these standards help federal courts avoid intruding on the policymaking function and retain the credibility they need to serve in our democracy as the arbiter of constitutional issues and the ultimate protector of constitutional rights. Courts that disregard these principles abuse their power. They contribute, as Justice Potter Stewart once put it, to "the popular misconception that this institution is little different from the two political branches of the Government."[15] "No misconception," Justice Stewart warned, "could do more lasting injury to this Court and to the system of law which it is our abiding mission to serve."[16]

I am asked frequently whether I find these methodological principles constraining. Of course I do, but I also find them immensely reassuring. Most D.C. Circuit cases involve difficult and complex policy questions. Will limits on the number of subscribers that any one cable company may reach increase diversity of information or promote competition? Are restrictions on picketing and demonstrating near the Capitol needed in our post–September 11th world to protect members of Congress? At what level should national air quality standards be set to promote public health? Although my colleagues and I have personal views about such questions, we have neither the expertise to resolve them nor accountability to the electorate for doing so. What we are good at and what we are accountable for is determining whether policymakers responsible for resolving such issues have done so lawfully. Judges may not know whether a cap on the number of subscribers any cable company may reach is necessary to promote diversity, but by applying relevant Supreme Court and circuit decisions, we know how to determine whether a statute authorizing such caps is consistent with the First Amendment.[17] Judges may be ill-equipped to assess the Capitol's security needs, but we do know how to determine whether a particular restriction on picketing meets constitutional standards established by controlling case law.[18] And although judges may lack expertise to select national air pollution standards, we certainly know how to assess whether in doing so the Environmental Protection Agency satisfied the requirements of the Administrative Procedure Act.[19]

These methodological constraints mean that we judges sometimes sustain actions we think make little sense, invalidate programs we like, or apply precedents we believe were wrongly decided. For example, I once wrote an opinion for the court upholding a congressional ceiling on attorneys' fees in special education cases brought against the District of Columbia public school system. Though believing that law quite unwise, I was unable to conclude that it was "irrational"—the applicable standard in such cases.[20] In another case, my opinion for the court sustained a police stop based on a rather vague description of a suspect obtained from an emergency 911 caller because the stop was consistent with circuit case law, even though I thought our precedents insufficiently protected Fourth Amendment rights.[21] In still another case, my opinion for the court sustained a challenge to a creative state program that made low-cost drugs available to the poor because, applying canons of statutory construction, my fellow judges and I concluded that the agency lacked authority for the program.[22] I could list just as many opinions that sustained programs or policies that I thought were sound, many of which were joined by colleagues who may not have been as pleased as I about the outcomes but who nonetheless followed basic principles of judging. In all these cases, though we may have been troubled by the outcomes, we knew that vindicating the rule of law was far more important to our constitutional system than the issues at stake in any particular case. Oliver Wendell Holmes Jr. put it this way: "It has given me great pleasure to sustain the Constitutionality of laws that I believe to be as bad as possible, because I thereby helped to mark the difference between what I would forbid and what the Constitution permits."[23]

Measured against these principles—principles that, because of the Supreme Court's virtual unaccountability, apply to it with even greater force than to the "inferior courts"—*Dowell* and *Jenkins* are flawed. They are flawed in multiple ways, but particularly with respect to their departure from principles of stare decisis.[24] The decisions sharply departed from two of the Supreme Court's most important post-*Brown* desegregation cases, *Green v. County School Board of New Kent County*[25] and *Swann v. Charlotte-Mecklenburg Board of Education*,[26] which set demanding desegregation standards for southern school systems and for federal courts, yet neither *Dowell* nor *Jenkins* acknowledged, let alone explained, its disregard for those two precedents. The two decisions certainly produced *politically* conservative outcomes—they cut back on one of the Warren Court's most dramatic assertions of judicial power—but do not confuse that result with their methodology, for as I will show, *Dowell* and *Jenkins* arrived at their conservative outcomes through decidedly unconservative means.

Before analyzing the two decisions, this paper begins with some history. Part I examines the origins of *Green* and *Swann* and summarizes the powerful desegregation principles they announced. Understanding these principles is critical to seeing how far *Dowell* and *Jenkins* strayed from precedent. Part II discusses Richard Nixon's 1968 presidential campaign and his effort, once elected, to limit *Green* and *Swann* and to curtail court-ordered desegregation. Although unnecessary to understanding *Dowell*'s and *Jenkins*'s methodological flaws, this history provides the background against which the public may perceive the two decisions and, ultimately, the courts themselves. Parts III, IV, and V—the heart of this paper—then undertake a detailed, methodological analysis of *Dowell* and *Jenkins*.

Three last introductory points. First, although this article deals with school desegregation, it is not about busing. It is about judicial methodology. The fundamental problem with *Dowell* and *Jenkins* is not their outcome—the curtailing of school desegregation remedies—but the manner by which they reached that result.

Second, in offering this critique, I realize that by comparison to the lower federal courts, the Supreme Court faces far more issues for which precedent provides little or no guidance. That said, this simply means that other principles of judging—in particular, the requirement to provide rational explanations for holdings—become even more critical to ensuring that the Supreme Court is not perceived as a policymaking institution.

Finally, some friends who read drafts of this paper wondered why a sitting appeals court judge would criticize the court that reviews his opinions—or as my dear friend Judge Louis Oberdorfer puts it, the court that "grades his papers." That is a good question, and I have thought long and hard about it. But after ten years as a federal judge, I too am increasingly concerned about the growing public perception that courts are blurring the distinction between judging and policymaking. This perception is reinforced by the results-focused criticism of judicial decisions, by the increasingly bitter and, again, results-focused confirmation process, and sometimes by the courts themselves. I hope this analysis of *Dowell* and

Jenkins will help refocus the national debate about the role of Article III courts and persuade combatants in the "judicial wars" to pay attention to methodology. Rigorous judicial methodology is not only essential to the legitimacy of any opinion, but it also protects the judiciary's integrity, the public's confidence in the courts, and the rule of law. It is in that spirit that I offer this year's Madison Lecture.

I.

I could begin this paper at several points in American history: the Constitution's failure to abolish slavery; *Dred Scott v. Sandford*;[27] the passage of the Thirteenth, Fourteenth, and Fifteenth Amendments; the *Civil Rights Cases*;[28] or *Plessy v. Ferguson*.[29] Although my topic has its roots in all these critical events, this paper begins a little later, with *Brown v. Board of Education*[30] and the condition of schools that black children attended in the years leading to *Brown*.

Although *Plessy v. Ferguson* had held that separate but equal public facilities did not offend the Fourteenth Amendment,[31] the segregated black schools that were mandated or authorized by state law in the seventeen former slave and border states were notoriously unequal to those that white students attended. By the 1950s, southern school systems spent on average twice as much to educate white children as they did to educate black children.[32] The percentage of whites finishing high school was four times higher than the percentage of blacks.[33]

In his seminal book, *Simple Justice*, Richard Kluger describes conditions in Clarendon County, South Carolina, one of the four school systems at issue in *Brown*.[34] Some 276 white children attended two brick schools whose combined value (including buildings, grounds, and furnishings) was four times that of the three wooden schools attended by more than eight hundred black children.[35] One black school had no running water; another had no electricity. While both white schools had indoor flush toilets, the black schools had only outhouses and, according to Kluger, "not nearly enough of them."[36] The white schools had desks for all children, while one of the black schools had no desks at all. The two white schools offered bus transportation, but the three black schools, located in rural, isolated areas, offered none; to attend school, two black six-year-olds had to walk ten miles each day.[37] The white elementary school had one teacher for every twenty-eight children; the student-teacher ratio at the black schools was forty to one.[38]

The condition of black schools throughout the South was deplorable, but when the Supreme Court reconsidered *Plessy* in *Brown*, it did not rely on such inequalities, instead recognizing a more basic harm: Even in the rare districts where facilities were in fact equal,[39] compulsory segregation itself stigmatized black students by "generating a feeling of inferiority as to their status in the community that may affect their hearts and minds in a way unlikely ever to be undone."[40] "We conclude," the Court therefore declared unanimously, "that in the field of public education the doctrine of 'separate but equal' has no place. Separate educational facilities are inherently unequal."[41]

The South responded to *Brown* with Massive Resistance. Led by race-baiting demagogues like George Wallace—who later declared in his 1963 inaugural address as Alabama governor, "Segregation now! Segregation tomorrow! Segregation forever!"[42]—political leaders responded with a series of actions that rejected *Brown*'s very legitimacy. For instance, Louisiana's so-called "interposition resolution" rejected federal authority to exercise power over state and local officials, forbidding such officials from complying with court desegregation decrees.[43] At the national level, in 1956 Senator Strom Thurmond and ninety-five other members of Congress signed the infamous Southern Manifesto, decrying *Brown* as an "exercise [of] naked judicial power" and pledging "to use all lawful means to bring about a reversal of this decision . . . and to prevent the use of force in its implementation."[44] The signers "commended the motives of those States which had declared the intention to resist forced integration by any lawful means."[45]

Although the Supreme Court's second *Brown* decision in 1955 (*Brown II*) directed school officials and federal district courts to plan "a transition to . . . racially nondiscriminatory school systems" with "all deliberate speed,"[46] many southern states instead radically altered their education laws to thwart desegregation. Several states adopted pupil assignment laws that used facially "objective" factors such as student preparation, dangers to public order, and the supposed interests of children and parents to assign students to the same effectively segregated schools that they had attended before *Brown*.[47] Some states abandoned compulsory attendance altogether, authorizing local officials to close schools rather than integrate them,[48] and adopted publicly funded tuition payment plans and other measures to make it easier for white children to attend segregated private academies.[49] Georgia made it a felony for local officials to spend public money on desegregated

schools, while Mississippi and Louisiana outlawed attendance at integrated schools.[50]

Massive Resistance reached a new level in 1957 when Arkansas governor Orval Faubus dispatched the National Guard to block school desegregation in Little Rock.[51] Americans watched on television while whites,
their faces filled with hatred, screamed at nine black youngsters attempting to enter Central High School. Violence continued until the Little
Rock federal court ordered the Guard withdrawn,[52] and a reluctant President Eisenhower deployed one thousand paratroopers from the 101st Air-
borne, the first time since Reconstruction that military force was used to
protect black citizens in the South.[53] When the issue reached the Supreme
Court in *Cooper v. Aaron*,[54] the Court responded with an assertion of the
supremacy of federal judicial power as emphatic as its cornerstone pronouncement in *Marbury v. Madison*.[55] Holding that the governor and the
Arkansas legislature were both bound by *Brown*, the Court declared that
its 1954 decision was "now unanimously reaffirmed" and that "[its] principles . . . [were] indispensable for the protection of the freedoms guaranteed by our fundamental charter for all of us."[56] Emphasizing their unanimity, the nine Justices individually signed the opinion[57]—the only time
that has ever happened.

After *Cooper*, segregationists gradually shifted from overt defiance
to feigned acquiescence. In some states, public officials gerrymandered
school district lines to create smaller, majority-white "carve-out" districts—predominantly white jurisdictions that seceded from larger,
desegregating school systems.[58] Other school systems made desegregation as unpleasant as possible for the few black students who chose to
attend desegregated schools. Such students often were subjected to exces-
sively long bus rides, assigned to segregated classes within their new
schools, harassed by white students and teachers, and unfairly expelled.[59]

The most common form of continued resistance to *Brown* was "freedom-of-choice," a popular tactic through which children were assigned
to their original segregated schools unless they "chose" otherwise.[60]
Freedom-of-choice appeared facially neutral, yet in many communities it
produced, just as intended, far less integration than would have occurred
had school districts simply adopted neighborhood schools. Faced with
byzantine bureaucratic obstacles, social pressure, and even physical
intimidation, few black parents "chose" to send their children to historically white schools.[61] The recollections of a young black student, Stanley
Trent, are telling. Asked by his parents which school he wished to attend,

young Trent replied, "I don't want to go to no white school." Reflecting on
the experience later in life, Trent explained that his parents readily agreed
because they worried that enrollment in a white school "would place us
in physical, psychological, and emotional danger [and t]hey feared that
our mere presence in one of the newly integrated schools would aggra-
vate and intensify the hatred that had maintained our segregated communities, our segregated existence, for centuries."[62]

In reality, "freedom" to choose meant freedom for white children to
attend all-white schools and, in the words of one black parent, freedom
for black children to "go where you been going."[63] Proponents embraced
freedom-of-choice as a sacred and historic right, but in fact, prior to
Brown no southern students freely chose their own schools: Whites were
assigned to neighborhood schools, while blacks were assigned to separate schools, often in remote areas.[64] Moderate white southerners well
understood the true nature of the system: "You may be assured," wrote
renowned *Atlanta Constitution* editor Ralph McGill, "that the freedom of
choice plan is, in fact, neither freedom nor a choice. It is discrimination."[65]

Beginning in the mid-1960s, the Supreme Court, building on the
principles of *Brown*, issued a series of decisions that unanimously and
emphatically rejected these efforts to avoid desegregation. In *Griffin v.
County School Board*, the Court held that a Virginia school district violated the Fourteenth Amendment's equal protection guarantee by shut-
ting down its public schools and providing whites with tuition grants and
tax breaks to attend segregated private academies.[66] In *United States v.
Scotland Neck City Board of Education*, the Court upheld an injunction
that prevented a largely white North Carolina city from seceding from a
predominantly black county school system to avoid desegregation.[67] In
Alexander v. Holmes County Board of Education, the Court rejected Mississippi's plea to delay court-ordered desegregation, declaring that where
"the denial of fundamental rights to many thousands of school children"
was at stake, *Brown II*'s "standard of allowing 'all deliberate speed' for
desegregation is no longer constitutionally permissible."[68] Instead, "the
obligation of every school district is to terminate dual school systems at
once and to operate now and hereafter only unitary schools."[69]

The two most important cases in this series were *Green v. County
School Board*[70] and *Swann v. Charlotte-Mecklenburg Board of Education*.[71]
Green rejected a freedom-of-choice plan under which eighty-five percent
of black children still attended historically black schools,[72] and *Swann*, the
first desegregation case involving a major urban school system, sustained

a district court order requiring extensive busing beyond neighborhood attendance zones.[73] The two cases charged southern school authorities with an "affirmative duty to take whatever steps might be necessary to convert to a unitary system in which racial discrimination would be eliminated root and branch"[74] and held that facially neutral student assignment policies were constitutionally unacceptable if they failed to produce promptly a "system without . . . 'white' schools and . . . 'Negro' schools, but just schools."[75] Declaring that the objective of school desegregation was not just to strike down laws requiring segregated schools but also "to eliminate from the public schools all vestiges of state-imposed segregation,"[76] the Court directed that if local officials failed to desegregate all aspects of school operations, federal district courts must themselves craft and implement effective desegregation plans.[77] *Green* and *Swann* established three key principles for district judges to use in evaluating local desegregation efforts:

1. Southern school boards bear the burden of proof. Courts must presume that all remaining one-race schools are vestiges of segregation and hold school boards responsible for desegregating them unless officials demonstrate that the schools are products of neither past nor present discrimination.[78] School officials also bear a "heavy burden" to justify choosing less effective desegregation methods (like freedom-of-choice) over more effective alternatives (like busing).[79]

2. Good faith is not enough. Federal courts must evaluate desegregation plans on the basis of their effectiveness in eliminating vestiges of segregation, not on the school boards' intent.[80] A plan is not acceptable simply because it is facially neutral since it may fail to counteract the continuing effects of prior discriminatory decisions concerning school size and location that can affect residential segregation for years.[81]

3. Federal courts must tailor desegregation decrees to match the scope of the constitutional violations. Courts have "'not merely the power but the duty'" to craft remedies that eliminate the effects of segregation,[82] for "once a right and a violation have been shown, the scope of a district court's equitable powers to remedy past wrongs is broad . . . and flexible."[83] Courts must retain jurisdiction "until it is clear that state-imposed segregation has been completely removed."[84]

Applied by federal courts throughout the South in hundreds of lawsuits brought by the Department of Justice, the NAACP Legal Defense & Educational Fund, and other civil rights organizations, these three principles proved extremely effective in hastening desegregation, particularly when augmented by Title VI of the Civil Rights Act of 1964, which required the U.S. Department of Health, Education, and Welfare (HEW) to terminate federal funds to school districts refusing to desegregate.[85] In the seventeen states covered by *Brown* where segregation had been mandated or authorized by law, the percentage of black children attending school with whites jumped from just eleven percent in 1964-65, a decade after *Brown*, to eighty-four percent in 1970-71.[86] Yet the principles of *Green* and *Swann*, responsible for so much desegregation, would not survive the political and especially the judicial forces that would soon be marshaled against them.

II.

The political forces opposing court-ordered school desegregation had their origins in Massive Resistance, but they gained national potency during the 1968 presidential campaign and its aftermath. Although presidential hopeful Richard Nixon had taken relatively progressive civil rights stands early in his career—for example, he had supported the Civil Rights Acts of 1957 and 1964[87]—he decided that his presidential hopes and the Republican Party's future lay in a calculated "Southern Strategy"—an attempt to forge a new, long-term majority by combining northern and western suburban Republicans with blue-collar workers and white southerners dissatisfied with the Democratic Party's focus on civil rights.[88] On May 31, 1968, just four days after the Supreme Court announced its decision in *Green*, Nixon flew to Atlanta to court two of the South's most influential politicians, Republican senators Strom Thurmond of South Carolina and John Tower of Texas.[89] To secure their support for the nomination, Nixon promised to protect the South's declining textile industry, to provide more money for defense, and to slow the pace of school desegregation. In particular, he promised to ease federal pressure on southern schools, to limit the use of busing, and to appoint "strict constructionists" to the Supreme Court.[90]

Once Nixon secured the Republican nomination, he set out to differentiate himself from the openly segregationist George Wallace by declaring that he supported "an orderly transition" to desegregation, meaning the removal of formal legal obstacles to integrated schools, but opposed "instant integration," by which he meant court-ordered measures to end segregation.[91] Nixon told campaign workers that the "Court was right on *Brown* and wrong on *Green*."[92] Late in the campaign, Nixon publicly supported freedom-of-choice and declared that he opposed withholding money from schools refusing to desegregate.[93]

Upon taking office, Nixon began by curtailing HEW's critical enforcement role,[94] ordering the department to make desegregation plans "inoffensive" to the "people" of the southern states.[95] HEW's laxity was so great that U.S. district judge John Pratt found the Department guilty of subverting the Civil Rights Act of 1964.[96] Affirming the district court's decision unanimously, the D.C. Circuit called HEW's inaction a "dereliction of duty."[97]

Then, in part to gain Mississippi senator John Stennis's support for the anti–ballistic missile treaty, Nixon directed his HEW secretary to ask the federal court in *Alexander v. Holmes County Board of Education*[98] to give Mississippi school districts more time to desegregate.[99] For the first time since *Brown*, Justice Department lawyers sat on the opposite side of the courtroom from lawyers for black schoolchildren. Ultimately, the administration's efforts failed, for in *Alexander*, a unanimous Supreme Court rejected any delay, declaring that the obligation of every school district was to terminate dual school systems "at once."[100]

Rather than risk open confrontation with the Supreme Court, Nixon convened a Cabinet working group[101] and issued a statement that, like so much of his rhetoric, walked a fine line between endorsing *Brown*'s broad principles and signaling to the South that he meant to minimize *Green*'s and *Alexander*'s impact on white students.[102] The statement enunciated three basic points.

First, the statement declared a preference for neighborhood schools, despite the fact that neighborhood-based assignments would perpetuate many of the all-black schools created under the dual system.[103] As revealed in the Nixon tapes, many of which I reviewed to prepare this paper, Nixon's private views were more blunt. For example, in an Oval Office meeting, Nixon told aides: "I want to take a flat-out position against busing, period. . . . I am against busing! I am for neighborhood schools!"[104]

Second, whereas the Supreme Court demanded a remedy for the victims of *segregation*, Nixon's statement demanded a remedy for the so-called "victims" of *desegregation*.[105] Throughout the tapes, Nixon's constant theme was that busing was educationally harmful.[106]

Third, the statement asserted that "good faith is critical"[107] and that school boards should have "substantial latitude" to desegregate as long as they demonstrate good faith.[108] The Oval Office tapes reveal a President more concerned with limiting federal government involvement in local school districts than with achieving the effective desegregation required by *Green* and *Swann*.[109] While Nixon did call on local leaders to ensure that desegregation proceeded smoothly,[110] his statement implied that minimal local efforts would be sufficient even if significant vestiges of segregation remained.[111]

In the fall of 1970, many hold-out southern districts finally implemented desegregation plans, as Nixon had urged,[112] but in *Swann* the Supreme Court rejected Nixon's plea to protect neighborhood schools, unanimously affirming district court authority to order extensive busing, including of young children.[113] Reacting to *Swann* and other desegregation decisions, Nixon instructed domestic policy adviser John Ehrlichman to "get legislation or a constitutional amendment ready."[114]

Seeing busing as an ideal reelection issue, Nixon decided to propose a legislative moratorium on busing because he worried that a constitutional amendment, favored by many southerners, would take too long.[115] Any delay, he told Cabinet members,

> means that school children who are truly [unintelligible] in the next school year and possibly the next school year, the hundreds of thousands will be the victims of new massive busing orders by the courts. So, therefore, it's too slow. I think that this issue, an issue that all of you know from your mail, all of you know from watching what is happening around the country, this issue is one that requires action now. It requires it because you just can't have a generation of children that are the victims, if you believe that busing's wrong, [unintelligible] are the victims of this kind of thing.[116]

Even if the Supreme Court were to invalidate the legislative moratorium, Nixon reasoned, "We wouldn't have lost everything. We'll just come up with a constitutional amendment. Period. And let the Democratic candidate be against it. It'll polarize the country. I'm telling you we're going to fight this battle, we're going to fight it."[117]

Supporting anti-busing legislation and curtailing federal government desegregation enforcement activities were not President Nixon's only efforts to limit school desegregation. As he had promised Senators Thurmond and Tower, Nixon also attempted to use Supreme Court nominations to change the Court's direction, though his first efforts failed. After successfully appointing Chief Justice Warren Burger, Nixon nominated Fourth Circuit judge Clement Haynsworth, who had written one opinion upholding a freedom-of-choice plan that was unanimously reversed in a companion case to *Green*,[118] and another opinion allowing a Virginia county to close its schools to avoid court-ordered desegregation that was unanimously reversed by *Griffin*.[119] The Senate, concerned (among other things) about Judge Haynsworth's commitment to *Brown*, rejected his nomination.

Undaunted and angry, Nixon told aides to look "farther South and further right."[120] They did, and they found a little-known federal judge from Florida named G. Harrold Carswell. After the press revealed that Carswell had once stated, "I yield to no man . . . in the firm, vigorous belief in the principles of white supremacy, and I shall always be so governed,"[121] the Senate rejected this nomination as well.[122]

When two additional Supreme Court seats opened up in 1971, Nixon told Attorney General Mitchell that he was determined to appoint at least one southerner:

> It would be a slap to the South not to try for a southerner. So I would say that our first requirement is a southerner. The second requirement: He must be a conservative southerner. . . . Third, within the definition of conservative, he must be . . . against busing and against forced housing integration. Beyond that, he can do what he pleases.[123]

For the other vacancy, Nixon was more concerned about ideology than geography, explaining:

> I just feel so strongly about that. I mean when I think about what the busing decision has done to this thing in the South and when I think of what it could do if they get into de facto busing and forced integration in housing, I just, I just feel that, I just feel that if it's the last thing we do, we've got to have a conservative.[124]

The President directed Mitchell to talk personally with the final candidate to get an absolute commitment on busing:

> I want you to have a specific talk with whatever man we consider and I have to have an absolute commitment from him on busing and integration. I really have to. All right? Tell him we totally respect his right to do otherwise, but if he believes otherwise, I will not appoint him to the Court.[125]

After considering several candidates, Nixon ultimately selected Lewis Powell, formerly an American Bar Association president and chairman of the Richmond, Virginia, school board.[126] Powell had opposed Massive Resistance, but Nixon told aides that Powell was against busing. Referring to Powell, as well as to Senator Howard Baker, whom the President was considering for the other open seat, Nixon told aides: "Let me go over all of this, this issue of busing. Both these men are against busing. And that will help us like hell."[127]

III.

Before turning to *Dowell* and *Jenkins*, I think it worth observing that signals of the Supreme Court's departure from *Brown* and its progeny appeared years earlier, starting with the internal deliberations over *Swann* itself. Although most Justices believed that the district court's desegregation order should be upheld, Chief Justice Burger's initial draft of *Swann* criticized the lower court because of "strong intimations" that it had relied on a "fixed mathematical racial balance."[128] Retreating from *Green*, the draft stated that "some of the problems . . . arise from viewing *Brown I* as imposing a requirement for racial balance, i.e., integration, rather than a prohibition against segregation."[129] Other Justices objected to the draft, but the Chief Justice, apparently misreading their objections, produced a second draft that was even more critical of the district court.[130] After Justice Stewart and others renewed their objections, Burger gradually refocused the opinion to affirm district courts' authority to craft effective desegregation remedies and to reject the challenge to the busing order at issue, explaining that "we are unable to conclude that the order of the District Court is not reasonable, feasible and workable."[131]

Burger's authorship of *Swann* disappointed Nixon, who worried that the South would hold him accountable.[132] Indeed, Nixon had been so concerned about *Swann* that he actually lobbied the Chief Justice while the case was pending. In an Oval Office meeting, Nixon told aides that three weeks before *Swann* was handed down, he had met with the Chief Justice: "Mitchell and Burger and I had breakfast about three months ago and I lit into Burger. I said, 'Now look here, I'll be honest with you, if you insist on busing. . . .' So I was sorta disappointed."[133]

A year later, the President again met with the Chief Justice, telling him that the Warren Court had led "the people" to "lose confidence. They see these, you know, they see these hippies, and frankly, the Negro problem[,] . . . and then there's busing. That just drives them up the damn wall."[134] Apparently getting the message but not mentioning that *Swann* had approved busing of even young children, Chief Justice Burger told Nixon: "That *Swann* case was thoroughly misrepresented by the press. . . . They wanted it to be just a busing decision. . . . It was the first time the Court could put limits on busing."[135]

Later in 1972, Burger's discomfort with the principles he had enunciated in *Swann* surfaced publicly when, joined by Justices Blackmun, Powell, and Rehnquist, he authored the first dissent in a school desegregation case. *Wright v. City of Emporia*[136] involved Greensville County, Virginia, where, before *Brown*, white students had attended white schools in Emporia, the county's only city, and most black children, including those living in Emporia, had attended black schools in rural areas.[137] Two weeks after the district court, responding to *Green*, imposed a countywide desegregation plan,[138] Emporia's city council suddenly announced that it would begin operating its schools as an independent system.[139] The district court enjoined Emporia's secession, finding that it would "plainly cause a substantial shift in the racial balance" and would "prejudice the prospects for unitary schools for county" students.[140] The Fourth Circuit reversed and remanded with instructions to dissolve the injunction.[141]

Justice Stewart, joined by four other Justices who also had participated in several key post-*Brown* decisions, including *Green* and *Swann*, authored the Court's majority opinion in *Wright*.[142] Concluding that the district court had acted within its equitable powers, the majority adhered to the principle established in *Green* and *Swann* that to be constitutionally acceptable a desegregation plan, measured by its effects, must produce "a school system in which all vestiges of enforced racial segregation have been eliminated."[143] Although the Fourth Circuit had concluded that the dominant purpose of the Emporia secession was "benign,"[144] the Supreme Court majority rejected that conclusion as inconsistent with *Green*'s effects test.[145] Explaining that the district court's factual findings had adequate support in the record,[146] the majority found that the Emporia secession would have "purchased [a quality education for city students] only at the price of a substantial adverse effect upon the viability of the county system."[147] The majority acknowledged that "direct control over decisions vitally affecting the education of one's children is a need that is strongly felt in our society,"[148] and stated that once the combined county system was unitary, Emporia would be free to establish an independent district.[149]

Although the four dissenters had joined the majority in a companion case that rejected a similar carve-out plan where the record contained direct evidence that public officials intended to perpetuate segregation,[150] they emphasized in their *Wright* dissent that no such evidence existed with regard to Emporia and concluded that sufficient desegregation would occur even if the city seceded.[151] Under such circumstances, the dissent stated, the district court was obligated to accept Emporia's carve-out plan, "unless there are strong reasons why a different plan is to be preferred," in order to protect what it called the "overriding importance" of local control of public schools.[152] In other words, contrary to *Green* and *Swann*, the dissent sought to protect local control even if that meant less effective desegregation and to impose on *plaintiffs* the burden of demonstrating the need for more effective desegregation measures.

The *Wright* dissent not only foreshadowed the Court's later change in direction but also deviated from key principles of judicial methodology. In addition to disregarding precedent (i.e., *Green*), the dissent substituted its own judgment for the district court's on the key factual question at the heart of the case—the desegregative effects of the competing Emporia plans—and ignored *Swann's* recognition that "'because of [district courts'] proximity to local conditions . . . [they] can best perform the judicial appraisal'" of the efficacy of a desegregation plan.[153] The district judge had found that Emporia's secession would "substantially" skew racial distributions and anticipated that white students moving to and from private academies could exacerbate such disparities.[154] The dissent viewed the facts very differently, dismissing the possibility of resegregation as "at best, highly speculative."[155] Then, itself speculating about the effect of the Emporia secession, the dissent accused both the district court and the majority of an inordinate focus on "racial balance."[156]

The following year, then-Justice Rehnquist authored a lone dissent in the Denver school desegregation case, *Keyes v. School District Number 1*, the first decision in which the Supreme Court extended *Brown* beyond southern states that had operated school systems segregated by law.[157] After explaining his disagreement with the majority, Justice Rehnquist called *Green* a "marked," "drastic," "significant," and "barely, if at all, explicated" extension of *Brown*.[158] He explained:

> To require that a genuinely "dual" system be disestablished, in the sense that the assignment of a child to a particular school is not made to depend on his race, is one thing. To require that school boards affirmatively

undertake to achieve racial mixing in schools where such mixing is not achieved in sufficient degree by neutrally drawn boundary lines is quite obviously something else.[159]

In the school district involved in *Green*, however, the problem was not that "neutrally drawn boundary lines" had produced insufficient levels of integration. Instead, the school system had assigned students by default to their previously segregated schools—hardly neutral—giving them the "choice" to transfer to a school where they would be in the minority.[160] But because the district had little residential segregation, assigning students to the school nearest their homes—a "neutral" assignment plan— would have produced far more integration.[161]

For nearly two decades following *Keyes*, the Supreme Court remained focused on northern and western school desegregation. Unlike in the South, where racial segregation had been imposed systematically by law[162] and where the courts' primary focus since *Brown* had been on devising effective remedies for the vestiges of segregation,[163] courts in the north and west were required to determine whether racial imbalances stemmed from deliberate school board discrimination, from factors beyond school officials' control, or from a mixture of the two. Focusing on the value of local control of education, the Court emphasized that school boards cannot be deprived of authority absent a proven constitutional violation and that district courts should tailor remedies to match the scope of the violation.[164] Although the details of the northern cases are unnecessary to this paper, the cases are significant because, as I will show, *Dowell* and *Jenkins* transported the northern cases' concern for protecting local control into the southern context without ever acknowledging the critical differences between southern and northern segregation.[165]

IV.

In the early 1990s, with Justice Rehnquist as Chief Justice and the addition of five Reagan and Bush appointees, the Court turned its attention back to southern desegregation, issuing *Board of Education v. Dowell*[166] in 1991 and *Missouri v. Jenkins*[167] in 1995. Like the Charlotte-Mecklenburg school system involved in *Swann*, the Oklahoma City and Kansas City school systems had been segregated by law prior to *Brown* and had resisted desegregation even after *Green*. By the time the two cases reached the Supreme Court, however, the systems had operated under court-ordered desegregation plans for thirteen and seven years, respectively.[168] The cases presented two questions critical to the future of southern school desegregation. May a school system that has operated under a court-ordered desegregation plan for several years unilaterally scrap the plan and return to all-black neighborhood schools?[169] May states be ordered to fund magnet schools and other programs designed to attract white suburban students to inner-city schools?[170]

Students of the Supreme Court's early desegregation case law might have thought that the Court would not hesitate to resolve these issues in favor of black students and their parents. After all, under *Green* and *Swann*, southern school systems had a heavy burden to justify desegregation plans that included one-race schools if more effective options were available.[171] *Green* and *Swann* also had emphasized repeatedly that district courts possess broad power not only to scrutinize desegregation plans proposed by school officials but also to order whatever additional steps were needed to redress the remaining vestiges of segregation.[172] Although in a later case involving the Detroit schools, *Milliken v. Bradley* (*Milliken I*), the Supreme Court had held that district courts could not compel innocent suburban districts to participate in metropolitan-wide desegregation plans,[173] the Court had never before suggested that district courts might lack authority to order constitutional violators to fund programs that encouraged suburban students to transfer voluntarily to city schools. Indeed, for many urban school systems that had become predominantly black, such voluntary programs represented one of the few ways to promote desegregation.

Such courtwatchers, however, would be surprised by the Court's holdings in *Dowell* and *Jenkins*. As the *Wright* and *Keyes* dissents had foreshadowed,[174] by the time the Court returned to southern school cases in the early 1990s, its view of court-ordered desegregation had changed. In opinions written by Chief Justice Rehnquist for himself and four other Justices (Justices White, O'Connor, Scalia, and Kennedy in *Dowell*, and Justices O'Connor, Scalia, Kennedy, and Thomas in *Jenkins*), the Court shifted its focus from redressing the harms of segregation, as required by *Brown*, *Green*, and *Swann*, to restoring control to state and local school officials.

A. Dowell

Admitted to the Union in 1907 as a Jim Crow state, Oklahoma mandated segregation in public vehicles and places.[175] Most Oklahoma City neighborhoods were also segregated because deeds included restrictive covenants that prohibited the sale of lots to and property ownership by African Americans.[176] Thus, from 1907 until at least 1954, "the Oklahoma [City] School District was completely and fully segregated."[177] During that period, Article XIII of the state constitution provided: "Separate schools for white and colored children with like accommodations shall be provided by the Legislature and impartially maintained."[178] Although the Supreme Court had declared race-based restrictive covenants unenforceable in 1948[179] and would outlaw school segregation six years later,[180] the damage in Oklahoma City was done. In 1963, the district court found that "the patrons of the School District had lived under a dual school system and the children's residential areas were fixed by custom, tradition, restrictive covenants and laws."[181] As a result, when the city's school board adopted a neighborhood school plan, ostensibly to bring the school system into compliance with *Brown*, the plan merely imposed local attendance zones on highly segregated neighborhoods. Indeed, the district court found that by destroying integrated neighborhoods and reinforcing residential segregation, the school board's actions had worsened the problem.[182]

In 1972, after nearly two decades of school board resistance, the district court ordered complete desegregation of the school system.[183] But by 1985, shifting residential patterns had made the court-ordered plan burdensome for black students.[184] Rather than revising the plan to make it more equitable, however, the school board ended busing and returned to neighborhood schools. Because many neighborhoods were highly segregated, the board's action recreated at least seven of the very same all-black elementary schools that had existed prior to court-ordered desegregation.[185] In all, twenty-two elementary schools became ninety percent or more white (or nonblack minorities), and nearly half of the district's black elementary students were assigned to eleven virtually all-black schools[186]—their only alternative being an entirely ineffective voluntary transfer program.[187]

Although the plaintiffs agreed that some adjustment to the court-ordered plan was needed, they objected to the resurrection of one-race schools.[188] This time, however, the district court agreed with the school board, holding that the school system had achieved unitary status and releasing it from further supervision.[189] According to the court, current residential patterns were too attenuated to be considered a vestige of segregation and school officials had not acted with discriminatory intent when they adopted the new neighborhood school plan.[190] The Tenth Circuit reversed, holding that the school system failed to meet its burden to justify dissolving the original desegregation order, that the district court findings regarding the causes of residential segregation were clearly erroneous, and that the district court should have focused on the *effects* of the neighborhood school plan, as required by *Swann*, rather than on school officials' *intent*.[191]

Reversing the Tenth Circuit, the Supreme Court began by holding that the appeals court had applied the wrong legal standard in determining when to end a school desegregation decree.[192] Although all eight Justices who took part in the case agreed on this issue, the five-Justice majority went on, in a seemingly innocuous remand instruction, to eviscerate several of *Green*'s and *Swann*'s key principles.

To begin with, in a footnote to the remand instruction, the majority discussed whether the residential segregation that was responsible for the reincarnation of one-race schools following the board's adoption of the neighborhood school plan could be considered a vestige of official discrimination.[193] The district court, in support of its conclusion that school officials had no duty to continue the desegregation plan, had found that modern residential segregation stemmed from economics and personal choice and was too attenuated to be considered a vestige of past official conduct.[194] The Tenth Circuit reversed, remanding the case for the district court to fashion an appropriate remedy,[195] but the Supreme Court majority then reversed the Tenth Circuit, explaining:

> Respondents contend that the Court of Appeals held that this finding was clearly erroneous, but we think its opinion is at least ambiguous on this point. The only operative use of "clearly erroneous" language is in the final paragraph of Subpart VI-D of its opinion, and it is perfectly plausible to read the clearly-erroneous findings as dealing only with the issues considered in that part of the opinion. To dispel any doubt, we direct the District Court and the Court of Appeals to treat this question as *res nova* upon further consideration of the case.[196]

This directive requires close scrutiny. It is true that the Tenth Circuit used "clearly erroneous" terminology once near the end of its analysis, in section VI.D. of the opinion, but it is not "perfectly plausible" that the court's clearly erroneous conclusion dealt exclusively with the issues considered in that subpart. Although the Tenth Circuit's opinion is hardly a model of lucidity, one thing is clear: The appeals court concluded that the district court's findings regarding the current causes of neighborhood segregation were clearly erroneous. In the opinion's background section, the Tenth Circuit, after summarizing the experts' conclusion that residential segregation was no longer a vestige of past discrimination,[197] expressly observed that appellants (the black schoolchildren) were challenging the district court ruling on the grounds that it had "abused its discretion by relying on clearly erroneous findings of fact."[198] Then, in its analysis sections, the Tenth Circuit used language that appellate courts typically employ when analyzing trial court fact findings pursuant to the clearly erroneous standard and embarked on a detailed, four-page critique of the expert testimony and the experts' voluminous exhibits.[199] The court pointed to defects in the experts' data and methodology, to conflicts in their testimony, and to contrary expert testimony unmentioned by the district court.[200] In the end, the Tenth Circuit explained—as appellate courts must in order to reject a district court's finding as clearly erroneous—that it was "'left with the definite and firm conviction that a mistake had been committed.'"[201] This conclusion appeared in the opinion's penultimate section for a very good reason: The Tenth Circuit obviously knew it had an obligation to "total all of the evidence" on which the district court had relied—evidence relating not just to demographic changes but also to such matters as faculty desegregation, the burden the court-ordered plan placed on black students, the system's majority-to-minority transfer policy, and the school board's intent in adopting the neighborhood school plan.[202] Where else would one expect the Tenth Circuit to state its ultimate conclusion about the district court findings than at the end of its analysis?[203] Equally significant, all parties agreed that the Tenth Circuit had overturned the district court's residential segregation finding as clearly erroneous. The school board devoted an entire section of its opening brief to demonstrating that, in its view, the Tenth Circuit had erred in finding clearly erroneous the district court's conclusion that blacks were voluntarily choosing to live in segregated neighborhoods;[204] for their part, the schoolchildren devoted almost as much space in their brief to defending the Tenth Circuit's finding.[205]

Instead of reviewing the expert testimony, the district court's findings, and the Tenth Circuit's analysis in order to determine whether the appeals court itself had erred, the Supreme Court majority simply directed the lower courts to consider the issue "*res nova.*"[206] In doing so, the majority swept aside a major obstacle to ending court-ordered

desegregation—after all, if residential segregation were a vestige of official discrimination, the district court would have had to continue the
desegregation process.

Next, despite citing *Green* and *Swann* as apparent authority, the majority proceeded in its remand instruction to weaken some of those cases'
most important principles. Specifically, the majority directed the district
court to

> decide, in accordance with this opinion, whether the Board made a suffi-
> cient showing of constitutional compliance as of 1985, when the [neighbor-
> hood plan] was adopted, to allow the [1972] injunction to be dissolved. The
> District Court should address itself to whether the Board had complied in
> good faith with the desegregation decree since it was entered, and whether
> the vestiges of past discrimination had been eliminated to the extent
> practicable. . . . After . . . deciding whether the Board was entitled to have
> the decree terminated, . . . [the district court] should proceed to decide
> respondents' challenge to the [neighborhood plan].[207]

We need a microscope to see the significance of what actually happened here. Notice first that the majority indicated that unitary status
should depend on good-faith compliance, as well as on whether the vestiges of segregation had been eliminated "to the extent practicable."[208]
What became of *Green*'s and *Swann*'s directive to district courts to evaluate desegregation efforts based on their effects[209]—rather than school
board intent—and to retain jurisdiction until "state-imposed segregation
has been *completely* removed"?[210] In its remand instruction, the majority subtly shifted the emphasis from ensuring that black students receive
a complete remedy for the harms of segregation to protecting the prerogatives of local officials who act in good faith.[211] The majority declared:
"Dissolving a desegregation decree after the local authorities have operated in compliance with it for a reasonable period of time properly recognizes . . . 'necessary concern for the important values of local control of
public school systems. . . .'"[212]

Notice also the remand instruction's use of the date 1985, the year the
school system ended busing and reestablished one-race schools.[213] By
directing the district court to decide unitariness as of 1985 and only *then*
to consider plaintiffs' challenge to the resurrection of one-race schools,
the majority separated the two issues. Instead of requiring the school
system to justify a less effective assignment plan, as *Green* and *Swann*

required,[214] the district court could declare the Oklahoma City school district unitary without regard to the reappearance of one-race schools—the primary vestige of the dual system.[215] If the system were unitary as of 1985, moreover, the district court would then evaluate the new assignment plan not on the basis of its effects, as required by *Green*, but rather under an intent test, the result of which was a foregone conclusion given the district court's finding that the school board had not acted with a discriminatory motive.[216]

Taken as a whole, *Dowell* strongly suggested that regardless of the resurrection of one-race schools, a finding of unitariness would be justified because the school system had complied with the desegregation order in good faith and because black students had been exposed to the court-ordered plan for some period of time. Yet the opinion contained no explanation, or even acknowledgment, of how the majority transformed the *Green* and *Swann* mandates to eliminate the vestiges of segregation into a temporary requirement that school boards must comply with, however briefly, before they may be released from court desegregation orders. This silence is particularly striking in light of Justice Marshall's dissent, which expressly warned that "the majority risked subordination of the constitutional rights of Afro-American children to the interest of school board autonomy" despite "our jurisprudence requiring . . . that the job of school desegregation be fully completed and maintained" before court supervision may be lifted.[217]

B. Jenkins

Having thus permitted the reestablishment of one-race schools in systems once segregated by law, the Supreme Court majority continued its departure from precedent in *Missouri v. Jenkins*.[218] As in Oklahoma City and Charlotte-Mecklenburg, schools in Kansas City were, by operation of state constitutional and statutory provisions, segregated by race prior to 1954.[219] After *Brown*, the Missouri attorney general declared those provisions unenforceable, but the state failed to repeal them for years.[220] Although the school system took some steps to desegregate, those efforts were largely ineffective, and, by 1974, eighty percent of black schoolchildren still attended one-race schools.[221] In the mid-1980s, some thirty years after *Brown*, the district court found that severe vestiges of segregation remained: Twenty-five of the system's sixty-six schools were still ninety percent or more black, school facilities were "literally rotting," and

segregation had "caused a system-wide reduction in student achievement."[222] More than eighty percent of the district's elementary schools
were below national levels in reading, and only fifty-one percent of secondary students passed standardized tests.[223] The district court also found
that the defendants' actions had contributed to "white flight."[224]

The *Jenkins* plaintiffs had originally sought to require eleven suburban school districts to participate in a metropolitan-area desegregation
plan.[225] The district court rejected that effort, relying on *Milliken I*, which
held that suburban districts surrounding Detroit could not be compelled
to participate in a desegregation remedy if they had neither committed
nor been affected by intentional interdistrict segregation.[226] According to
the district court, although prior to 1954 suburban school districts had
transferred black students to Kansas City rather than providing their
own segregated schools, those actions no longer had significant segregative effects.[227] The court also found that the suburban districts were
not responsible for white flight from Kansas City and so dismissed them
from the litigation.[228]

After hearing additional evidence, however, the district court concluded that actions by both the state and the Kansas City school system
had caused white flight to suburban districts and ordered them both to
share the costs of magnet schools and transportation to encourage white
students to transfer voluntarily from private schools and suburban districts into the Kansas City schools.[229] Relying on its finding that state and
local school officials were responsible for the system-wide reduction in
student achievement, the court also ordered them to fund remedial programs to address the system's educational deficiencies.[230] The Eighth Circuit upheld these remedial orders in large part,[231] but the Supreme Court
reversed.[232] In doing so, the majority disregarded *Green's* and *Swann's*
holdings that district courts have "'not merely the power but the duty to
render . . . decrees which will so far as possible eliminate the discriminatory effects'" of past segregation,[233] and distorted several later precedents
in the process.

The majority's reversal of the portion of the district court's order that
required the state to fund remedial academic programs was problematic
for several reasons. Not only did the majority address issues not fully
framed by the parties,[234] but it strongly hinted—contrary to *Green* and
Swann—that seven years of exposure to desegregation remedies was by
itself sufficient to justify ending court-ordered desegregation.[235] Also,
although Missouri had not challenged the district court's underlying

finding that segregation had caused "a system wide reduction in student achievement," the majority took the district court to task for "never . . . identifying the incremental effect that segregation has had on minority student achievement or the specific goals of the quality education programs."[236] This is in striking contrast to *Milliken v. Bradley* (*Milliken II*), the first case in which the Supreme Court upheld a district court order requiring—on the basis of findings no more specific than those in *Jenkins*—state and local defendants to pay for remedial academic programs.[237] In rejecting the district court findings, moreover, the *Jenkins* majority cited just one case, *Dayton Board of Education v. Brinkman* (*Dayton I*),[238] a northern case in which the Supreme Court had held that, where a school board engaged in only isolated acts of discrimination affecting student assignment patterns, district courts should determine the incremental segregative effects of those actions and tailor remedies accordingly.[239] In later cases, however, the Court held that district courts need not make incremental-effects findings if they conclude that school board discrimination had a system-wide effect.[240] Although all desegregation remedies—northern and southern—must be tailored to match the scope of the constitutional violations,[241] the *Jenkins* majority never explained why it applied the demanding *Dayton I* standard to a southern school system where uncontested findings showed that segregation had had a system-wide effect on student achievement. Perhaps the majority thought that detailed findings were needed because unlike one-race schools, which were the direct result—indeed, the very goal—of the dual system, academic deficiencies stem from multiple forces, only some of which are traceable to actions of school officials. If so, the majority never explained this distinction.[242]

As for the voluntary transfer program that the district court had ordered the state to fund, the Supreme Court majority held categorically that the district court lacked authority to increase the "desegregative attractiveness" of Kansas City schools.[243] According to the majority, *Milliken I* did not permit an "interdistrict" remedy in response to an "intradistrict" violation.[244] In effect, the majority declared, "the District Court has devised a remedy to accomplish indirectly what it admittedly lacks the remedial authority to mandate directly: the interdistrict transfer of students."[245]

To reach this result, the majority first had to address the district court's key finding, repeatedly affirmed by the Eighth Circuit, that the defendants' failure to remedy the vestiges of segregation had stimulated white flight and thus produced interdistrict effects.[246] As in *Dowell*, this finding proved no obstacle. Once again failing to conduct a detailed analysis of the record,[247] the majority summarily dismissed the district court's finding, calling it "inconsistent internally, and inconsistent with the typical supposition, bolstered here by the record evidence, that 'white flight' may result from desegregation, not *de jure* segregation."[248] This statement ran counter to two principles of appellate judging: First, trial court fact findings affirmed by a court of appeals are generally reviewable by the Supreme Court only where there is an exceptional showing of obvious error,[249] and, second, an appellate court reviewing district court findings of fact must determine whether those findings are supported by record evidence, not whether evidence exists to support the appellate court's contrary view.[250]

Having engaged in its own fact finding, the majority went on to distort both *Milliken I*[251] and a later decision, *Hills v. Gautreaux*, in which a unanimous Supreme Court had made clear that *Milliken I* hinged on "the limits on the federal judicial power to interfere with the operation of state political entities that were not implicated in unconstitutional conduct."[252] As long as the order coerced no innocent governmental units, *Gautreaux* explained, nothing in *Milliken I* created a per se rule forbidding a federal court to order constitutional wrongdoers to undertake remedial programs throughout a metropolitan area.[253] Because the Kansas City district court order likewise coerced no innocent school systems and was tailored to address the white flight caused by school officials' actions, one would have thought that it too did not exceed the district court's remedial authority. According to the *Jenkins* majority, however, because *Gautreaux* involved a federal defendant—the U.S. Department of Housing and Urban Development—that case had not raised "the same federalism concerns that are implicated when a federal court issues a remedial order against a State."[254] This statement is surprising given then-existing precedent.

To begin with, *Gautreaux* and *Milliken I* held that federalism protects *innocent* state and local actors, not governmental entities that *violate* the Constitution. In fact, *Gautreaux* specifically explained that in cases in which a metropolitan area remedy would otherwise be appropriate,[255] "to foreclose such relief solely because [the defendant's] constitutional violation took place within the [central] city limits . . . would transform *Milliken*'s principled limitation on the exercise of federal judicial authority into an arbitrary and mechanical shield for those found to have engaged in unconstitutional conduct."[256]

In *Jenkins*, however, the majority never even acknowledged that, as Justice Souter observed in his dissent, it had "not only rewritten *Milliken I*" but also "effectively overruled. . . . *Hills v. Gautreaux*."[257] Indeed, the majority insisted that its decision was "fully consistent with *Gautreaux*."[258]

Moreover, the only case on which *Jenkins* relied for the importance of federalism concerns—*Milliken II*[259]—fell far short of holding that federalism imposes substantive limits on federal court authority to order effective remedies for Fourteenth Amendment violations by states or their political subdivisions. In *Milliken II*, the Supreme Court directed that in crafting desegregation decrees, federal courts must (1) ensure that the remedy matches the "nature and scope of the constitutional violation"; (2) design the order "'as nearly as possible' to restore the victims of [segregation] to the position they would have occupied" absent such discrimination; and (3) "take into account the interests of state and local authorities in managing their own affairs, consistent with the Constitution."[260] Although *Milliken II* certainly suggested that courts should avoid unnecessary interference with school district operations, nothing in the opinion either stated that state and local concerns trumped the interests of the victims of segregation or otherwise overruled *Green's* and *Swann's* holdings that federal courts must ensure that constitutional violators implement effective remedies for the vestiges of segregation.[261] Indeed, in upholding the district court order requiring state defendants to share the costs of remedial educational programs as sufficiently tailored to remedy the constitutional violation,[262] *Milliken II* rejected the state defendants' argument that the order violated the Tenth Amendment and general principles of federalism:

> The Tenth Amendment's reservation of nondelegated powers to the States is not implicated by a federal court judgment enforcing the express prohibitions of unlawful state conduct enacted by the Fourteenth Amendment. Nor are principles of federalism abrogated by the decree. The District Court has neither attempted to restructure local governmental entities nor to mandate a particular method or structure of state or local financing.[263]

Yet in *Jenkins*, the majority relied on *Milliken II* to limit the scope of federal court remedial authority under the Fourteenth Amendment. Notwithstanding this distortion of *Milliken II*, the *Jenkins* majority stated that its "conclusion followed directly from *Milliken II*,"[264] and then went on to declare local school autonomy a "vital national tradition."[265]

C. Dowell *and* Jenkins *Together*

Stepping back from the details of *Dowell* and *Jenkins*, I am struck by the virtual absence in either opinion of any concern about the seriousness of the Fourteenth Amendment violations or the educational harms of segregation, particularly when compared to the majority's emphasis on the virtues of local control. This new focus represented a significant departure from *Brown*, *Green*, and *Swann*—a departure that began many years earlier in Chief Justice Burger's dissent in *Wright v. City of Emporia*, in which he chided the district court for failing to recognize the "overriding importance" of local control.[266]

What is particularly significant about the majority's engineering of this important shift in focus is that it did so in disregard of fundamental principles of judging. To begin with, the Court majority never acknowledged its transformation of *Brown*, *Green*, and *Swann*; it simply adopted the restoration of local control as a new national goal. In support, moreover, the majority relied on northern cases, which dealt not with statutory segregation—the issue in the southern cases—but with far more complex situations involving racial imbalances stemming from a mix of school-district discrimination and factors beyond school district control.[267] Unlike in these northern cases, the constitutional violations in southern cases were both clear and system-wide, and *Green* and *Swann* imposed upon school officials an affirmative duty to eliminate the vestiges of those violations.[268] To be sure, *Brown II* referred to "the primary responsibility" of local school boards, but in doing so, the Court was referring to a school board's responsibility to help courts devise effective remedies.[269] And while acknowledging that "responsibility for public education is primarily the concern of the States," *Cooper v. Aaron* made clear that this responsibility "must be exercised consistently with federal constitutional requirements."[270] Distorting both *Brown II* and *Cooper* and ignoring the fundamental differences between northern and southern school segregation, the *Dowell* and *Jenkins* majorities imported the northern cases' concern for local control into the southern context.

The majority's eagerness to restore local control is particularly questionable given the history of the two cases. Like many other southern communities, Oklahoma City and Kansas City resisted *Brown* and so had experienced little desegregation by the mid-1970s. When finally begun, the process of remedying decades of systemic discrimination proved difficult in both cities.[271] Indeed, by the time the Supreme Court decided the cases, Oklahoma City's desegregation plan had been in place for only thirteen years and Kansas City's for just seven.[272] As Justice Ginsburg pointed out in her *Jenkins* dissent, such remedies were "evanescent" in comparison to Missouri's two centuries of mandatory segregation going back to the reign of Louis XV of France.[273] Notwithstanding this history, and without examining the record to determine whether the vestiges of dual systems had been eliminated, the *Dowell* and *Jenkins* majorities repeatedly suggested that temporary exposure to desegregation was enough, and that ending district court supervision was long overdue. As Justice Marshall once wrote of another school desegregation opinion, *Dowell* and *Jenkins* leave the impression that their outcomes were "more a reflection of a perceived public mood that we have gone far enough in enforcing the Constitution's guarantee of equal justice than [they were] the product of neutral principles of law."[274]

V.

The Court's sharp change in direction is particularly striking when *Dowell* and *Jenkins* are compared to *Brown* itself. All three decisions had dramatic, though quite different, impacts on the victims of segregation and on constitutional doctrine. By overruling the "separate but equal" doctrine that had governed American race relations for over half a century,[275] *Brown* opened the doors for thousands of black children throughout the South to attend integrated schools. *Green* and *Swann* implemented *Brown*'s command.[276] In contrast, *Dowell* and *Jenkins* undermined the powerful principles articulated in *Green* and *Swann* that had brought about so much desegregation. *Dowell* made it possible for the Oklahoma City school system to return to a pre-*Green* world of one-race schools— some of which were the very same all-black schools that had existed under the dual system. The students' only alternative was an ineffective voluntary transfer program—in essence, a freedom-of-choice plan—that produced even less integration than the plan struck down in *Green*.[277] In Kansas City, where thousands of students still attended all-black schools decades after *Brown*, *Jenkins* made it more difficult for district courts to order remedial education programs and, in addition, blocked a purely voluntary interdistrict transfer program—one of the only remaining avenues for promoting further integration.[278]

Methodologically, *Dowell* and *Jenkins* also stand in sharp contrast to *Brown*. Although *Brown* has attracted scholarly criticism,[279] the

Supreme Court at least left no doubt about what it had done: The Court expressly acknowledged that *Brown*'s conclusion contradicted *Plessy*'s holding and declared that "any language in *Plessy v. Ferguson* [to the] contrary . . . is rejected."[280] By contrast, in *Dowell* and *Jenkins* the powerful desegregation principles of *Green* and *Swann*—the obligation to eliminate the vestiges of segregation "'root and branch,'"[281] the duty to convert to systems "without . . . 'white' schools and . . . 'Negro' schools, but just schools,"[282] the burden on school systems to justify the adoption of less effective desegregation plans,[283] and the proposition that "a district court's equitable power[] to remedy past wrongs is broad . . . and flexible"[284]—simply vanished. Neither distinguished nor overruled, they were just overwhelmed by the new mandate to restore local control.[285]

Perhaps the *Jenkins* and *Dowell* majorities viewed busing as a failed social experiment. If so, they did not say so, nor would the record in either case have supported such a conclusion.[286] Or perhaps they believed, as then-Justice Rehnquist wrote in his *Keyes* dissent, that *Green* represented a "drastic" and "significant" departure from *Brown*.[287] But *Dowell* and *Jenkins* identified no flaws in *Green*'s reasoning, much less acknowledged that they were effectively overruling it.

When courts expressly overrule precedent, even on debatable grounds, we at least know that the law has changed and have a basis for evaluating the court's reasoning. One may or may not agree with *Brown*, or for that matter with *Garcia v. San Antonio Metropolitan Authority*,[288] *Agostini v. Felton*,[289] or *Lawrence v. Texas*,[290] but no one can doubt that those decisions overruled precedent. In *Dowell* and *Jenkins*, by comparison, the majority never explained its sharp departure from precedent or acknowledged the dramatic change it was executing in longstanding, carefully developed, Fourteenth Amendment remedial principles.

This lack of explanation is particularly surprising, given that there may well have been principled reasons for modifying the *Green* and *Swann* standards or for applying them differently in Oklahoma City and Kansas City. For example, the urban complexities of Oklahoma City probably warranted more attention to the precise causes of segregated schools. Because of advances in magnet programs since *Green* and *Swann*, perhaps busing in Oklahoma City could have been replaced with equally effective magnet schools. In Kansas City, the complex causes of academic deficiencies probably warranted requiring the district court to make more detailed findings concerning the incremental effects of segregation than are required with regard to student assignments. And perhaps the Kansas City district court had surpassed the limits of its ability to oversee long-term, complex institutional reform.

The passage of time also probably warranted reexamining the key holdings of *Green* and *Swann* that school officials have the burden of demonstrating that current racial imbalances are no longer a vestige of segregation.[291] Justice Scalia made this point in a concurrence to another desegregation decision, *Freeman v. Pitts*,[292] in which he suggested that as the passage of time makes it increasingly difficult to determine whether past segregation contributed to modern residential patterns, the allocation of the burden of proof will become outcome-determinative.[293] His statement that "it has become absurd to assume, without any further proof, that [constitutional violations] dating from the days when Lyndon Johnson was President, or earlier, continue to have an appreciable effect upon current [school] operations" has a certain facial appeal.[294] But neither *Dowell* nor *Jenkins* confronted this issue directly; indeed, doing so would have required the development of a considerably more sophisticated record and a principled decision on the merits.

Conclusion

I conclude by returning to where I began—the debate about judicial activism. Defenders of the Rehnquist Court cite *Dowell* and *Jenkins*, pointing out that the two decisions cut back on the Warren Court's expansive exercise of federal judicial power. Arguing just the opposite, critics insist that *Dowell* and *Jenkins* reflect the anti-desegregation policy views of the members of the majority and of the Presidents who appointed them.

In my view, neither observation properly assesses the two decisions as acts of judging. Such an assessment cannot turn on the results of the two decisions, nor on the Court's motive or on the views of the appointing Presidents. We have no way of ascertaining the motives of a five-Justice majority, and the Justices that made up the majorities in these two cases were appointed by four different Presidents, one of whom was a Democrat.

As I explained at the outset, whether decisions qualify as acts of judging, as opposed to policymaking, turns on whether their results evolved from the application of legal principles to established fact. For this reason, legitimate acts of judging—decisions that follow rules of stare decisis and that are fully and openly explained—do not lose their legitimacy just because they may coincide with the policy views of the judges or their appointing presidents.

Viewed methodologically, *Dowell* and *Jenkins* are flawed as acts of judging. As I have demonstrated, they never explain, much less acknowledge, their overruling of precedent, they discard lower court fact-findings and engage in fact-finding of their own, and they fail to provide "principled justifications"[295] for their outcomes. These methodological defects have additional consequences given *Dowell*'s and *Jenkins*'s historical context, in particular, the extent to which the two decisions could be seen as having accomplished what the political process could not: limiting court-ordered school desegregation and doing so, like President Nixon two decades earlier, by shifting the focus from providing effective remedies for the victims of segregation to restoring local control. By failing to anchor these results in principles of judicial methodology, I fear the Court may have contributed to the "popular misconception that this institution is little different from the two political branches of the Government."[296]

NOTES

1. 5 U.S. (1 Cranch) 137, 177 (1803).
2. The Slaughter-House Cases, 83 U.S. (16 Wall.) 36 (1873).
3. *See, e.g.*, Lochner v. New York, 198 U.S. 45 (1905).
4. *See, e.g.*, A.L.A. Schechter Poultry Corp. v. United States, 295 U.S. 495 (1935).
5. 410 U.S. 113 (1973).
6. *See, e.g.*, DONALD GRIER STEPHENSON JR., CAMPAIGNS AND THE COURT: THE U.S. SUPREME COURT IN PRESIDENTIAL ELECTIONS 181 (1999) (noting Nixon's promise to nominate Supreme Court Justices who "would be strict constructionists who saw their duty as interpreting law and not making law" and who "would see themselves as caretakers of the Constitution and servants of the people, not super-legislators with a free hand to impose their social forces and political viewpoints on the American people"); *Campaign Notes, Reagan: Look at "Philosophy" for High Court*, WASH. POST, Oct. 2, 1980, at A3 (noting Reagan's promise to appoint judges who would interpret Constitution without "cross[ing] over the line, as many times the Supreme Court has in recent years, and usurp[ing] legislative functions"); David Hoffman & T. R. Reid, *Bush, Dukakis Duel over Ideology, Identity*, WASH. POST, Oct. 14, 1988, at A1 (noting George H. W. Bush's promise to select judges who will "interpret the Constitution" and "not legislate from the bench").
7. *See, e.g.*, KENNETH W. STARR, FIRST AMONG EQUALS: THE SUPREME COURT IN AMERICAN LIFE (2002) (distinguishing post–Warren Court activism as lacking zeal for reshaping society and as more principled and cautious); *Is the Senate's Current Reconsideration of the Confirmation Process*

Justified?, 6 TEX. REV. L. & POL. 245, 265-73 (2001) (asserting that Rehnquist Court has reestablished proper limits on Congress's Commerce Clause power).

8. 531 U.S. 98 (2000).

9. *See, e.g.*, THE REHNQUIST COURT: JUDICIAL ACTIVISM ON THE RIGHT (Herman Schwartz ed., 2002) (presenting critical analyses by several authors); Jack M. Balkin & Sanford Levinson, *Understanding the Constitutional Revolution*, 87 VA. L. REV. 1045 (2001) (criticizing Rehnquist Court decisions as amounting to new constitutional revolution and creating partisan entrenchment); Larry D. Kramer, *The Supreme Court, 2000 Term—Foreword: We the Court*, 115 HARV. L. REV. 4 (2001) (arguing that Rehnquist Court has interpreted judicial supremacy to mean that executive and legislative understandings of Constitution carry no weight); William L. Taylor, *Racial Equality: The World According to Rehnquist, in* THE REHNQUIST COURT: JUDICIAL ACTIVISM ON THE RIGHT, *supra*, at 52-54 (concluding that Rehnquist Court's civil rights decisions cannot be justified as strict constructionist or respectful of precedent and that they often rely on "arid legalisms").

10. 498 U.S. 237 (1991).

11. 515 U.S. 70 (1995). The case discussed in this paper is often referred to as *Jenkins III*, since the Supreme Court had ruled on other aspects of the Kansas City litigation on two prior occasions. *See* Missouri v. Jenkins, 495 U.S. 33 (1990) (*Jenkins II*); Missouri v. Jenkins, 491 U.S. 274 (1989) (*Jenkins I*).

12. In the interest of full disclosure, I should add that although I was personally involved in neither case, I did serve as counsel for the school district in earlier stages of the *Jenkins* litigation, and some arguments I advanced in a similar case in St. Louis were eventually rejected by *Jenkins*.

13. 347 U.S. 483 (1954) (*Brown I*).

14. Planned Parenthood v. Casey, 505 U.S. 833, 865 (1992).

15. Mitchell v. W.T. Grant Co., 416 U.S. 600, 636 (1974) (Stewart, J., dissenting).

16. *Id.* Justice Stewart expressly addressed stare decisis, commenting that "unless we respect the constitutional decisions of this Court, we can hardly expect that others will do so." *Id.* at 634.

17. *See, e.g.,* Time Warner Entm't Co. v. United States, 211 F.3d 1313, 1320-22 (D.C. Cir. 2000); *see also* Time Warner Entm't Co. v. FCC, 240 F.3d 1126, 1129-30 (D.C. Cir. 2001).

18. *See, e.g.*, Lederman v. United States, 291 F.3d 36, 41, 44 (D.C. Cir. 2002).

19. *See, e.g.*, Am. Trucking Ass'ns v. EPA, 283 F.3d 355, 362 (D.C. Cir. 2002).

20. Calloway v. District of Columbia, 216 F.3d 1, 9 (D.C. Cir. 2000) (upholding attorney fee cap under Individuals with Disabilities Education Act after applying rational-basis review).

21. United States v. Davis, 235 F.3d 584, 586 (D.C. Cir. 2000) (stating that *Terry* stops are constitutional if police can show "'minimal level of objective justification'" (quoting INS v. Delgado, 466 U.S. 210, 217 (1984))).

22. Pharm. Research & Mfrs. of Am. v. Thompson, 251 F.3d 219 (D.C. Cir. 2001).

23. LOUIS MENAND, THE METAPHYSICAL CLUB 67 (2001) (internal quotation marks omitted).

24. Although stare decisis is not an "inexorable command,"

> when [a] court reexamines a prior holding, its judgment is customarily informed by a series of prudential and pragmatic considerations designed to test the consistency of overruling a prior decision with the ideal of the rule of law, and to gauge the respective costs of reaffirming and overruling a prior case. Thus, for example, [it] may ask whether the rule has proven to be intolerable simply in defying practical workability; whether the rule is subject to a kind of reliance that would lend a special hardship to the consequences of overruling and add inequity to the cost of repudiation; whether related principles of law have so far developed as to have left the old rule no more than a remnant of abandoned doctrine; or whether facts have so changed, or come to be seen so differently, as to have robbed the old rule of significant application or justification.

Planned Parenthood v. Casey, 505 U.S. 833, 854-55 (1992) (citations omitted).

25. 391 U.S. 430 (1968).

26. 402 U.S. 1 (1971).

27. 60 U.S. (19 How.) 393 (1856).

28. 109 U.S. 3 (1883).

29. 163 U.S. 537 (1896).

30. 347 U.S. 483 (1954) (*Brown I*).

31. 163 U.S. at 544, 548.

32. RICHARD KLUGER, SIMPLE JUSTICE: THE HISTORY OF BROWN V. BOARD OF EDUCATION AND BLACK AMERICA'S STRUGGLE FOR EQUALITY 256-57 (1975); *see also* LEON E. PANETTA & PETER GALL, BRING US TOGETHER: THE NIXON TEAM AND THE CIVIL RIGHTS RETREAT 38 (1971).

33. KLUGER, *supra* note 32, at 257.

34. *Id*. at 331-32.

35. *Id*. at 332.

36. *Id*.

37. *Id*.

38. *Id*.

39. *Brown* involved four consolidated cases from three federal courts and one state court. Brown v. Bd. of Educ., 347 U.S. 483, 486-88 n.l.

40. *Id*. at 494.

41. *Brown I*, 347 U.S. at 495.

42. JAMES T. PATTERSON, BROWN V. BOARD OF EDUCATION: A CIVIL RIGHTS MILESTONE AND ITS TROUBLED LEGACY 94 (2001) (internal quotation marks omitted) (citation omitted). Others baldly tapped into the worst racial stereotypes and southern fears of miscegenation. Such leaders saw integration as threatening the natural order of society. *See generally* FRANCIS M. WILHOIT, THE POLITICS OF MASSIVE RESISTANCE 85-90 (1973) (discussing demagogues' role in Massive Resistance).

43. J. W. PELTASON, FIFTY-EIGHT LONELY MEN: SOUTHERN FEDERAL JUDGES AND SCHOOL DESEGREGATION 234-35 (Univ. of Ill. Press 1971) (1961); WILHOIT, *supra* note 42, at 46, 69-70, 137-41.

44. 102 Cong. Rec. 4515-16 (1956), *reprinted in* WILHOIT, *supra* note 42, app. at 286-87. The constitutional theory of "interposition," revived in response to *Brown*, has a long pedigree dating from the famous Virginia and Kentucky Resolutions, which were passed in opposition to the Alien and Sedition Acts. The doctrine's basic premise is that the Constitution is a compact among sovereign states that delegates strictly limited powers to the federal government. According to the theory, when the federal government exceeds those limits, states have a right to "interpose" their authority between the federal government and their citizens. *See* NUMAN V. BARTLEY, THE RISE OF MASSIVE RESISTANCE: RACE AND POLITICS IN THE SOUTH DURING THE 1950S, at 127-44, 335-38 (1969); Judith A. Hagley, *Massive Resistance: The Rhetoric and Reality*, 27 N.M. L. REV. 167, 171-72 & n.24, 190-95 & n.177 (1997). The Supreme Court rejected the doctrine as "without substance" in *United States v. Louisiana*, 364 U.S. 500, 501 (1960).

45. 102 Cong. Rec. 4516 (1956), *reprinted in* WILHOIT, *supra* note 42, app. at 287.

46. *Brown II*, 349 U.S. at 301.

47. BARTLEY, *supra* note 44, at 77-78; PELTASON, *supra* note 43, at 78-92; WILHOIT, *supra* note 42, at 139-40, 143, 173-74. Many statutes contained transfer procedures that were so intentionally convoluted that southern school boards could deny transfer requests for technical reasons, such as a failure to have signatures notarized or even more minor mistakes in filling out forms. PELTASON, *supra* note 43, at 79-80. Initially, some district courts upheld the laws against facial challenges. *See, e.g.*, Shuttlesworth v. Birmingham Bd. of Educ., 162 F. Supp. 372 (N.D. Ala.), *aff'd per curiam*, 358 U.S. 101 (1958).

48. PATTERSON, *supra* note 42, at 99-100; PELTASON, *supra* note 43, at 193-220; WILHOIT, *supra* note 42, at 35-36, 137-40, 143, 145-46, 149; *see, e.g.*, Griffin v. County Sch. Bd., 377 U.S. 218, 222 n.4 (1964); Jackson v. Sch. Bd., 203 F. Supp. 701, 706 (W.D. Va. 1962); Bush v. Orleans Parish Sch. Bd., 188 F. Supp. 916, 936-38 (E.D. La. 1960).

49. PELTASON, *supra* note 43, at 193-220; WILHOIT, *supra* note 42, at 137, 139-40, 145, 149, 153-55; *see, e.g.*, Griffin, 377 U.S. at 218, 221-22; Lee v. Macon County Bd. of Educ., 231 F. Supp. 743, 749 (M.D. Ala. 1964); *Jackson*, 203 F. Supp. at 706; Hall v. St. Helena Parish Sch. Bd., 197 F. Supp. 649, 653-55 (E.D. La. 1961).

50. BARTLEY, *supra* note 44, at 74-77; PATTERSON, *supra* note 42, at 99. *See generally* WILHOIT, *supra* note 42, at 34-36, 44-45, 136-51, tbl.A (cataloguing Massive Resistance legislation by state).

51. The school system had voluntarily adopted a desegregation plan a few days before the Supreme Court handed down *Brown II* in 1955. Cooper v. Aaron, 358 U.S. 1, 7-8 (1958). A group of black plaintiffs sought faster implementation, but the federal courts upheld the original plan. Aaron v. Cooper, 143 F. Supp. 855 (E.D. Ark. 1956), *aff'd*, 243 F.2d 361 (8th Cir. 1957). After Governor Faubus called out the Arkansas National Guard and declared Central High School "off limits"

to black students, the district court ordered the school system to proceed with desegregation anyway. *Cooper*, 358 U.S. at 9-11. *See generally* BARTLEY, *supra* note 44, at 251-69, 273-74, 327-32 (discussing Little Rock desegregation process and Supreme Court's *Cooper* decision); PATTERSON, *supra* note 42, at 109-13 (same); PELTASON, *supra* note 43, at 154-57, 161-92, 195-207 (same); WILHOIT, *supra* note 42, at 170-71, 177-82 (same).

52. Aaron v. Cooper, 156 F. Supp. 220 (E.D. Ark. 1957).

53. *Cooper*, 358 U.S. at 11-12; ROBERT A. CARO, MASTER OF THE SENATE: THE YEARS OF LYNDON JOHNSON 1002 (2002).

54. 358 U.S. 1 (1958). The school board filed a petition seeking to suspend all desegregation until 1960. Aaron v. Cooper, 163 F. Supp. 13, 14 (E.D. Ark. 1958). Insisting that it had acted in good faith, the board argued that the actions of Governor Faubus and the Arkansas Legislature had created "'chaos, bedlam and turmoil'" by encouraging desegregation opponents to resist implementation. *Id.* at 21 (quoting school-board testimony). Although the board was concerned that local police could not provide necessary protection and that the education of both black and white children was suffering, the Supreme Court rejected the board's legal position, declaring that "[t]he constitutional rights of [black children] are not to be sacrificed or yielded to the violence and disorder which have followed upon the actions of the Governor and Legislature." 358 U.S. at 16.

55. Indeed, *Cooper* invoked *Marbury* for the propositions that the Constitution is "the fundamental and paramount law of the nation" and that "it is emphatically the province and duty of the judicial department to say what the law is." 358 U.S. at 18 (quoting Marbury v. Madison, 5 U.S. (1 Cranch) 137, 177 (1803)). The Court concluded that "it follows that the interpretation of the Fourteenth Amendment enunciated by this Court in the *Brown* case is the supreme law of the land, and Art. VI of the Constitution makes it of binding effect on the States." *Id.*

56. *Cooper*, 358 U.S. at 19-20. The Court stressed that its adherence to *Brown's* principles remained constant even though "three new Justices have come to the Court. They are at one with the Justices still on the Court who participated in [*Brown*] as to its correctness. . . ." *Id.* at 19.

57. *Id.* at 4.

58. *See, e.g.*, Stout v. Jefferson County Bd. of Educ., 448 F.2d 403 (5th Cir. 1971); Haney v. County Bd. of Educ., 410 F.2d 920 (8th Cir. 1969); Aytch v. Mitchell, 320 F. Supp. 1372 (E.D. Ark. 1971).

59. WILHOIT, *supra* note 42, at 155.

60. PANETTA & GALL, *supra* note 32, at 39-42; PATTERSON, *supra* note 42, at 100-01.

61. PATTERSON, *supra* note 42, at 100; *cf. supra* note 47 (discussing similar procedural barriers under pupil assignment laws).

62. PATTERSON, *supra* note 42, at 101 (citation omitted).

63. PANETTA & GALL, *supra* note 32, at 41 (internal quotation marks omitted).

64. In fact, many school systems in Mississippi, Georgia, and Florida found that total busing miles actually *decreased* after desegregation because students no longer had to be bused to separate white and black schools. GARY ORFIELD, MUST WE BUS? SEGREGATED SCHOOLS AND NATIONAL POLICY 140-41 (1978).

65. Ralph McGill, *Listen, Please, Sec. Finch*, ATLANTA CONST., Feb. 4, 1969, at A1.
66. 377 U.S. 218, 231 (1964).
67. 407 U.S. 484, 489 (1972). After negotiations with the Department of Justice, Halifax County agreed to desegregate, but the North Carolina legislature enacted a bill authorizing the creation of a separate city system. The Scotland Neck city schools would have been fifty-seven percent white, but an appointed school board approved transfers to and from the county system that would have boosted the white majority to seventy-four percent. *Id.* at 486-87. The Supreme Court held that carve-outs in the midst of desegregation must be judged on the basis of their effects and may be enjoined where, as in *Scotland Neck*, they would impede the "dismantling [of] a dual school system." *Id.* at 489.
68. 396 U.S. 19, 20 (1969) (per curiam). *Alexander* was decided one year after *Green v. County School Board*, 391 U.S. 430 (1968).
69. *Alexander*, 396 U.S. at 20.
70. 391 U.S. 430 (1968).
71. 402 U.S. 1 (1971).
72. 391 U.S. at 441.
73. 402 U.S. at 28-31. For a detailed discussion of the case's background, the lower court decisions, and the Supreme Court's deliberations, see BERNARD SCHWARTZ, SWANN'S WAY: THE SCHOOL BUSING CASE AND THE SUPREME COURT (1986).
74. *Green*, 391 U.S. at 437-38.
75. *Id.* at 442.
76. *Swann*, 402 U.S. at 15.
77. *Id.* at 16.
78. *Id.* at 26.
79. *Green*, 391 U.S. at 439-41.
80. *Swann*, 402 U.S. at 25, 28; *Green*, 391 U.S. at 439.
81. *Swann*, 402 U.S. at 28 (stating that facially neutral plans "may fail to counteract the continuing effects of past school segregation resulting from discriminatory location of school sites or distortion of school size in order to achieve or maintain an artificial racial separation").
82. *Green*, 391 U.S. at 438 n.4 (quoting Louisiana v. United States, 380 U.S. 145, 154 (1965)).
83. *Swann*, 402 U.S. at 15.
84. *Green*, 391 U.S. at 439.
85. 42 U.S.C. § 2000d-1 (1970); *see also* ORFIELD, *supra* note 64, at 279-85, 319-23 (describing HEW and Justice Department enforcement efforts during Johnson administration).
86. U.S. BUREAU OF THE CENSUS, U.S. DEP'T OF COMMERCE, STATISTICAL ABSTRACT OF THE UNITED STATES: 1974, at 124 tbl.200 (1974).
87. In contrast, Ronald Reagan and George H. W. Bush opposed the Civil Rights Act of 1964. DEAN J. KOTLOWSKI, NIXON'S CIVIL RIGHTS: POLITICS, PRINCIPLE, AND POLICY 24 (2001).

88. As explained by Kevin Phillips, an aide to Nixon's campaign manager (and later Attorney General) John Mitchell, the key to Nixon's Southern Strategy was to attract and energize white southerners without alienating the traditional Republican base of Sun Belt conservatives and rural and suburban northerners. KEVIN P. PHILLIPS, THE EMERGING REPUBLICAN MAJORITY 26-36, 187-289 (1969).

89. See STEPHEN E. AMBROSE, NIXON: VOLUME TWO, THE TRIUMPH OF A POLITICIAN, 1962-1972, at 155 (1989); Bruce H. Kalk, *Wormley's Hotel Revisited: Richard Nixon's Southern Strategy and the End of the Second Reconstruction,* N.C. HIST. REV., Jan. 1994, at 85, 88.

90. AMBROSE, *supra* note 89, at 155; Kalk, *supra* note 89, at 88.

91. KOTLOWSKI, *supra* note 87, at 24 (internal quotation marks omitted) (citation omitted).

92. WILLIAM SAFIRE, BEFORE THE FALL: AN INSIDE VIEW OF THE PRE-WATERGATE WHITE HOUSE 232 (1975) (internal quotation marks omitted).

93. STEPHENSON, *supra* note 6, at 180; Brad Snyder, *How the Conservatives Canonized* Brown v. Board of Education, 52 RUTGERS L. REV. 383, 416 & n.194 (2000).

94. After the White House engineered the firing of Leon Panetta, the director of HEW's Office for Civil Rights, for being a "disloyalist[]" because he supported desegregation efforts, HEW significantly reduced pressure on southern school districts to desegregate. Memorandum from Harry Dent, to H. R. Haldeman (Feb. 23, 1970) (Box 23, Folder: "Panetta, [Leon]," John D. Ehrlichman Files, White House Special Files, Nixon Presidential Materials, National Archives, College Park, Md.) (questioning whether Panetta should be allowed to stay in office for one more week and asking, "why not get rid of other disloyalists and limit their access to info that will be used against us eventually").

95. KOTLOWSKI, *supra* note 87, at 29 (internal quotation marks omitted) (citation omitted).

96. Adams v. Richardson, 351 F. Supp. 636 (D.D.C. 1972), *aff'd en banc, rev'd on other grounds,* 480 F.2d 1159 (D.C. Cir. 1973). *See generally* ORFIELD, *supra* note 64, at 291-97 (describing litigation and its aftermath).

97. Adams v. Richardson, 480 F.2d 1159, 1163 (D.C. Cir. 1973).

98. 396 U.S. 19, 20 (1969) (per curiam).

99. KOTLOWSKI, *supra* note 87, at 30-31; ORFIELD, *supra* note 64, at 325-27; PANETTA & GALL, *supra* note 32, at 249-66, 295-300; Kalk, *supra* note 89, at 95.

100. *Alexander,* 396 U.S. at 20.

101. Again, Nixon sent mixed messages, appointing Vice President Spiro Agnew, a vocal desegregation critic, to chair the group. *See* LEONARD GARMENT, CRAZY RHYTHM: MY JOURNEY FROM BROOKLYN, JAZZ, AND WALL STREET TO NIXON'S WHITE HOUSE, WATERGATE, AND BEYOND . . . , at 203-17 (2001); KOTLOWSKI, *supra* note 87, at 34-37; George P. Shultz, *How a Republican Desegregated the South's Schools,* N.Y. TIMES, Jan. 8, 2003, at A23.

102. Statement About Desegregation of Elementary and Secondary Schools, 1970 PUB. PAPERS 304 (Mar. 24, 1970).

103. Statement About Desegregation of Elementary and Secondary Schools, *supra* note 102, at 315; *see, e.g., id.* at 305 (criticizing some lower court decisions for

raising fears that "the neighborhood school [is] virtually doomed"); *id.* at 307-08 (expressing continuing opposition to "compulsory busing . . . beyond normal geographic school zones"); *id.* at 314 (advocating part-time activities as alternative to busing so that "no one would be deprived of his own neighborhood school"); *id.* at 315 (stating that busing of students "beyond normal geographic school zones" would not be required).

104. Audio tape: Conversation between Richard Nixon, John Mitchell, and John D. Ehrlichman, Oval Office of the White House, Washington, D.C. (Oct. 8, 1971) (Nat'l Archives Nixon White House Tape Conversation 587-3). The public statement made the same point in more politic language: "I believe it is preferable, when we have to make the choice, to use limited financial resources for the improvement of education . . . rather than buying buses, tires, and gasoline to transport young children miles away from their neighborhood schools." Statement About Desegregation of Elementary and Secondary Schools, *supra* note 102, at 309.

105. In conversations with his staff, Nixon said that schoolchildren—meaning white children—were the "victims" of busing. *See, e.g., infra* note 116 and accompanying text. The statement, however, did not use that term, instead portraying busing as frequently harmful, schools as overburdened, and children as extremely vulnerable to disruption and injury. *See, e.g.,* Statement About Desegregation of Elementary and Secondary Schools, *supra* note 102, at 308 (denouncing some lower court rulings because they would "divert such huge sums of money to non-educational purposes, and would create such severe dislocations of public school systems, as to impair the primary function of providing a good education"); *id.* at 312 ("Our children are highly sensitive to conflict, and highly vulnerable to lasting psychic injury."); *id.* at 314 (describing busing as "taking children out of the schools they would normally attend, and forcing them instead to attend others more distant, often in strange or even hostile neighborhoods").

106. *See, e.g.,* Audio tape: Conversation between Richard Nixon and various members of Cabinet and staff, Cabinet Room of the White House, Washington, D.C. (Mar. 17, 1972) (Nat'l Archives Nixon White House Tape Conversation 95-1) ("But when you bus children, particularly young children, away from their neighborhood schools, that results—more often than not—in inferior education. So the question is, are you going to address one harm by compounding it with another wrong?"); Audio tape: Telephone Conversation between Richard Nixon and John D. Ehrlichman (Mar. 12, 1972) (Nat'l Archives Nixon White House Tape Conversation 21-47) ("Transportation which is excessive and which is detrimental to a child's education is wrong, because one year out of a child's life may be too important to be lost."); Audio tape: Conversation between Richard Nixon and various advisers, Cabinet Room of the White House, Washington, D.C. (Mar. 10, 1972) (Nat'l Archives Nixon White House Tape Conversation 94-3) ("And certainly education that is the result of busing in an excessive amount is an inferior education.").

107. Statement About Desegregation of Elementary and Secondary Schools, *supra* note 102, at 314.

108. *Id.* at 309; *see also id.* at 310 (describing "'rule of reason' . . . in which school boards, acting in good faith, can formulate plans of desegregation which best suit the needs of their own localities"); *id.* at 314 ("If the essential element of good faith is present, it should ordinarily be possible to achieve legal compliance . . . through a plan designed to be responsive to the community's own local circumstances."); *id.* at 315 ("In devising local compliance plans, primary weight should be given to the considered judgment of local school boards—provided they act in good faith, and within constitutional limits.").

109. *See, e.g.*, Audio tape: Conversation between Richard Nixon and various members of Cabinet and staff, Oval Office of the White House, Washington, D.C. (Apr. 21, 1971) (Nat'l Archives Nixon White House Tape Conversation 484-2) ("I don't want any initiative undertaken by HEW or by Justice to go in and break up the plans. . . . I just do not want us, as the federal government, in this highly explosive area, to try to be heroic and rush down there and kick the South around.").

110. *See, e.g.*, Statement About Desegregation of Elementary and Secondary Schools, *supra* note 102, at 316 ("The leaders of the communities [facing desegregation orders] will be encouraged to lead—not in defiance, but in smoothing the way of compliance. . . . Where local leadership has failed, the community has failed—and the schools and the children have borne the brunt of that failure.").

111. *See, e.g., id.* at 314 (suggesting that part-time educational programs on "'neutral'" sites would be sufficient); *id.* at 315 (calling for immediate elimination of deliberate racial segregation, yet stating that neighborhood schools are most appropriate basis for student assignment and that busing beyond normal geographic school zones would not be required).

112. GARMENT, *supra* note 101, at 215-18; KOTLOWSKI, *supra* note 87, at 15; TOM WICKER, ONE OF US: RICHARD NIXON AND THE AMERICAN DREAM 505-07 (1991); Shultz, *supra* note 101.

113. 402 U.S. 1 (1971).

114. KOTLOWSKI, *supra* note 87, at 39 (quoting Nixon's notes on annotated news summary); *see also* The President's News Conference of February 10, 1972, 1972 PUB. PAPERS 347, 354-55 (stating that Nixon was considering both legislative moratorium and constitutional amendment proposals to protect neighborhood schools and curtail "busing for the purpose of racial balance").

115. Nixon did so despite a warning from aide Leonard Garment that "Congress may not restrict or dilute a Constitutional right." Memorandum from Leonard Garment, to John D. Ehrlichman 1 (Jan. 13, 1972) (Box 52, Folder: "Busing—Constitutional amendment [2 of 3]," Leonard Garment Files, White House Central Files, Nixon Presidential Materials, National Archives, College Park, Md.).

116. Audio tape: Conversation between Richard Nixon and various members of his Cabinet and staff, Cabinet Room of the White House, Washington, D.C. (Mar. 17, 1972) (Nat'l Archives Nixon White House Tape Conversation 95-1). After telling Ehrlichman of his initial decision, Nixon warned him against leaking anything to desegregation moderates such as Elliott Richardson and Leonard Garment: "Don't tell 'em I've made a decision, . . . I don't want them to lobby

me in this damn thing. You know, I've heard all the arguments." Audio tape: Telephone Conversation between Richard Nixon and John D. Ehrlichman (Mar. 12, 1972) (Nat'l Archives Nixon White House Tape Conversation 21-47).

117. Audio tape: Conversation between Richard Nixon, H. R. Haldeman, and Charles W. Colson, Oval Office of the White House, Washington, D.C. (Mar. 30, 1972) (Nat'l Archives Nixon White House Tape Conversation 697-29). Nixon also directed the Justice Department to begin intervening in cases where lower courts had ordered desegregation plans that the department considered particularly burdensome. Address to the Nation on Equal Educational Opportunities and School Busing, 1972 PUB. PAPERS 425, 427 (Mar. 16, 1972).

118. Bowman v. County Sch. Bd., 382 F.2d 326 (4th Cir. 1967) (en banc), *vacated by* Green v. County Sch. Bd., 391 U.S. 430, 442 (1968); *see also Green*, 391 U.S. at 434 n.3 ("[*Green*] was decided *per curiam* on the basis of the opinion in [*Bowman*], decided the same day. Certiorari has not been sought for the *Bowman* case itself.").

119. Griffin v. County Sch. Bd., 322 F.2d 332 (4th Cir. 1963), *rev'd*, 377 U.S. 218 (1964).

120. Kalk, *supra* note 89, at 102 (internal quotation marks omitted).

121. *See also id.* (internal quotation marks omitted).

122. Nixon responded to the 51-45 vote by declaring that his next nominee would be a northerner because it was impossible to "successfully nominate to the Supreme Court any Federal Appellate Judge from the South who believes as I do in the strict construction of the Constitution." TOM WICKER, ONE OF US: RICHARD NIXON AND THE AMERICAN DREAM 498 (1991) (internal quotation marks omitted). Nixon's press release went on to state, "I understand the bitter feeling of millions of Americans who live in the South about the act of regional discrimination that took place in the Senate yesterday." *Id.* at 499 (internal quotation marks omitted).

123. Audio tape: Conversation between Richard Nixon and John Mitchell, Oval Office of the White House, Washington, D.C. (Sept. 18, 1971) (Nat'l Archives Nixon White House Tape Conversation 576-6).

124. *Id.*

125. *Id.*

126. *See generally* Snyder, *supra* note 93, at 431-49 (describing nomination process and candidates considered).

127. Audio tape: Conversation between Richard Nixon and Richard Moore, Executive Office Building, Washington, D.C. (Oct. 20, 1971) (Nat'l Archives Nixon White House Tape Conversation 282-26). When Baker dithered over financial and political considerations, Nixon chose Assistant Attorney General William Rehnquist instead. *See* Snyder, *supra* note 93, at 432 (describing selection of Rehnquist).

128. SCHWARTZ, *supra* note 73, app. A at 217 (reprinting draft opinion).

129. SCHWARTZ, *supra* note 73, app. A at 215; *cf.* Winston-Salem/Forsyth County Bd. of Educ. v. Scott, 404 U.S. 1221, 1227 (Burger, Circuit Justice 1971) (finding it "disturbing" that lower courts might have read *Swann* too broadly as requiring precise racial balancing of individual schools).

130. *See* SCHWARTZ, *supra* note 73, at 130-36.

131. *Swann*, 402 U.S. at 31; *see* SCHWARTZ, *supra* note 73, at 118-84 (outlining objections of other Justices and discussing Burger's subsequent drafts); MARK V. TUSHNET, MAKING CONSTITUTIONAL LAW: THURGOOD MARSHALL AND THE SUPREME COURT, 1961-1991, at 78-82 (tracing evolution of Burger's opinion).

132. Aide Harry Dent warned Nixon that Chief Justice Burger might "become the new Earl Warren." Audio tape: Conversation between Richard Nixon, Harry Dent, John Mitchell and others, Oval Office of the White House, Washington, D.C. (Apr. 21, 1971) (Nat'l Archives Nixon White House Tape Conversation 484-2).

133. *Id.*

134. Audio tape: Conversation between Richard Nixon and Warren Burger, Oval Office of the White House, Washington, D.C. (June 14, 1972) (Nat'l Archives Nixon White House Tape Conversation 733-10).

135. *Id.*

136. 407 U.S. 451, 471-83 (1972) (Burger, C.J., dissenting).

137. *Id.* at 455.

138. *Id.* at 455-56.

139. *Id.* at 456.

140. Wright v. County Sch. Bd., 309 F. Supp. 671, 678, 681 (E.D. Va. 1970).

141. Wright v. Council of City of Emporia, 442 F.2d 570, 574-75 (4th Cir. 1971).

142. The majority consisted of Justices Douglas, Brennan, Stewart, White, and Marshall. Justice Douglas had participated in *Brown*, while Justices Brennan and Stewart were among the new Justices who signed on to *Cooper*. Justice Marshall argued *Brown* on behalf of the plaintiff schoolchildren.

143. *Wright*, 407 U.S. at 462-63.

144. 442 F.2d at 574.

145. *Wright*, 407 U.S. at 461-63.

146. *Id.* at 463-66.

147. *Id.* at 468.

148. *Id.* at 469.

149. *Id.* at 470.

150. *See* United States v. Scotland Neck City Bd. of Educ., 407 U.S. 484, 491-92 (1972) (Burger, C.J., concurring in result); *supra* note 67 (discussing Supreme Court opinion).

151. 407 U.S. at 477, 482-83 (Burger, C.J., dissenting).

152. *Id.* at 477 (Burger, C.J., dissenting).

153. Swann v. Charlotte-Mecklenberg Bd. of Educ., 402 U.S. 1, 12 (1971) (quoting Brown v. Bd. of Educ., 349 U.S. 294, 299-300 (1955) (*Brown II*)); *see also* Dayton Bd. of Educ. v. Brinkman, 443 U.S. 526, 534 n.8 (1979) (*Dayton II*) (noting that "there is great value in appellate courts showing deference to the fact-finding of local trial judges" in desegregation cases); *Wright*, 407 U.S. at 466 (emphasizing that assessment of various desegregation proposals "is aided by a sensitivity to local conditions, and . . . is primarily the responsibility of the district judge").

154. Wright v. County Sch. Bd., 309 F. Supp. 671, 678, 680 (E.D. Va. 1970).

155. *Wright*, 407 U.S. at 474 (Burger, C.J., dissenting).
156. *Id.* at 473-74.
157. 413 U.S. 189 (1973).
158. *Id.* at 257-58 (Rehnquist, J., dissenting). Compare an earlier memo written by
     Assistant Attorney General Rehnquist calling *Green* and its companion cases
     "muddy" and "'disingenuous'" and stating that

> in view of what appears to be a large body of public support for the
> idea of neighborhood schools, free from supervision by the federal
> courts, it would appear to be sound policy to couple with any amend-
> ment validating "freedom of choice" plans a related provision validat-
> ing "neighborhood school" plans.

     Memorandum from William H. Rehnquist, Assistant Attorney General, Office
     of Legal Counsel, to Egil Krogh, Jr., Deputy Assistant to the President for
     Domestic Affairs, Re: Constitutional Amendment to Validate "Freedom of
     Choice" and "Neighborhood Schools" 3-5 (Mar. 3, 1970) (Box 19, Folder "School
     desegregation," Egil G. Krogh Files, White House Special Files, Nixon Presiden-
     tial Materials, National Archives, College Park, Md.) [hereinafter Memorandum
     to Egil Krogh].
159. 413 U.S. at 258 (Rehnquist, J., dissenting).
160. Green v. County Sch. Bd., 391 U.S. 430, 434 (1968).
161. *See id.* at 442 & n.6.
162. *See supra* notes 47-65 and accompanying text.
163. *See, e.g.*, Cooper v. Aaron, 358 U.S. 1, 24 (1958); *see supra* note 54 and accompa-
     nying text.
164. *See, e.g.*, Bd. of Educ. v. Brinkman, 443 U.S. 526 (1979) (*Dayton II*) (holding that
     plaintiffs need not prove incremental effects of individual constitutional viola-
     tions where they have demonstrated that school board discrimination has had
     system-wide effect); Columbus v. Penick, 443 U.S. 449 (1979) (same); Dayton
     Bd. of Educ. v. Brinkman, 433 U.S. 406 (1977) (*Dayton I*) (holding that where
     school board has engaged in only isolated acts of discrimination, district courts
     should determine incremental segregative effects of those actions and style
     their remedies accordingly); Milliken v. Bradley, 433 U.S. 267 (1977) (*Milliken
     II*) (holding that desegregation remedies should be tailored to fit nature of viola-
     tion, should strive to return victims of segregation to position they would have
     enjoyed absent discrimination, and should take into account state and local
     interests in managing their own affairs, consistent with Constitution); Milliken
     v. Bradley, 418 U.S. 717 (1974) (*Milliken I*) (holding that mandatory interdistrict
     remedies are only justified where interdistrict constitutional violations have
     caused interdistrict effects).
165. *See infra* notes 254-70 and accompanying text.
166. 498 U.S. 237 (1991).
167. 515 U.S. 70 (1995).
168. *Jenkins*, 515 U.S. at 74-80, 102; *Dowell*, 498 U.S. at 240-42.
169. *Dowell*, 498 U.S. at 248-50.

170. *Jenkins*, 515 U.S. at 89-99.
171. Swann v. Charlotte-Mecklenberg Sch. Bd., 402 U.S. 1, 25-26 (1971) ("Schools all or predominantly of one race in a district of mixed population will require close scrutiny to determine that school assignments are not part of state-enforced segregation."); Green v. County Sch. Bd., 391 U.S. 430, 439 (1968) (stating that availability of more promising desegregation plan places "heavy burden" on school board to explain its choice of less effective plan); *see supra* notes 72-73, 78-79, and accompanying text.
172. *Swann*, 402 U.S. at 15; *Green*, 391 U.S. at 438 n.4; *see supra* notes 77, 82-84, and accompanying text.
173. 418 U.S. 717, 744-45 (1974) (*Milliken I*). *See infra* note 251 and accompanying text for further discussion of the Supreme Court's holding.
174. *See supra* notes 150-59 and accompanying text.
175. Dowell v. Sch. Bd., 219 F. Supp. 427, 431 (W.D. Okla. 1963).
176. *Id.* at 433.
177. *Id.* at 431.
178. OKLA. CONST. art. XIII, § 3 (repealed 1966).
179. Shelley v. Kraemer, 334 U.S. 1 (1948).
180. Brown v. Bd. of Educ., 347 U.S. 483 (1954) (*Brown I*).
181. *Dowell*, 219 F. Supp. at 434.
182. Dowell v. Sch. Bd., 244 F. Supp. 971, 976-77 (W.D. Okla. 1965); *see also* Bd. of Educ. v. Dowell, 498 U.S. 237, 240-41 (1991) (noting this finding).
183. Dowell v. Bd. of Educ., 338 F. Supp. 1256 (W.D. Okla. 1972).
184. Because the court order exempted from busing "stand-alone" elementary schools in integrated neighborhoods and because residential integration had increased in some areas, black inner-city students had to be bused greater distances to reach predominantly white schools in outlying suburbs. *See Dowell*, 498 U.S. at 242; Brief for Respondents at 10-12, *Dowell* (No. 89-1080).
185. The parties did not agree on the precise number of one-race schools. *Compare* Brief for Respondents at 15-16, *Dowell* (No. 89-1080) (listing ten such schools), *with* Brief of Petitioner at 6 n.8, *Dowell* (No. 89-1080) (listing seven).
186. *Dowell*, 498 U.S. at 242; *id.* at 255 (Marshall, J., dissenting).
187. *See* Dowell v. Bd. of Educ., 890 F.2d 1483, 1500-01 (10th Cir. 1989); *id.* at 1510 n.4 (Baldock, J., dissenting).
188. Dowell v. Bd. of Educ., 677 F. Supp. 1503, 1517 (W.D. Okla. 1987).
189. *Id.* at 1519, 1522.
190. *Id.* at 1511-13, 1516-17.
191. *Dowell*, 890 F.2d at 1502-04.
192. All of the Justices agreed that school desegregation decrees were not intended to extend in perpetuity and that the Tenth Circuit's approach was too rigid. *See Dowell*, 498 U.S. at 240; *id.* at 256 (Marshall, J., dissenting) ("I agree with the majority that the proper standard for determining whether a school desegregation decree should be dissolved is whether the purposes of the desegregation litigation, as incorporated in the decree, have been fully achieved."). Justice Souter did not participate in the case. *Id.* at 251.

193. *Id.* at 250 n.2.

194. *Dowell*, 677 F. Supp. at 1515-22.

195. *Dowell*, 890 F.2d at 1506.

196. *Dowell*, 498 U.S. at 250 n.2. In contrast, Justice Marshall believed that the record amply demonstrated "complicity in residential segregation on the part of the Board." *Id.* at 264 (Marshall, J., dissenting). He also believed that the district court should have put more weight on the

> roles of the State, local officials, and the Board in creating what are now self-perpetuating patterns of residential segregation. . . . [The district court also should have considered] the *unique* role of the School Board in creating "all-Negro" schools clouded by the stigma of segregation— schools to which white parents would not opt to send their children.

Id. at 265 (Marshall, J., dissenting).

197. *Dowell*, 890 F.2d at 1487-88.

198. *Id.* at 1489.

199. *Id.* at 1493-97.

200. *Dowell*, 890 F.2d at 1493-97.

201. *Id.* at 1504 (quoting United States v. U.S. Gypsum Co., 333 U.S. 364, 395 (1948)).

202. *Id.*

203. The majority's suggestion that the Tenth Circuit's conclusion applied only to the factual findings it discussed in subpart VI.D. cannot be accurate. The findings discussed in Part VI related solely to faculty desegregation and to various aspects of the new reassignment plan. *See id.* at 1498-1504.

204. *See* Brief of Petitioner at 48-50, *Dowell* (No. 89-1080). Although Petitioner initially suggested that "*Dowell*'s failure to defer to the district court's findings [on residential segregation] 'is difficult to fathom,'" *id.* at 50 (quoting Amadeo v. Zant, 486 U.S. 214, 227 (1988)), it asserted in a footnote to its Reply Brief that the Tenth Circuit's holding was "ambiguous," Reply Brief for the Petitioner at 16 n.14, *Dowell* (No. 89-1080).

205. *See* Brief for Respondents at 42-47 & n.31, *Dowell* (No. 89-1080).

206. *Dowell*, 498 U.S. at 250 n.2.

207. *Id.* at 249-50 (footnotes omitted).

208. *Id.* at 250.

209. *See* Swann v. Charlotte-Mecklenburg Bd. of Educ., 402 U.S. 1, 28 (1971); Green v. County Sch. Bd., 391 U.S. 430, 439 (1968).

210. *Green*, 391 U.S. at 439 (emphasis added).

211. *Green* clearly had held that the "obligation of the district courts, as it always has been, is to assess the effectiveness of a proposed plan in achieving desegregation." *Id.* Though *Green* mentioned good faith in passing, *id.* ("Where the court finds the board to be acting in good faith *and* the proposed plan to have real prospects for dismantling the state-imposed dual system at the earliest practicable date, then the plan may be said to provide effective relief.") (emphasis added) (internal quotation marks omitted), *Green* and later cases judged school desegregation plans according to whether they would eliminate vestiges of

segregation from all aspects of school operations, *see, e.g.*, *Swann*, 402 U.S. at 15, 26.

212. *Dowell*, 498 U.S. at 248 (quoting Spangler v. Pasadena City Bd. of Educ., 611 F.2d 1239, 1245 n.5 (9th Cir. 1979) (Kennedy, J., concurring)).

213. *Id.* at 249.

214. *See Green*, 391 U.S. at 439 ("The availability to the board of other more promising courses of action may indicate a lack of good faith. . . ."); *Swann*, 402 U.S. at 25-26 ("Schools all or predominantly of one race in a district of mixed population will require close scrutiny to determine that school assignments are not part of state-enforced segregation."); *supra* notes 72-73, 78-79, and accompanying text.

215. The dissenters, led by Justice Marshall in his last desegregation opinion, asserted that because one-race schools were "one of the primary vestiges of state-imposed segregation," the decree should remain in place as long as there were reasonable alternatives available to combat such vestiges. *Id.* at 262 (Marshall, J., dissenting) (quoting Milliken v. Bradley, 418 U.S. 717, 802 (1974) (Marshall, J., dissenting) (*Milliken I*)).

216. Dowell v. Bd. of Educ., 677 F. Supp. 1503, 1515-17 (W.D. Okla. 1987).

217. *Dowell*, 498 U.S. at 266-67 (Marshall, J., dissenting).

218. 515 U.S. 70 (1995).

219. MO. CONST. art. IX, §1 (repealed 1976); MO. REV. STAT. §§163.130, 165.117 (repealed 1957); *see also* Jenkins v. Missouri, 807 F.2d 657, 690 (8th Cir. 1987).

220. *Jenkins*, 593 F. Supp. at 1490.

221. *Id.* at 1492-93.

222. Jenkins v. Missouri, 672 F. Supp. 400, 411 (W.D. Mo. 1987); *Jenkins*, 639 F. Supp. at 36, 24 (emphasis omitted).

223. *Jenkins*, 639 F. Supp. at 24-25.

224. Jenkins v. Missouri, No. 77-0420-CV-W-4, slip op. at 1 (W.D. Mo. Aug. 25, 1986). Although the court did not explain this finding, the plaintiff schoolchildren had introduced evidence that Kansas City officials had attempted to limit desegregation of historically white schools in the western part of the city at the expense of white neighborhoods in the southeast, prompting rapid demographic changes in and significant white flight from the latter areas into private schools and nearby suburban districts. Brief of Appellants at 32-35, 45, 51, Jenkins v. Missouri, 807 F.2d 657 (8th Cir. 1987) (Nos. 85-1765WM, -1949WM, -1974WM) (providing extended citations to district court record); *see also Jenkins*, 593 F. Supp. at 1494-95 (finding that "whites moved out" as blacks moved to or were bused to schools in southeastern neighborhoods and that defendants had failed to adopt effective district-wide stabilization plans). The Eighth Circuit upheld the district court's white-flight finding. Jenkins v. Missouri, 855 F.2d 1295, 1302-03 (8th Cir. 1988).

225. *Jenkins*, 807 F.2d at 661-62 & n.6; *Jenkins*, 593 F. Supp. at 1488; *Sch. Dist.*, 460 F. Supp. at 430.

226. Jenkins v. Missouri, No. 77-0420-CV-W-4, slip op. at 6-42 (W.D. Mo. June 5, 1984) (repeatedly citing Milliken v. Bradley, 418 U.S. 717 (1974) (*Milliken I*)).

227. *Id.*, slip op. at 15-19.

228. Plaintiffs had argued that post-1954 housing discrimination and white flight from Kansas City had interdistrict effects, but the district court concluded that such "white flight[] does not implicate any [suburban school district] and must be rejected" as a basis for a mandatory interdistrict remedy because the suburban districts had not lured white families, discouraged black family migration, or contributed to residential segregation allegedly caused by various state and federal actors. *Id.* at 34-42; *see also id.* at 39 ("White flight is simply not a constitutional violation by any [suburban school district].***").** In discussing specific high-school transfer statistics, the court stated that "the numbers involved are too insignificant to have had a segregative impact on the [Kansas City school district] or the [suburban school districts]," *id.* at 38-39, but it made no findings with regard to the total amount or significance of white flight from the Kansas City system.

229. Jenkins v. Missouri, 639 F. Supp. 19, 34 (W.D. Mo. 1986) (magnet program); *id.* at 38-39 (voluntary interdistrict program); *id.* at 39-41 (capital improvements); *see also* Jenkins v. Missouri, 672 F. Supp. 400, 404-08 (W.D. Mo. 1987) (capital improvements).

230. *Jenkins*, 639 F. Supp. at 26-35 (mandating funding for various academic programs, including magnet schools).

231. Jenkins v. Missouri, 855 F.2d 1295, 1301-06 (8th Cir. 1988), *cert. denied*, 484 U.S. 816 (1987); *Jenkins*, 807 F.2d at 682-86.

232. Green v. County Sch. Bd., 391 U.S. 430 (1968).

233. *Id.* at 438 n.4 (1968) (quoting Louisiana v. United States, 380 U.S. 145, 154 (1965)); *see also* Swann v. Charlotte-Mecklenburg Bd. of Educ., 402 U.S. 1, 15 (1971) ("Once a right and a violation have been shown, the scope of a district court's equitable powers to remedy past wrongs is broad, for breadth and flexibility are inherent in equitable remedies.").

234. The specific question relating to academic deficiencies on which the Supreme Court had granted certiorari was whether the remedial educational programs ordered by the district court "'failed to satisfy the Fourteenth Amendment (thus precluding a finding of partial unitary status) solely because student achievement in the District, as measured by results on standardized test scores, had not risen to some unspecified level.'" Missouri v. Jenkins, 515 U.S. 70, 144 (1995) (Souter, J., dissenting) (quoting Petition for a Writ of Certiorari, at i (No. 88-1150)). But the challenged order made no reference to test scores, and defendants never attempted to show that the district had achieved partial unitary status with regard to the academic vestiges of segregation. *Id.* at 148-50 (Souter, J., dissenting).

235. 515 U.S. at 102 (emphasizing that "insistence upon academic goals unrelated to the effects of legal segregation unwarrantably postpones the day when the [school district] will be able to operate on its own" and that "the District Court also should consider that many goals of its quality education plan already have been attained").

236. 515 U.S. at 101 (emphasis omitted).

237. 433 U.S. 267 (1977).
238. 433 U.S. 406 (1977).
239. *Id.* at 420.
240. *See, e.g.*, Dayton Bd. of Educ. v. Brinkman, 443 U.S. 526, 540 (1979) (*Dayton II*) (describing as "a misunderstanding of *Dayton I*" contention that plaintiffs must "prove with respect to each additional act of discrimination precisely what effect it has had on current patterns of segregation").
241. *See, e.g.*, Swann v. Charlotte-Mecklenburg Bd. of Educ., 402 U.S. 1, 16 (1971) ("As with any equity case, the nature of the violation determines the scope of the remedy.").
242. The majority left room, however, for the district court to continue the remedial programs, provided that it made sufficiently precise findings to support such relief. *Jenkins*, 515 U.S. at 101-02. On remand, the district court did make such findings regarding the incremental effects of segregation and continued many of the remedial programs. Jenkins v. Missouri, 959 F. Supp. 1151 (W.D. Mo. 1997), *aff'd*, 122 F.3d 588 (8th Cir. 1997).
243. 515 U.S. at 84 (citation omitted); *see also id.* at 83-100.
244. *Jenkins*, 515 U.S. at 92-93.
245. *Id.* at 92.
246. *See supra* note 224 (discussing holding and Eighth Circuit's initial affirmance); *see also* Jenkins v. Missouri, 11 F.3d 755, 767-68 (8th Cir. 1993) (reexamining and upholding "the finding . . . that 'segregation has caused a system wide *reduction* in student achievement in the schools of the KCMSD'" as well as departures of whites to private schools and suburbs" as supported by "substantial evidence" (quoting Jenkins v. Missouri, 855 F.2d 1295, 1300 (8th Cir. 1988)).
247. *Cf. supra* note 206 and accompanying text (describing similar behavior in *Dowell*).
248. *Jenkins*, 515 U.S. at 95 (footnotes omitted).
249. *See, e.g.*, Goodman v. Lukens Steel Co., 482 U.S. 656, 665 (1987); Graver Tank & Mfg. Co. v. Linde Air Prods. Co., 336 U.S. 271, 275 (1949). Four members of the *Jenkins* majority cited this rule in a dissent they issued just a few months before *Jenkins*. *See* Kyles v. Whitley, 514 U.S. 419, 456-57 (1995) (Scalia, J., dissenting); *see also* Bradley W. Joondeph, Missouri v. Jenkins *and the De Facto Abandonment of Court-Enforced Desegregation*, 71 WASH. L. REV. 597, 642-45 & nn.251 & 254 (1996) (discussing "'two court rule,' under which the Court 'ordinarily' will not review factual findings made by a district court and approved by the court of appeals," and noting other cases in which members of *Jenkins* majority had invoked it).
250. *See, e.g.*, Anderson v. City of Bessemer City, 470 U.S. 564, 573-74 (1985).
251. Milliken v. Bradley, 418 U.S. 717 (1974) (*Milliken I*).
252. 425 U.S. 284, 298 (1976).
253. 425 U.S. at 297-98.
254. 515 U.S. at 98.
255. 425 U.S. at 299-300.
256. 425 U.S. at 300.

257. *Jenkins*, 515 U.S. at 169 (Souter, J., dissenting).

258. *Id.* at 97.

259. *Id.* at 98 (citing Milliken v. Bradley, 433 U.S. 267 (1977) (*Milliken II*)).

260. *Milliken II*, 433 U.S. at 280-81 (citations omitted).

261. Indeed, *Milliken II* specifically reiterated *Swann*'s holding that "once invoked, 'the scope of a district court's equitable powers to remedy past wrongs is broad, for breadth and flexibility are inherent in equitable remedies.'" 433 U.S. at 281 (quoting Swann v. Charlotte-Mecklenburg Bd. of Educ., 402 U.S. 1, 15 (1971)).

262. On remand after *Milliken I*, the district court ordered the implementation of several educational programs that it found were "needed to remedy effects of past segregation, to assure a successful desegregative effort and to minimize the possibility of resegregation." Bradley v. Milliken, 402 F. Supp. 1096, 1118 (E.D. Mich. 1975).

263. *Milliken II*, 433 U.S. at 291 (citations omitted).

264. 515 U.S. at 97.

265. *Id.* at 99 (citing Freeman v. Pitts, 503 U.S. 467, 489 (1992); Bd. of Educ. v. Dowell, 498 U.S. 237, 247 (1991); Dayton Bd. of Educ. v. Brinkman, 433 U.S. 406, 410 (1977) (*Dayton I*)).

266. 407 U.S. 451, 477 (1972).

267. The *Jenkins* majority relied on *Dayton I* for the proposition that "local autonomy of school districts is a vital national tradition," 515 U.S. at 99 (citing *Dayton I*, 433 U.S. at 410), and relied on *Freeman* for the rule that district courts' end purpose in desegregation cases must be "to restore state and local authorities to the control of a school system that is operating in compliance with the Constitution" in addition to remedying vestiges of segregation to the extent practicable, *id.* at 102 (citing *Freeman*, 503 U.S. at 489). The *Dowell* majority relied on *Milliken II* and *Spangler* for the proposition that ending court supervision after school systems have complied for a reasonable time period recognizes the "necessary concern for the important values of local control." 498 U.S. at 248 (citing Milliken v. Bradley, 433 U.S. 267, 280-82 (1977) (*Milliken II*) and Spangler v. Pasadena City Board of Education, 611 F.2d 1239, 1245 n.5 (9th Cir. 1979) (Kennedy, J., concurring)).

268. *See supra* notes 70-77 and accompanying text.

269. Brown v. Bd. of Educ., 349 U.S. 294, 299 (1955) (*Brown II*) ("Full implementation of these constitutional principles may require solution of varied local school problems. School authorities have the primary responsibility for elucidating, assessing, and solving these problems; courts will have to consider whether the action of school authorities constitutes good faith implementation of the governing constitutional principles."); *see supra* note 47.

270. 358 U.S. 1, 19 (1958).

271. *Jenkins*, 515 U.S. at 74-80; *Dowell*, 498 U.S. at 240-44.

272. *Jenkins*, 515 U.S. at 102; *Dowell*, 498 U.S. at 249.

273. *Jenkins*, 515 U.S. at 175-76 (Ginsburg, J., dissenting).

274. Milliken v. Bradley, 418 U.S. 717, 814 (1974) (*Milliken I*) (Marshall, J., dissenting).

275. 347 U.S. 483 (1954) (*Brown I*); *see supra* notes 39-41 and accompanying text.

METHODOLOGY, DESEGREGATION, AND THE RULE OF LAW >> 105

276. Swann v. Charlotte-Mecklenburg Bd. of Educ., 402 U.S. 1 (1971); Green v. County Sch. Bd., 391 U.S. 430 (1968); *see supra* notes 72-86 and accompanying text.

277. *See supra* notes 185-87 and accompanying text.

278. *See supra* notes 229-33, 243-48, and accompanying text.

279. *See, e.g.,* ROBERT H. BORK, THE TEMPTING OF AMERICA: THE POLITICAL SEDUCTION OF THE LAW 74-84 (1990) (characterizing decision as disingenuous and "inconsistent with the original understanding of the equal protection clause"); WHAT BROWN V. BOARD OF EDUCATION SHOULD HAVE SAID: THE NATION'S TOP LEGAL EXPERTS REWRITE AMERICA'S LANDMARK CIVIL RIGHTS DECISION (Jack M. Balkin ed., 2001) (providing nine scholars' alternate opinions); Michael W. McConnell, *Originalism and the Desegregation Decisions*, 81 VA. L. REV. 947, 1131-40 (1995) (criticizing *Brown*'s treatment of history and emphasis on education and social science); Herbert Wechsler, *Toward Neutral Principles of Constitutional Law*, 73 HARV. L. REV. 1, 22, 31-34 (1959) (criticizing Court's failure to view *Brown* in terms of associational rights); Louis H. Pollak, *Racial Discrimination and Judicial Integrity: A Reply to Professor Wechsler*, 108 U. PA. L. REV. 1, 24-31 (1959) (presenting draft of alternate "adequate" opinion).

280. 347 U.S. at 494-95.

281. Swann v. Charlotte-Mecklenburg Bd. of Educ., 402 U.S. 1, 15 (1971) (quoting Green v. County Sch. Bd., 391 U.S. 430, 438 (1968)).

282. *Green*, 391 U.S. at 442.

283. *Id.* at 437-38.

284. *Swann*, 402 U.S. at 15.

285. Missouri v. Jenkins, 515 U.S. 70, 99, 102 (1995); Bd. of Educ. v. Dowell, 498 U.S. 237, 248 (1991).

286. In fact, the effectiveness of school desegregation and its benefits to both minority and non-minority students remain the subject of intense debate. *Compare Jenkins*, 515 U.S. at 120 n.2 (Thomas, J., concurring) (citing various conflicting studies for proposition that "there simply is no conclusive evidence that desegregation either has sparked a permanent jump in the achievement scores of black children, or has remedied any psychological feelings of inferiority black schoolchildren might have had"), DAVID J. ARMOR, FORCED JUSTICE: SCHOOL DESEGREGATION AND THE LAW 221 (1995) (describing evidence of achievement gains as "mixed at best"), *and* CHRISTOPHER JENCKS & MEREDITH PHILLIPS, THE BLACK-WHITE TEST SCORE GAP: AN INTRODUCTION, IN THE BLACK-WHITE TEST SCORE GAP 1, 9 (Christopher Jencks & Meredith Phillips eds., 1998) (reporting that schools' racial composition does not appear to affect math scores at any age or reading scores after sixth grade), *with* GARY ORFIELD, HARVARD UNIV. CIVIL RIGHTS PROJECT, SCHOOLS MORE SEPARATE: CONSEQUENCES OF A DECADE OF RESEGREGATION 9-11 (2001), *available at* http://www.civilrightsproject. harvard.edu/research/deseg/Schools More Separate.pdf (citing various studies concluding that desegregation has improved test scores and college attendance rates), Rita E. Mahard & Robert L. Crain, *Research on Minority Achievement in*

Desegregated Schools, in THE CONSEQUENCES OF SCHOOL DESEGREGA-
TION 103, 103-25 (Christine H. Rossell & Willis D. Hawley eds., 1983) (concluding on the basis of review of ninety-three studies that desegregation has positive
effect on student achievement when it begins in early primary grades, involves
"critical mass" of black students, and is performed on metropolitan-area basis),
and Janet Ward Schofield, *Review of Research on School Desegregation's Impact
on Elementary and Secondary School Students, in* HANDBOOK OF RESEARCH
ON MULTICULTURAL EDUCATION 597, 605-07 (James A. Banks ed., 1995)
(summarizing recent long-term studies suggesting that desegregated schools
increase "life outcomes" of black students).

287. Keyes v. Sch. Dist. No. 1, 413 U.S. 189, 258 (1973) (Rehnquist, J., dissenting); *see
supra* note 158 and accompanying text; *see also* Memorandum to Egil Krogh,
supra note 158, at 3 (criticizing *Green* in similar language).

288. 469 U.S. 528, 557 (1985) ("National League of Cities v. Usery, 426 U.S. 833 (1976),
is overruled.").

289. 521 U.S. 203, 206 (1997) ("The doctrine of stare decisis does not preclude us
from recognizing the change in our law and overruling *Aguilar* [*v. Felton*, 473
U.S. 402 (1985)].").

290. 123 S. Ct. 2472, 2484 (2003) ("*Bowers* was not correct when it was decided, and
it is not correct today. It ought not to remain binding precedent. *Bowers v. Hardwick* should be and now is overruled.").

291. Green v. County Sch. Bd., 391 U.S. 430, 439 (1968); Swann v. Charlotte-Mecklenburg Bd. of Educ., 402 U.S. 1, 26 (1971); *see supra* note 78 and accompanying
text.

292. 503 U.S. 467 (1992).

293. *Freeman*, 503 U.S. at 506 (Scalia, J., concurring).

294. *Id.*

295. *See supra* text accompanying note 14.

296. Mitchell v. W.T. Grant Co., 416 U.S. 600, 636 (1974) (Stewart, J., dissenting).

4

Our Eighteenth-Century Constitution in
the Twenty-First-Century World

DIANE P. WOOD

Introduction

Fine wines and Stradivarius violins improve with age, taking on greater
richness and depth as the years go by. For many, if not most, other things
in today's frenetic world, value is evanescent. To be old is all too often
to be out of date and ready for disposal. In this paper, I explore which
conception of age better describes our Constitution—now 215 years old.
Is this eighteenth-century document, along with its eighteenth-century
Bill of Rights and its other seventeen Amendments, still up to the job?
How well is it serving the demands we are placing upon it, particularly
in the area of individual rights, or what international scholars call human
rights?

One's answer depends critically on which model of constitutional
interpretation one chooses: the originalist approach or the dynamic
approach. While there may be a certain attraction to so-called "plain language" literalism, the Constitution, when viewed in that light, fares badly
as a charter for twenty-first-century America. On the other hand, while
the dynamic approach has prevailed over time, for the most part, and
allowed the Constitution to adapt to the demands of a modern society,
this approach has proven vulnerable to criticism.

How serious is that criticism? Has the time now come for us to consider amending our basic charter to bring it up to date, taking to heart the
advice that so many American scholars have so assiduously given over
the last decade and a half to countries emerging from the Communist

This lecture was delivered on October 18, 2004, and appeared in *80 N.Y.U. L. Rev.*
1079 (2005).

shadow? One who advocates a narrow, text-based approach to the Constitution would be compelled to answer that the Constitution has reached the end of its rope, for reasons I shall explain in this paper. If, on the other hand, one is willing to give the broad provisions in the Constitution and its Amendments a generous reading, thereby validating the many adaptations that the Court and country have endorsed over the years, our old Constitution has stood the test of time admirably. The basic charter that suited a small, relatively powerless, rural economy with a population of 3.9 million now serves a global superpower of nearly three hundred million citizens,[1] where economically the relevant stage is the entire world, where national and global communications are instantaneous, and where it is easier to get from New York to Honolulu than it once was to get from New York to Philadelphia.

But not all have welcomed this achievement. The doctrines the Supreme Court has used to allow the Constitution to grow with the times have been hotly contested. Many people today question whether the Court has strayed too far from the original intent of the Framers. They also assert that it is not proper to look to foreign experience when we consider which human rights have constitutional status. While critics are right to note that some of the most important constitutional developments rest on what some have called the "unwritten Constitution,"[2] this does not mean that we should reject them. The price of doing so would be far too high both for the structural provisions of the Constitution and our commitment—both domestically and internationally—to the protection of human rights. Rejection would be tantamount to an unnecessary conclusion that the Constitution has indeed outlived its usefulness. It is time, therefore, to end the long-standing and unproductive methodological debate over "originalism" versus "dynamism" or "evolution" and focus instead on how, as a substantive matter, we should interpret the Constitution in the twenty-first century, and what it has to say on questions unimaginable to our eighteenth-century Framers.

I. What Do We Expect of the Constitution?

In order to set the stage, let me begin by reviewing what we rightly expect the Constitution to do, and how well it manages to meet those expectations. It is well understood that the United States Constitution, like most constitutions, contains both provisions that allocate powers among the institutions of government and provisions that protect individual rights.

A quick overview of both areas is enough to illustrate how far we have evolved in each one from the literal text of the Constitution and how much we depend upon the elaboration that has largely come from the Supreme Court.

A. Structural Rules

Because the original Constitution was primarily concerned with the structure of the new federal government, and because its first three articles are almost exclusively about structure, let me begin there. We are all familiar with the basic outline. Despite the absence of an article or clause announcing that the new United States would adopt a modified structure of separation of powers, where a system of checks and balances would operate, it is plain from Articles I, II, and III of the Constitution that this is exactly what was being done. Moreover, as everyone knows, the Constitution spells out numerous ways in which each branch was to interact with its fellows. To name just a few examples, the Vice President presides over the Senate;[3] the Senate tries all impeachments;[4] before a bill becomes law, the President must sign it, or a supermajority of Congress must pass it over his veto;[5] the President's appointment and treaty powers are limited by the need to obtain the Senate's advice and consent;[6] and the appellate jurisdiction of the Supreme Court is subject to "such Exceptions, and . . . Regulations as the Congress shall make."[7] The last of these has been in the news recently in connection with legislation passed by the House of Representatives that would strip the Supreme Court of jurisdiction to hear cases challenging the phrase "under God" in the Pledge of Allegiance.[8]

There are additional structural rules found in the Constitution and its Amendments. Congress's power to tax was the subject of the Sixteenth Amendment;[9] the Seventeenth Amendment changed the way in which senators are chosen;[10] and the Twenty-Seventh Amendment governs laws affecting the compensation of members of Congress.[11] The text of the Constitution also contains rules about federal elections in the Twelfth Amendment,[12] the Fourteenth Amendment,[13] the Twentieth Amendment (which sets the dates from which the terms of the President and the Congress run),[14] the Twenty-Second Amendment (which limits a person to two terms as President),[15] and the Twenty-Fifth Amendment (which outlines what happens upon the disability or death of the President).[16]

Finally, the Constitution has a few things to say about the federal structure of the nation, although not as much as one might think. Principal among these textual provisions is Article IV of the original Constitution, which contains such important guarantees as the Full Faith and Credit Clause,[17] the Privileges and Immunities Clause,[18] the Extradition Clause,[19] and the rules for admitting new states and governing territories.[20] Article VI contains the Supremacy Clause, which addresses the place of federal law in the hierarchy of federal and state law.[21] In addition, the Tenth Amendment underscores the fact that the federal government is indeed a government of limited and delegated powers, and that the powers not specifically given to it are reserved to either the States or the people.[22] Last, there is the Eleventh Amendment, which, to a literalist, says that federal judicial power does not extend to cases brought against a State by a citizen of another State.[23]

That all sounds comprehensive, but it has turned out not to be enough for a growing country. I list here some of the more important structural doctrines that developed, particularly in the twentieth century, to help the United States adapt to its changing size and to the changing world.

Justice Byron White eloquently took note of these changes in his dissenting opinion in *INS v. Chadha*,[24] which held the single-house legislative veto unconstitutional. Explaining why he would have upheld this device, which by that time appeared in nearly two hundred statutes, he wrote as follows:

> From the summer of 1787 to the present the Government of the United States has become an endeavor far beyond the contemplation of the Framers. Only within the last half century has the complexity and size of the Federal Government's responsibilities grown so greatly that the Congress must rely on the legislative veto as the most effective if not the only means to insure its role as the Nation's lawmaker. But the wisdom of the Framers was to anticipate that the Nation would grow and new problems of governance would require different solutions. Accordingly, our Federal Government was intentionally chartered with the flexibility to respond to contemporary needs without losing sight of fundamental democratic principles.[25]

Even though Justice White made this point in dissent, its basic truth has been reflected many times over in the Court's majority opinions. Justice White himself commented in his separate opinion in *Buckley v. Valeo* that "there is no doubt that the development of the administrative agency in response to modern legislative and administrative need has placed severe strain on the separation-of-powers principle in its pristine formulation."[26] But, he went on, there is similarly no doubt that the independent agency has come to be accepted as an important and lawful part of the federal government. The New Deal ushered in the administrative state, and along with it the Court's decisions rejecting constitutional challenges to the so-called "independent agency." In *Crowell v. Benson*,[27] the Court considered the constitutionality of certain provisions of the Longshoremen's and Harbor Worker's Compensation Act[28] that called for the use of a deputy commissioner to find critical jurisdictional facts. It came to the brink of holding the statute unconstitutional as an impermissible infringement of the powers of the judicial branch. It pulled back at the last minute, saving the statute with a narrow construction, under which the ultimate fact of employment would be determined by a court.[29] Even more frankly, in *Sunshine Anthracite Coal Co. v. Adkins*,[30] it found that the Bituminous Coal Act of 1937[31] did not contain an invalid delegation of legislative or judicial powers to the Bituminous Coal Commission, noting pragmatically that "the effectiveness of both the legislative and administrative processes would become endangered if Congress were under the constitutional compulsion of filling in the details beyond the liberal prescription here."[32] In a similar vein, the Court a few years earlier had held in *Humphrey's Executor v. United States*[33] that a commissioner of the Federal Trade Commission was not a "purely" executive officer and thus could not be removed at the President's pleasure. The Court wrote, somewhat vaguely, that the FTC was constituted to perform "legislative and judicial" duties and thus could not be viewed exclusively as an arm of the executive branch.[34]

Congress has continued to create agencies and officials that are neither fish nor fowl, and the Court has continued to evaluate them for consistency with the structure of the Constitution. Thus, in 1989 the U.S. Sentencing Commission dodged the constitutional bullet when the Court found in *Mistretta v. United States*[35] that Congress had neither impermissibly delegated legislative power to the Commission (which was described as an "independent commission in the judicial branch of the United States") nor violated separation-of-power principles.[36] Once again, a practical approach pervades the Court's discussion of both the nondelegation doctrine and the separation-of-powers argument.

This does not mean that the Court now takes an "anything goes" approach to separation of powers. The majority in *Chadha*, as noted earlier, found the device of the one-house legislative veto to be incompatible with the constitutional design, but the four separate opinions reveal a deeply felt concern over the appropriate role for the Court in reconciling the modern federal system with the literal assignment of functions found in the constitutional text.[37] In *Metropolitan Washington Airports Authority v. Citizens for the Abatement of Aircraft Noise*,[38] the Court struck down a board of review that Congress created to administer certain aspects of the operation of the two Washington, D.C., area airports on the ground that a board composed of nine members of Congress with veto power over the Airport Authority represented too great a legislative encroachment upon judicial and executive powers, as well as state law. Three Justices dissented from the Court's unwillingness to accept what they called "yet another innovative and otherwise lawful governmental experiment."[39]

Two other areas where unwritten rules have profoundly affected the current constitutional balance are also worth noting. Both excited passionate debate thirty years ago, and to varying degrees they have since gained public acquiescence. I am referring to the ability of the President to refuse to spend funds appropriated by Congress, using the practice known as "impoundment," and the ability of the President to commit U.S. troops to hostilities without a formal declaration of war by the Congress. With respect to the former, the constitutional question was whether, as part of his duty faithfully to execute the laws, the Chief Executive was required to spend the monies appropriated by Congress in accordance with the governing legislation. Presidents over the years had exercised the authority to refrain from such expenditures when they found it in the country's interest, but when President Richard Nixon took this practice to new heights, controversy erupted. It was resolved for the most part by the Congressional Budget and Impoundment Control Act of 1974,[40] Title X of which begins with a disclaimer: "Nothing contained in this Act, or in any amendments made by this Act, shall be construed as . . . asserting or conceding the constitutional powers or limitations of either the Congress or the President."[41] Professor Gerald Gunther refers to the Act as "quasi-constitutional in nature, for it seeks to clarify and define basic relationships among the branches of government."[42] Indeed the Act does seek to do this: It permits the President to defer spending appropriated funds, unless either house of Congress passes a resolution disapproving the deferral; it permits the President to refuse altogether to spend funds for a particular purpose or beyond a fiscal year only with the affirmative concurrence of both houses of Congress.

War powers bring into even sharper focus the difference between today's Constitution and the text adopted in 1789. Article I, Section 8, Clause 11 confers on the Congress the power "to declare War." One could be forgiven for thinking that this short phrase must mean that the country cannot enter into hostilities without first obtaining a formal declaration from Congress, and that this declaration will specify with what country or group of countries the United States is at war. Neither of those suppositions is true in the post–Vietnam War period. First, the Congress specifically recognized the power of the President to commit U.S. troops to hostile action without a formal declaration of war in the War Powers Resolution of 1973.[43] It provides that not only a declaration of war but also "specific statutory authorization" or a national emergency created by an attack on the United States is enough to justify the President as Commander-in-Chief to initiate action. Second, the idea of "war" itself has become hopelessly fuzzy. In an era where one can have "wars" on phenomena like terrorism or organized crime—in which there is no enemy with whom to negotiate, no power capable of surrender, and thus no way to know when the "war" is over—the text of the Constitution is not very helpful.

Perhaps the most important stretch beyond the literal language of the Constitution that affects the structure of the federal government has come in the last decade, in the area of state sovereignty. The Framers knew perfectly well that the Constitution they crafted took important powers away from the States (in response to the unsatisfactory experience under the Articles of Confederation), yet left many powers still in state hands. With the latter especially in mind, they were careful (at least in the Tenth Amendment) to dissipate any impression of a negative inference about state power from the existence of the enumerated powers. But the express provisions of the Constitution leave much unsaid. They do not spell out, for example, answers to such important questions as whether Congress, acting pursuant to its Article I powers, may enact legislation creating rights that private parties may enforce against the States; whether, if there is a pre-constitutional doctrine of sovereign immunity of the States, the scope of that immunity was absolute or restricted; and whether the state sovereign immunity doctrine will evolve over the years in the same way as the foreign sovereign immunity doctrine has done.

The Supreme Court has found that the Eleventh Amendment provides the answers to these questions, despite the narrowness of its language. Indeed, the Court has been remarkably frank about the lack of a textual basis for its doctrine in this field. Justice Anthony Kennedy, for instance, commented in *Alden v. Maine*[44] that the phrase "Eleventh Amendment immunity" was "convenient shorthand but something of a misnomer,"[45] because State sovereign immunity "neither derives from nor is limited by the terms of the Eleventh Amendment."[46] To similar effect, Justice Clarence Thomas wrote in *Federal Maritime Commission v. South Carolina State Ports Authority*[47] that "the Eleventh Amendment does not define the scope of the States' sovereign immunity; it is but one particular exemplification of that immunity."[48] For present purposes, I am willing to say "so be it." The important point is that this vital part of our governmental structure rests on extra-textual constitutional doctrine that delineates the relative power of the central government and the states.

B. Individual Rights

When we turn from the Constitution's structural provisions to the area of individual rights—the places where the Constitution, as amended, seeks to ensure, as James Madison put it in *Federalist No. 10*, that "an interested and over-bearing majority" does not trample on "the rules of justice, and the rights of the minor party"[49]—we find a similar elaboration of the express text. Even at the time the ratification debates were underway after 1787, it was well recognized that the original Constitution contained very few explicit provisions on this topic. The brief list included the qualified guarantee against suspension of the writ of habeas corpus in Article I, Section 9, Clause 2—suspension only "when in Cases of Rebellion or Invasion the public Safety may require it"; the prohibition in Article I, Section 9, Clause 3 against bills of attainder and ex post facto laws; the guarantee of a jury trial in the place where the crime was committed in Article III, Section 2, Clause 3; and the Privileges and Immunities clause in Article IV, Section 2. The impression the *Federalist Papers* leave is that the Framers believed that individual rights did not need to be spelled out, both because of the structural protections they had built into the foundational document and because the constitutions of most states had bills of rights.[50]

As we all know, this point was not ultimately persuasive to the ratifying conventions in the states, and thus we gained a ten-article, Federal Bill of Rights in 1791. There is no need here to go through an exhaustive review of each Amendment—they are already quite well known. A few examples are enough to make the point about written versus unwritten understandings. The First Amendment literally says that "Congress shall make no law" abridging the various freedoms that it enumerates, but it does not say anything about state laws that may have the same effect. (Nor, for that matter, do any of the other Amendments.) The first phrase of the Second Amendment speaks of "a well regulated Militia, being necessary to the security of a free State," before the Amendment goes on to say anything about a right to keep and bear arms. Are those phrases independent, as the National Rifle Association believes, or are they interlinked, as almost all courts have thought thus far?[51] Another kind of interpretive question arises with the Amendments that use broad terms like "unreasonable,"[52] "due process of law,"[53] "just" compensation,[54] "speedy" trial,[55] and "excessive" bail and "cruel and unusual" punishment.[56] What do those terms mean? Is their meaning constant over time, or does something like "reasonableness" change as society itself changes? Finally, there are the Ninth and Tenth Amendments. Taken together, they certainly seem to indicate that there are some rights that do not reside in any governmental body. Instead, this admittedly undefined set of rights is "retained by the people," according to the Ninth Amendment, or is "reserved . . . to the people," under the Tenth Amendment. At a minimum, these texts make it impossible to apply the maxim *expressio unius est exclusio alterius* (to express one thing is to exclude others) to the preceding articles of the Bill of Rights. Whether they mean anything else in addition is another matter about which, as we like to say in the law, reasonable people have disagreed.

The Bill of Rights obviously does not exhaust the Constitution's protections for individual rights. There are, in addition, the three pivotal Civil War Amendments that not only ensured that slavery would be abolished[57] and that the right to vote could not be denied on the basis of race[58] but also that the states were forbidden to pass certain kinds of laws: those abridging the privileges and immunities of citizens of the United States (defined in the same Amendment to include every person born in the United States and all persons who become naturalized citizens); laws depriving *any* person of "life, liberty, or property, without due process of law"; and laws that "deny to *any* person within [the State's] jurisdiction the equal protection of the laws."[59] All three Amendments also confer upon Congress the right to enforce them by "appropriate legislation." In addition to the Civil War Amendments, one should add to the list the Nineteenth Amendment,[60] guaranteeing that the right to vote shall not be abridged on account of sex; the Twenty-fourth Amendment,[61] forbidding poll taxes; and the Twenty-sixth Amendment,[62] giving eighteen-year-olds the right to vote.

Much of the sound and fury that has arisen since World War II over constitutional developments has centered not on judicial elaborations concerning constitutional structure, but instead on judicial elaborations of the meaning of the individual-rights guarantees. Not very many people outside the legal academy will have passionate feelings about the growth of the administrative state, or the revival of states' rights in the name of the Eleventh Amendment. But they do feel strongly about many of the individual rights I am about to mention, although some excite more attention than others, and some are now seen as so obvious or so mundane that it is hard to recall why they were ever contested.

Let us start with the obvious or mundane rights that the Supreme Court has recognized over the years as implicit in the "liberty" recognized by both the Fifth and the Fourteenth Amendments. The Court has held that the protection against deprivation of "liberty" without due process has a substantive floor—a point where even the best "process" in the world would not be "due." I am referring, of course, to the oft-criticized doctrine of "substantive due process"—a phrase that some think is oxymoronic, and others think reflects a fundamental truth about the American system of government—namely, that there are some areas that are so personal to the individual that no aspect of government can intrude into them. American constitutional law started down this path in a way that has since become disavowed, with *Lochner v. New York* and its decision to strike down the state's maximum-hour law in the name of the substantive right of freedom of contract.[63] The Court's concerns are worth recalling, because they are not entirely wrong even today:

> It must, of course, be conceded that there is a limit to the valid exercise of the police power by the State. There is no dispute concerning this general proposition. Otherwise the Fourteenth Amendment would have no efficacy and the legislatures of the States would have unbounded power, and it would be enough to say that any piece of legislation was enacted to conserve the morals, the health, or the safety of the people. . . . The claim of the police power would be a mere pretext—become another and delusive name for the supreme sovereignty of the State to be exercised free from constitutional restraint.[64]

This was hardly the first time in constitutional history that someone expressed concern about a doctrine that would lead to the ability of one organ of government—here the states collectively—to exercise unrestrained power. And whatever one might think of *Lochner's* holding, this concern was a serious one.

Several years later and, interestingly, before the late 1930s saw the end of *Lochner*-style economic substantive due process, the Court considered whether a Nebraska statute forbidding the teaching of foreign languages in any school in the state violated the Federal Constitution.[65] Unlike many newer constitutions in the world, the U.S. Constitution does not mention the topic of languages.[66] Nonetheless, the Court, over dissents from Justices Holmes and Sutherland, held that the statute was unconstitutional. In a passage that became famous more than fifty years later when the infinitely more contentious issue of abortion was before the Court, Justice McReynolds wrote the following on behalf of the majority:

> While this Court has not attempted to define with exactness the liberty thus guaranteed [by the Fourteenth Amendment], the term has received much consideration and some of the included things have been definitely stated. Without doubt, it denotes not merely freedom from bodily restraint but also the right of the individual to contract, to engage in any of the common occupations of life, to acquire useful knowledge, to marry, establish a home and bring up children, to worship God according to the dictates of his own conscience, and generally to enjoy those privileges long recognized at common law as essential to the orderly pursuit of happiness by free men.[67]

The Court went on to say that, important though the state interest was in the physical, moral, and mental health of its citizens, "the individual has certain fundamental rights which must be respected. The protection of the Constitution extends to all, to those who speak other languages as well as to those born with English on the tongue."[68]

The Court continued with this theme a few years later in *Pierce v. Society of Sisters*.[69] This time it held unanimously that a state law requiring all children to receive their education in a public school—on pain of finding the parent or guardian guilty of a misdemeanor—was unconstitutional. It announced in rather grand language that "the fundamental theory of liberty upon which all governments in this Union repose excludes any general power of the State to standardize its children by forcing them to accept instruction from public teachers only."[70]

For a variety of reasons, the theories articulated in *Meyer* and *Pierce* lay dormant for many years, until the Supreme Court turned once again to them in the group of cases that dealt with privacy rights, reproductive rights, and issues concerning the family unit starting in the 1960s. The case that has always struck me as telling in this group is not the obvious one—*Roe v. Wade*—but is instead *Moore v. City of East Cleveland*.[71] That case involved a city ordinance that was undoubtedly inspired by the desire of city leaders to stamp out hippie communes. To do so, the City of East Cleveland enacted an ordinance that began by limiting occupancy of a dwelling unit to members of one family, and then defined the term "family" with extraordinary parsimony. The appellant, Mrs. Inez Moore, was convicted of a misdemeanor under the ordinance and sentenced to five days in jail and fined twenty-five dollars because she had living under her roof both of her sons and their respective sons. The ordinance violation came about because the grandchildren were cousins rather than brothers. The Ohio courts rejected her constitutional challenge to the ordinance, and so the case arrived at the U.S. Supreme Court on appeal.[72]

What is notable about the case is how the Justices struggled with it. Four members of the Court, led by Justice Lewis Powell, concluded that the ordinance was unconstitutional under the line of cases including *Meyer*, *Pierce*, and many others.[73] Justice William Brennan, joined by Justice Thurgood Marshall, wrote separately to emphasize that the idea of the "family" is itself culturally dependent and that there were serious (and negative) racial and economic undertones in the East Cleveland ordinance.[74] Justice John Paul Stevens provided the crucial fifth vote to strike down the ordinance, but he saw it as an undue restriction of the property rights of the owner that was invalid under the Court's zoning jurisprudence.[75] Chief Justice Warren Burger dissented on the ground that there could be no constitutional violation until Mrs. Moore exhausted her local administrative remedies by seeking a variance (an odd view, given the fact that the state courts themselves did not think that such a requirement existed).[76] Justice Potter Stewart, joined by then-Justice William Rehnquist, saw nothing unconstitutional about the ordinance, which in his view was just one of the ways that the city was entitled to define permissible property use.[77] Finally, Justice White wrote a thoughtful dissent in which he tried to come to grips with the entire line of substantive due process cases.[78] While he was not advocating that any particular case recognizing a substantive due process right be overruled, he did stress that the Court would be well-advised "to restrict the liberties protected by the Due Process Clause to those fundamental interests 'implicit in the concept of ordered liberty,'"[79] quoting *Palko v. Connecticut*.[80] The majority might have replied that it believed that it was doing exactly that, in declaring something as elemental as the family unit to be off-limits to restrictive legislative measures. But perhaps this merely illustrates how hard it is to draw lines, and how vulnerable any such judicially drawn lines are to outside criticism.

"Critical" is the mildest word one could choose to describe the reaction to the Supreme Court's recognition that the "liberty" clauses of the Constitution protect a private sphere surrounding intimate personal decisions such as the obtaining of contraceptives, abortion, and the choice of sexual partner without regard to criteria like race or sexual orientation.[81] For the sake of argument, let us assume that these questions have been resolved for now, though at least the reproductive choice right may leave the constitutional lists depending on what changes take place in the Supreme Court's membership, or it may even become constitutionalized in the opposite direction. Other freedoms may yet achieve constitutional recognition, even if we, as a society, and the Supreme Court, as the responsible institution, continue to move cautiously. It is possible, for example, that we have not heard the last word on personal autonomy over end-of-life decisions, even though the Court for now has left that delicate area to further development in the states.[82]

The idea that government must refrain altogether from some takings, no matter·how much compensation is offered, because they are not for a public purpose, is another perennial. In *Kelo v. City of New London*,[83] the Court reaffirmed the principle that government may not take property solely for the purpose of conferring a private benefit on a particular private party, nor may it take property under a mere pretext of public use.[84] On the other hand, it adopted a broad interpretation of the term "public use," and in so doing, it upheld the right of a city to take private property for purposes of an economic development plan, even though some of that property would wind up in private hands.[85] It is doubtful that this will be the last word on how to draw the line between permissible and impermissible uses of eminent domain to transfer private property to different private hands. Finally, of course, some would argue that implicit in the Second Amendment is an unqualified right to bear arms, without any necessary connection to a "Well-Regulated Militia."

While this brief review is hardly an exhaustive exploration of judicially elaborated constitutional provisions—both structural and individual— it suffices to illustrate the point that we are relying today on far more than the literal written Constitution in the area of individual rights. This is not surprising, especially when we recall that the Framers (like most draftsmen) deliberately left some things unresolved, in order to obtain the consensus needed for ratification. Moreover, we would sorely miss these constitutional elaborations, if I may call them that, if they were to be swept away with the stroke of a pen or the tap of a "delete" key. The United States has been rightfully proud of the example it has set for the world in the field of human rights, particularly since the end of World War II. It was Eleanor Roosevelt, after all, who led the successful effort for the United Nations to adopt the Universal Declaration of Human Rights.[86] Building from that nonbinding General Assembly resolution, many other international human rights conventions followed. Although the United States has not adhered to all of them, it has joined many of the most important ones.[87] Invariably in doing so, the ratification documents have proclaimed that the obligations that the nation is undertaking are already reflected in U.S. domestic law—especially in our constitutional law.[88] When we take a look at those obligations, we will see that our legal recognition of many of the core human rights recognized by the international community as a whole depends critically on the judicially recognized rights we have just reviewed.

C. Individual Rights on the International Stage

Of all these conventions, the one with the most general sweep and the one that shows most dramatically how much we depend on our evolving Constitution is the International Covenant on Civil and Political Rights. The Covenant, which currently has 152 State Parties,[89] expressly recognizes the following rights: equal rights of men and women;[90] the "inherent right to life" and protection against arbitrary deprivation of life;[91] the prohibition against torture or "cruel, inhuman or degrading treatment or punishment";[92] a ban on slavery;[93] a prohibition on arbitrary arrest or detention;[94] a right to travel;[95] procedural rights in a criminal trial,[96] including a right to an appeal;[97] a prohibition on ex post facto laws;[98] a right to privacy;[99] freedom of thought, conscience, and religion;[100] freedom of opinion and expression;[101] protection of the family;[102] the right of "men and women of marriageable age" to marry and found a family;[103] the protection of children;[104] the right to vote and take part in public affairs;[105] a broad nondiscrimination obligation;[106] and the right of minority groups to associate and maintain their culture and religion, and to use their own language.[107]

The Declarations and Understandings of the United States quite clearly reserve the right of the United States to derogate from some of these obligations—for instance, the United States has reserved the authority (though certainly not the obligation, as the Court's 2005 decision in *Roper v. Simmons*[108] has now made clear as a matter of domestic law) to impose the death penalty on a person below the age of eighteen— but just as clearly those Declarations and Understandings reflect the assumption that United States law already protects everything to which an express reservation was not made.[109] Accordingly, the United States disavowed any need to create separate private rights of action under the Convention.[110]

While some have bemoaned the Declarations and Understandings because they appear to cabin the United States' commitment to the Convention, the implication that U.S. law is already doing the job should be seen in a positive light. Nonetheless, the United States cannot support this assertion without relying on the unwritten constitutional protections we have been reviewing. The Constitution does not explicitly mention equal rights of men and women; a right to travel; a right to be free from arbitrary interference with one's privacy, family, and home; protection of the family; the right to marry; or cultural rights of minority groups. Yet as presently understood, U.S. law affords protection to most, if not all, of these rights as a matter of constitutional law. For examples, one need think only of cases like *United States v. Virginia*,[111] *Shapiro v. Thompson*,[112] *Moore v. City of East Cleveland*,[113] *Loving v. Virginia*,[114] *Lawrence v. Texas*,[115] and *Whalen v. Roe*.[116] The cultural rights of minority groups often involve nothing more nor less than the right to practice a particular religion, which the First Amendment protects, or the right to speak a particular language, which *Meyer* addressed, or the right to follow a particular lifestyle, which *Wisconsin v. Yoder*[117] and *Church of the Lukumi Babalu Aye, Inc. v. City of Hialeah*[118] both addressed, though through a religious lens. If our understanding of our own Constitution were more cramped, we would be forced to admit that there is no secure constitutional foundation in United States law for these international human rights norms. Although one might hope that statutes could be passed that would fill the gap, there is first a question whether Section 5 of the Fourteenth Amendment would suffice as a basis for a nationally enforceable code of human rights. Recall, in this connection, the fate of the Violence Against Women Act in *United States v. Morrison*[119] and ask whether the understanding of the treaty power expressed in *Missouri v. Holland*[120] would be enough to support legislation enacting the Covenant's rights in the eyes of a strict constructionist. In addition, there is always the risk that unpopular minorities might be left behind.

II. Devices Used to Find Unwritten Rules

No one in the United States thought that we had come to such a pass during the heyday of American leadership in the field of human rights, which began right after World War II and continued through at least the end of the Cold War era. Our strong national commitment to individual rights, however, depended during that period and continues to depend on several crucial constitutional understandings that have always had their critics, and more recently have come under sharper attack.[121] Those understandings include the following: (1) broad language may legitimately be interpreted broadly, in a manner informed by evolving notions of a decent society; (2) as a matter of federal constitutional law, some liberties are beyond the power of any governmental entity to deny; (3) most parts of the Bill of Rights, in particular through the doctrine of selective incorporation, apply to state action as well as to federal action; (4) constitutional principles can be inferred from sources such as the structure of the overall document and preconstitutional understandings. I will elaborate on these points in order.

First and most important is the idea that we should take seriously the fact that the text of the Constitution tends to reflect broad principles, not specific prescriptions. Neither James Madison, for whom this lecture is named, nor any of the other Framers of the Constitution were oblivious, careless, or otherwise unaware of the words they chose for the document and its Bill of Rights. The papers they left behind leave no doubt that they hoped to be writing for the ages.

There is no more reason to think that they expected the world to remain static than there is to think that any of us holds a crystal ball. The only way to create a foundational document that could stand the test of time was to build in enough flexibility that later generations would be able to adapt it to their own needs and uses.

That is exactly what the Framers did. Rather than spelling out every last detail of the structure of government and of the way that government would relate to individual citizens, they chose to enshrine only the broadest principles in the Constitution. Whether they were doing so for lofty reasons or, as appears to be the case in some instances, out of political expediency, hardly matters; what does matter is the language that was ultimately adopted. One need not write in this way, of course, and we can see the alternative approach reflected in the constitutions of some states. Perhaps the ultimate example of this is the Constitution of Texas, which today runs more than two hundred pages long, and, as of 2003, has been amended 432 times (out of a total of 606 possible amendments passed by the Texas legislature).[122] Had the Federal Constitution followed that model, it would undoubtedly by now contain a comparable number of amendments. It is even possible that those amendments would protect the very same individual rights that have emerged instead through constitutional interpretation. But there was no need to burden the Federal Constitution with endless amendments, because it was supple enough to accommodate this growth without them.

The jurisprudence of the Eighth Amendment provides a good example. The words "excessive" in the fines clause and "cruel and unusual" in the punishments clause are relative words. If one were to take the view that the only fines it prohibits are those that would have been thought excessive in 1791,[123] there would be no meaningful ceiling on criminal fines today. Civil punitive damages might be outside the reach of the Amendment as well, if one thought the word "fine" implies criminal enforcement. More to the point, the Amendment might as well not exist if the only punishments that were deemed to be "cruel and unusual" were the ones that an eighteenth-century audience would have abhorred. The Court in *Weems v. United States*[124] referred to Blackstone's understanding that executions of various types were permissible, but that disemboweling, drawing and quartering, and torture were not. But in *Weems*, the Court struck down as incompatible with the Eighth Amendment the far "milder" punishment of twelve years' hard and painful labor and imprisonment for the crime of falsifying two entries in public records. Later, in *Trop v. Dulles*,[125] the Court said that it had recognized in *Weems* "that the words of the [Eighth] Amendment are not precise, and that their scope is not static. The Amendment must draw its meaning from the evolving standards of decency that mark the progress of a maturing society."[126]

That is the approach that the Court has continued to take, as it has steadily narrowed the circumstances under which the death penalty may be imposed: first establishing strict procedural requirements for any sentence of death, in a quintuplet of cases decided in 1976,[127] then rejecting death for any crime that did not itself result in death, in *Coker v. Georgia*,[128] and still later categorically rejecting the death penalty for mentally retarded persons, in *Atkins v. Georgia*.[129] In the spring of 2005, the Court decided in *Roper v. Simmons* that the Eighth Amendment prohibits the death penalty for an offender who committed murder at the age of seventeen.[130] Just as in *Atkins*, the Court was closely divided. Justice Scalia, writing for himself, Chief Justice Rehnquist, and Justice Thomas, reiterated his opposition to the *Trop* idea that the Amendment must be understood in the light of evolving standards of decency.[131] Both the majority and Justice O'Connor in dissent, however, were willing to undertake an inquiry into what it means in 2005 to be "cruel and unusual." In doing so, the majority relied on a national consensus against the death penalty for juveniles, as evidenced both by the states that have abolished the death penalty altogether and those that maintain it but exclude juveniles from its reach.[132] The Court also noted that the United States was "the only country in the world that continues to give official sanction to the juvenile death penalty,"[133] even as it carefully pointed out that this fact was "not controlling our outcome."[134] In doing so, the Court appropriately chose to enrich its understanding of the issue by reviewing international practice, acknowledging implicitly that the American people are indeed part of the broader human community and at least presumptively share its core values.

The willingness to give content to other broad terms, such as "due process," or "equal protection of the laws," or "liberty," or "unreasonable," has allowed recognition of the other core rights the Court has identified. Inferences from constitutional structure have also played their role, as in the case of the often-disputed but still-recognized constitutional right to travel.[135] Perhaps critics of the latter right would think better of it if they took a look at the profound restrictions on liberty that arise in countries that have denied it to their citizens, such as the former Soviet Union.

The reason why these debates have been so contentious in the United States is, quite simply, that many of our most precious rights have achieved federal protection through the incorporation doctrine,[136] through the substantive component of the Fourteenth Amendment's Due Process Clause,[137] or through the equal protection component of the Fifth Amendment's Due Process Clause.[138] These were the critical constitutional moves, and each one requires a broad understanding of the words that appear on the page.

I am willing to make that move, in spite of the fact that it carries with it a risk of error on the part of the Supreme Court—error in the sense that the Court may from time to time push out in a direction that is inconsistent with the constitutional plan, and error in the sense that the Court may be too far out of step with American society and the elected branches of government. Over the medium to long run, the Court corrects those errors, or (occasionally) the Constitution is amended. That, in my view, is the best we can do. We would not be better off with constant amendments to the Constitution, because such a process would ultimately devalue the Constitution and make it the same kind of repository of special interest rules that one can observe in all too many state constitutions. And, as I will argue in Part III, we even more clearly would not be better off with a strict constitutional reading that jettisoned all of the unwritten extrapolations that have occurred since the beginning of the Republic.

III. What Would the Literal Constitution Look
Like, and Why Has Everyone Rejected It?

The literal Constitution, for which some have argued, would be a woefully inadequate document for the American people today. As a matter of constitutional structure, it would require a radical restructuring of the administrative state, placing a nearly unbearable legislative burden on the Congress to specify in detail exactly what powers it was conferring on executive branch agencies and to monitor the minutiae through some kind of oversight mechanism. Presidents would lose the flexibility to make adjustments in the rate of federal spending. The ability of the Commander-in-Chief to take rapid action to protect the United States against unusual threats that do not correspond to any eighteenth-century model would be severely compromised if we were required always to wait for the Congress to pass a resolution declaring war. Taking a strict view of the Commerce Clause (and taking cases like *United States v. Lopez*[139] and *United States v. Morrison*[140] to their logical extreme), it would be impossible for the United States to function as a single integrated economic entity. This would be ironic indeed, given the fact that the European countries have steadily been increasing the size of their own common market from the original six countries that founded what has become the European Union (EU) in 1958 to the powerhouse of twenty-five countries today. They have done so by conferring upon EU institutions the power to enact EU-wide regulations in all areas affecting trade between member states. The United States achieved this goal almost two centuries earlier, thanks to the early Commerce Clause decisions of Chief Justice

John Marshall,[141] but all that would be up for grabs if one were to try to discern and adopt the strictest possible reading of the eighteenth-century document.

The story would be even more disturbing in the area of individual rights. Like many people, I thought it was regrettable at best, absurd at worst, when the United States lost its place on the United Nations Commission on Human Rights in 2002, after continuous membership from 1947 through 2001, even though it then resumed membership from 2003 to the present.[142] This was hardly a reflection of the actual record of leadership in the field of human rights that the United States has built. The fact that there are blemishes on this record only says that we have not been perfect. But the legal tools are in place to correct problems when they arise, if we have the political will to use them. That toolbox would be sorely depleted if we were to decide now that the Constitution cannot protect the full range of individual rights after all.

But, one might say, the states also have their Bills of Rights and judiciaries ready and willing to implement them. That is true, but irrelevant. It ignores the lessons of history that brought us the Civil War Amendments: States may fail at times to respect due process and to give equal protection of the laws, and these are exactly the times when, in a unified nation, federal law must step in.[143] It also ignores the fact that it is usually local prejudices that must be overcome, and a national perspective is the best way to accomplish that task. From the standpoint of protecting international human rights, the only relevant actor is the United States as a whole. The Constitution confers the entirety of the foreign affairs power on the federal government[144] and thus places the entire responsibility for compliance with international norms at the federal level.

If we really had a narrow, literal Constitution, it would be ready for the dustbin unless it was amended significantly. But logical consistency should force even the most zealous advocates of "original intent" and "plain language" to admit that we have long since crossed the Rubicon. No principle allows one to draw a distinction between asserting the legitimacy of a living constitution when it comes to structural matters, and denying the validity of the same approach when it comes to individual rights. This means that we face a stark choice: disregarding the strong textual and historical evidence indicating that the Framers themselves used broad language to facilitate constitutional growth and turning the clock back two centuries for all purposes, or accepting the fact that elaborations of all parts of the Constitution will occur over the years. The former choice is, in my opinion, exceedingly unattractive. It would lead in the long run to a federal constitution that looks like the most detailed of today's state constitutions—for example, the constitution of my adopted home state of Texas, for which the word "micromanagement" was invented.[145]

If we were doomed to go down that path by something we could find in the constitutional text, we would have to live with it. But we are not. The *Federalist Papers* and other documents from the Founding period make it abundantly clear that the Framers knew that they were creating a set of constitutional standards, not prescribing rigid constitutional rules. They knew that courts would need to define and interpret words like "liberty," "cruel and unusual," "due" process, and "equal" protection. They also knew, having given Congress the power to pass "necessary and proper" legislation, that the reach of federal legislation was likely to change over time. The fact that the federal government of 2005 does not look much like the federal government of 1789, and the fact that the list of recognized individual rights has expanded, should not cause weeping and gnashing of teeth.

Conclusion

Instead, those developments demonstrate that the Constitution has proven to be up to the job. It has realized the fondest hopes of its creators, and it has put to rest their worst fears. Debate over its meaning is inevitable whenever something as specific as the Bankruptcy Clause or the Titles of Nobility Clause is not at issue, but the existence of debate does not imply that one side's position is illegitimate, unpatriotic, or otherwise unworthy, while the other side's position is foreordained.

Both courts and society would be stronger if we stopped arguing over the interpretive conventions of so-called original intent versus purposive or dynamic interpretation[146] and focused instead on content. This does not mean that courts should or could legitimately ignore the constitutional text. Far from it; the text will always be the proper starting point. It does mean, however, that we should understand both the words in the text and the structure of the constitutional system at a high level of generality. When it is presented with the question of whether a punishment is "cruel and unusual," or whether a state is denying "equal protection of the laws," or whether a certain right should be regarded as a constitutionally protected "liberty," the Court ought to consider what those terms mean in today's world, cognizant of the norms Americans have adopted, whether those norms flow from our membership in the human race as a whole or are more particularized. It must then explain how the more specific rules flow from the constitutional language and framework. In that way, evolution will continue to occur through adjudication. There is no reason to suppose that it will move systematically in either a "liberal" or a "conservative" direction, as any observer of the change from the original *Roe v. Wade* decision to the current regime governing abortion represented by decisions like *Planned Parenthood v. Casey*,[147] *Maher v. Roe*,[148] and *Harris v. McRae*[149] knows well. The same point is reflected in the evolution from *Plessy v. Ferguson*[150] to *Brown v. Board of Education*,[151] or the contrast between *Korematsu v. United States*[152] and *Rasul v. Bush*[153] and *Hamdi v. Rumsfeld*.[154]

If the interactive process that occurs through dialogue among the Supreme Court, the lower courts, legal scholars, and society at large, coupled with the occasional changes in personnel on the Court over time, is not fast enough for modern tastes, then and only then would it be advisable to consider amending the Constitution. But, taking a page from the Founders, the way to amend it would not be to add long laundry lists of recognized rights and prohibitions that enshrine one generation's pet issues into the document forever and doom it to obsolescence. Suppose, for example, we had written the original Pledge of Allegiance of 1942[155] into the Constitution. It then would have taken a constitutional amendment in 1954 to add the words "under God" to the text, rather than simply changing it by legislation.[156] Or, more seriously, what if the Constitution had enshrined the Jim Crow system, or the view of women expressed in such infamous decisions as *Bradwell v. Illinois*[157] or *Goesaert v. Cleary*?[158] Over the long run, even though it can sometimes be frustrating to wait for the long run, it has been better to allow constitutional understandings to grow with the times.

If, and only if, one were to conclude that there is a broad, systematic problem with the pace of constitutional change, should one consider how to address that (hypothetical) problem. On this point also, we would be well advised to take a page from the book of the Framers and to look to structural mechanisms. If the problem is, as President Franklin Roosevelt once thought, the lack of turnover on the Supreme Court, then one might reconsider whether there should be some outer limit for the number of years any particular Justice can serve. If the amendment process is not enough (though it is worth noting that the Constitution has been amended six times since 1950),[159] then we might look north and adopt some mechanism like the power of the legislature in Canada to override constitutional holdings in extraordinary circumstances—a power that is rarely used, to be sure, but that stands as yet another democratic safeguard.[160] However radical these options might seem—and I do not wish to be understood as advocating either of them—they would be far preferable to the expedient of refusing to recognize any constitutional right or structure that has not been spelled out in black and white in the document itself, abandoning the timeless principles that have served us so well, for so long. Our eighteenth-century Constitution, while a bit cryptic at the edges, is nonetheless a treasure. Approached the right way, there is every reason to be confident that the dynamic process that has sustained it will continue to do so through the years, decades, and even centuries to come.

NOTES

1. The population of the United States is now 294,379,807, according to the website maintained by the U.S. Census Bureau. *See* U.S. Census Bureau, Population Clocks, http://www.census.gov (last visited September 27, 2004). [As of March 19, 2012, the population of the United States was 313,210,254. —Ed.]
2. *See generally* Suzanna Sherry, *The Founders' Unwritten Constitution*, 54 U. CHI. L. REV. 1127 (1987).
3. U.S. CONST. art. I, § 3, cl. 4.
4. U.S. CONST. art. I, § 3, cl. 6.
5. U.S. CONST. art. I, § 7, cl. 2.
6. U.S. CONST. art. II, § 2, cl. 2.
7. U.S. CONST. art. III, § 2, cl. 2.
8. *See* H.R. 2028, 108th Cong. (2004).
9. U.S. CONST. amend. XVI.
10. U.S. CONST. amend. XVII.
11. U.S. CONST. amend. XXVII.
12. U.S. CONST. amend. XII.
13. U.S. CONST. amend. XIV.
14. U.S. CONST. amend. XX.
15. U.S. CONST. amend. XXII.
16. U.S. CONST. amend. XXV.
17. U.S. CONST. art. IV, § 1.
18. U.S. CONST. art. IV, § 2, cl. 1.
19. U.S. CONST. art. IV, § 2, cl. 2.
20. U.S. CONST. art. IV, § 3.
21. U.S. CONST. art. VI, cl. 2.
22. U.S. CONST. amend. X.

23. U.S. CONST. amend. XI ("The Judicial power of the United States shall not be construed to extend to any suit in law or equity, commenced or prosecuted against one of the United States by Citizens of another State, or by Citizens or Subjects of any Foreign State.").

24. 462 U.S. 919, 967 (1983) (White, J., dissenting).

25. *Id.* at 978.

26. 424 U.S. 1, 280-81 (1976) (White, J., concurring in part and dissenting in part).

27. 285 U.S. 22 (1932).

28. 33 U.S.C. §§ 901 to 950 (2000).

29. 285 U.S. at 62-63.

30. 310 U.S. 381, 397, 400 (1940).

31. 15 U.S.C. §§ 828 to 852 (repealed 1966).

32. 310 U.S. at 398.

33. 295 U.S. 602 (1935).

34. *Id.* at 631, 630 (emphasis added).

35. 488 U.S. 361 (1989).

36. *Id.* at 368. In the wake of *United States v. Booker*, 543 U.S. 220 (2005), the Commission's role has changed from enacting legally binding sentencing rules to writing advisory guidelines. Its structural legitimacy, however, was unaffected by that decision.

37. Chief Justice Warren Burger wrote for the six-person majority; Justice Lewis Powell filed an opinion concurring only in the judgment; Justices White and Rehnquist each filed a dissenting opinion, with Justice White joining Justice Rehnquist's dissent. 462 U.S. 919, 922 (1983).

38. 501 U.S. 252 (1991).

39. *Id.* at 277 (White, J., dissenting).

40. 2 U.S.C. §§ 681-688 (2000).

41. *Id.* 681.

42. GERALD GUNTHER, CONSTITUTIONAL LAW 332 (12th ed. 1991).

43. Pub. L. No. 93-148, 87 Stat. 555 (1973) (codified as amended at 50 U.S.C. §§ 1541-1548 (2000)).

44. 527 U.S. 706 (1999) (holding that Congress has no power under Article I to subject nonconsenting states to private suits for damages in state courts).

45. *Id.* at 713.

46. *Id.*

47. 535 U.S. 743 (2002) (holding that state sovereign immunity precludes federal administrative agency from adjudicating private party's complaint against state entity).

48. *Id.* at 753.

49. THE FEDERALIST NO. 10 (James Madison).

50. *See, e.g.,* WILLI PAUL ADAMS, THE FIRST AMERICAN CONSTITUTIONS 299 (2001) (referring to *The Federalist No. 84*, where Alexander Hamilton defended the omission of a bill of rights).

51. *Compare* United States v. Miller, 307 U.S. 174 (1939) (construing Second Amendment as protecting right to bear arms only insofar as it relates to maintenance

of militia), United States v. Parker, 362 F.3d 1279, 1283 (10th Cir. 2004) (same), *and* United States v. Hale, 978 F.2d 1016, 1019 (8th Cir. 1992) (same), *with* United States v. Emerson, 270 F.3d 203 (5th Cir. 2001) (rejecting so-called "collective rights model" and finding individual right to bear arms). *See also* Printz v. United States, 521 U.S. 898, 938 n.2 (1997) (Thomas, J., concurring) (citing literature advocating individual rights model).

52. U.S. CONST. amend. XIV.
53. U.S. CONST. amend. V.
54. *Id.*
55. U.S. CONST. amend. VI.
56. U.S. CONST. amend. VIII.
57. U.S. CONST. amend. XIII.
58. U.S. CONST. amend. XV.
59. U.S. CONST. amend. XIV (emphasis added).
60. U.S. CONST. amend. XIX.
61. U.S. CONST. amend. XXIV.
62. U.S. CONST. amend. XXVI.
63. 198 U.S. 45 (1905).
64. *Id.* at 56.
65. Meyer v. Nebraska, 262 U.S. 390 (1923).
66. *But see* Arizonans for Official English v. Arizona, 520 U.S. 43 (1997) (dismissing on standing and mootness grounds case challenging 1988 amendment to Arizona Constitution making English official language of Arizona).
67. *Id.* at 399.
68. *Id.* at 401.
69. 268 U.S. 510 (1925).
70. *Id.* at 535.
71. 431 U.S. 494 (1977).
72. At the time, 28 U.S.C. § 1257 (1988) provided for appellate jurisdiction in cases where the state courts had upheld a state law against a federal constitutional challenge. This changed in 1988 with the passage of the Supreme Court Case Selections Act, Pub. L. No. 100-352, § 3, 102 Stat. 662, 662 (1988) (codified at 28 U.S.C. § 1257(a) (2000)), which repealed the U.S. Code sections creating appellate jurisdiction and substituted certiorari for all requests to review decisions from state courts.
73. 431 U.S. at 499.
74. *Id.* at 506-13.
75. *Id.* at 513-21.
76. *Id.* at 521-31.
77. *Id.* at 531-41.
78. *Id.* at 541-52.
79. *Id.* at 546.
80. 302 U.S. 319 (1937).
81. *See, e.g.,* Lawrence v. Texas, 539 U.S. 558 (2003) (finding unconstitutional criminalization of adult consensual homosexual unions); Planned Parenthood

v. Casey, 505 U.S. 833 (1992) (concerning abortion); Carey v. Population Servs. Int'l, 431 U.S. 678 (1977) (regarding distribution and advertising of nonprescription contraceptives to minors); Roe v. Wade, 410 U.S. 113 (1973) (abortion); Eisenstadt v. Baird, 405 U.S. 438 (1972) (concerning distribution of contraceptives to unmarried individuals); Griswold v. Connecticut, 381 U.S. 479 (1965) (concerning access of married couples to contraceptives). Compare the preceding cases with *Loving v. Virginia*, 388 U.S. 1 (1967), which struck down Virginia's anti-miscegenation law on equal protection grounds, despite the fact that at least from one point of view, the racial classification by definition affected whites and blacks identically. Interestingly, the Court observed along the way that "the State does not contend . . . that its powers to regulate marriage are unlimited notwithstanding the commands of the Fourteenth Amendment. Nor could it do so in light of *Meyer* . . . and *Skinner v. Oklahoma.*" *Id.* at 7 (internal citations omitted). The Court in *Skinner* struck down Oklahoma's forced sterilization of certain criminals as a violation of the Equal Protection Clause. 316 U.S. 527, 538 (1942).

82. *See* Washington v. Glucksberg, 521 U.S. 702 (1997); Vacco v. Quill, 521 U.S. 793 (1997); *see also* Oregon v. Gonzales, 368 F.3d 1118 (9th Cir. 2004), *cert. granted*, 125 S. Ct. 1299 (2005) (presenting question whether attorney general may interpret federal law to prohibit distribution of federally controlled substance to facilitate suicide, regardless of state law authorizing such distribution). After this lecture was delivered, the nation's attention became riveted by the case of Theresa Marie Schiavo, where the question was whether any law, federal or state, prevented Mrs. Schiavo's husband from ordering that her feeding tube be disconnected, in light of medical advice that she had for many years been in a persistent vegetative state. *See* Schiavo ex rel. Schindler v. Schiavo, 403 F.3d 1223 (11th Cir. 2005); Schiavo ex rel. Schindler v. Schiavo, 404 F.3d 1270 (11th Cir. 2005), *stay denied*, No. 04 A844, 125 S. Ct. 1722 (2005). Although the Supreme Court did not intervene, and Mrs. Schiavo was allowed to die, it appears as of the time of this paper that the issues presented are far from resolved.

83. 125 S. Ct. 2655 (2005).

84. *Id.* at 2661.

85. *Id.* at 2663-66.

86. G.A. Res. 217, U.N. GAOR, 3d Sess., pt. 1, 183d plen. mtg., at 71, U.N. Doc. A/810 (1948).

87. The following list of human rights conventions presently in force in the United States is taken from TREATY AFFAIRS STAFF, U.S. DEP'T OF STATE, TREATIES IN FORCE: A LIST OF TREATIES AND OTHER INTERNATIONAL AGREEMENTS OF THE UNITED STATES IN FORCE ON JANUARY 1, 2004, *available at* http://www.state.gov/s/l/38294.htm: (1) Convention Against Torture and Other Cruel, Inhuman or Degrading Treatment or Punishment, Dec. 10, 1984, 23 I.L.M. 1027, 24 I.L.M. 535 (entered into force June 26, 1987; for U.S. Nov. 20, 1994); (2) Protocol Relating to the Status of Refugees, Jan. 31, 1967, 19 U.S.T. 6223, 606 U.N.T.S. 267 (entered into force

Oct. 4, 1967; for U.S., Nov. 1, 1968); (3) International Covenant on Civil and Political Rights, Dec. 19, 1966, S. Exec. Doc. E (1978), 999 U.N.T.S. 171 (entered into force Mar. 23, 1976; for U.S., Sept. 8, 1992); (4) International Covenant on the Elimination of All Forms of Racial Discrimination, Dec. 21, 1965, S. Exec. Doc. C (1978), 660 U.N.T.S. 211 (entered into force Jan. 4, 1969; for U.S., Nov. 20, 1994); (5) Convention on the Prevention and Punishment of the Crime of Genocide, Dec. 9, 1948, 102 Stat. 3045, 78 U.N.T.S. 277 (entered into force Jan. 12, 1951; for U.S., Feb. 23, 1989); (6) Inter-American Convention on the Granting of Political Rights to Women, May 2, 1948, 27 U.S.T. 3301, 1438 U.N.T.S. 63 (entered into force Mar. 17, 1949; for U.S., May 24, 1976); (7) Convention on the Nationality of Women, Dec. 26, 1933, 49 Stat. 2957, 3 Bevans 141 (entered into force Aug. 29, 1923; for U.S., Aug. 29, 1934).

88. *See, e.g.*, International Covenant on Civil and Political Rights, 6.A. Res. 2200A (XXI), U.N. GAOR, 21st Sess., 1496th plen. mtg. at 168-74, U.N. Doc. A/631b (1966), United States, Understandings and Declarations (describing in greater detail relation between U.S. law and Convention obligations).

89. *See* Office of the United Nations High Comm'r for Human Rights, *Status of Ratifications of the Principal International Human Rights Treaties* (June 9, 2004), *available at* www. unhchr.ch/pdf/report.pdf.

90. International Covenant on Civil and Political Rights, art. 3, *supra* note 87, S. Exec. Doc. E at 24, 999 U.N.T.S. at 174.

91. *Id.*, art. 6.1, S. Exec. Doc. E at 25, 999 U.N.T.S. at 174.

92. *Id.*, art. 7, S. Exec. Doc. E at 25, 999 U.N.T.S. at 175.

93. *Id.*, art. 8, S. Exec. Doc. E at 25, 999 U.N.T.S. at 175.

94. *Id.*, art. 9.1, S. Exec. Doc. E at 26, 999 U.N.T.S. at 175.

95. *Id.*, art. 12, S. Exec. Doc. E at 27, 999 U.N.T.S. at 176.

96. *Id.*, art. 14, S. Exec. Doc. E at 27, 999 U.N.T.S. at 176.

97. *Id.*, art. 14.5, S. Exec. Doc. E at 28, 999 U.N.T.S. at 177.

98. *Id.*, art. 15.1, S. Exec. Doc. E at 28, 999 U.N.T.S. at 177.

99. *Id.*, art. 17, S. Exec. Doc. E at 29, 999 U.N.T.S. at 177 ("No one shall be subjected to arbitrary or unlawful interference with his privacy, family, home or correspondence, nor to unlawful attacks on his honour and reputation.").

100. *Id.*, art. 18, S. Exec. Doc. E at 29, 999 U.N.T.S. at 178.

101. *Id.*, art. 19, S. Exec. Doc. E at 29, 999 U.N.T.S. at 178. But see *id.*, art. 20, S. Exec. Doc. E at 29, 999 U.N.T.S. at 178, which provides that there is no right to advocate national, racial, or religious hatred that constitutes incitement to discrimination, hostility, or violence. The United States has taken an exception to this language, insofar as it might prohibit speech that is protected by the First Amendment.

102. *Id.*, art. 23.1, S. Exec. Doc. E at 30, 999 U.N.T.S. at 179.

103. *Id.*, art, 23.3, S. Exec. Doc. E at 30, 999 U.N.T.S. at 179.

104. *Id.*, art. 24, S. Exec. Doc. E at 30, 999 U.N.T.S. at 179.

105. *Id.*, art. 25, S. Exec. Doc. E at 30, 999 U.N.T.S. at 179.

106. *Id.*, art. 26, S. Exec. Doc. E at 31, 999 U.N.T.S. at 179.

107. *Id.*, art. 27, S. Exec. Doc. E at 31, 999 U.N.T.S. at 179.

108. *See* Roper v. Simmons, 125 S. Ct. 1183, 1198 (2005) (holding that Eighth Amendment prohibits execution of person who committed his or her crime before reaching age of eighteen).

109. *See supra* note 88, United States Declarations and Understandings.

110. *Id.*

111. 518 U.S. 515 (1996) (striking down all-male admissions policy at Virginia Military Institute).

112. 394 U.S. 618 (1969) (acknowledging constitutional dimension to right to travel); *see also* Attorney General of New York v. Soto-Lopez, 476 U.S. 898, 902-03 (1986); Saenz v. Roe, 526 U.S. 489 (1999) (citing *Shapiro*).

113. 431 U.S. 494 (1977) (striking down single-family zoning restriction).

114. 388 U.S. 1 (1967) (protecting right to interracial marriage).

115. 539 U.S. 558 (2003) (striking down statutes criminalizing adult consensual homosexual acts).

116. 429 U.S. 589 (1977) (protecting right to confidential doctor-patient relationship).

117. 406 U.S. 205, 214 (1972) (holding that Free Exercise Clause protects "the traditional interest of parents with respect to the religious upbringing of their children").

118. 508 U.S. 520 (1993) (finding ordinances restricting Santerian religious practices unconstitutional).

119. 529 U.S. 598 (2000) (striking down Violence Against Women Act as unauthorized by either Commerce Clause or Section 5 of Fourteenth Amendment).

120. 252 U.S. 416 (1920) (Holmes, J.) (holding that if treaty is valid, then statute that provides necessary and proper means for executing treaty is also valid; rejecting argument that subject matter covered by treaties must be limited to same subjects on which Congress is permitted to legislate).

121. *See generally* ROBERT H. BORK, COERCING VIRTUE: THE WORLDWIDE RULE OF JUDGES (2003).

122. Legislative Reference Library of Texas, Constitutional Amendments, http://www.lrl. state.tx.us/legis/constAmends/lrlhome.cfm (last visited Apr. 14, 2005).

123. Not only is it possible that ideas of excessiveness have changed, but it is also undisputed that the value of a dollar has changed. For example, $20 in 1791 would have been worth $389.49 in 2003 using the Consumer Price Index, but it would have been worth a whopping $882,489.05 using the relative share of GDP. *See* Econ. History Servs., What Is Its Relative Value in US Dollars?, http://www.eh.net/hmit/compare/. This suggests that there is no meaningful way to apply an historical approach to the idea of excessive fines.

124. 217 U.S. 349, 357-58, 381 (1910) (holding that punishment of fifteen years' imprisonment, civil interdiction, lifetime surveillance, deprivation of office, loss of voting rights and right to acquire honors, and loss of retirement pay was cruel and unusual in light of offense of falsifying public document).

125. 356 U.S. 86 (1958) (finding that loss of United States citizenship as punishment for crime of wartime desertion violated Eighth Amendment).

126. *Id.* at 100-01.

127. Gregg v. Georgia, 428 U.S. 153 (1976); Proffitt v. Florida, 428 U.S. 242 (1976); Jurek v. Texas, 428 U.S. 262 (1976); Woodson v. North Carolina, 428 U.S. 280 (1976); Roberts v. Louisiana, 428 U.S. 325 (1976).

128. 433 U.S. 584 (1977) (finding unconstitutional death penalty for rape not resulting in death of victim).

129. 536 U.S. 304 (2002) (holding that executions of mentally retarded criminals constitute "cruel and unusual punishments").

130. 125 S. Ct. 1183 (2005).

131. *Id.* at 1217-18 (Scalia, J., dissenting).

132. *Id.* at 1192-94.

133. *Id.* at 1198.

134. *Id.* at 1200.

135. *See* Shapiro v. Thompson, 394 U.S. 618 (1969) (holding state statutory provisions that deny benefits to residents of less than one year unconstitutional).

136. *See* Palko v. Connecticut, 302 U.S. 319, 323-27 (1937) (rejecting wholesale incorporation of first eight Amendments through Fourteenth Amendment; discussing which Amendments have been incorporated and which have not); *see, e.g.,* Malloy v. Hogan, 378 U.S. 1 (1964) (incorporating Fifth Amendment privilege against compulsory self-incrimination); Mapp v. Ohio, 367 U.S. 643 (1961) (incorporating Fourth Amendment protections against unreasonable searches and seizures); Gideon v. Wainwright, 372 U.S. 335 (1963) (incorporating Sixth Amendment right to counsel in criminal cases).

137. *See supra* notes 63-83 and accompanying text.

138. *See* Bolling v. Sharpe, 347 U.S. 497 (1954).

> The Fifth Amendment . . . does not contain an equal protection clause. . . . But the concepts of equal protection and due process, both stemming from our American ideal of fairness, are not mutually exclusive. The "equal protection of the laws" is a more explicit safeguard of prohibited unfairness than "due process of law," and, therefore, we do not imply that the two are always interchangeable phrases. But, as this Court has recognized, discrimination may be so unjustifiable as to be violative of due process.

> *Id.* at 499.

139. 514 U.S. 549 (1995) (holding that Gun-Free School Zones Act exceeded Congress's authority under Commerce Clause).

140. 529 U.S. 598 (2000) (holding that Violence Against Women Act exceeded Congress's authority under either Commerce Clause or Section 5 of Fourteenth Amendment).

141. *See, e.g.,* Gibbons v. Ogden, 22 U.S. (9 Wheat.) 1 (1824) (reading Commerce Clause to reach all navigation within states, to extent that it is connected at all to interstate, foreign, or Indian commerce); McCulloch v. Maryland, 17 U.S. (4 Wheat.) 316 (1819) (upholding power of Congress to establish Bank of the United States, based on Necessary and Proper Clause).

142. *See* The United Nations Commission on Human Rights website for a list of the years during which every country has held a seat on the Commission, http://www.ohchr.org/eng lish/bodies/chr/docs/membership.doc (last visited Apr. 24, 2005).

143. For early articulations of this view of federalism, see THE FEDERALIST NO. 9 (Alexander Hamilton) and THE FEDERALIST NO. 10 (James Madison).

144. *See, e.g.,* Crosby v. Nat'l Foreign Trade Council, 530 U.S. 363 (2000) (striking down Massachusetts law aimed at trade with Burma (also known as Myanmar) as unconstitutional under Supremacy Clause).

145. The Texas Constitution regulates such minutiae as assistance to local fire departments, TEX. CONST. art. III, § 51-a-1; the establishment of a State Medical Educational Board, TEX. CONST. art. III, § 50-a; the establishment of numerous other boards, such as the Water Development Board, to which it devotes more than seven pages and eleven articles, TEX. CONST. art. III, §§ 49-c to 49-d; the provision of student loans, TEX. CONST. art. III, §§ 50-b-4 to 50-b-5; and, famously to graduates of the University of Texas, the establishment of a state university "of the first class," TEX. CONST. art. VII, § 10.

146. *See, e.g.,* Aharon Barak, *Foreword: A Judge on Judging: The Role of a Supreme Court in a Democracy,* 116 HARV. L. REV. 16, 64-84 (2002) (arguing that purposive interpretation is appropriate method for all legal texts).

147. 505 U.S. 833 (1992) (replacing trimester framework of *Roe v. Wade* with rule forbidding state regulations that place undue burden on women's right to choose abortion before fetus attains viability; subsequent to viability state may regulate or prohibit abortion, as long as law has exception for preservation of life or health of mother).

148. 432 U.S. 464 (1977) (holding that Constitution does not require state participating in Medicaid program to pay for nontherapeutic abortions of indigent women, even if it chooses to pay for prenatal care and childbirth).

149. 448 U.S. 297 (1980) (holding that title XIX of Social Security Act does not require state government to pay for medically necessary abortions for which federal reimbursement is unavailable under Hyde Amendment, Pub. L. 96-123, § 109, 93 Stat. 923, 926 (1979) (codified as amended in scattered sections of 42 U.S.C.), thus further restricting de facto access to abortions for indigent women).

150. 163 U.S. 537 (1896).

151. 347 U.S. 483 (1954).

152. 323 U.S. 214 (1944) (upholding constitutionality of military order requiring exclusion from described West Coast areas of all individuals of Japanese ancestry).

153. 124 S. Ct. 2686 (2004) (finding federal courts not barred from hearing claims of aliens held at Guantanamo Bay).

154. 124 S. Ct. 2633 (2004) (holding unconstitutional detention of United States citizen as enemy combatant without meaningful opportunity to contest).

155. *See* Act of June 22, 1942, Pub. L. No. 623, § 7, 56 Stat. 380 (1942).

156. *See* Act of June 14, 1954, Pub. L. No. 396, 68 Stat. 249 (1954) (codified as amended at § 4 U.S.C. 4 (2000)).
157. 83 U.S. 130 (1872) (Miller, J.) (upholding Illinois statute denying women right to be licensed as attorneys).
158. 335 U.S. 464 (1948) (upholding Michigan statute prohibiting women from bartending unless they were wives or daughters of liquor establishment owners), *overruled by* Craig v. Boren, 429 U.S. 190, 210 (1976) (overruling *Goesaert* insofar as it upheld sex-based classifications related to sale of alcoholic beverages).
159. U.S. CONST. amend. XXVII (1992); U.S. CONST. amend. XXVI (1971); U.S. CONST. amend. XXV (1967); U.S. CONST. amend. XXIV (1964); U.S. CONST. amend. XXIII (1961); U.S. CONST. amend XXII (1951).
160. *See, e.g.,* Constitution Act, 1982, sched. B, pt. I (citing Canadian Charter of Rights and Freedoms, § 33, which details power of Parliament or legislature of province to make overriding declarations).

5

Judging under the Constitution

Dicta about Dictum

PIERRE N. LEVAL

A judge's power to bind is limited to the issue that is before him; he cannot transmute dictum into decision by waving a wand and uttering the word "hold."
—Henry J. Friendly, *United States v. Rubin*[1]

I. Thesis

In the quaint language of eighteenth-century England, when judges elevated their status and authority by conducting their business in Latin, it was known as "obiter dictum"—in the plural, "dicta." This referred to a judge's insignificant aside remark—something to be treated lightly or, frankly, ignored. Cardozo in his time expressed amazement that judges, of all people, might "put their faith in dicta."[2]

Why would I talk about something so insignificant? The problem is that dicta no longer have the insignificance they deserve. They are no longer ignored. Judges do more than put faith in them; they are often treated as binding law. The distinction between dictum and holding is more and more frequently disregarded. Although I think most agree in the abstract with the proposition that dictum does not establish binding law, this rule is now honored in the breach with alarming frequency. Today more and more, dicta flex muscle to which, I submit, they are not entitled by constitutional right.

We judges regularly undertake to promulgate law through utterance of dictum made to look like a holding—in disguise, so to speak. When we do so, we seek to exercise a lawmaking power that we do not rightfully possess. Also, we accept dictum uttered in a previous opinion as if it were

This lecture was delivered on October 18, 2005, and appeared in *81 N.Y.U. L. Rev.* 1249 (2006).

binding law, which governs our subsequent adjudication. When we do so, we fail to discharge our responsibility to deliberate on and decide the question that needs to be decided.

A. *Two Examples*

Consider two representative recent instances exemplifying two facets of the problem.

1. *BARAPIND V. ENOMOTO*[3]

Recently, one of the circuit courts of appeals convened en banc to review an order to extradite a Sikh militant to India to answer murder charges.[4] In an earlier extradition case involving an Irishman, Quinn, a panel of the same circuit, in dictum, had expressed views on one issue while deciding the case on a different basis.[5] The lower court judge in the Sikh's case disagreed with the Quinn panel's dictum and declined to follow it, as dictum is not binding.[6] The court of appeals chastised the judge for failing to follow its earlier dictum. "The [lower] court operated under a mistaken understanding of what constitutes circuit law. . . . Our articulation [in Quinn] . . . became law of the circuit, regardless of whether it was in some technical sense 'necessary'[7] to our disposition of the case. The [lower court was] . . . required to follow [it]."[8]

According to this view, a court has the power to make binding law, at least on an issue argued by the parties, simply by announcing a rule, irrespective of whether the rule plays any functional role in the court's decision of the case—a very considerable power, and without constitutional justification.

2. *MYERS V. LOUDOUN COUNTY PUBLIC SCHOOLS*[9]

Also recently, another circuit decided (or should I say, "failed to decide") a constitutional challenge to the Pledge of Allegiance.[10] The plaintiff, Myers, the father of a child in public school, contended that school recitation of the Pledge of Allegiance, with its invocation of God, violates the Establishment of Religion Clause of the First Amendment.[11] The Supreme Court had considered a similar attack just the previous term in *Elk Grove v. Newdow.*[12] In *Newdow,* the Supreme Court had dodged the divisive issue and dismissed the suit on the ground that the plaintiff, the divorced noncustodial parent of the affected schoolchild, lacked standing to challenge the practice.[13]

Notwithstanding that the Supreme Court had expressly left open the constitutional question, the majority of the circuit panel in *Myers* reasoned that it was compelled by prior Supreme Court opinions to uphold the Pledge—not by Supreme Court holdings, but by Supreme Court dicta.[14] One judge even made clear that, were it not for the binding force of the dicta, the judge would find the question very difficult because the Supreme Court's holdings were in conflict.[15]

I express no views about the merits of that case. My point is simply that the court had a duty to decide the case in accordance with law. If established law governed the question, the court was bound to follow the established precedent. If the established law was inconclusive, the court was obligated in the discharge of its constitutional duties to adjudicate the question—to wrestle with the issue and reach its own conclusion. It did neither.

B. Not Opposed to Dicta

It is difficult to make the point I advocate without being misunderstood as opposing the use of dictum. Let me make as clear as I can that I do not in the least oppose the careful use of dictum in judicial opinions. To the contrary, I believe that dicta often serve extremely valuable purposes. They can help clarify a complicated subject. They can assist future courts to reach sensible, well-reasoned results. They can help lawyers and society to predict the future course of the court's rulings. They can guide future courts to adopt fair and efficient procedures. What is problematic is not the utterance of dicta, but the failure to distinguish between holding and dictum.

C. So What?

You might well ask, "So what? Are you wasting our time, Judge Leval, carping about technicalities? What does it matter whether a proposition becomes established as law when it is first uttered in a court's dictum, or later when it is uttered as a holding justifying the court's ruling?"

The distinction is not a mere technicality. It is by no means inevitable that rules initially expressed in gratuitous, nonbinding dictum would be ultimately adopted when it came time for the court to decide the issue. An important aspect of my point is that courts are more likely to exercise flawed, ill-considered judgment, more likely to overlook salutary cautions and contraindications, more likely to pronounce flawed rules, when uttering dicta than when deciding their cases. The practices I discuss impair the quality and reliability of our performance. Giving dictum the force of law increases the likelihood that the law we produce will be bad law.[16]

My criticism is directed no less against myself than others. Insufficient attention to the distinction between holding and dictum and to the importance of the distinction has become endemic. This comes perhaps in part from a gradual change in the self-image of courts. Once, the perception of the judicial function was relatively modest—to settle disputes under an existing body of rules; judges were not seen as making law through their opinions, but rather as finding the common law, which existed already, waiting only to be discovered.[17]

Gradually, first with the advent of stare decisis, and with the central role courts have increasingly played in resolving important social questions, we have come to see ourselves as something considerably grander—as lawgivers, teachers, fonts of wisdom, even keepers of the national conscience. This change of image has helped transform dicta from trivia into a force. The second aspect of the problem—the acceptance of prior dictum as if it were binding law—results in some part from time pressures on an overworked judiciary, the ever-increasing length of judicial opinions, and the precision-guided weaponry of computer research—all of which contribute to our taking previously uttered statements out of context, without a careful reading to ascertain the role they played in the opinion.

D. Definition

I should pause to make sure we are on the same page as to the meaning of "dictum." A dictum is an assertion in a court's opinion of a proposition of law that does not explain why the court's judgment goes in favor of the winner. If the court's judgment and the reasoning that supports it would remain unchanged, regardless of the proposition in question, that proposition plays no role in explaining why the judgment goes for the winner. It is superfluous to the decision and is dictum. The dictum consists essentially of a comment on how the court would decide some other, different case, and has no effect on its decision of the case before it. If the court's function is to decide the case in accordance with the rules of law, explaining what are the rules that govern the decision, and explaining the interaction between those rules and the facts of the case, the utterance of such dictum is superfluous to the court's performance of its function.

To identify dictum, it is useful to turn the questioned proposition around to assert its opposite, or to assert whatever alternative proposition the court rejected in its favor. If the insertion of the rejected proposition into the court's reasoning, in place of the one adopted, would not require a change in either the court's judgment or the reasoning that supports it, then the proposition is dictum. It is superfluous. It had no functional role in compelling the judgment.

I illustrate by reference to a hypothetical card game, with rules not yet clearly understood. Let's call it "Poker." The plaintiff has three Jacks; the defendant holds a pair of Queens. Each claims to have the winning hand. The court rules for three Jacks. In explanation, the court writes, "When held in equal numbers, Queens beat Jacks. But three-of-a-kind always beats a pair." The statement that Queens beat Jacks is superfluous to the court's reasoning, which explained the grant of judgment to the plaintiff by reason of the plaintiff's having three-of-a-kind. Were the statement turned around to state the opposite—that Jacks beat Queens—the court's grant of judgment in favor of the three Jacks, on the ground that three-of-a-kind beats a pair, would nonetheless stand unaltered. The statement of priorities between Jacks and Queens played no role in its award of judgment in favor of the three-Jack hand and was accordingly dictum.

To say that a court's statement is a dictum is to say that the statement is not the holding. Holding and dictum are generally thought of as mutually exclusive categories. However, it is not always immediately apparent at a glance whether a pronouncement of law is holding or dictum. One cannot tell by reading the statement in isolation, without reference to the overall discussion. The distinction requires recognition of what was the question before the court upon which the judgment depended, how (and by what reasoning) the court resolved the question, and what role, if any, the proposition played in the reasoning that led to the judgment. A dictum is not converted into holding by forceful utterance, or by preceding it with the words "We hold that. . . ."[18] Judge Friendly cautioned, "A judge's power to bind is limited to the issue that is before him; he cannot transmute dictum into decision by waving a wand and uttering the word 'hold.'"[19]

I do not mean to imply that in all cases it is easy, or even possible, to reach a confident conclusion whether a statement should be considered dictum or holding. At times a proposition advanced by the court will support the court's decision to grant judgment to the plaintiff or defendant, but indirectly or remotely. There is no line demarcating a clear boundary between holding and dictum. What separates holding from dictum is better seen as a zone, within which no confident determination can be made whether the proposition should be considered holding or dictum.[20]

Nonetheless, to say that the distinction between holding and dictum is sometimes murky does not mean that it is always murky. In many instances there can be no doubt that the proposition in question played no role in the court's justification of its judgment. Court opinions today are crammed full of such superfluous declarations of law. The remarks in this lecture are directed primarily to these vast deposits of dictum in contemporary jurisprudence.

E. Why Does This Matter?

Why do we care whether a rule announced by a court is dictum? The distinction between holding and dictum was always important to the common law tradition of fidelity to prior holdings. It took on a heightened importance with the adoption of the prudential rule known by the Latin phrase "stare decisis" (meaning "to remain decided"). This rule requires that once a court has decided a case based on a proposition of law, the court must thereafter adhere to that proposition of law, deciding like cases in like manner (unless it takes the rare step of disavowing and overruling the proposition).

Stare decisis inevitably results in courts having some lawmaking power. If the court is obliged to adhere to its prior decisions, every decision becomes a part of binding law. But it was not the purpose of stare decisis to increase court power. To the contrary, the rule was intended as a limitation on the courts. It was designed to keep courts principled and consistent—to prevent courts from acting arbitrarily or capriciously, deciding the same facts one way in Jones's case and another way in Smith's case. The idea behind it was that courts would better perform their assigned function of deciding cases if compelled to decide them consistently.

Stare decisis requires a court to adhere only to its decisions—its holdings—not to any utterance the court may make. It thus becomes of great importance to distinguish between a court's holdings, which become binding law for the future, and its dicta, which at least in theory do not.

F. Questions

I pose two questions. First: Is judicial lawmaking through dictum consistent with the powers and duties of courts prescribed by the Constitution? Second: Is the treatment of dictum as established, binding law consistent with common sense and sound judicial practice? I believe the answer to both questions is "No."

II. The Constitution

What does the Constitution have to say that bears on making law by dictum? It does not address the subject directly. Nonetheless, the Constitution's message is forceful, if oblique and terse. The only role granted to the federal courts in Article III was to exercise "the judicial power" in "Cases" and "Controversies."[21] What does this mean? The constitutional function of the courts is to adjudicate—to decide cases. The Constitution does not explicitly grant to courts the power to make law. The power to make law generally is encompassed in the words, "All legislative powers," and was vested by Article I, Section 1, in the Congress.[22]

Needless to say, courts do legitimately make law under the Constitution. But they do so not because the Constitution conferred lawmaking power on them. It didn't. They do so only because the rule of stare decisis evolved to require that courts judge consistently. Given that the court's sole constitutional authority is to decide cases, what should we make of the constitutional legitimacy of lawmaking through proclamation of dicta? It is simply without justification. Courts make law only as a consequence of the performance of their constitutional duty to decide cases. They have no constitutional authority to establish law otherwise.

What if we in the Second Circuit, without any filed dispute between parties, were to publish a tract entitled *In re Securities Litigation*, in which we promulgated a compendium of rules to govern securities cases? I think all would agree that we lack constitutional authority to establish binding law in this fashion.

Then what if, when a securities dispute comes before us, after giving judgment on the disputed issue, we go on to say, "Having focused our attention on the subject of securities litigation, we will go beyond the particular issue in dispute and proclaim a set of rules to be followed." Is this meaningfully different from the previous example?

The ordinary instance of courts making law through dictum is less bla-tant—better disguised, more interwoven with the issues in dispute—but essentially not different. It is beyond our authority.

III. Practical Considerations of Structural Limitations

I turn now to practical considerations, which reinforce the wisdom of this constitutional structure. How well do courts do their job when dictum is treated as holding? In their structure and manner of operation, courts are poorly equipped to promulgate law, and even more poorly equipped to do so in dictum. When they make law in dictum, the likelihood is high that it will be bad law.[23]

A. Structure of Courts as Lawmakers

Brandeis observed that "courts are ill-equipped to make the investiga-tions which should precede" legislation.[24] Think what a lawmaking body should do before promulgating laws. By their structure and manner of operation, courts lack the ability to perform those tasks. If we were designing an ideal body to promulgate laws for society, it would not look at all like a federal court.

The ideal lawmaking body would be designed to undertake a broad, integrated study of the area requiring attention. It would issue public notices so that affected persons could make submissions and participate in hearings. It would seek advice from experts. It would employ a staff to make a detailed, independent study. It would deliberate and wait as long as it considered useful before promulgating a new rule.

A court functions very differently. It focuses on whatever fragmentary portion of an area of law the case of the moment happens to place before it. Usually, the only input the court receives is from the litigants.[25] The court is barred from researching the facts privately on its own.[26] It rarely employs neutral experts.[27] It works with a tiny staff, whose attention is spread over the multitude of cases and areas on which the court will need to rule. And the court is under pressure to make its adjudication promptly after the submission of the case.

The poor design of courts for the task of lawmaking suggests that law-making by courts is best limited to where the lawmaking inescapably results from the court's performance of its duty to decide the case. This is never true when law is made by dictum, which is always—by definition—superfluous to the court's performance of its job.

B. Structure with Regard to Dictum

However poorly courts are designed for lawmaking generally, their structural limitations particularly disfavor lawmaking through dictum. Why? A number of reasons:

1. ABSENCE OF BRIEFING AND ADVERSITY

Our readiness to trust a court's rulings of law depends on the assumption that the adverse parties will each vigorously assert the best defense of its positions. The court reaches its decision only after confronting conflicting arguments powerfully advanced by both sides. When, however, the court asserts rules outside the scope of its judgment, that salutary adversity is often absent. In many instances the court will have no briefing whatsoever on the issue, because the parties usually have no interest in a question whose resolution will not affect the result of their case.

2. CONCRETENESS

Conditions that best favor lawmaking by courts are those where the dispute is framed by concrete facts. Two of the most difficult challenges in lawmaking are understanding the facts that call for regulation and understanding what effect the imposition of any rule will have on those facts. When the assertion of a proposition of law determines a case's outcome, the court necessarily sees how that proposition functions in at least one factual context, at least with respect to the immediate result.

In contrast, when a court asserts a rule of law in dictum, the court will often not have before it any facts affected by that rule. In addition, the lack of concrete facts increases the likelihood that readers will misunderstand the scope of the rule the court had in mind.

3. THE LACK OF APPEAL

Another weakness of law made through dicta is that there is no available correction mechanism. No appeal may be taken from the assertion of an erroneous legal rule in dictum. Frequently, what's more, no party has a motive to try to get the bad proposition corrected. No party will even ask the court to reconsider its unfortunate dicta.

4. INSUFFICIENT JUDICIAL SCRUTINY

My experience as a judge has shown me that assertions made in dictum are less likely to receive careful scrutiny, both in the writing chambers and in the concurring chambers. When a panel of judges confers on a case, the judges generally focus on the outcome and on the reasoning upon which the outcome depends. Judges work under great time pressure. When the concurring chambers receive the writing judge's draft for their review, they are likely to look primarily at whether the opinion fulfills their expectations as to the judgment and the reasoning given in support. There is a high likelihood that peripheral observations, alternative explanations, and dicta will receive scant attention.

Of cardinal importance to this point is Leval's rule of restaurant selection: If a restaurant's location assures that customers will come whether the food is good or bad, it will be bad. This is a corollary of a broader rule: Stuff you get for free ain't worth more than you paid for it. The rule applies loosely to dicta.

When a court justifies a judgment in favor of the plaintiff or the defendant, the court necessarily confronts the cautionary realization that the rule relied upon determines the outcome of the litigation. The court metaphorically "pays the price" of the rule it has declared. When a rule is uttered in dictum, the court pays no price; the statement comes free, as it has no consequence for the case. In my experience, when courts declare rules that have no consequence for the case, their cautionary mechanism is often not engaged. They are far more likely in these circumstances to fashion defective rules, and to assert misguided propositions, which have not been fully thought through.

I cannot tell you how many times I have read briefs asserting an improbable proposition of law and citing a case as authority. The proposition sounds so dubious that I immediately look it up to see if the cited court can really have made this ruling. So often I find the proposition is indeed there, but was uttered in dictum—where the court paid no price, and consequently paid little attention.

IV. Where Dicta Are Found

We will now explore briefly where abuses of dictum are commonly found—and why.

A. Question beyond the Case

Among the most common manifestations of disguised dictum occurs where the court ventures beyond the issue in controversy to declare the solution to a further problem—one that will arise in another case, or in a later phase of the same case.

Why do we judges do this? Don't we have enough work deciding the controversies before us? The reasons are numerous and grow in part out of our human frailties. (1) At times our exuberance for a point of view gets out of hand. (2) At times we may devise a strategic gambit in ideological warfare. We may reach beyond the case in order to preempt colleagues who might later decide a further issue in a manner not to our liking. (3) You will surely be amazed at the further suggestion that judges may at times be prey to vanity. Like professors, we have not been encouraged to view ourselves modestly. (We judges at least are reversed from time to time.) A judge tends to think, "I've looked at this stuff closely and I understand it. It will come out better if I cover these questions now, rather than leaving them to whatever (perhaps less thoughtful) judge comes along next." (4) We are tempted also by the seductive lure of establishing the landmark precedent, which, like the great opinions of Hand and Friendly, will be repeatedly cited as the authoritative guidepost for the area. We think the further we venture in the opinion, the more likely it is to achieve landmark status. We fail to recognize how likely we are to make mistakes when addressing issues beyond the scope of the decision.

Let's look at an illustrative instance. A banner event in the annals of disguised dictum was one of the Supreme Court's first examinations of the antidiscrimination legislation known as Title VII—*McDonnell Douglas Corp. v. Green.*[28] The plaintiff alleged that the company's refusal to hire him was the result of race discrimination, but the district court dismissed the claim on the ground that the EEOC had not found reasonable cause supporting the allegation.[29] The district court's dismissal depended both on the conclusion that the EEOC had not found reasonable cause and on the determination that such a finding was a prerequisite to suit.[30] The Supreme Court found there was no such prerequisite. It was therefore necessary to vacate the judgment of dismissal and remand for trial.[31]

That should have been the end of the case. The Court might have simply waited to review subsequent litigation emerging under Title VII, affirming good decisions and reversing bad ones. It might, in other words, have behaved as a court. Instead it undertook, gratuitously, in legislative

fashion, and in dictum, to declare new standards to govern Title VII litigation.[32] The Court concocted a three-stage construct, worthy of Rube
Goldberg. It starts with a unique minimalist prima facie case, which can
be satisfied without any evidence of discrimination.[33] The plaintiff's satis-
faction of this minimalist prima facie standard gives rise to a first burden
shift—a temporary presumption in favor of the plaintiff.[34] The defendant's
presentation of an explanation for its action then gives rise to a second
burden shift—dissipating the initial temporary presumption.[35] Thereafter
the plaintiff must satisfy a conventional prima facie standard of proof,
offering evidence sufficient to support a finding of discrimination.[36] This
construct has confused—nay bewildered—lawyers, judges, juries, and
everyone who has tried to deal with it (including the Supreme Court) for
now over thirty years.[37] Wouldn't the law have developed more sensibly
had the Supreme Court simply decided cases as they arose?[38]

B. The Counterfactual Hypothesis

Another version is the contrary-to-fact hypothetical. While explaining a
ruling in favor of the winner, courts often add that if the facts had been
otherwise, the court would have ruled the other way. At times, judges
seem to be motivated by an emotional need to demonstrate that they are
not biased against such claims; had the facts only been slightly different,
the ruling would have been for the adversary. This is a dangerous practice, which can easily engender bad law.

An interesting example is *Sony Corp. of America v. Universal City
Studios, Inc.*[39] In determining whether the emerging technology for vid-
eotaping television transmissions should be considered a contributory
infringement of copyrighted programs, the Supreme Court considered
whether fair use would protect a family's recording of a program, so as to
permit the family to watch it at a more convenient hour.[40] Emphasizing
that such copying would be done without commercial exploitation, the
Court concluded it would not be considered infringing.[41] It added unnecessarily that "every commercial use of copyrighted material is presumptively an unfair exploitation of the [copyright] privilege."[42]

This last observation was pure dictum and involved all of dictum's
weaknesses. It sounded good, but it seriously misunderstood the law. The
vast majority of publications are commercial. Whether commercial copying of copyrighted material infringes or is a fair use depends on context.
Newspapers, book reviews, biographies, histories—they are all published

commercially for profit. They regularly quote from protected material in such manner that the quoting work does not compete in the original work's market and receives fair use protection.

This unfortunate dictum in *Sony*—stated as if the Supreme Court were proclaiming a rule of law—introduced confusion that plagued the understanding of copyright doctrine for ten years, until the Court finally mopped up the mess in *Campbell v. Acuff-Rose Music, Inc.*[43]

Without doubt, in some circumstances there can be good reason for suggesting the limitations of the rule that compels the particular judgment—to lessen the risk that the holding will be read too broadly. While the practice is surely useful, it carries the risks I have described of inadequate consideration. The court should make clear that its specification of the limits of the doctrine is dictum, and thus open for rethinking.[44]

C. Erudite Opinions and Gratuitous Statement of Standards

Another pernicious stimulus for making law through dictum lies in the desire of us judges to appear erudite and to demonstrate our subservience to law by copious recitation of legal rules. Rather than focus simply on the identification of what is in dispute and the explanation of our decision, buttressed by citation of supporting authority, we engage in unnecessary, discursive, scholarly discussions of doctrine; we gratuitously recite standards of law that are not in dispute and have no effect on the judgment.

As a tiny, but recurring example, for every issue considered in courts of appeals, we pronounce ritualistically that our review is "de novo," or "for abuse of discretion," even where it makes no difference in the case because we conclude there was no error of any sort. It is the fashion in appellate decisions today to proclaim the standard that governs the type of questions, even when the particular standard announced will have no bearing on the resolution of the dispute. Characteristically, a statement of a standard will be lifted without examination from a prior opinion. We think this practice is harmless. After all, we are doing nothing more than correctly stating a rule of law.

If these superfluous pronouncements were indeed always correct, there would be no problem. Unfortunately, however, law is endlessly complex and subtle. You surely recall Seneca's undying maxim, "*Contextum omnia est.*" (How's that for a judge's erudition? If you do not recall it, that is because I made it up. Whatever Seneca may have said, as the context changes, the meaning changes.) When we thoughtlessly copy a statement of law from a prior opinion in a manner that determines nothing in the case before us, we risk misunderstanding the context and getting it wrong, introducing confusion and error.

Particularly to be feared is the scholarly, treatise-type opinion, which for no good reason lectures on the nature and origins of the doctrine, making pronouncements that have no consequence for the dispute. Although the court generally believes it is correctly explaining non-controversial matters, the practice is risky.

D. Other Non-Dispositive Determinations

The dangers of dictum uttered without "paying the price" are also present in two other common circumstances: first, when an appellate court asserts that a ruling below was error, but goes on to affirm because the error was harmless; and second, when the court asserts there was no error as to some of the claims on appeal, but ultimately goes on to reverse on another basis. None of the original assertions affects the judgment. They come for free. Because they have no consequences for the judgment, such pronouncements are often glibly uttered, without careful scrutiny, and are therefore often mistaken.

Courts should recognize these types of statements as dictum and so label them. Indeed in some cases, unless the court is confident that what was done below was error, it might in some circumstances be best to hedge the assertion of error, or omit it.

V. Acceptance of Dicta

I have discussed problems a court creates by generating disguised dictum. However grievous the errors a court commits when it writes dictum disguised as holding, those errors would be neutralized if the next court would recognize the prior dictum as nonbinding and go on to grapple with and decide the issue. In this regard, however, we have been woefully inadequate. As a general proposition, if it is set down in black and white in a prior court opinion, we treat it as a holding—even to the point of using the words, "We held in such and such case." Unless a court disagrees with the earlier statement and is eager to reject it, the court often does not make the effort to determine whether the proposition was in fact a holding. So, as Frankfurter put it, with "progressive distortion," "a hint becomes a suggestion, is loosely turned into dictum and finally elevated to a decision."[45]

Why do subsequent courts accept earlier dicta as holding? Once again, we are human. Part of being human is to be pleased when an exceedingly demanding job is made a little easier. Cardozo observed, "Cases do not unfold their principles for the asking. They yield up their kernel slowly and painfully."[46] Determining whether a statement of law is holding or dictum can be a time-consuming task. You must read the full opinion, understand what were the facts, what question was in dispute, how the court resolved it, and what role the proposition played in justifying the judgment. Far easier to have the magic carpet of computer research whisk you straight to the pertinent sentence of the prior opinion and to write, "In such and such case, the court held. . . ." We do it unaware. I am sure I have done this a thousand times.

A second foible that encourages the practice is a lower court's worry that a higher court may react harshly if its pronouncement is rejected as dictum. Remember in *Barapind v. Enomoto*,[47] the Sikh extradition case, the scolding the circuit court gave the lower court when it properly declined to follow a circuit dictum it believed was wrong.[48]

The Supreme Court's decision in *Boykin v. Alabama*[49] demonstrates the mess that can result from failure to identify the holding of a meandering opinion that makes assertions on questions not before the court. In *Boykin*, the defendant, who had been sentenced to death in the Alabama courts based on his plea of guilty to charges of robbery, appealed, contending that his plea was void because he lacked the requisite state of mind to enter a guilty plea.[50] At the taking of the plea, the trial judge had "asked no questions of petitioner concerning his plea, and petitioner did not address the court."[51] The issue before the Court was whether the sufficiency of the defendant's mental state must be demonstrated at the time of the taking of the guilty plea, as the defendant argued and the Supreme Court held, or could be demonstrated in an after-the-fact hearing, as the State and the dissenters argued. In an opinion written by Justice Douglas, the Supreme Court set aside the conviction.[52]

As the Supreme Court explained in a later case,[53] the requirement that a plea of guilty must be intelligent and voluntary had long been recognized. The new element added in *Boykin* was the requirement that this state of mind be established in the record at the taking of the plea. From a reading of the majority opinion, however, it is nearly impossible to discern what question was in dispute and what was the holding. Much of the majority opinion is dedicated to a confusing discussion of the mental state required to support a plea and the importance of the rights a defendant surrenders by pleading guilty.

At least twice the opinion refers to the traditional requirement that the plea be entered intelligently and voluntarily.[54] In the middle of the opinion, however, the Court turns to the importance of three constitutional rights the defendant would have enjoyed at trial had he not pleaded guilty. The Court stated:

> Several federal constitutional rights are involved in a waiver that takes place when a plea of guilty is entered in a state criminal trial. First, is the privilege against compulsory self-incrimination guaranteed by the Fifth Amendment and applicable to the States by reason of the Fourteenth. Second, is the right to trial by jury. Third, is the right to confront one's accusers. We cannot presume a waiver of these three important federal rights from a silent record.[55]

Although the dispute before the Supreme Court did not involve specification of the mental state a defendant must possess in order to enter a valid plea of guilty or the points that must be covered in the allocution,[56] the quoted paragraph seems to imply that the plea proceeding must include a showing that the defendant "waived" the three trial rights mentioned.[57] As the issue in dispute implicated only the timing of inquiry into the defendant's mental state and not the elements of the required mental state, the dissenting opinion does not even mention the seeming suggestion that the plea proceeding must include mention of those three rights.

The majority presumably did not intend to lay down a new constitutional rule on the required mental state; if it had, the sudden requirement that the defendant understand the trial rights regarding jury, confrontation, and self-incrimination, over and above the traditional requirement that the plea be intelligent and voluntary, would have been extremely odd and arbitrary. At trial a defendant exercises numerous constitutional rights. These include the due process rights to the presumption of innocence,[58] need for proof beyond a reasonable doubt,[59] right to present a defense,[60] and the right to testify,[61] as well as Sixth Amendment rights to a speedy and public trial,[62] compulsory process,[63] notice of the charges,[64] and assistance of counsel.[65] While the trial rights mentioned in *Boykin* regarding jury, confrontation, and self-incrimination are undoubtedly important, they are no more important than several of the other constitutional trial rights. The *Boykin* opinion offered no explanation for requiring mention of those particular rights in preference to others.[66]

The *Boykin* majority probably had no intention to alter the understanding of the state of mind necessary to enter a guilty plea. But the meandering opinion, which at times seems to assert new rules on the subject, together with the failure of subsequent readers to focus on what was at issue in the case, has left a wake of confusion. While the courts of appeals and the Supreme Court have not read *Boykin* as mandating that the plea procedure demonstrate waiver of the specific rights mentioned in *Boykin*,[67] Congress amended the Federal Rules of Criminal Procedure in 1975 in the belief that *Boykin* required a court to establish a defendant's understanding of particular trial rights at a guilty plea colloquy.[68] Numerous states have followed suit, requiring their courts to establish a defendant's understanding of the rights mentioned in *Boykin* before accepting a guilty plea. In short, the *Boykin* dictum has generated tremendous confusion and misunderstanding as to what is constitutionally required at a guilty plea proceeding.

As another less consequential example, I sat on a panel recently that considered the sufficiency of a pleading of a stockholder's derivative action. Back in 1978, a panel of our court said in dictum that this particular issue of sufficiency was reviewed for "abuse of discretion."[69] Thereafter, several panels repeated the phrase in dictum, sometimes incorrectly adding, "We have repeatedly held. . . ."[70] The proposition is surely wrong. It cannot be a matter of a district judge's discretion whether a complaint is legally sufficient to state a claim.[71] Thoughtless repetition should not convert a dictum into law, but it manages to do so.

VI. Supreme Court Dicta

What about Supreme Court dicta? Some who would agree with my point as applied to the inferior courts would assert that things are different when it comes to the Supreme Court. It is sometimes argued that the lower courts must treat the dicta of the Supreme Court as controlling.[72] Various reasons are given: Great respect is owed to the Supreme Court; it always sits en banc, assuring that all of its Justices have participated in whatever it decides; its small docket means it will not likely hear enough cases to cover any area of law by its holdings.[73]

I certainly agree that great respect is owed to the Supreme Court. It is indisputably supreme among courts. By the same token, however, it is but a court. It may make law only in the ways in which a court may make law. Its constitutional function is to adjudicate. Its holdings are without doubt the law of the land. Its dicta? Anything the Supreme Court says should be considered with care; nonetheless, there is a significant difference between statements about the law, which courts should consider with care and respect, and utterances that have the force of binding law. The Supreme Court's dicta are not law. The issues so addressed remain unadjudicated. When an inferior court has such an issue before it, it may not treat the Supreme Court's dictum as dispositive. It must adjudicate.

I am not counseling disrespect for a higher court, least of all the Supreme Court. I am saying only that a lower court has a constitutional responsibility to decide the case in accordance with law. Dictum is not law. The court must decide a previously undecided question.

VII. Good Faith Immunity

I conclude with a puzzling misadventure in constitutional dictum, commanded by the Supreme Court—the *Saucier* rule in claims of constitutional tort.[74] The background is as follows: When a plaintiff sues a government officer—let's say a police officer—for damages, alleging a constitutional tort, the defendant officer is entitled to have the case dismissed if, at the time of his conduct, there was no clear authority that his conduct violated the Constitution. This is a rule of "good faith immunity," which deems it unfair to hold the officer liable for doing what he reasonably perceived to be his job.[75]

We dismiss a large number of these cases, probably the great majority, at the outset because it is immediately apparent that there are no rulings establishing the unconstitutionality of the officer's conduct.

Then, a few years ago, the Supreme Court conceived a new and mischievous rule: Before granting the officer's motion to dismiss for good faith immunity, the trial court must first decide whether the officer's alleged conduct, assuming that it happened, violated a constitutional right—a question, mind you, which will have no impact on the adjudication of the case.[76] In other words, before dismissing the case on the ground of good faith immunity, the court must first either gratuitously declare a new constitutional right in dictum or decide that the claimed right does not exist.[77]

What is more, on appeal from the dismissal, before affirming an obviously correct dismissal for good faith immunity, the appellate court must similarly pass in dictum on the theoretical question whether the constitutional right exists.

This rule involves so many and such serious problems that I am not sure where to begin. For generations, the Supreme Court has wisely cautioned against unnecessary constitutional rulings. It is a long-honored principle that a court should decide a constitutional question only when there is no other basis for resolving the dispute.[78] Yet in this context, the Supreme Court now requires that courts glibly announce new constitutional rights in dictum that will have no effect whatsoever on the case.[79]

The practice will inevitably produce bad constitutional law. Why so? Let us look at how the issue arises in a characteristic case.

The defendant moves at the outset for dismissal by reason of good faith immunity: "Judge, my client is entitled to have this case dismissed because, at the time of the events, he had no warning from court decisions that his conduct was unconstitutional. This is all spelled out in my brief."

"I've looked at the cases," the judge responds, "and you're right. Still today there are no such rulings. But the Supreme Court requires that before I grant you dismissal, I must determine, as an abstract question, whether the alleged right exists. Your papers have not said much about that. May I ask you to brief that issue more extensively?"

"Judge," the attorney answers, "my client couldn't care less what you decide on that point. He has no interest in it. I can't charge for writing a brief the client has no interest in. He is entitled to the dismissal no matter what you conclude about the theoretical existence of the right."

"I know," says the judge, "but counselor, have a heart. The Supreme Court says I have to do this. Give me a break. I need briefing from both sides."

"Whatever!" responds the lawyer. "I have a great idea. If it will help your Honor out, we'll concede unconstitutionality. We really don't care."

Of course my dialogue is caricature. But the fact is, in many cases neither the judge nor the defendant has any practical interest in the theoretical question of constitutionality. Both know it can have no effect on the inevitable dismissal of the case.[80] The court's conclusion on this question will come at no price.[81]

A further problem lies in the fact, as we discussed before, that there is no appeal from the trial court's declaration in dictum that the officer's conduct violated the Constitution—nor from the appeals court's dictum.[82]

One Supreme Court justice proposed to cure this latter problem by permitting the defendant to petition for Supreme Court review of the declaration of a right in dictum.[83] That cure is seriously deficient. Even if the defendant officer could appeal from the dictum, in many cases he would not do so. He has won the case. Unless he has an interest in freedom to continue the conduct, he does not care. People do not appeal from abstract statements they don't care about.

What is more, even if the defendant did care and did appeal, at this point the plaintiff would likely have no interest in the appeal. If the plaintiff sees he will be unable to convince the court that the right was established at the time, he knows the dismissal will be affirmed. He knows he will get nothing out of persuading the higher court that the right now exists.

Saucier is a blueprint for the creation of bad constitutional law.[84]

Why has the Supreme Court commanded this bizarre practice? The best justification is that the rule is intended to prevent continually repeated unconstitutional conduct from successfully evading judicial review through repeated dismissals for immunity.[85]

The problem of illegal conduct repeatedly escaping judicial review is not imaginary. But it is present in only a very narrow class of cases. Those are the cases where (1) the conduct was not a one-time event, but is likely to be repeated, and (2) it is likely to evade judicial review through repeated dismissals for good faith immunity.

In many cases, one or both of these conditions is not present. Often the challenged conduct was a one-time event—not a matter of policy, and not likely to be repeated. When the conduct is likely to be repeated, it is often not likely to repeatedly escape review. This is because in many types of litigation, especially the types that occur when the conduct is a matter of continuing policy, good faith immunity does not apply. It does not apply, for example, where an injunction is sought to prevent repetition of the conduct,[86] nor where the suit is against a municipality based on municipal policy.[87] It also does not apply where suppression of evidence is sought. When such proceedings can be anticipated, there is no reasonable likelihood that the conduct will continue without judicial scrutiny.[88]

The Supreme Court's remedy, with its toxic side effect, is prescribed far too broadly—for cases where there is no disease.[89] At the very least, this risky, unreliable declaration of constitutional rights in dictum should be reserved for the class of cases where a pattern of repetition, escaping review, is likely.

Even in that narrow class of cases, there is a better solution. If the conduct is egregious, or has already escaped review and is probably unconstitutional, the court would warn of the probable unconstitutionality—without taking a definitive position. Government officials who persist in the conduct after receipt of such a warning (at least in an opinion of the Supreme Court or a court of appeals) are either acting in bad faith disregard of the court's warning or taking a calculated risk that their conduct will ultimately be vindicated. They should not be entitled to rely on good faith immunity.[90] In the next case, immunity would be denied, and the court would adjudicate the question of constitutional right—as holding—after proper litigation by parties who had an interest in the outcome.[91]

Conclusion

If any of what I have said makes sense, what course does this suggest for professors, students, practitioners, and judges?

To professors I would say: You have a responsibility to make sure your students understand and are alert to the distinction between holding and dictum—and its importance. It is not something to be discussed only in a brief, first-year intro-to-law lecture. Students who graduate without a grasp of it are not well trained for the profession.

To students and practitioners I would say that, in arguing to courts, you will need to be keenly aware what is holding and what is dictum. It is often the best way to undermine unfavorable language in a prior opinion. By the same token, it can alert you that your argument is built on a house of cards.

To myself and other judges I would say three things: First, dictum can serve useful purposes. We have no need to purge dictum from our opinions and we shouldn't be embarrassed by its presence. We must only remember that it is not law. To avoid trespassing beyond the territory confided to us by the Constitution, to avoid creating law in circumstances likely to produce bad law, and to avoid creating confusion, we should not disguise dictum, but should forthrightly label it as what it is. Second, rather than reciting rules of law, which are not in dispute in the case, we should focus sharply on exactly what is in dispute and set forth rules in our opinions only as rulings on the disputed questions. Third, before relying on a formulation of law in a prior opinion, we must determine whether it was holding or dictum. We must make that inquiry even when the prior court was the Supreme Court. If a rule was declared only in dictum, the question remains undecided, and we have a constitutional duty to make our own determination of the answer. Unless we do, we have not done our job.

NOTES

1. 609 F.2d 51, 69 (2d Cir. 1979) (Friendly, J., concurring).
2. BENJAMIN N. CARDOZO, THE NATURE OF THE JUDICIAL PROCESS 29 (1921).
3. 400 F.3d 744 (9th Cir. 2005) (en banc).
4. *Id.* at 746-48.
5. *See* Quinn v. Robinson, 783 F.2d 776, 810-14 (9th Cir. 1986). The *Quinn* opinion rejected Quinn's defense to extradition because he had failed to show the existence of an "uprising." The court also digressed in a lengthy discussion of when criminal conduct can be deemed "incidental" to an uprising, which discussion had no effect on the court's decision and was therefore dictum.
6. In re Extradition of Singh, 170 F. Supp. 2d 982, 998 (E.D. Cal. 2001) ("The portion of *Quinn* that addresses the 'incidental to' prong is dicta and is only persuasive, non-binding authority.").
7. Had the *Quinn* court's discussion of the meaning of "incidental" supported its judgment, this position would have been reasonable, even if the discussion was not strictly "necessary" to the *Quinn* decision. However, the *Quinn* court's articulation of the meaning of "incidental" was not only not "necessary" to its disposition; in fact, it played no role whatsoever in supporting the decision.
8. *Barapind*, 400 F.3d at 750-51 (citations omitted).
9. 418 F.3d 395 (4th Cir. 2005).
10. *Id.*
11. *Id.* at 397.
12. Elk Grove Unified School Dist. v. Newdow, 542 U.S. 1 (2004).
13. *Id.* at 17-18.
14. The three-judge panel issued three opinions. The lead opinion gave its own reasons for its decision, explaining that "the history of our nation, coupled with repeated dicta from the Court respecting the constitutionality of the Pledge, guides our exercise of that legal judgment in this case." *Myers*, 418 F.3d at 402. While the second opinion said that it joined the first in part, it explicitly disclaimed reliance on the historical analysis of the first opinion and explained its conclusion by reference to Supreme Court dicta to the effect that the Pledge does not violate the Establishment Clause and that its recitation is not a religious activity. *Id.* at 409 (Duncan, J., concurring) (citing dicta in *Newdow*, 542 U.S. at 5-6). The third opinion made clear it believed the plaintiff's attack on the Pledge was foreclosed by Supreme Court dicta. *See id.* at 410 (Motz, J., concurring) (acknowledging dicta and denying that court "need . . . search further than these assurances to resolve the issue before us").
15. *See id.* at 409-11 (Motz, J., concurring) ("Without the Court's explicit guidance, this could be an extremely close case, requiring navigation through the Supreme Court's complicated Establishment Clause jurisprudence.").

16. In Cohens v. Virginia, 19 U.S. (6 Wheat.) 264 (1821), the Supreme Court wrote:

> It is a maxim not to be disregarded, that general expressions, in every opinion, are to be taken in connection with the case in which those expressions are used. If they go beyond the case, they may be respected, but ought not to control the judgment in a subsequent suit when the very point is presented for decision. The reason of this maxim is obvious. The question actually before the Court is investigated with care, and considered in its full extent. Other principles which may serve to illustrate it, are considered in their relation to the case decided, but their possible bearing on all other cases is seldom completely investigated.

Id. at 399-400.

17. See, e.g., Willis v. Baddeley, (1892) 2 Eng. Rep. 324, 326 (Q.B.D.) ("There is in fact no such thing as judge-made law, for the judges do not make the law, though they frequently have to apply existing law to circumstances as to which it has not previously been authoritatively laid down that such law is applicable."); R. W. M. DIAS, JURISPRUDENCE 151 (5th ed. 1985) ("The orthodox Blackstonian view . . . is that judges do not make law, but only declare what has always been the law.").

18. Nor can the classification of a pronouncement of law be determined based on whether a subsequent court has described it as holding or dictum. The words, "In Smith v. Jones, the court held . . ." are often written without the slightest attention to whether the proposition was a holding or dictum. Frequently, it means no more than "the court wrote. . . ." And a subsequent court's description of an earlier proposition as dictum is often attributable to a motivation to diminish the status of the prior pronouncement, rather than to a reasoned justification.

19. United States v. Rubin, 609 F.2d 51, 69 (2d Cir. 1979) (Friendly, J., concurring).

20. As to utterances falling within this zone, it is unclear to what degree a future court should consider itself bound by them. When the statement forms a part of the line of reasoning supporting the judgment, but a remote or tangential part, subsequent rulings are less clearly bound to adhere to it than to a statement that lies at the core of the court's reasoning. The same may be true when the court relies on two or more lines of reasoning to support judgment, so that the judgment would be the same regardless of the second line of reasoning. Courts often give less careful attention to propositions uttered in support of unnecessary alternative holdings. Conversely, the closer an assertion comes to the court's justification for its ruling, the less easily it may be avoided, even if it can, with arguable justification, be considered dictum.

21. U.S. CONST. art. III, § 1.

22. Id. art. I, § 1.

23. I will not discuss in this lecture the problems for democratic governance that arise if judges, appointed for life, exercise the power to make law simply by writing it into their decisions, regardless of whether the newly declared rule plays a role in the decision of the case.

24. Int'l News Serv. v. Associated Press, 248 U.S. 215, 267 (1918) (Brandeis, J., dissenting).

25. In limited circumstances, courts also receive briefing from amici. See FED. R. APP. P. 29.

26. The court may call its own witness to the stand. See FED. R. EVID. 614(a)-(b). But the court is not at liberty to do private fact research to discover who has knowledge of the facts and what they know.

27. The court may appoint an expert pursuant to Rule 706 of the Federal Rules of Evidence or its inherent authority. See Ex Parte Peterson, 253 U.S. 300, 312 (1920) (Brandeis, J.) (upholding decision of Judge Augustus Hand to appoint auditor because "courts have . . . inherent power to provide themselves with appropriate instruments required for the performance of their duties"). However, this power is exercised infrequently. See JOE S. CECIL & THOMAS E. WILLGING, COURT-APPOINTED EXPERTS: DEFINING THE ROLE OF EXPERTS APPOINTED UNDER FEDERAL RULE OF EVIDENCE 706, at 7-23 (1993).

28. 411 U.S. 792 (1973).

29. Id. at 797.

30. Id. at 798-800.

31. Id. (agreeing with court of appeals that "absence of a Commission finding of reasonable cause cannot bar suit under an appropriate section of Title VII and that the District Judge erred" and "accordingly . . . remanding the case for trial of respondent's claim of racial discrimination consistent with the views set forth below").

32. Id. at 800-06.

33. Id. at 802-03; Reeves v. Sanderson Plumbing Prods., Inc., 530 U.S. 133, 142 (2000); see also Fisher v. Vassar Coll., 114 F.3d 1332, 1335 (2d Cir. 1997) (en banc). A plaintiff may establish the minimalist prima facie case by showing membership in a protected class, qualification for the job, an adverse employment action, and a preference given to a person not of the preferred class. See Farias v. Instructional Sys., Inc., 259 F.3d 91, 98 (2d Cir. 2001); Fisher, 114 F.3d at 1335. Unlike other areas of the law, under this framework, the prima facie case is a minimal requirement, which is met without evidence sufficient to establish the essential element of discriminatory motivation. See Fisher, 114 F.3d at 1337.

34. Tex. Dep't of Cmty. Affairs v. Burdine, 450 U.S. 248, 254 (1981); Fisher, 114 F.3d at 1335.

35. St. Mary's Honor Ctr. v. Hicks, 509 U.S. 502, 506-07 (1993); Burdine, 450 U.S. at 255; Fisher, 114 F.3d at 1335-36. To shift the burden back to the plaintiff, the defendant must "come[] forward with a non-discriminatory reason for the action complained of," failing which, judgment will be awarded to the plaintiff. Fisher, 114 F.3d at 1335.

36. See Hicks, 509 U.S. at 507; Fisher, 114 F.3d at 1336. Once the defendant articulates its non-discriminatory reason, all presumptions drop away. "The question becomes the same question asked in any other civil case: Has the plaintiff shown, by a preponderance of the evidence, that the defendant is liable for the

alleged conduct?" *Id.*; *see Reeves*, 530 U.S. at 142; James v. N.Y. Racing Ass'n, 233 F.3d 149, 153-54 (2d Cir. 2000).

37. *See, e.g.*, U.S. Postal Serv. Bd. of Governors v. Aikens, 460 U.S. 711, 713-14 (1983).

> Because this case was fully tried on the merits, it is surprising to find the parties and the Court of Appeals still addressing the question whether Aikens made out a prima facie case. We think that by framing the issue in these terms, they have unnecessarily evaded the ultimate question of discrimination vel non.

Id.; *see also* Sanders v. N.Y. City Human Res. Admin., 361 F.3d 749, 758 (2d Cir. 2004) ("Explaining [the burden shifting framework] to the jury in the charge, we believe, is more likely to confuse rather than enlighten the members of the jury.").

38. "The purpose of the *McDonnell Douglas* framework is to force the defendant to give an explanation for its conduct, in order to prevent employers from simply remaining silent while the plaintiff founders on the difficulty of proving discriminatory intent." *Fisher*, 114 F.3d at 1335. This elaborate, confusing construct, which the Supreme Court devised in dictum, could have been completely avoided had the Court simply specified, in an appropriate case, that a plaintiff is entitled to discovery of the defendant's purported reason for the adverse employment action before having to defend against a motion for summary judgment. In the end, the McDonnell Douglas construct, with all its complications, accomplishes nothing more than forcing the defendant to give a reason for its adverse action before the plaintiff must defend against such a motion.

39. 464 U.S. 417 (1984).

40. *See id.* at 443-55.

41. *See id.* at 451.

42. *Id.* (emphasis added) ("Thus, although every commercial use of a copyrighted material is presumptively an unfair exploitation of the monopoly privilege that belongs to the owner of the copyright, noncommercial uses are a different matter.").

43. 510 U.S. 569, 583-85 (1994).

44. *See supra* note 17 and accompanying text.

45. United States v. Rabinowitz, 339 U.S. 56, 75 (1950) (Frankfurter, J., dissenting), *overruled by* Chimel v. California, 395 U.S. 752, 760 (1969).

46. Cardozo, *supra* note 3, at 29.

47. 400 F.3d 744 (9th Cir. 2005) (en banc).

48. *See supra* Part I.A.1.

49. 395 U.S. 238 (1969).

50. *Id.* at 239-41.

51. *Id.* at 239.

52. *Id.* at 244.

53. Brady v. United States, 397 U.S. 742 (1970).

54. *Boykin*, 395 U.S. at 242, 244.

55. *Id.* at 243 (citations omitted).

56. Boykin's brief to the Supreme Court, while arguing that the record did not demonstrate that his plea was knowing and voluntary, never suggests that the trial court was required to establish the waiver of particular trial rights. Brief for the Petitioner at 25-31, *Boykin*, 395 U.S. 238 (No. 642), 1968 WL 129462, at 25-31.

57. Such a reading is at odds with other passages in *Boykin* that seem to require only that the plea be intelligent and voluntary, without any mention of particular rights. It also is in tension with footnote seven of the *Boykin* opinion, in which the Court quoted with apparent approval a state court description of what a guilty plea allocution should include, which did not include any mention of the rights of confrontation and against self-incrimination. See *Boykin*, 395 U.S. at 244 n.7 (quoting Commonwealth ex rel. West v. Rundle, 237 A.2d 196, 197-98 (Pa. 1968)).

58. *See* Estelle v. Williams, 425 U.S. 501, 503 (1976).

59. In re Winship, 397 U.S. 358, 364 (1970).

60. Washington v. Texas, 388 U.S. 14, 19 (1967).

61. *See* Rock v. Arkansas, 483 U.S. 44, 49 (1987).

62. U.S. CONST. amend. VI.

63. *See Washington*, 388 U.S. at 18.

64. *See, e.g.*, In re Ruffalo, 390 U.S. 544, 550-51 (1968).

65. *See, e.g.*, Gideon v. Wainwright, 372 U.S. 335 (1963).

66. The *Boykin* opinion no doubt singled out those three rights because, two months earlier, the Court had stated in *McCarthy v. United States*, 394 U.S. 459 (1969), with respect to guilty pleas governed by Rule 11 of the Federal Rules of Criminal Procedure, that "[a] defendant who enters such a plea simultaneously waives several constitutional rights, including his privilege against compulsory self-incrimination, his right to trial by jury, and his right to confront his accusers," *id.* at 466. However, the *McCarthy* Court was simply giving examples of rights waived by a guilty plea; it did not suggest that a guilty plea must include the waiver of those particular rights. In *McCarthy* itself, the Court reversed a judgment of conviction pursuant to a guilty plea because the district court had failed to address the defendant personally as required by Rule 11. *Id.* at 464, 471-72. As in *Boykin*, the question of whether specific rights had to be waived in a guilty plea was not before the Court. At the time of the *McCarthy* decision, Rule 11 did not require mention of the three rights identified by the Court. See *McCarthy*, 394 U.S. at 462; FED. R. CRIM. P. 11, 18 U.S.C. app. IV (1970) (indicating that rule last amended on February 28, 1966). Nonetheless, there is no indication that the *McCarthy* Court considered that version of Rule 11 to be constitutionally unsound.

67. *See, e.g.*, Brady v. United States, 397 U.S. 742, 756 (1970); Hanson v. Phillips, 442 F.3d 789, 798 (2d Cir. 2006) (citing *Boykin* for proposition that guilty plea must be intelligent and voluntary and noting that *Boykin* does not impose "any particular interrogatory 'catechism'" on state courts).

68. When *Boykin* was decided, Rule 11 required a federal judge to establish that a "plea is made voluntarily with understanding of the nature of the charge and the consequences of the plea." *Brady*, 397 U.S. at 744 n.3. In 1974, the Supreme

Court approved a new version of Rule 11 and sent that proposed version to Congress. The Rule 11 colloquy requirements suggested by the Supreme Court required that a judge establish the defendant's understanding of the right to trial, but did not require that there be any mention of the right to confront witnesses or the privilege against self-incrimination. PROPOSED AMEND-MENTS TO FEDERAL RULES OF CRIMINAL PROCEDURE FOR THE UNITED STATES DISTRICT COURTS, 62 F.R.D. 271, 275 (1974). However, the language finally adopted by Congress, in conformity with the recom-mendations of the House of Representatives Judiciary Committee, required a federal judge accepting a guilty plea to establish that the defendant under-stands not only his right to plead not guilty, his right to be tried by a jury, and his right to assistance of counsel, but also the right to confront witnesses and the privilege against self-incrimination. *See* FED. R. CRIM. P. 11(c)(3). The Judiciary Committee explained that "it believed that the warnings given to the defendant ought to include those that *Boykin v. Alabama*, 395 U.S. 238 (1969), said were constitutionally required." H.R. Rep. No. 94-247, at 7 (1975), *as reprinted in* 1975 U.S.C.C.A.N. 674, 679.

69. Elfenbein v. Gulf & W. Indus., Inc., 590 F.2d 445, 451 (2d Cir. 1978).
70. *See, e.g.*, Kaster v. Modification Sys., Inc., 731 F.2d 1014, 1018 (2d Cir. 1984); Lewis v. Graves, 701 F.2d 245, 248 (2d Cir. 1983).
71. *See* Scalisi v. Fund Asset Mgmt., L.P., 380 F.3d 133, 137 n.6 (2d Cir. 2004) (sug-gesting that review should be de novo).
72. *See, e.g.*, McCoy v. M.I.T., 950 F.2d 13, 19 (1st Cir. 1991) (finding itself "both unable . . . and unwilling" to ignore "considered" Supreme Court dic-tum); Faheem-El v. Klincar, 841 F.2d 712, 731 (7th Cir. 1988) (Easterbrook, J., concurring) (finding Supreme Court discussion—"wise or not"—to be authoritative).
73. *See, e.g.*, Barapind v. Enomoto, 400 F.3d 744 (9th Cir. 2005) (en banc) (Rymer, J., dissenting in part).

> It is one thing for a court of last resort to announce that whatever it says in a published opinion is binding, for a court of last resort regu-larly sits en banc, has ultimate responsibility for the efficient adminis-tration of justice within its province, and may not have enough cases to flesh out the rule being articulated.

Id. at 759.
74. Saucier v. Katz, 533 U.S. 194 (2001).
75. *See* Harlow v. Fitzgerald, 457 U.S. 800, 818 (1982) ("If the law at [the time the action occurred] was not clearly established, an official could not reasonably be expected to anticipate subsequent legal developments, nor could he fairly be said to 'know' that the law forbade conduct not previously identified as unlawful.").
76. *Saucier*, 533 U.S. at 194 (2001).
77. Judge Calabresi has forcefully made the point that when a court dismisses by reason of good faith immunity, its pronouncement that the alleged right exists

is dictum. *See* Wilkinson v. Russell, 182 F.3d 89, 112 (2d Cir. 1999) (Calabresi, J., concurring) ("All statements about constitutional rights made in the *Sacramento* framework (i.e., where qualified immunity exists notwithstanding the violation of a right since the right was not clearly established at the time the conduct allegedly occurred), are dicta. . . .").

78. *See* Ashwander v. Tenn. Valley Auth., 297 U.S. 288, 346-47 (1936) (Brandeis, J., concurring); *see also* Tory v. Cochran, 544 U.S. 734, 740 (2005) (Thomas, J., dissenting) ("As a prudential matter, the better course is to avoid passing unnecessarily on the constitutional question."); Christopher v. Harbury, 536 U.S. 403, 417 (2002) ("The need to resolve . . . constitutional issues ought to be avoided where possible. . . .").

79. *See Brosseau*, 543 U.S. at 201 (Breyer, J., joined by Scalia and Ginsburg, JJ., concurring) (expressing concern that *Saucier* rule "rigidly requires courts unnecessarily to decide difficult constitutional questions when there is available an easier basis for the decision (*e.g.*, qualified immunity) that will satisfactorily resolve the case before the court"); *County of Sacramento*, 523 U.S. at 859 (Stevens, J., concurring) (arguing that court should address constitutional question when answer is clear, but that "when, however, the question is both difficult and unresolved, I believe it wiser to adhere to the policy of avoiding the unnecessary adjudication of constitutional questions"); *id.* at 858-59 (Breyer, J., concurring) (arguing that in qualified immunity cases courts should not be required to address "constitutional issues that are either difficult or poorly presented"); *Siegert*, 500 U.S. at 235 (Kennedy, J., concurring) ("If it is plain that a plaintiff's required malice allegations are insufficient but there is some doubt as to the constitutional right asserted, it seems to reverse the usual ordering of issues to tell the trial and appellate courts that they should resolve the constitutional question first."); *see also Lyons*, 417 F.3d at 582-83 (Sutton, J., concurring) (arguing that in some circumstances *Saucier* rule is "difficult to justify" and that Supreme Court should "permit lower courts to make reasoned departures" from that rule); Horne v. Coughlin, 191 F.3d 244, 246 (2d Cir. 1999) ("There are powerful arguments against reaching out in dictum to establish new constitutional rights in circumstances where the reasoning plays no role whatsoever in the disposition of the action.").

80. *See Horne*, 191 F.3d at 247. For example, in *Vives*, 405 F.3d 115, plaintiff claimed that his arrest for aggravated harassment under New York law violated his First and Fourth Amendment rights, and that the arresting officers were not entitled to qualified immunity because they had fair notice that the New York aggravated harassment statute would be declared unconstitutional. *Id.* at 116. Before the district court, the officers argued only that they did not have fair notice regarding the statute's alleged unconstitutionality, and took no position on whether the statute was constitutional. After the district court held that defendants were not entitled to qualified immunity, the officers appealed and once again only argued the notice question. The Second Circuit concluded that the officers did not have fair notice of the statute's alleged unconstitutionality and granted qualified immunity. *Id.* at 118. The court did not address whether

the statute was actually constitutional, explaining that "we do not reach the constitutional question because we are reluctant to pass on the issue in dicta and because the parties did not genuinely dispute the constitutionality of [the state law] either in the District Court or on appeal." *Id.* at 118 n.7.

81. In support of this doctrine, the Supreme Court has asserted that the two questions are inescapably interwoven. According to the Court, "[a] necessary concomitant to the determination of whether the constitutional right asserted by a plaintiff is 'clearly established' at the time the defendant acted is the determination of whether the plaintiff has asserted a violation of a constitutional right at all." *Siegert*, 500 U.S. at 232. By the Court's reasoning, a judge deciding whether a right was clearly established will necessarily first have to decide whether the right exists.

I believe this is quite mistaken. It is often immediately apparent that the claimed right was not clearly established at the time of the defendant's conduct, while it may be very difficult to determine whether the claimed right should be found to exist. Moreover, in some instances a court concludes that a right was not clearly established, but that whether the right exists in a particular context requires further fact-finding. *See, e.g.*, Kalka v. Hawk, 215 F.3d 90, 97 (D.C. Cir. 2000) ("Whether [defendant's] humanism is a religion under the First Amendment could not be decided in the abstract."); Mollica v. Volker, 229 F.3d 366, 372-73 (2d Cir. 2000) (concluding that unconstitutionality of checkpoint was not clearly established but that determination whether checkpoint was constitutional would require fuller record). It is difficult to believe that "the Supreme Court intended that trial courts would direct parties to participate in additional unnecessary evidence-gathering proceedings in which the parties had no practical interest—solely to enable the court to utter advisory dicta on constitutionality." *Mollica*, 229 F.3d at 373.

82. *See Horne*, 191 F.3d at 247-48.

> If those governmental actors defer to the courts' declarations and modify their procedures accordingly, new constitutional rights will have effectively been established by the dicta of [the] lower court without the defendants having the right to appellate review. . . . Officials may be placed in the untenable position of complying with the lower court's advisory dictum without opportunity to seek appellate review, or appearing to defy the lower court's assertion and thus exposing themselves to a risk of punitive damages.

> *Id.*; *see also Lyons*, 417 F.3d at 582 (Sutton, J., concurring) ("By multiplying constitutional holdings that are not subject to review in the normal course, a rigid application of the two-step inquiry may do as much to unsettle the law as to settle it.").

83. *See* Bunting v. Mellen, 541 U.S. 1019, 1023, 1025 (2004) (Scalia, J., dissenting from denial of certiorari).

84. The *Saucier* rule also increases the workload of an already overburdened judiciary. *See* Brosseau v. Haughen, 543 U.S. 194, 201-02 (2004) (Breyer, J.,

concurring) ("When courts' dockets are crowded, a rigid 'order of battle' makes little administrative sense and can sometimes lead to a constitutional decision that is effectively insulated from review."").

85. In *Saucier*, the Court stated:

> In the course of determining whether a constitutional right was violated on the premises alleged, a court might find it necessary to set forth principles which will become the basis for a holding that a right is clearly established. This is the process for the law's elaboration from case to case, and it is one reason for our insisting upon turning to the existence or nonexistence of a constitutional right as the first inquiry. The law might be deprived of this explanation were a court simply to skip ahead to the question whether the law clearly established that the officer's conduct was unlawful in the circumstances of the case.

Saucier v. Katz, 533 U.S. 194, 201 (2001).

86. *See* Harlow v. Fitzgerald, 457 U.S. 800, 819 n.34 (1982) (noting qualified immunity may not be applicable to injunctions); Charles W. v. Maul, 214 F.3d 350, 360 (2d Cir. 2000) (finding that qualified immunity is not defense against injunctions).

87. *See* Owen v. City of Independence, 445 U.S. 622, 638 (1980) (holding that "the municipality may not assert the good faith of its officers or agents as a defense to liability" if there is municipal policy or custom).

88. *See, e.g.*, African Trade & Info. Ctr. Inc. v. Abromaitis, 294 F.3d 355, 359-60 (2d Cir. 2002) (declining, pre-*Saucier*, to reach existence of constitutional right in qualified immunity case where "the merits of this issue are scarcely mentioned in the briefs on appeal, let alone adequately briefed" and noting that existence of constitutional right might be addressed on remand in that very case, as plaintiff was also seeking injunctive relief); Koch v. Town of Brattleboro, 287 F.3d 162, 166 (2d Cir. 2002) (refraining from deciding constitutional question that was not unique to 1983 cases and likely to be litigated during motion to suppress in criminal trial).

89. For more examples of types of cases where the *Saucier* requirement does not make sense, see *Lyons*, 417 F.3d at 582 (Sutton, J., concurring).

90. *See* Wilkinson v. Russell, 182 F.3d 89, 112 (2d Cir. 1999) (Calabresi, J., concurring) ("By providing that the first statement about a given right will usually be in dicta that is explicit enough to put state actors on notice, Sacramento creates a situation in which the next time that particular right is alleged, qualified immunity will not be a defense.").

91. The Court may be ready to rethink the *Saucier* rule. In his recent concurrence in *Brosseau*, Justice Breyer, together with Justice Ginsburg and Justice Scalia, called upon the court to reconsider *Saucier*. *Brosseau*, 543 U.S. at 201-02 (Breyer, J., joined by Scalia and Ginsburg, JJ., concurring).

6

Judge Henry Friendly and the Mirror of Constitutional Law

MICHAEL BOUDIN

Henry Friendly served as a judge on the U.S. Court of Appeals for the Second Circuit from 1959 until his death in 1986. During that period, he wrote almost one thousand opinions,[1] several books,[2] thirty or so full-scale articles,[3] and many tributes and book reviews.[4] The power and quality of his work made him the most admired legal scholar and craftsman then sitting on the federal circuit courts, dominating his era as Learned Hand had dominated the 1930s through the 1950s.

A number of Friendly's articles and a share of his opinions concern constitutional law, broadly taken to include not just issues of "rights" but also such matters as jurisdiction, federal common law, and the state action doctrine. Yet my subject today is not legal doctrine, but rather what Friendly's articles and opinions on the subject tell us about him and about appellate judging. Friendly's work in constitutional law is a mirror in which we may hope to catch his reflection and measure his greatness.

Friendly's education and his career in practice bore directly on his judging. He was born in 1903 and grew up in Elmira, New York, then a modest-sized community.[5] From the Elmira public schools, he entered Harvard College in 1919.[6] There, he studied history; it was, as Paul Freund has noted, a period in which Harvard was uncommonly rich in great teachers of the subject.[7] Charles McIlwain was of foremost importance to Friendly, whose special interest was medieval English history.[8]

This lecture was delivered on October 17, 2006, and appeared in *82 N.Y.U. L. Rev.* 975 (2007).

Graduating summa cum laude in 1923,[9] Friendly pondered an academic career as a historian.

Instead, Felix Frankfurter lured Friendly to law school, urging that he should try it for a year before making up his mind between law and history.[10] At Harvard Law School, which he entered in 1924 after a year abroad on a traveling fellowship,[11] Friendly became a legend. When the class was challenged by its professor to identify the language in which the old English cases were reported, Friendly answered correctly that the language was Law French and then offered to translate the example provided to him. Friendly was president of the *Harvard Law Review* and ranked first in his class. Again, he graduated with a rare summa degree and an astonishing average of 86[12]—approximately an A double plus.

Among his teachers at the Law School was Thomas Reed Powell, an early but subtle exponent of realism in constitutional law.[13] It was Powell who wrote that although law is to some extent "judicial whim or fiat[,] . . . [t]hose who see law as *only* this or *only* that see but narrowly."[14] And the spirit of James Bradley Thayer still hovered over the school with its message of judicial self-restraint in constitutional interpretation.[15] Thayer's view was one that Holmes and Hand championed on the bench. Yet the breadth of views within the faculty was remarkable, as able formalists like Samuel Williston and Joseph Beale contended with new tendencies of thought represented by professors such as Roscoe Pound, Felix Frankfurter, and Zechariah Chafee.

From Harvard Law School, Friendly went on to a clerkship with Justice Brandeis, at Frankfurter's recommendation.[16] Brandeis was himself a brilliant outsider who succeeded, as Friendly did thereafter, first at Harvard Law School, then in his law practice, and finally as a great judge. But Friendly, while mildly reformist in politics, had far less of a policy agenda than did Brandeis, whose law practice had mixed business representation with legal good works.[17] Nor did Friendly share Brandeis's crusading zeal.

At the end of the clerkship, Friendly faced a fork in the road: to teach law at Harvard or to enter law practice. Although Frankfurter urged him to return to Cambridge,[18] Friendly chose to practice in New York with Root, Clark, Buckner & Ballantine. Thirty years later, Friendly chided one of his own law clerks for making the same choice. To the clerk's obvious response that Friendly was the natural scholar, Friendly replied that law teaching was a lot less interesting in the 1920s: The common law subjects, he said, had been worked through, and the explosion of New Deal legislation, the rise of the agencies, and much else was hidden around the corner.

The presiding litigator at Root Clark in 1928 was Emory Buckner, who recruited his young lawyers not just from the regular cadre of conventional Ivy Leaguers but also from among Jewish students, like Friendly, and those whose law training had been obtained in England, like Hugh Cox and John Harlan.[19] Friendly's law practice came to combine administrative law, common-carrier regulation, and appellate practice. In 1946, he and others broke away from Root Clark and, with Hugh Cox returning to private practice after his work for the government, formed the Cleary Gottlieb firm—initially Cleary, Gottlieb, Friendly & Cox. In the same year, Friendly became the general counsel of his longtime client, Pan American World Airways, and thereafter held two full-time jobs.[20]

When Henry Friendly came to the bench in 1959, it was a "merit" selection. Hand had written a letter to President Eisenhower—a rare intervention for Hand—urging Friendly's appointment.[21] Friendly himself told a law clerk that the Republican politician who gave Friendly final clearance had said with dismay that he was tired of being sent candidates like Friendly who had done nothing for the party. A New York Times editorial referred glowingly to Friendly's "outstanding qualifications."[22]

The appointment was a salvation for a man who (as he later confided to a law clerk) had been rapidly tiring of large law firm practice. The judgeship opened not only a new perspective on law, which Friendly described in an early essay,[23] but also other opportunities. He joined the Council of the American Law Institute in 1961 and became active in its work; he was already a member of the Council on Foreign Relations and often attended its meetings. In addition, he began the career of extracurricular legal scholarship that dovetailed with his judicial work and much magnified his influence as a judge.

From 1959 onward, Friendly produced a set of major articles of extraordinary quality, as well as books, shorter articles, book reviews, and tributes.[24] Among the articles—to mention only constitutional subjects— are his Cardozo Lecture on *Erie v. Tompkins*[25] at the New York City Bar Association,[26] his Holmes Lectures at Harvard on administrative law,[27] another Holmes Lecture at Dartmouth on the public-private distinction in constitutional law,[28] and important articles on the Fifth Amendment,[29] the right to hearings,[30] criminal procedure,[31] and habeas corpus.[32]

Friendly's natural gifts—the mainspring of his achievements—began with the raw power of his mind. In the summer of 1959, while awaiting his Senate confirmation hearing, Friendly absorbed for the first time Hart and Wechsler's famous (and famously intricate) casebook, *The Federal Courts and the Federal System*,[33] saying afterwards: "The book, while not exactly summer reading, proved to be the most stimulating and exciting law book I had encountered since Wigmore's *Evidence*."[34] The invited mental picture of the young law student plowing steadily through the five volumes of Wigmore's 1923 edition may not be wholly imaginary.

Nor did Friendly forget very much of what he read. He could say to a clerk, "I think the passage to support this proposition is in such and such decision, in volume 274 U.S., somewhere near the end of the opinion." His essays, even his book reviews, glimmer with aphorisms and quotations, especially to works of legal history and philosophy, that were stored in his head. An early book review of Mark de Wolfe Howe's biography of Justice Holmes shows Friendly's intimidating command of legal history and jurisprudence.[35]

Writing ability was another gift: The connection between quality of writing and influence as an appellate judge cannot be overstated. Friendly wrote his own opinions from scratch and so maintained a distinctive voice. Although without the poetic magic of Holmes or the King James resonances of Hand or Jackson, Friendly had a command of metaphor, a stock of literary and operatic references, a deft use of sarcasm, and a crisp way of summing up a matter. Consider this classic first line in an opinion: "Our principal task, in this diversity of citizenship case, is to determine what the New York courts would think the California courts would think on an issue about which neither has thought."[36] To watch Friendly crafting an opinion was to feel sorry for the Learned Hand depicted in Gerald Gunther's magnificent biography.[37]

Hand prepared meticulously, even to the point of modeling or diagramming ship collisions on his desk, often wrote draft after draft, and visibly agonized in hard cases.[38] Friendly, writing on a pad with briefs and law books stacked around him, normally produced a single draft—often over a period no longer than a weekend. It was then typed, edited by the judge in a single session with a law clerk who had read the cases cited in the opinion, and dispatched for a final retyping and circulation to his colleagues.

This disciplined energy probably owed something to the demands of law practice and, without it, Friendly could not have led the double life of a judge and a scholar. If nothing else, a successful lawyer is an overworked and therefore usually efficient lawyer. The reflective tone of

Hand's opinions, such as his brilliant soliloquy on the Sherman Act,[39] is less common with Friendly; Friendly's thinking was deep but swift, and his sometimes cryptic sentences mirror the train of his actual thinking as words flowed from his mind through his pen. Consider this dense gem from an opinion discussing a hearsay exception:

> True, inclusion of a past event motivating the plan adds the hazards of defective perception and memory to that of prevarication; but this does not demand exclusion or even excision, at least when, as here, the event is recent, is within the personal knowledge of the declarant and is so integrally included in the declaration of design as to make it unlikely in the last degree that the latter would be true and the former false.[40]

These gifts were merely the ingredients. What mattered most about Friendly as a judge was the pattern of thinking that his opinions and other writing revealed. Out of a number of Friendly's characteristics, let us dwell briefly on four: his intense respect for precedent and the other constraints of the craft; his immense practicality; his intellectual seriousness and integrity; and his essential moderation.

In the common law tradition, judges—especially appellate judges—occupy a curious position. In the course of deciding cases, often the judge is not just applying law but making law in miniature. Yet, in principle, such lawmaking is not free-form legislative action: It is constrained lawmaking. There is room to create and alter, but it is limited room. As Willard Hurst once wrote: "[T]he wisdom of the great judge consists in a grasp both of the potentialities and the limitations of the kind of power that he wields."[41] And the integrity of the process—indeed, the legitimacy of the judge's action—depends upon respecting the constraints and acting within the boundaries they set.

The constraints are the familiar stuff of first-year law school: the language of statutes and constitutions, history and precedent, public and legislative policy, stare decisis, canons of construction and legal maxims, neutral principles, and all the rest. Still, these are elastic constraints whose force varies from one case to another. Nor is it easy to weigh one hard-to-measure variable against another of a different kind. And the formal constraints may vie with practical considerations.

Friendly was a master of the formal constraints and, what is more important, he took them very seriously, perhaps more seriously than our own jaded age allows. True, the ability to operate inventively within the constraints is one of the marks of great and creative judges. To take this as saying that clever judges can get around the rules is a mistranslation. Rather, a judge like Friendly can justify an improving change while at the same time shaping and limiting the change to maintain continuity, to minimize disruption, and to mark its limits in the interest of a new stability.

To Friendly, precedent was a constraint as central as any. Recall that Friendly was trained at Harvard College as a historian. Decided cases are themselves history comprised of the real-world events, the litigation, and the rules thus generated. Precedents, and the wisdom encoded in them, are one of the central motivating forces of the common law but also one of the great constraints. Law, said Hand, "is the precipitate of a long past of active controversy."[42]

Friendly's most dramatic excursion into precedent and large-scale history is his tour de force Cardozo Lecture at the New York City Bar Association, titled *In Praise of* Erie—*and of the New Federal Common Law*.[43] The lessons of this lecture were that *Erie*[44] had been correctly decided, that Brandeis had been correct to declare *Swift v. Tyson*[45] at odds with the Constitution, and that by obliterating *Swift*'s "spurious uniformity" the decision opened the way "for the truly uniform federal common law on issues of national concern."[46] What was extraordinary about the lecture was the conceptual basis of this assessment, which displays (among other virtues) Friendly's use of history at every level.

He begins with a terse recounting of the scholarly backlash against the reasoning of the *Erie* decision. Then, with a study of precedent and constitutional history, he demolishes two of the less ambitious lines of reasoning that *Erie*'s critics proposed to substitute for that of Brandeis: namely, a withering-away approach to *Swift*[47] and a broad construction of section 34 of the Judiciary Act of 1789.[48] The withering-away approach Friendly shows to be medicine worse than the disease;[49] the expansion of section 34, Friendly refutes—in a neat move of confession and avoidance—by assuming the accuracy of Charles Warren's account of the statute's original intent but showing that Story's reading of the statute was too settled to disturb.[50]

This leads him to consider the constitutional rightness of *Swift v. Tyson*, constitutional errors being more open to correction by the Court despite their age than statutes, where errors of interpretation can always be repaired by Congress. Friendly embarks on a demonstration of the soundness of *Erie* as constitutional law, grappling with section 34, pertinent case law, and the implications of the "necessary and proper" clause.[51] The conclusion, temperate but forceful, is vintage Friendly and gives one some sense of the powerful generalizations to which his elegant and detailed analysis led him:

> A great constitutional decision is not often compelled in the sense that a contrary one would lie beyond the area of rationality. I shall not insist that *Erie* was the rare exception. But it provided a far better fit with the scheme of the Constitution as that had developed over the years than do the assertions that the "necessary and proper" clause empowers Congress to establish substantive law for the federal courts in fields otherwise reserved to the states, or that federal courts themselves may do so—thereby not merely permitting but insuring unequal justice under law.[52]

This lecture was on a grand scale; but many of Friendly's opinions, constitutional and otherwise, contain remarkable essays that trace, summarize, and explain the evolution of precedent on the subject in question. A memorable example is his treatment of the "arising under" test for federal jurisdiction in *T.B. Harms Co. v. Eliscu*,[53] neatly distinguishing between the phrase's use in the Constitution and the narrower reading given to the same phrase in the statute and offering this gracious gloss on Holmes's own incomplete "cause of action" test: "It has come to be realized that Mr. Justice Holmes' formula is more useful for inclusion than for the exclusion for which it was intended."[54]

Precedent is only one of the constraints with which Friendly dealt masterfully. Others of particular importance to him were statutory language and institutional competence, and on both subjects he wrote thoughtful articles.[55] Needless to say, Friendly learned much else from his training as a historian, including a commitment to factual accuracy and the need to underpin generalizations, surely reinforced by his work with Brandeis. But we must pass on to another subject: practical judgment.

Ordinarily, a judge faced with a legal problem starts with the directions or clues provided by language, historical context, precedent, and the underlying policies imputed to the constitutional provision or statute involved or derived from prior common law decisions. If these were enough, judging would be a self-contained, if still demanding, discipline. In truth, more worldly considerations bear upon decision: They range from broad-canvas judgments of social problems, institutions, and tolerable rates of change, to more specific mental pictures as to what goes on in police stations, union meetings, or households, and as to what remedies will fix an existing problem.

Friendly brought to his task something more than the ordinary, though invaluable, experience of a practicing lawyer who had spent three decades addressing real-world problems. His work for Pan American had exposed him not only to federal regulation and administrative practice but also to international issues and war-related matters and a certain amount of work with Congress and state legislatures. He once remarked to a law clerk that Justice Brandeis, always enthusiastic about local governance, might have been shocked by some of what Friendly had encountered in state legislatures.

Whatever the sources of his insights, Friendly rivaled Justice Jackson in giving readers the sense that his decisions were grounded in reality. An illustration is provided by a pair of Friendly's articles. The first is *The Bill of Rights as a Code of Criminal Procedure*,[56] which challenged (among much else) the Warren Court's selective incorporation doctrine, the mechanical application of provisions of the first eight amendments—by their terms applicable only to the federal government—to the states as well.[57] Friendly's concern was in part the inflexibility of the federal regime thereby imposed on the states and in part the questionable basis and reach of a number of the Warren Court's decisions interpreting specific Bill of Rights provisions.[58]

But what animates the article is Friendly's larger concern with the Supreme Court's seeming indifference to any countervailing interests and its unwillingness to place any limits on its newly expanded rights and remedies. As Friendly observed, "Maximizing protection to persons suspected of crime was hardly [the Framers'] sole objective; the famous words of the Preamble speak of establishing justice, insuring domestic tranquility, and promoting the general welfare."[59] He continued in even more practical terms, speaking of the line of precedent that would culminate in the *Miranda*[60] decision:

> Kidnapping raises the issue still more poignantly. If such a tragedy were to strike at the family of a writer who is enthused about extending the assistance of counsel clause to the station house, would he really believe the fundamental liberties of the suspect demanded the summoning of a lawyer, or at least a clear warning as to the right immediately to consult one, before the police began questioning in an effort to retrieve his child?[61]

The companion piece, *Is Innocence Irrelevant?*,[62] had a different target. The Warren Court was in the midst of a campaign to expand habeas corpus for state prisoners.[63] This took the form of extending the writ from its historic function of testing the authority of a jailer into a device for de novo review by lower federal courts of anything in a state court criminal case to which the label of constitutional error could be attached. And, as the Supreme Court was rapidly cultivating the garden of new rights so labeled, the effect was a revolution, only partly completed at the time that Friendly wrote.

The title of Friendly's habeas lecture raised the question whether the Warren Court had lost sight of the central objectives of criminal law: to convict the guilty so as to deter crime and to protect the public while taking all reasonable precautions to avoid conviction of innocent defendants. Many of the Warren Court's substantive rulings were concerned with neither of these goals but with other objectives: for example, with excluding illegally seized but often reliable evidence[64] and with giving the poor the same opportunities to thwart police interrogation as were enjoyed by the rich.[65]

Friendly thought it unsound that federal courts should spend their time undoing state court convictions of defendants whose trials had provided them with basic fairness and who made not the slightest pretense of actual innocence. Friendly's own remedy was that habeas should be restricted to cases of fundamental unfairness or, absent that, error coupled with some showing of potential innocence.[66] In time, the pendulum did swing back, although along a somewhat different axis.[67]

Friendly's concern with the real world was not limited to such large issues. Many of his decisions remind one of Jackson's arresting injections of common sense into his opinions.[68] For example, in explaining the rule allowing inconsistent jury verdicts in criminal cases, Friendly added that "[t]he vogue for repetitive multiple count indictments may well produce an increase in seemingly inconsistent jury verdicts, where in fact the jury is using its power to prevent the punishment from getting too far out of line with the crime."[69]

Similarly, in Friendly's article *"Some Kind of Hearing,"*[70] there is a passage in which he suggests differentiating between license denial and license revocation, adding that even the Magna Carta drew the distinction;[71] and, more broadly, he urges that some consequences in some contexts do not justify the cost of hearings and that the extent of a hearing should vary with need and cost.[72] He put these recipes into effect in his own management as chief judge of the special railroad court, whose achievements included assigning (within a relatively brief period) a dollar value to the entire northeastern railroad system, which was being taken over by the government.[73]

A story exists that the prospect of a district court judgeship had once been presented to Friendly and that, to inform himself, he spent some hours watching proceedings in the federal district court in Manhattan, concluding that the job was not for him. Yet when he took over the railroad court, he and his two colleagues managed the litigation, narrowing the legal issues in a series of opinions; and, without the use of special masters, they superintended the mammoth discovery of facts pertinent to the valuation puzzle. After four years of discovery, in a matter that could have lasted decades, a set of opinions on major issues precipitated settlements for all of the railroads but one (whose claim was then swiftly resolved on the merits).[74]

This brings us to a third element in Friendly's work: a combination of rigor, candor, and depth. Even the many admirers of the Warren Court must admit that its decisions in the 1960s and 1970s are not always models of serious reflection. Fiercer critics have pointed to doubtful assumptions of fact, rhetorical overstatement, law-office history, a wrenching of constitutional phrases from historical context, and an unwillingness to address contrary arguments or to acknowledge limits on the generalizations abundantly produced.[75]

"Conventional notions of finality of litigation," said Justice Brennan in a habeas case, "have no place where life or liberty is at stake and infringement of constitutional rights is alleged."[76] "Why do they have *no* place?" asked Friendly in his article on habeas, going on to point out the implications and weaknesses of Brennan's rhetoric.[77] In his *Bill of Rights* lecture, Friendly compared a sonorous pronouncement of Chief Justice Taft in defense of property rights with an almost identically phrased one by Justice Goldberg in a civil liberties case.[78]

By contrast, Friendly's own opinions sought to grapple with the underlying dilemmas in cases: to reveal the tensions between policies and the confusions in the precedents and to acknowledge that one goal often comes at the price of another. None of this made him doubt the capacity of reason to resolve an issue—he almost never showed Hand's unease[79]— nor was Friendly hesitant about coming to conclusions and laying down rules. After all, for decades as a lawyer he had made decisions or given advice on which others would act. And he had the skilled craftsman's confidence that the process of legal thinking would lead him in the right direction.

In this belief, Friendly in part reflected the outlook of the legal process movement that came to dominate Harvard Law School from World War II through the mid-1960s. Once again, the protean Thomas Reed Powell was a forerunner. Powell, who knew and admired John Dewey, had leanings both toward pragmatism and toward the weight that Thayer placed on self-restraint and stare decisis. But Powell, perhaps above all else, was concerned with the integrity of the process of judging. The minimum, Powell thought, was (in the words of a scholar)

> internal coherence, consistency with professed criteria, and fair treatment of the existing precedents, whether favorable or not. The most vital ingredient, however, was "intellectual rectitude"; judges must "support their judgments with that degree of candor" that will provide "adequate disclosure of the real steps by which they have reached where they are."[80]

The emphasis on these values came to represent a school of legal thought to which many figures contributed. The canonical text is Hart and Sacks's *The Legal Process*, and the hallmark phrase is "reasoned elaboration."[81] Of this technique Friendly was a master, and he was greatly admired by the Harvard Law School faculty of the 1960s. But Friendly was an exemplar and not a product of such thinking; as already noted, his own legal education had covered a period of greater ferment,[82] and it was probably the richer for it.

But why should rigor in reasoning and candor in expression matter in judicial opinions? Especially in constitutional law, as it has developed in this country, analysis can take one only so far—for example, in resolving matters for which the framers used general language but (so far as we can tell) gave no precise thought. In such instances an instinct for judicial statesmanship matters more than technical excellence. Even candor perhaps can occasionally be unwise: Would it have been better in *Brown v. Board of Education*[83] for the Court to have dwelled on the weight of precedent, or might this have been the wrong occasion to sound an uncertain trumpet?

Yet a sound decision, even if its origins lie (as they often do) in the instinct of the experienced judge, is usually confirmed and fine-tuned by good reasoning. Hand, it appears, sometimes wrote a decision both ways to see which one worked best. So, too, good reasoning tends to check bad results, overexpansive holdings, or unnecessary dicta. Thus, a judge may report back to colleagues that the tentative conclusion reached at *semble* after the oral argument "just would not write." To rest on rhetoric instead of analysis leads not merely to poor thinking but also to results that are poorer than they need be.

For example, if the exclusionary rule for illegally seized evidence in state courts had been developed thoughtfully, *Mapp v. Ohio*[84] would have been a better opinion and more widely accepted. As Friendly suggested,[85] the rule might well have directed the exclusion of evidence where it was seized in patent violation of the Fourth Amendment but not (in Cardozo's phrase) where the constable had merely blundered.[86] The deterrent value of exclusion is minimal for inadvertent fumbles, and the evidence remains reliable albeit wrongly seized. The Supreme Court has been inching in this direction.[87] How much better to have struck the balance at the outset.

Nowhere is the rigor of Friendly's thinking more in evidence than in his Dartmouth Holmes Lecture devoted to the so-called state action doctrine.[88] This is the label for a set of Supreme Court decisions determining when action is so governmental as to bring into play constitutional constraints that apply only to official (as opposed to private) conduct. Lowering the threshold could bring vast areas of previously private conduct within the Constitution and so within the reach of the federal courts.

At the time Friendly spoke, it was unclear whether the balance was going to tip in the direction of a major enlargement of this sphere, for example, by treating at least some corporations as state actors, so as to expand the kinds of activities treated as inherently governmental, or by extending the state action label to the state toleration of private discrimination. His lecture treats with exquisite subtlety the case law, the possibilities for line drawing, and the dangers of a promiscuous enlargement of the state action category.

Friendly saw that his own vision was more likely to prevail if the Supreme Court did not attempt to lay down the abstract doctrines that it had so favored in the criminal area but rather confined itself to results:

> Today's activist Court has thus far been treading rather cautiously in the area we have been discussing. . . . The lack of satisfactory theoretical explication may have been an advantage rather than the ground for criticism it seemed at first to be; on the whole it may be better that the Court should

plot a few reference points, even on what may be largely an intuitive basis, which can be erased if they prove unwise, before it attempts to project a curve to which all future determinations must conform.[89]

There may be some irony in having Friendly, himself a master of synthesis and the projection of doctrine, recommend that the Supreme Court concentrate on results rather than reasoning. But he was nothing if not practical and, as with criminal law, he trusted the Court's intuitive judgment more than its explanations. He had one more practical lesson in mind, warning that legislative action to resolve unrighted wrongs was the key: "[W]e can learn a lesson from the consequences of the long legislative default in the reform of criminal procedure if we only will."[90]

This Dartmouth Holmes Lecture, like much of his academic writings, showed a continuing interplay between Friendly's scholarship and his judicial writing.[91] An issue addressed in an opinion might spark further reflections in a talk or book review; a synthesis developed in a lecture could provide context for an opinion. With ease, Friendly bridged the gap, which has sadly grown wider since his time, between the twin worlds of legal scholarship and the law in action.

The same lecture, along with much else that he wrote, illustrates the final facet of Friendly's approach to constitutional issues on which we have time to dwell: temperance. Most of Friendly's writings on constitutional law aim at intermediate solutions: *Swift* was wrong but federal common law—a much narrower and better-justified variation on *Swift* —is right; the exclusionary rule is justifiable (perhaps) but not for reasonable violations of officers committed in good faith; habeas should go beyond jurisdictional error but with marked qualifications such as a threshold showing of potential innocence; the state action label should be applied beyond the classic case of the purely government actor but with great discretion.

This is what Paul Freund, speaking of Lewis Powell, called "the gift of moderation"[92] and, quoting Thomas Fuller, the "silken string running through the pearl-chain of all virtues."[93] So, too, the *Book of Common Prayer*, in a passage that might have been written for judges, lauds "the happy mean between too much stiffness in refusing, and too much easiness in admitting variations in things once advisedly established."[94] As Friendly himself said in the Dartmouth Holmes Lecture—the phrase was addressed to a particular issue but could have been a motto—"I prefer the midway course, with all its difficulties."[95]

The argument for temperance in making new constitutional law is familiar. A statutory interpretation, a reading of an agency rule, and a new direction in common law: all these can be overturned by legislation. A constitutional ruling, with limited exceptions,[96] tends to be final—regardless of what Congress or anyone else thinks about it—unless or until the Court changes its mind. It is therefore easy to argue for a presumption against interference. Hand said that a law that gets enacted is likely to be "not wholly unreasonable";[97] for federal enactments, it is probably constitutional as well.

Yet little in Friendly's writings or decisions shows a mechanical hostility to judicial intervention. Friendly knew that much of constitutional law was open ended and that choices were available to judges. And unlike Holmes, he was not a skeptic about betterment. On the contrary, his pragmatic impulse was strong. Speaking in praise of Frankfurter, he said: "[T]o [Frankfurter], as to Brandeis, law was preeminently an aspect of public affairs, an instrument for maximizing the goodness of life for all."[98] These were two of the men that Friendly most admired. Consider, as well, the following passage from the introduction to Friendly's *Bill of Rights* lecture:

> [T]here are few brighter pages in the history of the Supreme Court than its efforts over the past forty years to improve the administration of criminal justice. How can any lawyer not be proud of the decisions condemning convictions obtained by mob rule, testimony known to the prosecutor to be perjured, coerced confessions, or trial by newspaper? . . . [Or] insistence that persons charged with serious crime shall receive the assistance of counsel at their pleas and trials[?] . . . [T]he fingers of one hand would outnumber the instances where I disagree with decisions, as distinguished from opinions, in this area.[99]

But while Friendly believed that law was an instrument for social change, he also believed that, as Thayer had taught, legislators must take the lead in altering the law, and that courts should be slow to interfere with considered legislative judgments and cautious when they do so. This view reinforced his respect for the craft's constraints—which temper the pace and extent of intervention and changes in the law by judges. He was thus often counted as a conservative judge, but this label—so far as it implies conservative political values—is misleading.

Friendly's judicial career coincided with the Warren Court era—certainly the most liberal federal judiciary in American history—and against that backdrop his generally moderate views appear conservative. Critics of the Warren Court were free to seize on Friendly's pointed criticisms for their own ends, ignoring the fact that many were directed only to the breadth of the opinions and the weaknesses of analysis. They also ignored the truth that Friendly was often for reform but discriminated as to when it was within the province of judges.

One clue lies in Friendly's ever-present concern with relative competence. Judges are good at working out what kind of hearing the Constitution ought to—and therefore will—provide in diverse circumstances. Procedural rights in criminal cases are, and should be, a specialty of judges. But the bench, he thought, is perhaps less well equipped to decide when to innovate where divisive issues of social policy are at stake or where a solution requires the kind of information or line drawing in which Congress has the advantage.

Friendly's article subtitled *Judges Who Can't and Legislators Who Won't*[100] speaks directly to this subject. It is a thoughtful explanation—with roots in Thayer and Brandeis—of why legislatures, having superior information and a greater choice in solutions, are usually better than courts at solving large social problems. But, of course, the larger context is the ability of legislatures to reflect public preferences and the doubtful charter of judges to act as what Hand called "Platonic Guardians."[101] Elected officials, after all, can easily be replaced.

Friendly would readily have joined in *Brown v. Board of Education*,[102] sharing none of the doubts Hand expressed in his own Holmes Lecture.[103] Indeed, speaking of *Shelley v. Kraemer*,[104] Friendly later wrote: "[M]ost people would say of it, as Paul Freund is reputed to have said of *Brown v. Board of Education*, 'can you imagine it having been decided in the other way?'"[105] Whatever the claims of stare decisis, the Equal Protection Clause spoke directly to racial discrimination. Similarly, Friendly's notion of using the First Amendment against McCarthyesque abuses was more aggressive than the Warren Court's procedural tactics.[106] But, again, the language of the First Amendment and its historical concern with protecting political speech gave some warrant for what he proposed.

It is not surprising that Friendly, according to Judge Randolph's report, faced the abortion issue later resolved in *Roe v. Wade*[107] and tentatively came out the other way before the case was mooted by New York's repeal of the challenged statute.[108] Friendly's draft opinion makes the familiar arguments: for example, that the extension sought by the plaintiffs would imperil a good many other statutes not yet brought into question, such as those punishing attempted suicide, sodomy, bestiality, and perhaps drug use.[109] Friendly said that the Constitution did not enact "Mill's views on the proper limits of law-making."[110]

One closing observation in the opinion is of special interest, however, and is underscored by Friendly's own dislike of the New York anti-abortion statute, which is clearly expressed in the opinion. The opinion concludes with one of his signature multipart sentences:

> The contest on this, as on other issues where there is determined opposition, must be fought out through the democratic process, not by utilizing the courts as a way of overcoming the opposition of what plaintiffs assume but we cannot know to be a minority and thus clearing the decks, thereby enabl[ing] legislators to evade their proper responsibilities.[111]

No one can prove that a judge should take Friendly's temperate approach to changing settled rules of constitutional law. Self-restraint was Holmes's view of a judge's role, but it was not John Marshall's or Hugo Black's or Roger Traynor's. As it happens, Friendly had a grudging respect for Black, fighting successfully to get him an honorary degree from Harvard, and his tribute to Traynor, a liberal judge, was titled, *Ablest Judge of His Generation*.[112] What mattered most to Friendly was that Black and Traynor, although different from one another, each had a commitment to law.

What should be said in closing about Friendly's influence? In contrast to almost all other lower court judges, whose views rarely outlive them, Friendly did have an effect on the legal landscape in a few areas: for example, in crafting the template for the modern view of federal common law and in calling for a saner balance in criminal law between the interests of defendants and the needs of society. So also, Friendly's skeptical view in his Dartmouth College Holmes Lecture toward expansion of the state action doctrine[113] has largely prevailed, with only small back-and-forth shifts in where the line is drawn.[114]

Still, these results owe more to a shift in the tidal current than to any individual's views. And Friendly did not bequeath to us an explicit philosophy of law or, in contrast to Holmes and Cardozo, express much interest in the subject. His own attitude was a composite of the influences already described: his training as a historian and respect for precedent, a dose of legal realism, a pragmatic interest in outcomes, a respect for legal process, an insistence on relative competence, a sense of what is practical, and a concern with judicial overreaching.

Friendly tended to decide cases from the inside out; he knew, as the critic Louis Menand observed in his study of Holmes and his circle, that "a case comes to court as a unique fact situation" and enters a "vortex of discursive imperatives," an "unpredictable weather pattern" of diverse pressures to conform to precedent, to do justice, to achieve a socially useful result, and so on.[115] A judge's first take is often an intuitive response to these pressures. The obligation remains to test this first approximation against reasoning and to articulate an explanation. Judging is about exercising judgment, for which no mechanical formula has yet been found adequate.

Friendly's influence on the law, including constitutional law, is primarily of a different kind. He provides a model—of ability, of scholarship, of integrity in analysis, of practicality, and of balanced judgment—for others who labor in the same workshop. Even after years in the profession, one learns in reading a Friendly opinion what can be wrought out of such virtues, coupled with immense hard work, and what great judging can be.

Grant Gilmore once wrote that "the opinions of our better judges set a model for rational and humane discourse which the rest of us can only envy."[116] No one on the federal circuit courts ever did this better than Henry Friendly and Learned Hand. No one ever will.

NOTES

1. Professor Barnett identified 813 majority opinions for the circuit court. Stephen R. Barnett, *Henry Jacob Friendly, in* YALE BIOGRAPHICAL DICTIONARY OF AMERICAN LAW (Roger K. Newman ed., 2009). In addition to these opinions, Judge Friendly wrote majority opinions for three-judge district courts and for the railroad reorganization court whose work he described in his tribute to Judge Wisdom. Henry J. Friendly, *From a Fellow Worker on the Railroads*, 60 TUL. L. REV. 244, 246–54 (1985). A complete count of Friendly's opinions would also include his concurrences and dissents.

2. Friendly's books include HENRY J. FRIENDLY, FEDERAL JURISDICTION: A GENERAL VIEW (1973); his bound Holmes Lectures at Harvard, THE FEDERAL ADMINISTRATIVE AGENCIES: THE NEED FOR BETTER DEFINITION OF STANDARDS (1962) [hereinafter FRIENDLY, THE FEDERAL ADMINISTRATIVE AGENCIES] and at Dartmouth, THE DARTMOUTH COLLEGE CASE AND THE PUBLIC-PRIVATE PENUMBRA (1969)

[hereinafter FRIENDLY, THE DARTMOUTH COLLEGE CASE]; and a collection of essays, articles, and lectures entitled BENCHMARKS (1967) [hereinafter FRIENDLY, BENCHMARKS].

3. *See infra* notes 24–32 and accompanying text.

4. *See infra* note 35 and accompanying text.

5. LEO GOTTLIEB, CLEARY, GOTTLIEB, STEEN & HAMILTON: THE FIRST THIRTY YEARS 32 (1983).

6. *Id.*

7. Professor Freund refers, as examples, to McIlwain, Merk, and Langer—he could easily have added Turner—in comparing Hand's experience as a philosophy student with James, Royce, and Santayana in Harvard's golden age of philosophy. Paul A. Freund, Remarks at the Unveiling of the Bust of Judge Henry J. Friendly 5 (Mar. 27, 1989).

8. Friendly described McIlwain as the one who, more than anyone else, brought F. W. Maitland and his approach to America. Henry J. Friendly, *Mr. Justice Frankfurter*, 51 VA. L. REV. 552, 552 (1965).

9. GOTTLIEB, *supra* note 5, at 32.

10. Friendly, *supra* note 8, at 552.

11. GOTTLIEB, *supra* note 5, at 32.

12. *Id.*

13. For four descriptive tributes to Powell, see generally Felix Frankfurter, *Thomas Reed Powell*, 69 HARV. L. REV. 797 (1956); Paul A. Freund, *Thomas Reed Powell*, 69 HARV. L. REV. 800 (1956); Erwin N. Griswold, *Thomas Reed Powell*, 69 HARV. L. REV. 793 (1956); Henry M. Hart, Jr., *Thomas Reed Powell*, 69 HARV. L. REV. 804 (1956).

14. Thomas Reed Powell, *My Philosophy of Law, in* MY PHILOSOPHY OF LAW: CREDOS OF SIXTEEN AMERICAN SCHOLARS 269, 280 (Julius Rosenthal Found. ed., 1941); *see also* Freund, *supra* note 7.

15. *See* James B. Thayer, *The Origin and Scope of the American Doctrine of Constitutional Law*, 7 HARV. L. REV. 129, 136–38, 150–52 (1893).

16. *See* Henry J. Friendly, *Mr. Justice Brandeis: The Quest for Reason*, 108 U. PA. L. REV. 985, 992 (1960).

17. *See generally* ALPHEUS THOMAS MASON, BRANDEIS: A FREE MAN'S LIFE 4 (1946).

18. Professor Freund quotes Frankfurter's letter to Friendly: "Your fullest fruition would be not at the bar but in this school. . . . Such powers as you have call for their fulfillment as much as Kreisler's gifts call for playing the violin." Freund, *supra* note 7.

19. MARTIN MAYER, EMORY BUCKNER 141–44 (1968).

20. Leo Gottlieb, *Honorable Henry J. Friendly (1903–1986)*, 28 CLEARGOLAW NEWS 155, 158 (1986).

21. GERALD GUNTHER, LEARNED HAND: THE MAN AND THE JUDGE 650 (1994). Hand's letter spoke of Friendly's "unblemished reputation," "high scholarship," "balanced wisdom," and "wide outlook." *Id.*

22. Editorial, *Mr. Friendly for the Bench*, N.Y. TIMES, Mar. 11, 1959, at 34.

23. Henry J. Friendly, *Reactions of a Lawyer—Newly Become Judge*, 71 YALE L.J. 218, 219–22 (1961).

24. FRIENDLY, BENCHMARKS, *supra* note 2, contains many but by no means all of the lectures, articles, and tributes.

25. 304 U.S. 64 (1938).

26. Henry J. Friendly, *In Praise of* Erie—*And of the New Federal Common Law*, 39 N.Y.U. L. REV. 383 (1964).

27. FRIENDLY, THE FEDERAL ADMINISTRATIVE AGENCIES, *supra* note 2.

28. FRIENDLY, THE DARTMOUTH COLLEGE CASE, *supra* note 2.

29. Henry J. Friendly, *The Fifth Amendment Tomorrow: The Case for Constitutional Change*, 37 U. CIN. L. REV. 671 (1968).

30. Henry J. Friendly, *"Some Kind of Hearing,"* 123 U. PA. L. REV. 1267 (1975).

31. Henry J. Friendly, *The Bill of Rights as a Code of Criminal Procedure*, 53 CAL. L. REV. 929 (1965).

32. Henry J. Friendly, *Is Innocence Irrelevant? Collateral Attacks on Criminal Judgments*, 38 U. CHI. L. REV. 142 (1970).

33. HENRY M. HART & HERBERT WECHSLER, THE FEDERAL COURTS AND THE FEDERAL SYSTEM (1953).

34. Henry J. Friendly, *In Praise of Herbert Wechsler*, 78 COLUM. L. REV. 974, 974 (1978).

35. Henry J. Friendly, *A Shattering Book from Beacon Hill*, N.Y. TIMES, Aug. 11, 1963, § 7 (Book Review), at 6 (reviewing MARK DEWOLFE HOWE, JUSTICE OLIVER WENDELL HOLMES, VOL. II: THE PROVING YEARS, 1870–1882 (1963) and OLIVER WENDELL HOLMES, THE COMMON LAW (Mark DeWolfe Howe ed., 1963)).

36. Nolan v. Transocean Air Lines, 276 F.2d 280, 281 (2d Cir. 1960). Or consider another Friendly classic: "We cannot subscribe to plaintiffs' view that the Eighth Commandment 'Thou shalt not steal' is part of the law of nations." IIT v. Vencap Ltd., 519 F.2d 1001, 1015 (2d Cir. 1975).

37. GUNTHER, *supra* note 21.

38. *See id.* at 306–10.

39. United States v. Aluminum Co. of Am., 148 F.2d 416, 427–30 (2d Cir. 1945).

40. United States v. Annunziato, 293 F.2d 373, 378 (2d Cir. 1961).

41. Willard Hurst, *Who Is the "Great" Appellate Judge?*, 24 IND. L.J. 394, 399 (1949).

42. Learned Hand, *Mr. Justice Holmes at Eighty-five, in* THE SPIRIT OF LIBERTY 24, 24 (Irving Dilliard ed., 1952).

43. Friendly, *supra* note 26.

44. Erie R.R. v. Tompkins, 304 U.S. 64 (1938).

45. 41 U.S. 1 (1842).

46. Friendly, *supra* note 26, at 384.

47. Judge Clark had criticized Brandeis's supposed failure to realize that *Swift's* doctrine, "already tending toward decay and death, did not need the sledgehammer blows" of *Erie*. Charles E. Clark, *State Law in the Federal Courts: The Brooding Omnipresence of* Erie v. Tompkins, 55 YALE L.J. 267, 295 (1946).

48. Ch. 20, § 34, 1 Stat. 73, 92 (codified as amended at 28 U.S.C. § 1652 (2000)). This view, reading the Judiciary Act to bind federal courts to respect state common law as well as statutory law, had been endorsed by Justice Reed in his *Erie* concurrence. 304 U.S. at 91 (Reed, J., concurring).
49. Friendly, *supra* note 26, at 386–88.
50. *Id.* at 388–91.
51. *Id.* at 392–98.
52. *Id.* at 398.
53. 339 F.2d 823 (2d Cir. 1964).
54. *Id.* at 825.
55. On competence, see Henry J. Friendly, *The Gap in Lawmaking—Judges Who Can't and Legislators Who Won't*, 63 COLUM L. REV. 787 (1963) [hereinafter Friendly, *The Gap in Lawmaking*], and Friendly's Harvard Holmes Lectures, FRIENDLY, THE FEDERAL ADMINISTRATIVE AGENCIES, *supra* note 2. On statutory language, see Henry J. Friendly, *Mr. Justice Frankfurter and the Reading of Statutes, in* FELIX FRANKFURTER: THE JUDGE 30 (Wallace Mendelson ed., 1964).
56. Friendly, *supra* note 31.
57. *Id.* at 933–38 ("Whatever one's views about the historical support for Mr. Justice Black's wholesale incorporation theory, it appears undisputed that the selective incorporation theory has none.").
58. *See, e.g.,* Griffin v. California, 380 U.S. 609 (1965) (incorporating Fifth Amendment protection against commentary by prosecutor on silence of accused); Escobedo v. Illinois, 378 U.S. 478 (1964) (incorporating qualified Sixth Amendment guarantee of consultation with counsel); Mapp v. Ohio, 367 U.S. 643 (1961) (incorporating exclusionary rule for Fourth Amendment violations).
59. Friendly, *supra* note 31, at 948.
60. Miranda v. Arizona, 384 U.S. 436, 444 (1966) (holding that evidence obtained as a result of interrogation is inadmissible unless prosecution demonstrates that prescribed warnings were given).
61. Friendly, *supra* note 31, at 949.
62. Friendly, *supra* note 32.
63. *See, e.g.,* Fay v. Noia, 372 U.S. 391, 426–27, 435 (1963) (limiting federal habeas statute's exhaustion requirement to "state remedies still open to the habeas applicant at the time he files his application in federal court"); Townsend v. Sain, 372 U.S. 293, 312–13 (1963) ("Where the facts are in dispute, the federal court in habeas corpus must hold an evidentiary hearing if the habeas applicant did not receive a full and fair evidentiary hearing in a state court. . . .").
64. Mapp v. Ohio, 367 U.S. 643, 648–49 (1961).
65. *Miranda*, 384 U.S. at 472–73.
66. Friendly, *supra* note 32, at 160.
67. *See, e.g.,* Antiterrorism and Effective Death Penalty Act of 1996, Pub. L. No. 104-132, §§ 101–107, 110 Stat. 1214, 1217–26 (codified at 28 U.S.C. §§ 2244, 2253–55, 2261–66 (2000)) (establishing limits to habeas review); Wainwright v. Sykes, 433 U.S. 72, 90–91 (1977) (adopting cause-and-prejudice test for unpreserved claims of unconstitutional admissions of evidence); Stone v. Powell, 428 U.S. 465,

494–96 (1976) (holding that where state has provided full and fair opportunity to present Fourth Amendment claim, state prisoner cannot obtain habeas relief for admission of evidence obtained by unconstitutional search or seizure).

68. Especially memorable is Jackson's summing up of certain rules governing impeachment as "archaic, paradoxical and full of compromises and compensations," but then concluding, "[t]o pull one misshapen stone out of the grotesque structure is more likely simply to upset its present balance between adverse interests than to establish a rational edifice." Michelson v. United States, 335 U.S. 469, 486 (1948).

69. United States v. Maybury, 274 F.2d 899, 902 (2d Cir. 1960). For another example of Friendly's practicality, see his treatment of interlocutory appeals in *Parkinson v. April Industries, Inc.*, 520 F.2d 650, 659–60 (2d Cir. 1975) (Friendly, J., concurring).

70. Friendly, *supra* note 30.

71. *Id.* at 1295–96.

72. *Id.* at 1275–76.

73. *See* Friendly, *supra* note 1, at 244, 247, 253–54 (discussing work of special railroad court).

74. *Id.* at 253–54.

75. *See, e.g.*, ALEXANDER M. BICKEL, THE SUPREME COURT AND THE IDEA OF PROGRESS 45–101 (1978); PHILIP B. KURLAND, POLITICS, THE CONSTITUTION, AND THE WARREN COURT, 101–06 (1970); Alfred H. Kelly, *Clio and the Court: An Illicit Love Affair*, 1965 SUP. CT. REV. 119, 135–42 (1965).

76. Sanders v. United States, 373 U.S. 1, 8 (1963).

77. Friendly, *supra* note 32, at 149.

78. *See* Friendly, *supra* note 31, at 955 & n.141 (noting similarity of language used in Pointer v. Texas, 380 U.S. 400, 413 (1965) (Goldberg, J., concurring), and Truax v. Corrigan, 257 U.S. 312, 338 (1921) (Taft, C.J.)).

79. *See supra* note 38 and accompanying text (comparing writing styles of Friendly and Hand).

80. John Braeman, *Thomas Reed Powell on the Roosevelt Court*, 5 CONST. COMMENT. 143, 150 (1988) (quoting Thomas Reed Powell, *Some Aspects of American Constitutional Law*, 53 HARV. L. REV. 529, 549–50, 552 (1940)).

81. HENRY M. HART, JR. & ALBERT M. SACKS, THE LEGAL PROCESS: BASIC PROBLEMS IN THE MAKING AND APPLICATION OF LAW (tent. ed. 1958) was finally published in 1994 in an edition edited by William Eskridge and Philip Frickey whose introductory essay recounts the history of the movement in the context of its development in the United States. William N. Eskridge, Jr. & Philip P. Frickey, *An Historical and Critical Introduction to* The Legal Process, *in* HART & SACKS, *supra*, at li (William N. Eskridge, Jr. & Philip P. Frickey eds., 1994); *see also* Braeman, *supra* note 80, at 150 (describing Powell as intellectual father of "reasoned elaboration" school).

82. *See supra* text accompanying notes 13–15.

83. 347 U.S. 483 (1954).

84. 367 U.S. 643 (1961).

85. *See supra* notes 66–67 and accompanying text.

86. People v. Defore, 150 N.E. 585, 587 (N.Y. 1926).

87. *See* United States v. Leon, 468 U.S. 897, 926 (1984) (holding that exclusionary rule does not apply when officers rely in good faith on invalid warrant); Stone v. Powell, 428 U.S. 465, 482 (1976) (denying federal habeas relief for introduction of unconstitutional evidence at trial).

88. FRIENDLY, THE DARTMOUTH COLLEGE CASE, *supra* note 2.

89. *Id.* at 31 (citations omitted).

90. *Id.*

91. For example, Friendly also addressed state action issues in cases. *See* Jackson v. Statler Found., 496 F.2d 623, 636–41 (2d Cir. 1974) (Friendly, J., dissenting from denial of reconsideration en banc) ("A holding that an otherwise private institution has become an arm of the state . . . can have far more serious consequences than a determination that the state has impermissibly fostered private discrimination.").

92. Paul A. Freund, *Justice Powell—the Meaning of Moderation*, 68 VA. L. REV. 169, 169 (1982).

93. *Id.* at 170 (quoting 2 THOMAS FULLER, THE HOLY STATE AND THE PROFANE STATE 205 (Maximilian Graff Walten ed., AMS Press, Inc. 1966) (1642)).

94. *Preface* to THE BOOK OF COMMON PRAYER, at v, v (1928) (1789).

95. FRIENDLY, THE DARTMOUTH COLLEGE CASE, *supra* note 2, at 23 (advocating against all-or-nothing approach to Fourteenth Amendment state action restrictions on charitable institutions).

96. Although constitutional amendments and jurisdiction-stripping statutes are sometimes employed, the principal means of undoing mistaken constitutional decisions is the appointing of new Justices, an alternative with the disadvantages of uncertainty and delay.

97. Hand, *supra* note 42, at 28.

98. Henry J. Friendly, Mr. Justice Frankfurter, Remarks at a Memorial Meeting of the Bar of the Supreme Court of the United States (Oct. 25, 1965), *in* FRIENDLY, BENCHMARKS, *supra* note 2, at 320.

99. Friendly, *supra* note 31, at 931.

100. Friendly, *The Gap in Lawmaking*, *supra* note 55, at 791–92 (discussing legislative superiority to courts in fact gathering, generality, pragmatism, transformation, prospectivity, and legitimacy).

101. LEARNED HAND, THE BILL OF RIGHTS 73 (1958).

102. *See* Henry J. Friendly, *The Public-Private Penumbra—Fourteen Years Later*, 130 U. PA. L. REV. 1289, 1292 (1982) [hereinafter Friendly, *The Public-Private Penumbra*] ("The equal protection clause does not allow a state or a city to institutionalize Jim Crow."); Henry J. Friendly, *The Courts and Social Policy: Substance and Procedure*, 33 U. MIAMI L. REV. 22, 29 (1978) (arguing that psychological data in *Brown v. Board of Education*, 347 U.S. 483, 494–95 & n.11 (1954), were unnecessary in light of unconstitutionality of racial discrimination).

103. Hand, *supra* note 42, at 54–55 (arguing that *Brown* and *Bolling v. Sharpe*, 347 U.S. 497 (1954), were reappraisals of legislative decisions and expressing concern

that there was no principle to "explain when the Court will assume the role of a third legislative chamber").

104. 334 U.S. 1 (1948).

105. Friendly, *The Public-Private Penumbra, supra* note 102, at 1292.

106. *See* Friendly, *supra* note 29, at 696–97.

107. 410 U.S. 113 (1973).

108. A. Raymond Randolph, *Before* Roe v. Wade: *Judge Friendly's Draft Abortion Opinion,* 29 HARV. J.L. & PUB. POL'Y 1035, 1037, 1040 (2006).

109. *Id.* at 1038.

110. *Id.* at 1039.

111. *Id.* at 1061.

112. 71 CAL. L. REV. 1039 (1983). Friendly put Hand to one side, noting that Hand had begun his work many years before Traynor and ended it earlier. *Id.* at 1039 n.1.

113. FRIENDLY, THE DARTMOUTH COLLEGE CASE, *supra* note 2, at 11–12.

114. *Compare, e.g.,* Am. Mfrs. Mut. Ins. Co. v. Sullivan, 526 U.S. 40, 43–44 (1999) (holding that insurers acting pursuant to state workers' compensation scheme are not state actors), *with* Brentwood Acad. v. Tenn. Secondary Sch. Ass'n, 531 U.S. 288, 291 (2001) (holding that regulation of public school athletics by non-profit interscholastic association constitutes state action), *and* Lebron v. Nat'l R.R. Passenger Corp., 513 U.S. 374, 400 (1995) (holding that government-created and -controlled corporations are part of government for First Amendment purposes).

115. LOUIS MENAND, THE METAPHYSICAL CLUB 339 (2001).

116. GRANT GILMORE, THE AGES OF AMERICAN LAW 16 (1977).

7

Toward One America

A Vision in Law

J. HARVIE WILKINSON III

Introduction

The present age will go down in American history as a partisan and polarizing one. Indeed, that may be its defining characteristic. America has had deeply divisive eras before—the Federalist-Republican period and the Civil War spring to mind—but those eras divided over deeply consequential principles. The partisan differences of the present era are hardly insignificant, but these differences do not justify what can be described without exaggeration as the sheer magnitude of mutual hate. Thus again we have an America defined by colors—red and blue states—less portentous than the Civil War's blue and gray, but in their own way sapping the nation's common bonds and sense of strength.

It would be surprising if the acrimony of the political system had left the courts unscathed. Still no one anticipated *Bush v. Gore.*[1] "Although we may never know with complete certainty the identity of the winner of this year's Presidential election," reads the impassioned coda of Justice Stevens's dissent, "the identity of the loser is perfectly clear. It is the Nation's confidence in the judge as an impartial guardian of the rule of law."[2] The expression capped a judicial era of deep factional divisions, contrary to the founding years of our Republic, when the partisan strife

This lecture was delivered on October 2, 2007, and appeared in *83 N.Y.U. L. Rev. 323* (2008).

in the political arena was met by an extraordinary degree of unanimity in the Third Branch.[3]

If law is part of the problem of polarization, it should likewise be part of the solution. In other words, law should consciously aspire to promote a stronger sense of national cohesion. We have not traditionally thought of law in these terms. The great purposes of law have historically been the preservation of order in which freedom may flourish and the protection of liberty itself from overreaching by the State.

To these must now be added a third great purpose—that of maintaining a concept of American nationhood in a divisive and rapidly evolving age. It is hard to overstate the need for a national purpose in law. The gravity of our divisions demands it. The structural manifestations of our divisions—the gerrymandering of congressional districts to reflect each party's political base; the constant electioneering that leaves less time and opportunity for governance; the twenty-four-hour news cycle replete with cable, blogs, talk radio, and online news sites; the bitter judicial confirmation battles; the willingness of partisans to impeach or destroy character or to criminalize political differences—all these have led to the disintegration of civility and the ascendancy of partisanship.

The divisions in the body politic tell but part of the story. The changing demographics of this country augur a future of rich and challenging diversity, in which no ethnic group is a majority and the boundaries of race and ethnicity may become increasingly less distinct. In an age of varied national origins and ethnic heritages, it becomes important for law to celebrate commonality as well as to appreciate difference.

And in a nation where liberal and conservative, secular and sectarian, sunbelt and rustbelt, senior and junior, manual and informational, expose ever sharper fault lines, it becomes imperative that law bridge, not broaden, America's new gaps.

It is much easier to posit the need for a unifying role for law than to say how the law should unify. Where one person sees unity, another may see only division. Perhaps then it is best to draw prescriptions from various sides of the current legal debate. Even then, suggesting how national identity might thrive among competing racial, ethnic, regional, generational, religious, and other loyalties is a perilous task.

I nonetheless have seven recommendations. I arrived at seven not because it is the number of the wonders of the ancient world or even the first number of the famous convenience store, but because seven imperatives naturally suggest themselves to me as prerequisites to maintaining even a modest sense of national identity throughout the twenty-first century. I recognize that many of you may dispute this or that point in my talk. My hope, however, is that if adopted these suggestions, taken as a whole, will make us a stronger and healthier country.

I.

Let's respect judicial restraint. By restraint, I mean a healthy judicial regard for the roles and enactments of the coordinate branches of the federal government and the proper functioning of the states. Judicial restraint promotes the pursuit of national unity. The corollary is that judicial activism tends to undermine it.

In advancing this thesis, I have no wish to point a finger. Both right and left have had their fling. *Lochner v. New York* advanced the notion of a personal freedom of contract as part of the liberty protected by the Fourteenth Amendment.[4] *Roe v. Wade* transported substantive due process from the economic to the personal realm.[5] The Rehnquist Court did not break with the notion that substantive due process applied to state legislation,[6] and the Court struck down federal legislation as well under the commerce power[7] and Section 5 of the Fourteenth Amendment.[8] The point here is not whether some forms of activism are more or less justifiable than others. That question is surely debatable, but what is not debatable is that all forms of activism gild the scepter of judicial power.

But why is activism so inimical to national unity? One could argue that a national constitutional standard actually serves a unifying function on occasion by reminding us of the fundamental personal freedoms and governmental structures for which we stand. This is true to some extent— the invalidation of the poll tax, for example, is a valuable reminder that the franchise is something that is open to all.[9]

Taken sufficiently far, however, the idea of a unifying constitutionalism is nothing more than a neat rationalization for judicial supremacy. Such supremacy is deeply divisive, and not just because of the commonly given reason that unelected judges serving for life should not lightly displace the will of the people's chosen representatives.[10]

The underlying reason for the divisiveness of judicial activism is as much cultural as it is legal or political. Judges are drawn from the ranks of one profession only. There are no plumbers or flight attendants or school teachers or investment bankers or firefighters or insurance salesmen in our midst. It is odd, to say the least, that the members of one privileged profession should be making the most intimate and important decisions for the family and the workplace of all other professions. That one entire branch of government has been populated by the members of one profession only is no testament to the innate superiority of lawyers. It is a reminder that with great responsibility should go greater humility, lest the arrogance of legal authority drive resentments through our national heart.

Nor does the divisive potential of an activist bench end there. The courts reflect not only one profession, but the elite reaches of that profession to boot. Many judges—and I do not exempt myself—have been educated at the most exclusive colleges and law schools, have spent their careers in the upper ethers of legal practice or academia, and have served in the upper echelons of state and national government.

This training is superb. It may acquaint us with the workings of government and it may hone first-rate analytical and intellectual skills. It equips us well to perform the important interpretative and courtroom tasks we do. But our backgrounds have not by and large given birth to a breadth of human experience. We judges are as a class bereft of acquaintance with the variegated and pluralistic country that we serve. While we may project and empathize, that is no substitute for first-hand life experience or even the eye-and-ear contact with the electorate that a career in elective politics can bring. The courtroom and the bar conventions and the symposia and those proverbial embassy parties provide detachment and impartiality of a sort, but they regrettably shelter us from the bumps and bruises that attend our fellow citizens' daily lives. Those who enjoy the benefits of deference should not acquire the taste for dictation. Judicial activism is no long-run strategy for national wholeness; the inevitable elitism of a judicial ruling class will spawn a populist rancor in America that will frustrate the attempt to bridge our most basic divides.

II.

My next three recommendations have to do with how we regard our Constitution. This is critical, because how citizens regard their founding charter will influence how they view America itself.

Let's be sparing in what we seek to constitutionalize. Our Constitution sets forth a structure of governance and those basic rights the state may not abridge. It is a document of inclusion that welcomes all citizens into the American fold. Perhaps that is what makes the recent spate of same-sex marriage amendments (federal and state)[11] so at odds with the generous and unifying spirit any constitution must achieve. To forbid same-sex marriage through legislation is one thing. To assign second-class status to gay citizens in our founding charters is something else. Passing amendments whose character will so plainly be perceived as punitive is not the way to One America. Our constitutions must bind wounds, not rub them raw.

If law is to express a national purpose, a constitution must cover very few things. The Second Amendment doesn't need to be read to assign judges the final say over questions of gun control. The Equal Rights Amendment doesn't need to be passed to give judges the final word over relations between the sexes. National unity means a Constitution that embodies only surpassing common values around which citizens can unite. In fact, the Framers bequeathed a document that did not partake of most particulars because each generation must be free to seek its own way and because the most difficult subjects—volatile social issues, tax and budgetary disputes, even war and peace—are most amenable to political compromise that promises today's losers the prospect of tomorrow's change.

To constitutionalize our differences is to up the ante gravely. Legislation implies temporary winners and temporary losers. Constitutionalizing implies permanent winners and permanent losers, the most divisive of all worlds. Constitutionalizing tampers with our legal birthright and common heritage—with what we as a nation hold most dear. It is thus unfortunate when judges decree unenumerated rights to privacy or when legislators seek constitutional status for restrictions on personal rights. The American Constitution should not reflect the agenda of the NRA or NOW or Focus on the Family or NARAL Pro-Choice America. Interest-group politics are fine for Congress, but they threaten to tarnish national trust in the Constitution.

III.

Let's value the nationalism in our Constitution. It is, of course, too simple to say the Constitution is a nationalistic document. It is rather a charter of tensions, most notably among the three branches of federal government and between the federal government and the states. But the Constitution has a strong nationalist component—it was, after all, "to form a more perfect Union" that "[w]e the People of the United States" did "ordain and establish" the Constitution in the first place.[12]

At the core of constitutional nationalism are the enumerated powers of Congress in Article I, Section 8. And at the core of the enumerated powers are the commerce and spending powers, the latter being couched as a provision "for the common Defence and general Welfare."[13] The commerce power in particular has recently been the subject of debate, and its exercise by Congress has not received complete deference from the courts.[14]

So far, so good—a reminder that Congress's powers are enumerated, not residual, is a salutary thing. But there is also a danger here, best illustrated by efforts to weaken Congress's authority to protect the national environment. It is tempting, I suppose, to see the states as sovereigns of their own resources, be they land or animal species or bodies of water that have their chief locus within a single state. It is further tempting to say such things are not really commerce, at least in the sense that trucks and trains and roads and canals or production processes are. It is tempting finally to see federal officials as far-off policemen, out to handcuff property owners and developers from exercising basic rights.

There is force to these arguments, but pushed too aggressively they unwind the fabric of national life. The scarce and migratory quality of natural resources surely permits the constitutional exercise of national conservation measures. Inimical to national unity are judicial decrees that it is beyond the constitutional power of Congress to preserve resources that all of America may cherish.

The issue goes far beyond the environment. Imagine a scarce mineral or medicinal property found largely within the borders of one state. Imagine further that Congress further deems such resources important to the national defense or prevention of pandemic. The happenstance of property location should not place it beyond the power of Congress to act: The same Constitution that rightly limits government's ability to take property[15] likewise furnishes government the tools to guard against its dissipation and to preserve it for the longer haul and larger good.

And while we are at the business of constitutional nationalism, let's raise a toast to the dormant commerce clause. Often maligned as lacking an explicit textual basis or requiring judges to subjectively balance burdens against benefits,[16] the silent commerce clause is an indispensable ingredient of national unity. It has in fact persevered for generations,[17] a testament to its enduring utility as a unifying instrument. The last thing we need in a more global marketplace is a revival of parochialism at home. The vision of American states compelled to negotiate their own little NAFTAs with one another is no doubt an exaggerated fear. And yet it should sensitize us to the danger of burdening free trade within our national marketplace.[18]

It is the genius of our system that even a strong dose of constitutional nationalism will not enfeeble the states. The Supremacy Clause of Article VI and the preemption doctrines derived from it[19] provide a hefty boost for *economic* nationalism; it is far less certain that they should be utilized to assert a federal *cultural* supremacy or to erode the benefits of diversity and experimentation within our federal system. Constitutional nationalism will be most effective if, like good parenting, it does not attempt to regulate every subject under the sun.

IV.

Let's restore a constitutional respect for community. It is futile to expect a healthy nation in the absence of a healthy sense of community. Community instills within us the sense that we live for something larger and more meaningful than just ourselves. This sense of something larger than the self underlies the successful formation of all communities, be they the village or the nation. Communities are built around shared purposes and values, one of which is surely a respect and appreciation for individual rights. But there must likewise be the sense that individuals contribute to, as well as take from, this larger whole of which we as single persons are but parts.

Today the adjective "constitutional" is invariably associated with the noun "rights." The linkage itself is hardly automatic (the noun might be "structure" or "governance," for example), and the rights revolution that began not coincidentally in the 1960s has left the balance between the individual and society out of whack. For quite a while now, constitutional law has placed a strong emphasis upon rights, often at the expense of community, whether the rights be those of the accused or the victims of discrimination or the practitioners of intimate choice. The Warren Court began the constitutional rights revolution; the Burger Court extended it; and the Rehnquist Court did not curtail it, at least not in any significant way.

Much of this development was decidedly good, because a society that fails to accord respect and dignity to each of its members is not a society worthy of the name. It must still be asked whether the notion of free-floating, i.e., non-textual, constitutional rights of personal autonomy has not helped to deprive us of a sense of connectedness that is indispensable to the formation of collective identity. There is a limit to which individual intimacies should be at the sufferance of majorities, but there are likewise limits to the extent that democratic majorities in a state or nation can be deprived of the communal right to promote cherished values. To enshrine a sanctity of self in our founding charter without textual or historical warrant may be just as pernicious as the attempt to enshrine discrimination against those whose personal choices may for good and legitimate reason fail to conform to the majority's own.

On many of the great questions of the day, our Constitution is consciously agnostic. Its enumeration of rights is significant, but finite. Its grant of powers to representative government is formidable, but it does not prescribe what substantive ends the exercise of those powers must embody. To bend our Constitution in the direction of autonomy or collectivity is detrimental to our national health. I argued above that the rash of constitutional bans on same-sex marriage risks the destruction of the spirit of welcome and inclusiveness on which a sound republic rests.[20] Similarly, the judicially spearheaded rights revolution has left America in too much of a vacuum, where "I" and "me" trump all else.

Each of us can without much trouble compose a lengthy list of rights. But wish lists of rights may be grounded less in law than in desire. So while one might not wish to wear a seat belt, a community is not constitutionally precluded from asserting its prerogative to save others the costs of serious accidents.

When we next drive through the countryside or take a moment's pause, we might reflect on what we get from living in society: We did not build our own home; make our own car or clothes; or invent the computers, phones, lights, or appliances we now take so much for granted. Left alone, we could not enjoy a concert, educate our children, put out a fire, raise capital, or take a trip. We would, in short, be both miserable and helpless. So this unmoored, evolving constitutional notion of the supremacy of the individual is quite at odds with reality as we experience it. The great exhortation in President Kennedy's inaugural address[21] may seem to some an obsolete plea, but if so, the fault is not that of our forebears. It is not somehow anti-constitutional to think in terms of obligation and responsibility. That document protects democratic prerogative as well as individual liberty. In so doing, it enhances the collective consciousness on which a vital nation must in the end depend.

V.

The search for One America requires less polarization, but not necessarily less partisanship. The two must be distinguished. Polarization is the accumulation of personal animosities that is presently tearing us apart. Partisanship is more of a mixed bag. It can easily proceed too far, but it can also promote vigorous debate and frame electoral choices.

In a polarized age, the judiciary must assume the duty of lowering national temperatures. National unity requires that courts counteract both partisanship and polarization in the body politic. The judiciary fulfills this mission not only through allegiance to principles of law that transcend political division, but in its demeanor and approach, which should consciously lower volume as political discourse raises it.

It is good for a vital nation to be noisy; it is good for appellate courts to be places of some quiet. By quiet, I do not mean agreement, but civility, decorum, and restraint. The civility and restraint that should mark the judicial calling help satisfy the yearning for some institution of governance that serves the national interest in a non-ideological way.

Are we in the courts fulfilling our charge of counteracting the tendencies of a polarizing age? The answer would depend on whom you ask. On the one hand, it is reassuring that the rank partisanship of the day has not permeated judicial deliberation to a greater degree. On the other hand, the rhetoric in judicial opinions is sometimes personalized to an extent that obscures rather than clarifies real differences. The media identify judges as Republican or Democrat; the confirmation process sends nominees through bruising partisan disputes in which underlying merit is obscured; law clerks are too often chosen with their ideological proclivities uppermost in mind; and new statutes on controversial subjects, as well as eras of past activism, have brought an unprecedented level of interest-group participation in cases as well as confirmations.

All this makes it more difficult for courts to speak calmly, and to fulfill the civilizing and conciliatory function that national strength and unity require.

VI.

My sixth recommendation involves the reaffirmation that a unified nation cannot be one in which public allocations and benefits are premised on ethnicity and race. This principle should not be unfamiliar to us. Neutrality as to speech, neutrality as to faith, neutrality as to race. Our country rests on the pillars of neutrality that are the First and Fourteenth Amendments.

The temptations to compromise this principle are ever present. In the Michigan higher-education cases, the Supreme Court took notice of the need to develop diversity in the nation's future ranks of leadership.[22] And in the challenges to pupil assignment plans in the Louisville and Seattle public school systems, it was argued that race could be contemplated in non-meritocratic settings, and especially in elementary schools where the need to experience the benefits of diversity at a young age was undeniable.[23]

I respect this view. Many good people contend that affirmative action is unifying, not divisive, and that it will help America become a more integrated whole.[24] And others who may subscribe to the general or ultimate value of race neutrality nonetheless find compelling reasons to deviate from the principle in particular contexts,[25] including those noted above.

The need for contextual deviation is often argued sensibly in the singular, but the accumulation of contextual exceptions threatens to swallow the rule of race neutrality whole. Where does that leave us as a nation? It is the rapid diversification of our demographic profile that should render race-based preferences obsolete. Seeking to identify preferred groups and to parcel preferences among them will be a dangerous and divisive enterprise in our multi-ethnic nation. It will become a path to balkanization that America can ill afford. In fact, the increasing numbers of interracial and interethnic marriages make it ever more difficult to ascertain who belongs in what category. And the effort to categorize will prove in itself to be uncomfortably reminiscent of racial engineering efforts undertaken in the darkest hours of human history.

How much better to repair to the bright text and clear command of the Fourteenth Amendment, designed to rejoin us after the searing conflict of the Civil War. It says, ever so simply, that the State shall not "deny to any person within its jurisdiction the equal protection of the laws."[26] It does not speak of groups or of group entitlements. We should not suppose, however, that the Framers meant to embrace through this language a vision of radical individualism. Instead, the Amendment's explicit prohibition of the denial of equal protection to *any person* reflects the view that the strongest nation will be one in which each and every human being is freed from the yoke of identification and discrimination based on race. Only through this recognition of our common humanity and irreducible dignity will Americans come to see that each of us is one of us, that we journey together, not apart, along history's all too treacherous trail.

VII.

My last principle of unity lies in an appreciation of the importance of process. At times, process falls victim to impatience. It is in the nature of majorities to want results, and process just seems to get in the way. Process is a particular nuisance to authoritarian temperaments, a reproach to their theory that the end justifies the means. Why bother with warrants and hearings and procedures and trials? And, say the autocrats, why not just snuff out those opposition views and voices that might lead to something so embarrassing as an open debate? Process means accountability, which is why those who exercise power periodically try to hold it in contempt.

A democracy, of course, lives by process. Our nation is held together not only by common values and traditions, but by a mutual respect for the rules of the game. If process is respected, losers can absorb defeat and hope to be winners tomorrow. Process, properly understood, leaves even losers with power—the ability to form a vocal opposition and the chance to mobilize for the next election. Thus does process promote unity. With process open, the doors in a democracy never slam shut.

There has been a great deal of confusion lately about what process actually means. It definitely does not mean litigation above all else. Too much litigation is a distortion of process, because it takes decisions from Congress, from state and local governments, from school systems and business organizations, and plops them into federal court, where they often were never meant to be. There is a thin line between courts making sure that others abide by law and hijacking the decisionmaking process from them. It is also one thing to preserve civil liberties in wartime and quite another to distort the constitutional process for waging war and conducting foreign affairs. Process involves not only a respect for rights but also a respect for constitutional structure—a profound tension as we adapt the paradigms of criminal justice to suspects in our struggle against terror.

So the process that promotes unity does not have a love of litigation at its core. Rather, it embodies above all the idea of tolerance for others and their points of view. Process requires that legislative bodies, for example, respect the rights of the minority to offer floor amendments and to participate in conference committees, and that judicial bodies honor the rights of the dissenter in internal deliberation as well as external expression. Unity contemplates not some unattainable ideal of homogenization, but that we as a people afford process—that is to say opportunity—for those whose views and perspectives we may not share. When I hear someone say, "We are a Christian nation," that is not right. We are a nation that respects the expression of all religious faiths, including the faith of our Muslim friends. It is that process, that bedrock opportunity for expression of difference, that promotes unity through diversity, and it is that ideal of process that must animate both courts and country.

Conclusion

I end where I began. Law has two historic purposes: the protection of liberty and the preservation of order. It is time to add to those a third: the maintenance of One America. This is not a call for homogeneity or hollow patriotism. It is rather a plea for a legal framework within which the dynamics of diversity can be put to their most productive use.

In every way one can imagine, Americans are more different from one another than ever before. That is no cause for despair. It is simply a recognition that law can help us to acknowledge and appreciate all we have in common. Or it can drive us irretrievably apart.

Some may question why a sense of national unity is so necessary. It is not simply that national identification helps America present a stronger front against its global adversaries. It is not just that national allegiance helps to overcome the impulse of racial and ethnic separatism. What truly matters is that the great national goals of strength, prosperity, freedom, and humanity become impossible without the capacity to summon some sense of America itself.

It has long been assumed that the promotion of unity was purely a political task, and that law and the judiciary were meant to sit on the sidelines. That is no longer true. Promoting mutual respect, if not agreement, among Americans should figure in judicial judgment. A greater commitment to national unity can properly be expressed through the noble medium of the law. Indeed it must be. One America is too important for one entire branch of government to ignore.

NOTES

1. 531 U.S. 98 (2000).
2. *Id.* at 128–29 (Stevens, J., dissenting).
3. *See, e.g.,* Gibbons v. Ogden, 22 U.S. (9 Wheat.) 1 (1824); McCulloch v. Maryland, 17 U.S. (4 Wheat.) 316 (1819); Marbury v. Madison, 5 U.S. (1 Cranch) 137 (1803).
4. 198 U.S. 45, 53 (1905).
5. 410 U.S. 113, 153–54 (1973).
6. *See, e.g.,* Lawrence v. Texas, 539 U.S. 558 (2003); Planned Parenthood of Se. Pa. v. Casey, 505 U.S. 833 (1992).
7. *E.g.,* United States v. Morrison, 529 U.S. 598 (2000) (striking down civil damages provision of Violence Against Women Act); United States v. Lopez, 514 U.S. 549 (1995) (striking down federal statute regulating gun use).
8. *E.g.,* City of Boerne v. Flores, 521 U.S. 507 (1997) (holding that Religious Freedom Restoration Act exceeds Congress's power under Section 5).
9. *See* Harper v. Va. Bd. of Elections, 383 U.S. 663 (1966) (holding that poll tax imposes unconstitutional restriction on franchise).
10. *See, e.g.,* Connor v. Finch, 431 U.S. 407, 431 (1977) (Powell, J., dissenting) ("[L]egislative plans are likely to reflect a State's political policy and the will of its people more accurately than a decision by unelected federal judges.").
11. *See, e.g.,* Kevin Simpson, *Marriage, Gay Rights: Amend. 43 Supporters Revel in Double Victory,* DENVER POST, Nov. 9, 2006, at B06 (noting that seven states passed constitutional amendments banning same-sex marriages in 2006). While the proposed Federal Marriage Amendment has not passed, the fact that it has been so vigorously debated as a constitutional option was bound to deepen social division. *See* Alan Cooperman, *Gay Marriage as 'the New Abortion': Debate Becomes Polarizing as Both Sides Become Better Organized, Spend Millions,* WASH. POST, July 26, 2004, at A03 (describing debate).
12. U.S. CONST. pmbl.
13. U.S. CONST. art. I, § 8, cl. 1.
14. The Rehnquist Court invalidated the civil damages provision of the Violence Against Women Act and the entire Gun-Free School Zones Act as exceeding Congress's Commerce Clause powers. United States v. Morrison, 529 U.S. 598 (2000); United States v. Lopez, 514 U.S. 549 (1995). *But see* Gonzales v. Raich, 545 U.S. 1 (2005) (holding that federal Controlled Substances Act does not exceed Commerce Clause).
15. U.S. CONST. amend. V.
16. *See, e.g.,* Okla. Tax Comm'n v. Jefferson Lines, Inc., 514 U.S. 175, 200 (1995) (Scalia, J., concurring) ("[T]he 'negative Commerce Clause' . . . is 'negative' not only because it negates state regulation of commerce, but also because it does *not* appear in the Constitution.").
17. *See* Cooley v. Bd. of Wardens, 53 U.S. (12 How.) 299, 319 (1851) (recognizing dormant aspect of Commerce Clause).
18. *See* Gen. Motors Corp. v. Tracy, 519 U.S. 278, 287 (1997) ("The negative or dormant implication of the Commerce Clause prohibits state taxation or regulation that discriminates against or unduly burdens interstate commerce and thereby

impedes free private trade in the national marketplace." (internal citations and quotations omitted)).

19. *See* Gade v. Nat'l Solid Wastes Mgmt. Ass'n, 505 U.S. 88, 108 (1992) ("[U]nder the Supremacy Clause, from which our pre-emption doctrine is derived, 'any state law, however clearly within a State's acknowledged power, which interferes with or is contrary to federal law, must yield.'" (quoting Felder v. Casey, 487 U.S. 131, 138 (1988))).

20. *See supra* Part II.

21. "[A]sk not what your country can do for you—ask what you can do for your country." John F. Kennedy, Presidential Inaugural Address (Jan. 20, 1961) (transcript available at http://www.yale.edu/lawweb/avalon/presiden/inaug/kennedy.htm).

22. Gratz v. Bollinger, 539 U.S. 244, 268–71 (2003); Grutter v. Bollinger, 539 U.S. 306, 332 (2003).

23. Parents Involved in Cmty. Sch. v. Seattle Sch. Dist. No. 1, 551 U.S. 701 (2007).

24. For example, Justice Breyer predicated much of his dissent in *Parents Involved* on the idea that affirmative action would produce "one America." *Id.* at 2824 (Breyer, J., dissenting).

25. *See Grutter*, 539 U.S. at 343 ("We expect that 25 years from now, the use of racial preferences will no longer be necessary to further the interest approved today."); Regents of the Univ. of Cal. v. Bakke, 438 U.S. 265, 403 (1978) (Blackmun, J., concurring) ("At some time, however, beyond any period of what some would claim is only transitional inequality, the United States must and will reach a stage of maturity where action along this line is no longer necessary.").

26. U.S. CONST. amend. XIV, § 1.

8

Securing Fragile Foundations

Affirmative Constitutional Adjudication in Federal Courts

MARSHA S. BERZON

Introduction

I was so very pleased to have been invited to deliver the fortieth Madison
Lecture. This honor is an especially meaningful one for me, as one of my
predecessors in the Madison Lecture series was Justice William Brennan,
for whom I clerked on the Supreme Court. In fact, Justice Brennan is the
only person to have stood at this lectern twice—he gave the Madison
Lecture in 1961[1] and again in 1986.[2]

   In his first lecture, in 1961, Justice Brennan described a vigorous debate
then taking place in the courts about whether and to what extent the
federal Constitution constrains state, not just federal, power.[3] When he
returned to this podium to deliver his second lecture in 1986, he used
the occasion to reflect upon how much the legal world had changed in
the twenty-five years since he had first spoken. He recounted, on the one
hand, the step-by-step incorporation of the Bill of Rights' guarantees
as against the states, and, on the other, the increasing tendency of the
Supreme Court to decline to enforce those guarantees, often "in the name
of federalism."[4] Justice Brennan was heartened to find that state courts, in
interpreting their own constitutions, were "assum[ing] a leadership role
in the protection of individual rights and liberties."[5] Still, he cautioned,
federal courts are an "indispensable safeguard of individual rights against
governmental abuse,"[6] so that if federal courts abdicate that historic role,
both individuals and our federal system will suffer.

This lecture was delivered on November 10, 2008, and appeared in *84 N.Y.U. L. Rev.*
681 (2009).

In 2008, nearly another quarter-century later, we are still grappling with the role of federal courts in enforcing constitutional rights. When may an individual alleging a constitutional violation obtain access to federal court to seek relief? And, once the litigant is in court, what remedies may the court provide? These questions have a ring of contemporary urgency to them because of current controversies surrounding habeas corpus, § 1983, sovereign immunity, and standing doctrine.[7] Underlying those controversies are some of the most basic, vexing questions one can ask about a judicial system—the same questions James Madison and the other Founders faced as they devised our system of government.

Our Constitution is in many respects an extraordinarily laconic document, not least with respect to the judiciary's role in enforcing constitutional rights. Article III vests what it calls the "judicial Power" in "one supreme Court, and in such inferior Courts as the Congress may from time to time ordain and establish."[8] What *is* this judicial power? Various provisions of the Constitution set limitations upon the government; others confer rights upon individuals to be free of certain governmental actions—we see this most obviously in the Bill of Rights and the Reconstruction Amendments[9]—but in what fora, and by what means, are those limitations and rights to be enforced? The Constitution is mostly silent on the subject of remedies,[10] leaving unanswered difficult questions about the extent to which courts may fashion remedies suited to vindicating constitutional rights.

It is something of a truism that the task of interpreting the Constitution's provisions and applying them to particular facts is part of what the "judicial Power" is about. But there is a far more complex story to be told about when, and for whom, the federal courts' doors are open to affirmative constitutional claims in the absence of a statutorily created cause of action, and about the range of remedial powers available to the courts in redressing constitutional violations.[11] These are not new questions, of course, but I hope to demonstrate that the background assumptions upon which we operate today when answering them are quite different from what they were twenty-five and fifty years ago. In the last thirty years especially, the Supreme Court and lower federal courts have dramatically recast the role of the judiciary in adjudicating constitutional issues. In particular, courts are increasingly—but not consistently—insisting upon statutorily granted authority to hear constitutional claims and to fashion appropriate remedies.

As I will suggest, federal courts appear to have conflated the sensible desire for clear legislative direction with respect to enforcement of federal laws with the more dubious proposition that similar congressional authority is required for judicial enforcement of constitutional guarantees. But statutory causes of action (particularly so-called implied causes of action)[12] and direct, affirmative constitutional claims are largely distinct and are not usefully analyzed as though they were the same. In developing that point, I will examine the historical roots of direct constitutional actions and, with that history as backdrop, I will explore some inconsistencies in the modern approach to the judicial enforcement of constitutional rights. Ultimately, I conclude that the federal courts' recent hesitancy to hear certain kinds of cases when they arise directly under the Constitution cannot be reconciled with history, or with the judiciary's role of checking the other branches of the federal government and upholding the Constitution.

I. Affirmative Constitutional Litigation: Historical Foundations
A. Brown, Bolling, *and Direct Constitutional Actions at Mid-Century*

We now tend to think of affirmative constitutional litigation as beginning in the 1950s, 1960s, and 1970s. Those years did indeed see unprecedented numbers of lawsuits filed in federal court by individuals seeking to enforce their rights under the Constitution. In many of the earliest of these "mid-century cases," as I shall call them, litigants sought injunctive relief against state laws or actions asserted to be unconstitutional. The quintessential such case from the 1950s was, of course, *Brown v. Board of Education*, in which a group of black schoolchildren and their parents filed suit in federal district courts, arguing that segregation in the public schools violated their Fourteenth Amendment right to equal protection.[13] Other litigants sought injunctions against allegedly unconstitutional federal, rather than state, laws. For example, in *Bolling v. Sharpe*, decided with *Brown* in 1954, black schoolchildren and parents argued that segregation in the D.C. public schools violated their Fifth Amendment right to due process.[14] Still other litigants sought damages—not injunctive relief—to redress either state or federal violations of their constitutional rights. Perhaps most well-known among these cases is *Bivens v. Six Unknown Named Agents of the Federal Bureau of Narcotics*,[15] the 1971 case in which Webster Bivens sought to recover money damages from the federal officers who searched and arrested him in his home in violation of the Fourth Amendment.

In each of these mid-century cases—*Brown, Bolling,* and *Bivens*—the Supreme Court found for the plaintiffs on the merits and ordered that they be granted the relief sought. The Court's opinions in these cases shared some basic intuitions about the judicial role that I think typify the mood of the era. First, the opinions in the mid-century cases reflect a sense that the availability of *some* means of enforcement is implicit in the concept of a "right," and, more broadly, perhaps implicit in the nature of a constitution. Second, they reveal a pragmatic acknowledgment that, in some situations, the only effective way to enforce the Constitution will be through affirmative litigation. Third, and perhaps most strikingly, the opinions in these mid-century cases either presume or state outright that the lack of a statute expressly creating a federal cause of action does not prevent the federal courts from hearing such claims or from granting legal or equitable relief as appropriate. As long as Congress had conferred jurisdiction on the federal courts, the Court proceeded on the assumption that the courts had authority to hear cases arising directly under the Constitution.

So, for example, in *Brown* the plaintiffs grounded their claim for relief directly in the Fourteenth Amendment.[16] The Court's opinion did not mention whether the plaintiffs had properly stated a cause of action.[17] A lawyer today might assume that the *Brown* litigants filed their claims in federal court pursuant to what we now call § 1983, originally enacted as part of the Civil Rights Act of 1871.[18] But in the early 1950s, what is now § 1983 was a more or less dormant statute, limited by arcane case law concerning the meaning of the phrases "under color of [state law]" and "rights, privileges, or immunities secured by the Constitution," two key phrases in the statute.[19] The *Brown* litigants did not cite the precursor to § 1983 in their briefs, nor did the *Brown* Court cite what is now § 1983 in its opinion.

In *Bolling*, the Court again presumed that it could entertain direct constitutional claims without a statutory predicate. *Bolling* did not elaborate on why the plaintiffs were entitled to bring suit or to obtain a remedy, but, unlike in *Brown*, § 1983, even if it had not been languishing in dormancy, likely would not have applied at that time to authorize a suit against officials acting under color of District of Columbia law.[20] Most likely, the Court tacitly accepted that there was a cause of action directly under the Fifth Amendment—or, put another way, that the Fifth Amendment was self-executing and that the courts therefore had the authority to hear claims alleging violations of its terms and to determine the appropriate remedy.

In these mid-century cases, then, the Court evidently saw it as uncontroversial that the federal courts should be able to hear the plaintiffs' claims and grant the remedies sought without needing to locate a statutory source for the cause of action.[21] We tend now to think of mid-century cases like *Brown* and *Bolling* as marking a sea change in the Supreme Court's willingness to entertain the constitutional claims of individual petitioners. But, as I shall now suggest, the history of direct constitutional litigation in fact stretches back much further. The mid-century Court was in fact expanding upon a tradition with a long historical pedigree.

B. Early Claims under the Constitution

Throughout the 1800s and early 1900s, federal courts routinely recognized direct causes of action to enforce provisions of the Constitution.[22] These cases became quite common after 1875, when Congress conferred general federal question jurisdiction on the federal courts.[23] But even before the conferral of federal question jurisdiction, federal courts could exercise jurisdiction over cases involving constitutional issues in certain circumstances.[24]

Generally, courts in the early decades of the nation's history, as in the era of *Brown* and *Bolling*, seemingly viewed their power to interpret the Constitution at the behest of private litigants and to grant appropriate remedies if a constitutional violation was found as an unremarkable exercise of their inherent judicial functions. Although the courts certainly recognized other limits on their jurisdiction and their authority to provide affirmative relief, and although there was substantial dispute, once federal question jurisdiction was created, about what it meant for a claim to "aris[e] under" federal law,[25] courts assured of their jurisdiction generally did not concern themselves with finding a specific congressional grant of authority to decide constitutional issues affirmatively presented to them. This lack of concern was particularly evident in cases in which, as in *Brown* and *Bolling* decades later, the plaintiffs sought only prospective relief—traditionally referred to as cases "in equity." Such cases were far more common, but, as we shall see, a similar lack of concern with locating a congressional grant of authority was also evident in cases seeking damages relief—that is, cases "at law."

1. DIRECT CONSTITUTIONAL CASES IN EQUITY

The first notable case in equity in which the plaintiff sought relief directly under the Constitution was *Osborn v. Bank of the United States*,[26] decided in 1824. In *Osborn*, the Bank filed a suit in equity in federal court against the Auditor of the State of Ohio, Ralph Osborn, alleging that Osborn intended to collect an unconstitutional state tax from the Bank. The Supreme Court agreed with the Bank that the state tax offended Congress's Article I power to constitute the Bank, and, more important for our purposes, it saw "no plausible reason" why it should not grant the injunction "to restrain the [state] agent" from violating the Constitution, even though no statute expressly granted the Bank the right to challenge an unconstitutional state tax in court.[27]

Once Congress conferred general federal question jurisdiction on the lower federal courts in 1875, and continuing throughout the early 1900s, federal courts entertained numerous suits by individuals and corporations[28] who sought to protect their property rights under the Due Process Clause of the Fourteenth Amendment, the Commerce Clause, or the Contracts Clause in Article I, Section 10. For example, a South Carolina resident who imported liquor from other states for his own use brought suit to enjoin various state and county officers from seizing his liquor under an allegedly unconstitutional state law;[29] a railroad company brought suit to restrain a state auditor from seizing property under an allegedly unconstitutional state law forbidding payment of taxes with coupons;[30] and a business calling itself the "American School for Magnetic Healing" brought suit to enjoin the Missouri Postmaster's allegedly unconstitutional decision to withhold delivery of its mail.[31] In such cases, the federal courts applied the traditional rules of equity without difficulty: So long as the court had jurisdiction, the litigant demonstrated a risk of irreparable injury, and there was no adequate remedy available to him at law, the courts were able to fashion an appropriate equitable remedy.[32]

By far the best-known early example of a direct constitutional cause of action in equity is *Ex Parte Young*,[33] decided in 1908. We tend now to think of *Ex Parte Young* as a case about the limits of state sovereign immunity,[34] but it is equally remarkable as an explanation of why the federal courts' doors must be open, in appropriate situations, to affirmative suits in equity to enjoin constitutional violations.

The facts of *Young* were as follows: In 1907, the Minnesota state legislature enacted a law limiting the passenger and freight rates railroads were allowed to charge. To discourage railroads from defensively challenging the law's constitutionality, the law prescribed stern criminal penalties, including very high fines and jail time, for violations of the rates limitations. Edward Young, the attorney general of Minnesota at the time, indicated his intention to enforce the law vigorously.

Challenging the law defensively in criminal proceedings in state court was not feasible, given the draconian penalties. For that reason, and because they preferred the more hospitable federal forum, a group of railroad shareholders decided to challenge the law affirmatively in federal court. They sued Young, seeking an injunction against future enforcement of the rates legislation on the theory that it violated the Fourteenth Amendment's Due Process Clause and the Commerce Clause. When the federal court temporarily restrained Young from enforcing the law, Young disobeyed that order, was held in contempt, and was taken into federal custody. Once he was in custody—he was not in jail, but had to report to a marshal once a day[35]—Young sought habeas relief on an original writ to the Supreme Court. It was in this unusual posture that the constitutionality of the rates legislation was finally litigated.[36]

Obviously, if the court issuing the contempt order had lacked jurisdiction to do so, then Young would have had to be freed from the not-so-onerous "custody" he was in. So the Supreme Court turned to the question of jurisdiction. For our purposes, what is important is that the Court held that the federal court in which the shareholders originally filed suit did have jurisdiction to hear the case under § 1331 because the shareholders' claim for injunctive relief raised several "federal questions" arising directly under the Constitution.[37] The Court did not ultimately decide whether the rates legislation was confiscatory under the Fourteenth Amendment, but it did hold that "the provisions . . . imposing such enormous fines and possible imprisonment as a result of an unsuccessful effort to test the validity of the laws themselves[ ] are unconstitutional on their face, without regard to the question of the insufficiency of those rates."[38] For this reason, the Court dismissed Young's habeas petition and upheld the lower court's injunction.[39]

Whether Young reported to the marshal for the rest of his days or instead gave up trying to enforce the unconstitutional statute, I do not know. But *Ex Parte Young*'s legal legacy is still with us: It stands as an example of the importance of affirmative constitutional suits where requiring would-be litigants to wait and challenge an invalid law after its enforcement would be, in reality, to close the courthouse doors to any challenge at all. While *Ex Parte Young*'s facts are exceptional, the assumption that the federal court could entertain the case and grant relief was not. In *Young*, as in many cases before it, the courts were not concerned with whether Congress had created a statutory cause of action for the enforcement of the plaintiffs' constitutional rights. Instead, the Constitution itself, coupled with federal question jurisdiction, was enough to permit the federal courts to entertain the shareholders' suit and provide a remedy for the constitutional wrong.

To summarize, the federal courts had, from *Osborn* to *Young*, regularly entertained direct constitutional claims and granted injunctions when they found violations. By the time of *Brown* and *Bolling*, it was truly unremarkable for a court to grant injunctive relief for constitutional violations without seeking a legislatively created "cause of action."

2. DIRECT CONSTITUTIONAL CASES AT LAW

The federal "judicial Power" extends under Article III to suits "in Law and Equity," and the story I have just told about early exercises of federal "equity" jurisdiction has a lesser-known counterpart in "law." In fact, throughout the nineteenth and early twentieth centuries, federal courts entertained suits for damages and other legal remedies grounded directly on the Constitution, although these cases were considerably less plentiful than those in equity. There were a variety of reasons for this imbalance, but perhaps the most important was that, before law and equity were merged in 1938, the interaction of the well-pleaded complaint rule[40] and the differing pleading requirements for law and equity[41] made it relatively more difficult for a plaintiff at law who wished to raise a constitutional challenge to get into federal court if his constitutional challenge was styled not as an affirmative claim but as an anticipated response to the government officer's defense. Eventually, courts came to view the allegation that a government agent had acted unconstitutionally not just as a response to a government defense but also as the assertion of a claim arising under federal law, which could properly be stated in a plaintiff's complaint and thus support federal question jurisdiction.[42] But until that conceptual shift took hold, the pleading rules for suits at law meant that some litigants could not file suit in (and after 1894 could not remove to)[43] federal court despite having what we would now recognize as an affirmative constitutional claim.

I won't delve further into this question here, but I think it fair to say, as Professor Alfred Hill has suggested, that the relative infrequency of damages actions in the eighteenth and early nineteenth centuries can be attributed largely to contingent historical and procedural factors rather than to some inherent limitation on the power of federal courts to fashion legal, as opposed to equitable, remedies for constitutional violations.[44] When damages cases did reach the Supreme Court, the Court repeatedly affirmed federal courts' power to provide relief, without requiring any congressional authorization other than federal question jurisdiction.

As with the cases in equity, most of the early damages cases involved property rights. For example, in 1885, in *White v. Greenhow*, the Supreme Court reversed a lower federal court's dismissal of a Virginia resident's suit for $6,000 in damages against a state tax collector who seized his property pursuant to an allegedly unconstitutional state tax law.[45] Concluding that the plaintiff's claim "ar[ose] under the Constitution," the Court held that the suit was within federal question jurisdiction,[46] found in the plaintiff's favor on the merits, and remanded to the lower court to administer the remedy.[47] More recently, in *Jacobs v. United States*,[48] decided in 1933, the Supreme Court held that an individual who alleged that the federal government took his property for public use could sue for damages directly under the Fifth Amendment.[49] The Court's opinion made clear that "the right to recover just compensation . . . rest[s] upon the Fifth Amendment."[50]

Not all of the early direct constitutional damages cases involved property rights. Federal courts also granted damages remedies in other cases, including several concerning the right under Article I, Section 2 of the Constitution to vote in federal elections. Damages were the preferred remedy in the voting-rights context because injunctions—traditionally an extraordinary remedy to be used only when legal remedies were unavailable—were seen as an unduly intrusive means of assuring political rights.

In 1900, for example, in *Wiley v. Sinkler*, the Supreme Court considered the claim of a South Carolina resident who sought $2,500 in damages against the state election officials who refused to accept his vote in the federal election.[51] The Court found the plaintiff's pleadings insufficient because he never alleged that he was registered to vote, indicating that, had he so alleged, he would have stated a claim on which damages could issue under Article I, Section 2. The Court explained that "[t]he right to vote for members of the Congress . . . has its foundation in the Constitution of the United States."[52]

In short, throughout the late 1800s and early 1900s, the Court readily entertained claims for damages arising directly under the Constitution, even without any legislatively created cause of action. Yet the relative scarcity of such cases as compared with their counterparts in equity left several questions unanswered, including how the Supreme Court would approach damages actions brought directly under the Bill of Rights Amendments.

II. Constitutional Damages in the Modern Era: *Bell, Bivens,* and Beyond

The Supreme Court finally considered such a case in 1946, in *Bell v. Hood*.[53] *Bell* involved an affirmative claim for damages brought directly under the Fourth and Fifth Amendments. On one level, *Bell* did not decide much. But it set up the playing field for cases arising a quarter of a century later.

In *Bell v. Hood*, Arthur Bell brought a damages action in federal court against several FBI agents, alleging that they had violated his Fourth and Fifth Amendment rights by unlawfully arresting and imprisoning him. As with many of the earlier cases I have mentioned, there was no federal statute expressly giving Bell the right to sue; he relied instead directly on the Constitution. After holding that the district court did have "arising under" jurisdiction over Bell's case, the Supreme Court went on to distinguish between "jurisdiction" and "cause of action."[54] The Court ultimately left the question of whether there was a cause of action for damages under the Fourth or Fifth Amendments for the district court to decide. But the Court did note that there was an "established practice" of granting injunctive relief directly under the Constitution and suggested no reason why damages should be different.[55]

A. Bivens

The long-delayed answer to the question reserved in *Bell* finally came in 1971, in *Bivens v. Six Unknown Named Agents of the Federal Bureau of Narcotics*.[56] Bivens was unlawfully strip-searched, manacled, and arrested in his home by federal agents without a warrant. The Federal Bureau of Narcotics ultimately decided not to press charges against him, so the exclusion of any improperly seized evidence was not an available remedy. Nor could Bivens show that the violation was likely to occur again, so prospective injunctive relief was unavailable. For the injury Bivens sustained, it was "damages or nothing."[57] In an opinion written by Justice Brennan, the Supreme Court held that Bivens could bring suit directly under the Fourth Amendment against the federal officers who arrested him, and that damages were an appropriate remedy.

For our purposes, I want to focus on the difference between Justice Brennan's majority opinion and Justice Harlan's concurrence. And, despite my great respect and fondness for my old boss, I want to suggest that Justice Harlan's concurring opinion is the one that has had staying power and is essential for understanding why direct constitutional damages remedies—appropriately limited—remain both important to the vitality of our constitutional system and consistent with the nature of the federal judicial power.

Justice Brennan in *Bivens* read the Fourth Amendment, by its terms, to "guarantee[ ] to citizens of the United States the *absolute right* to be free from unreasonable searches and seizures carried out by virtue of federal authority."[58] Having identified a right, Brennan invoked *Marbury v. Madison*'s famous principle that any invasion of a right requires a remedy,[59] and concluded that while "the Fourth Amendment does not in so many words provide for its enforcement by an award of money damages[,] . . . 'it is . . . well settled that where legal rights have been invaded, and a federal statute provides for a general right to sue for such invasion, federal courts may use any available remedy to make good the wrong done.'"[60]

A damages remedy, Justice Brennan concluded, was appropriate in Bivens's case both because it is a remedy traditionally administered by the courts and because it was the only available remedy responsive to Bivens's injury. Justice Brennan's *Bivens* opinion rests upon an assumption that it is properly within the federal judiciary's role to supply the remedies necessary to vindicate federal rights, even without express congressional authorization. Why wait on Congress, when the Constitution clearly supplies an individual right, when the remedy sought is well within the courts' traditional competence to dispense, and when the courts' traditional and constitutionally mandated function is to match remedy with right?

This reasoning was consistent with that of many of the cases described thus far. The trouble with Justice Brennan's reasoning for modern-day readers is that some of the assumptions upon which it rested are no longer accepted in Supreme Court jurisprudence.

Recall the line from Justice Brennan's opinion that I just quoted, stating that "it is . . . well settled that where . . . a *federal statute* provides for a general right to sue for such invasion, federal courts may use any available remedy to make good the wrong done."[61] The federal statute Brennan had in mind was not § 1331, granting subject matter jurisdiction. Rather, Justice Brennan was referring to a particular sentence in *Bell v. Hood*,[62] which in turn referred to two early-twentieth-century cases that considered whether plaintiffs were entitled to monetary recoveries under various federal revenue laws that did not expressly provide such a right.[63] Justice Brennan's point in invoking this particular line from *Bell* was that if courts can find implied causes of action for retrospective monetary relief in federal statutes, certainly they can do the same with regard to the Constitution.

But the world in which such an analogy had resonance was soon to pass. Brennan's majority opinion in *Bivens* relied on *J.I. Case Co. v. Borak*,[64] a 1964 case that envisioned a relatively active role for the courts to play in applying statutes, explaining that "it is the duty of the courts to be alert to provide such remedies as are necessary to make effective the congressional purpose."[65] Notably, *Borak* did not use the term "implied cause of action,"[66] and I think that term fails to capture what the Court thought it was doing. In *Borak*, it was not so much that Congress "implied" a cause of action in the Securities Exchange Act as that the Court found a cause of action "implicit," in the quite different sense of finding it inherent because necessary to make the statutory scheme work.[67] So the Court in *Borak* recognized a cause of action despite the absence of any guidance from Congress. This process, in Justice Brennan's view, typified the sort of effectuating role that courts should play with regard to enforcing the Constitution as well, one that did not involve any mind-reading of the members of Congress in an effort to determine what they had intended.

Only a few years after *Bivens*, though, the Supreme Court abandoned the *Borak* approach in favor of one that did focus squarely on congressional intent. *Cannon v. University of Chicago*[68] was the turning point—particularly Justice Powell's dissent, which came to be influential in later years.[69] In 2001, *Cannon* in turn gave way to the still more stringent approach articulated in *Alexander v. Sandoval*,[70] whereby courts may infer the existence of a nonexpress cause of action in a federal statute only where they find affirmative evidence in the statute that Congress specifically intended private federal court enforcement.[71]

So, in retrospect, Justice Brennan's decision to rely on the implied statutory cause of action cases, rather than on the longer history of direct constitutional suits in equity and law that I described earlier,[72] left his majority opinion in *Bivens* vulnerable to limitation once the nonexpress statutory cause of action cases took the turns that they did.

It also seems apparent—again, in retrospect—that Justice Harlan was acutely aware of this vulnerability. Justice Harlan wrote a detailed concurrence in *Bivens*, shoring up the points at which, it appears, he feared the majority's foundations might give way. To support the majority's conclusion that federal courts have the power both to recognize causes of action directly under the Constitution and to provide damages remedies, Justice Harlan, after a quick nod to the recent history of nonexpress damages actions under federal statutes,[73] looked more generally to the Court's practice of recognizing causes of action directly under the Constitution.

Justice Harlan first noted, as had *Bell*, the long historical support for "the presumed availability of federal *equitable* relief against threatened invasions of constitutional interests."[74] He then attempted to bridge the divide between suits in equity and suits at law by reasoning that, as the Constitution allowed Congress to give the federal courts the "Power" to decide cases "in Law and Equity," and as Congress had in fact given the courts that power by enacting § 1331, it made little sense to suppose that the courts required additional congressional authorization to provide damages remedies but no additional authorization to provide equitable relief.[75] Justice Harlan further emphasized that damages awards are well within the courts' traditional remedial power and expertise in appropriate cases.[76]

Finally, and perhaps most importantly, Justice Harlan's concurrence hinted at a reason why courts in fact may have *more* latitude to recognize causes of action under the Constitution than under statutes. He wrote that "the judiciary has a particular responsibility to assure the vindication of constitutional interests. . . . [T]he Bill of Rights is particularly intended to vindicate the interests of the individual in the face of the popular will as expressed in legislative majorities. . . ."[77]

Justice Harlan's reasoning in *Bivens* provided the approach that Justice Brennan later adopted in his 1979 majority opinion in *Davis v. Passman*, a case allowing the former employee of a U.S. congressman to seek money damages for sex discrimination directly under the Fifth Amendment.[78] Justice Brennan wrote in *Davis* that, because of the greater textual simplicity of the Constitution and the judiciary's special responsibility to enforce the Constitution's provisions against legislative encroachments, an intent-focused method of identifying implied causes of action in federal statutes is inappropriate in the constitutional context.[79] Instead, in the absence of an "explicit congressional declaration" that a *Bivens*-type suit should *not* be available and that some other remedial scheme should replace it, courts presumptively have the authority to recognize direct causes of action under the Constitution and to develop appropriate remedies.[80]

B. Post-Bivens: *The Judiciary Retreats*

Despite Justices Harlan's and Brennan's efforts, *Bivens* today appears to be hanging by a thread. The Supreme Court has, in its own words, "responded cautiously to suggestions that *Bivens* remedies be extended into new contexts"[81] and has therefore allowed *Bivens*-type constitutional damages actions only three times since 1971.[82] Identifying various "special factors" counseling judicial restraint, the Court has declared itself powerless to recognize direct constitutional causes of action even where Congress has not explicitly set an alternative remedial scheme as the exclusive remedy, and even where the alternative scheme Congress has provided does not meaningfully compensate the individual bringing suit.[83]

A striking example is *Schweiker v. Chilicky*, in which the Court refused to permit individual recipients of disability benefits to bring a *Bivens*-style suit against Social Security Administration officials for violating their due process rights under the Fifth Amendment.[84] The plaintiffs alleged that the officials intentionally had subjected them to an impermissible review system that resulted in their benefits being wrongfully terminated. The Court recognized that the Social Security Act's remedial scheme provided no means of redressing the particular harms alleged and that the Act gave no affirmative indication that Congress had meant that scheme to foreclose a *Bivens*-style suit.[85] But the Court held that Congress's very failure to account for the redress of these injuries in its administrative remedial scheme appeared "not [to have] been inadvertent," and thus was a "special factor" that counseled against allowing a *Bivens*-type suit.[86]

In *Schweiker* and the other cases limiting *Bivens*, it is evident that the Court's increasing emphasis on Congress's intent in the realm of nonexpress statutory causes of action, from *Borak* to *Cannon* to *Sandoval*, has encroached—inappropriately so, in my view—upon the Court's understanding of direct constitutional causes of action. Thus, *Bivens* has come to be seen by some as an anomaly—in Justice Scalia's words, "a relic of the heady days in which this Court assumed common-law powers to create causes of action."[87] Justice Scalia wrote these words in 2001 in his concurrence in *Correctional Services Corp. v. Malesko*, in which the Court held that a federal prisoner in a privately operated facility could not bring a *Bivens*-type damages action against the facility operators for their neglect of his known medical needs.[88] Both the *Malesko* majority opinion by Justice Rehnquist and the concurrence by Justice Scalia cited *Alexander v. Sandoval* for the proposition that the Court was no longer willing liberally to recognize causes of action not expressly sanctioned by Congress, and both opinions indicated that this reluctance should apply equally in the statutory and constitutional contexts.[89] Justice Scalia's concurrence in *Malesko* went further, asserting that "[t]here is even greater reason to abandon [the practice of recognizing direct causes of action] in the constitutional field, since an 'implication' imagined in the Constitution can presumably not even be repudiated by Congress."[90]

My essential point is that, contrary to the position taken in these *Malesko* opinions, the two matters—nonexpress statutory causes of action and direct, affirmative constitutional enforcement by the courts— are entirely distinct, and are not profitably analyzed as though they were the same. Where Congress enacts legislation under one of its constitutionally conferred powers, it makes sense to look to the legislative intent with regard to how that enactment is to be enforced. Often, agreement as to how a statute is to be enforced comes about through the legislative give-and-take essential to the functioning of Congress. In the enactment of many statutes, agreement upon how the statute is to be enforced— whether through an administrative agency or in a court, before a jury or a judge, through prospective relief or retrospective monetary relief, through complaints to a government agency empowered to bring suit or through direct, private action—is hard to attain.[91] To divorce the agreed-upon remedies from the substantive enactment—especially now that the Court has told Congress, in *Cannon* and thereafter, that Congress can no longer assume it is legislating against a background norm favoring judicial inference of statute-based causes of action—is to disregard this feature of the legislative process, and so, often, to intrude upon the legislative role.

C. Constitutional Text, Separation of Powers Values, and the Role of Federal Courts in Constitutional Adjudication

These separation of powers considerations are not easily carried over into the constitutional realm, where other considerations come into play. As between the legislative and judicial branches, why should it be the *legislative* branch to which all decisions concerning the judicial enforcement of *constitutional* norms are entrusted?

This distribution of authority is not required by the text of the Constitution. All Article III says on the matter is that Congress has the power to constitute the lower federal courts, and, by implication, the power to confer or withhold the lower courts' subject-matter jurisdiction within the outer limits set by Article III. Within those limits, it is largely up to the courts to work out, as they go, the proper division of powers between the judiciary and the legislature.

Over time, courts have fashioned limitations on their own power, often articulating those limitations by reference to functions that are "essentially" judicial and functions that are "essentially" legislative. The Justices deciding *Bivens* differed sharply with regard to this distinction. Justices Brennan and Harlan described the federal courts, when entertaining affirmative constitutional suits, as exercising their constitutionally assigned power to interpret and enforce the Constitution and as providing traditional remedies where appropriate and necessary to its enforcement. The *Bivens* dissenters, in contrast, decried the majority's holding as "judicial legislation."[92] In other words, the dissenters viewed the recognition of causes of action, including constitutional causes of action, as a job primarily entrusted to Congress, a position that has now become in some respects—though not entirely, as we shall see—the prevailing view in the Supreme Court. Why should that be so?

Part of the answer is that we have become mesmerized by language, particularly with respect to the phrase "cause of action," a phrase that does not appear in Article III, or in the Judiciary Act of 1875, or in the Federal Rules of Civil Procedure of 1938. The term came into regular use in the era of code pleading, when it described what facts a litigant had to show in his "declaration," or his initial filing, in a suit at common law to invoke the court's jurisdiction.[93] This requirement grew increasingly formalistic and burdensome over time. As a result, when the Federal Rules of Civil Procedure merged law and equity and did away with the code-pleading system in 1938, the term "cause of action" was omitted. Instead, the Rules required that an injured party's complaint contain "a short and plain statement of the claim."[94] Courts continued to use the term "cause of action" after 1938, fairly loosely, "to refer roughly to the alleged invasion of 'recognized legal rights' upon which a litigant bases his claim for relief."[95]

In the last few decades, however, the Supreme Court has come to treat the "cause of action" concept with greater rigidity, as a threshold requirement for suit. And, increasingly, the Court has insisted that implicit in the concept is legislative—as opposed to judicial—instigation. This insistence on legislative primacy sometimes draws on a mistaken, but persistent, reading of the 1938 decision in *Erie Railroad v. Tompkins*, which famously held that "[t]here is no federal general common law."[96] In fact, *Erie* did not constrain federal courts' power to act as common law courts when adjudicating questions of federal law. Rather, its purpose was to abolish "federal [general] common law" in order "to secure in the federal courts, in diversity cases, the application of the same substantive law as would control if the suit were brought in the courts of the state where the federal court sits."[97]

Nevertheless, *Erie*'s language has repeatedly been marshaled in support of the entirely different proposition that federal courts now lack the power to recognize causes of action, whether statutory or constitutional, except as Congress directs. For example, one year after *Bivens*, in *Carlson v. Greene*, a majority of the Supreme Court extended *Bivens*'s rationale to allow suits by prisoners against federal prison officials for the denial of medical care directly under the Eighth Amendment.[98] Justice Rehnquist dissented, citing *Erie* for the proposition that "the authority of federal courts to fashion remedies based on the 'common law' of damages for constitutional violations . . . falls within the legislative domain, and does not exist where not conferred by Congress."[99] This invocation of *Erie* was echoed again in Justice Scalia's concurrence in *Malesko*, which characterized *Bivens*, as I mentioned, as "a relic of the heady days in which this Court assumed common-law powers to create causes of action."[100]

In my view, this analysis is premised on a misreading of *Erie*. *Erie* prohibited federal courts from generating substantive rules of decision while sitting in diversity jurisdiction in cases arising under state law.[101] But there is nothing in *Erie* that forbids courts, when addressing a question of federal law over which they have federal question jurisdiction, to employ the usual common law methodology to determine whether, given a certain substantive principle, a remedy is appropriate at the behest of a certain class of plaintiffs and, if so, to tailor the remedy to the facts before them. A federal court enforcing legal principles established by the federal Constitution or by federal statute is not generating general common law in the forbidden *Erie* sense.[102] Rather, it is interpreting and giving effect to federal law. Its doing so does not raise the worry that litigants with similar claims in state courts may receive substantively different outcomes than those in federal court, the "mischievous results" that prompted *Erie* in the first place.[103]

So, if we are to explain the recent trend in the *Bivens* line of cases of disfavoring judicial recognition of direct constitutional causes of action, we have to look elsewhere than *Erie*. The obvious candidates are separation of powers concerns and concerns about the constitutionally limited nature of federal court jurisdiction.

There is, indeed, a recent line of cases that relies squarely on separation of powers concerns to identify the limits of the federal courts' power in this realm. *Northwest Airlines v. Transport Workers Union*,[104] decided in 1981, is one such case. There, an airline that had previously been found to have discriminated against female flight attendants in terms of wages and that had been held liable for back pay filed suit seeking contribution from the union that had negotiated the collective bargaining agreement covering the flight attendants' wages. The Supreme Court declined to recognize a nonexpress cause of action for contribution under either the Equal Pay Act or Title VII. The majority opinion, written by Justice Stevens, emphasized "that the federal lawmaking power is vested in the legislative, not the judicial, branch of government; therefore federal common law is subject to the paramount authority of Congress."[105] As this quotation indicates, *Northwest Airlines*'s rejection of the common law tradition as a basis for judicial recognition of nonexpress causes of action was not premised on a misreading of *Erie*, but rather was grounded squarely in separation of powers concerns. The opinion explained that where a standard of liability "is entirely a creature of federal statute"[106] (in that case, the Equal Pay Act), the judicial creation of remedies that Congress did not provide may be a usurpation of the legislative function.[107]

But as I have indicated, separation of powers concerns necessarily look quite different in the context of constitutional enforcement than they do where the question is judicial recognition of a private action premised on a statute. The Constitution created and limits Congress, not the other way around. Where Congress did not create, but instead is bound by, the substantive rule that a plaintiff is attempting affirmatively to enforce in court, judicial deference to preserve a primary role for legislative control over the substantive standard and the means of enforcement makes little sense.[108] As between the legislative and judicial branches, there is no apparent separation of powers reason for entrusting all decisions concerning the judicial role in enforcing constitutional norms to the legislative branch.

Nor does the constitutionally limited nature of federal jurisdiction fully explain the recent trend of relegating entirely to Congress the shaping of the judicial role in enforcing constitutional standards. The Constitution gives Congress the power to constitute the inferior federal courts and to confer on them subject matter jurisdiction within the limits allowed by Article III. It does not follow from these powers, however, that in the areas where Congress *has* conferred subject matter jurisdiction, the courts may not identify proper litigants and fashion appropriate remedies without further, more specific congressional direction.

In fact, the Framers understood that the Constitution generally, and the Bill of Rights in particular, would be binding upon the federal legislative branch, and they understood that what Article III called the "judicial Power" would enable the courts to enforce the Constitution's provisions. Arguing in support of amending the Constitution to include the Bill of Rights in 1789, James Madison explained:

> If [the first ten amendments] are incorporated into the Constitution, independent tribunals of justice will consider themselves in a peculiar manner the guardians of those rights; they will be an impenetrable bulwark against every assumption of power in the Legislature or Executive; they will be naturally led to resist every encroachment upon rights expressly stipulated for in the Constitution by the declaration of rights.[109]

If the federal courts, once constituted by Congress, are to act as the "impenetrable bulwarks" against encroachment by the other two branches of the federal government, they cannot be entirely bound by the actions—let alone the inaction—of those two branches concerning the mode of enforcing those principles.

Justice Powell understood this critical point when he wrote his vehement dissent in *Cannon*. Justice Powell criticized the majority as going too far in recognizing statutory causes of action Congress had not created, but he emphasized that his criticism did not extend to constitutionally protected rights. In that context, he argued, "this Court's traditional responsibility to safeguard constitutionally protected rights, as well as the freer hand we necessarily have in the interpretation of the Constitution, permits greater judicial creativity with respect to implied constitutional causes of action."[110]

As Justice Powell's words suggest, the language of the Constitution itself—or the specific intent of its Framers with regard to the means of its enforcement—cannot limit judicial recognition of direct constitutional causes of action in the same manner as does the intent of Congress in the statutory context under today's post-*Cannon* case law. The Constitution is for the most part silent as to remedies, but not because the Framers meant for Congress to supply them. As Richard Fallon and Daniel Meltzer have suggested, "[t]o the framers, special provision for constitutional remedies probably appeared unnecessary, because the Constitution presupposed a going legal system, with ample remedial mechanisms, in which constitutional g[u]arantees would be implemented."[111] In other words, when they used the term "the judicial Power" in Article III, the Framers understood this phrase in the context of the power that English courts had traditionally exercised at law and in equity, including the power to exercise conferred jurisdiction to shape the contours of appropriate litigation and to fashion remedies as appropriate to new factual situations. Of course, the Constitution limits the federal courts' "judicial Power" to "Cases" and "Controversies," which means that plaintiffs must demonstrate that their claim is ripe and that they have standing to sue.[112] The Constitution also limits the federal courts' judicial power to cases involving certain subject matters, giving Congress the authority to confer jurisdiction—or not—within those designated subjects. But beyond these constitutional limitations, the tasks of identifying appropriate litigants and forms of action, and applying remedies to injuries, were seen as routine judicial tasks, inseparable from the Framers' concept of the judicial role generally.[113]

It was this fundamental understanding that underlaid *Ex Parte Young* and its predecessors, as well as what I have called the "mid-century cases," such as *Brown* and *Bolling*, in which the Court was entirely comfortable providing prospective relief for constitutional violations so long as there was, first, federal jurisdiction, and, second, a "Case" or "Controversy," as Article III requires. And, despite the Court's recent reluctance to recognize constitutional causes of action for damages in *Bivens*-type cases, it is this fundamental understanding, I suspect, that informs the many other cases to which I now turn—cases in which the Court has granted prospective relief for constitutional violations when the two requisites that do appear in the Constitution are met.

D. The Supreme Court's Continued Recognition of Three Categories of Direct Constitutional Claims

What is really intriguing here is that, in fact, the Supreme Court and the lower federal courts do still provide quite regularly for the enforcement of provisions of the Constitution without express congressional authorization. Even as *Bivens* is attacked as an anomaly and a departure from courts' supposedly normal passivity in the face of congressional inaction, the Supreme Court and the lower federal courts have continued their long history of entertaining affirmative suits directly under the Constitution in several categories of cases—three in particular—that have not attracted the same sort of backlash that *Bivens* and its progeny have.

1. SUPREMACY CLAUSE PREEMPTION CASES

First, direct constitutional causes of action are alive and well in Supremacy Clause cases against state actors. In the name of giving effect to the Supremacy Clause, federal courts routinely entertain suits brought by private actors—frequently corporations—arguing that a state law is invalid because it is preempted by federal law.[114] Federal courts regularly entertain these cases even when § 1983 is not available as a basis for suit.

Consider, for example, *Shaw v. Delta Air Lines*,[115] decided in 1983. In *Shaw*, a number of airline companies sued New York state agencies and officials, arguing that the state laws they intended to enforce—the Human Rights Law and Disability Benefits Law—were preempted by ERISA, the federal statute regulating pensions. The Supreme Court determined that federal courts had authority over the airline companies' claim:

> A plaintiff who seeks injunctive relief from state regulation, on the ground that such regulation is pre-empted by a federal statute which, by virtue of the Supremacy Clause of the Constitution, must prevail, thus presents a federal question which the federal courts have jurisdiction under 28 U.S.C. § 1331 to resolve.[116]

In other words, the Court held that federal jurisdiction existed precisely because the Supremacy Clause was involved.

Shaw did not discuss whether the airlines' cause of action originated in the Supremacy Clause—in fact, the opinion did not separately discuss the existence of a "cause of action" at all—but it certainly proceeded as if one existed, and it ultimately did grant the plaintiffs relief as to one of their claims. It seems that, like some of the direct constitutional cause-of-action cases from the late 1800s and early 1900s that I discussed at the outset,[117] *Shaw* was using the term "jurisdiction" as a loose proxy for "cause of action," and, based on the Supremacy Clause, it assumed a cause of action to exist.

In 2002, the Supreme Court addressed the cause-of-action question more squarely in *Verizon Maryland Inc. v. Public Service Commission of Maryland*,[118] in which a telephone company sued to enjoin a state agency from enforcing an order that allegedly was preempted by the federal Tele-communications Act. The Telecommunications Act did not clearly pro-vide Verizon with a private cause of action.[119] Rather, the asserted source of federal jurisdiction was § 1331, and the asserted cause of action, it appears, arose directly from the Supremacy Clause. Justice Scalia, writing for the Court, endorsed Verizon's assertion:

> We have no doubt that federal courts have jurisdiction under § 1331 to entertain such a suit. Verizon seeks relief from the Commission's order "on the ground that such regulation is pre-empted by a federal statute which, by virtue of the Supremacy Clause of the Constitution, must prevail," and its claim "thus presents a federal question which the federal courts have jurisdiction under 28 U.S.C. § 1331 to resolve."[120]

The Court then remanded the case so that Verizon's claims could be resolved on the merits. So *Verizon* necessarily recognized a direct con-stitutional cause of action allowing plaintiffs to seek prospective relief offensively for violations of the Supremacy Clause.[121] Many lower court cases have followed suit, on the understanding that such a cause of action exists.[122]

2. DORMANT COMMERCE CLAUSE CASES

A second category of cases in which the federal courts routinely recog-nize direct constitutional causes of action encompasses suits to enjoin allegedly unconstitutional laws brought by individuals or corporations against state officers under the so-called dormant Commerce Clause.

These claims traditionally were brought as direct constitutional causes of action based on the Commerce Clause itself. What is interesting is that, throughout the twentieth century, courts continued to entertain these cases without questioning the underlying source of the cause of action. It was not until *Dennis v. Higgins* in 1991 that the Court decided such suits could be brought under § 1983.[123] Until then, they came to the courts as direct constitutional claims.

Many of the best-known modern Commerce Clause cases came before the Supreme Court directly under the Constitution, including *Hunt v. Washington State Apple Advertising Commission*[124] in 1977. Hunt was not premised on a statutory cause of action. Yet the Court did not pause to seek rights-creating language or any other indication that Congress intended for particular litigants to be able to enforce the Commerce Clause in federal court. The Court later explained, in *South-Central Timber Development, Inc. v. Wunnicke*, that the Commerce Clause "has long been recognized as a self-executing limitation on the power of the States to enact laws imposing substantial burdens on such commerce."[125] Similarly, in *McKesson Corp. v. Division of Alcoholic Beverages & Tobacco*, the Court held that once a state tax was determined to violate the Commerce Clause, the state owed retrospective relief to those taxpayers who were required to pay taxes before challenging the statute to "cure any unconstitutional discrimination against interstate commerce during the contested tax period."[126]

3. SUITS AGAINST FEDERAL OFFICERS TO ENJOIN ALLEGEDLY UNCONSTITUTIONAL FEDERAL LAWS

The final category of direct constitutional causes of action consists of suits for prospective relief against federal officers, typically seeking to enjoin federal laws as violative of some structural provision or principle of the Constitution. For these suits, § 1983 is of course not available, as no action taken under color of state law is involved. Nevertheless, courts routinely hear these cases. Examples include the recent challenge to the federal Partial-Birth Abortion Act in *Gonzales v. Carhart*[127] and suits challenging certain applications of federal laws as beyond the federal government's regulatory power under the Commerce Clause, such as *Gonzales v. Raich*.[128] Much of the dispute in these cases centers on whether the plaintiffs have Article III standing, as required by Article III's Case or Controversy Clause.[129] But so long as Article III's prerequisites are met, and so long as there is jurisdiction, federal courts assume that they need no special authorization from Congress to entertain plaintiffs' constitutional claims and to provide appropriate remedies.

In the three categories of cases I have just described, the Supreme Court has not attempted to explain why it so assumes. But it has not looked for evidence of congressional intent to allow or disallow such cases before proceeding to exercise the judicial power.

III. Some Thoughts on the Reasons for the Court's Aversion to Retrospective Relief

How, then, does one explain the Court's much less hospitable approach in recent years to *Bivens*-type damages actions against both state and federal officers? What is the distinction between cases involving preemption (like *Shaw* and *Verizon*), the dormant Commerce Clause (like *Hunt*), and structural limits on federal officers' powers (like *Carhart* and *Raich*) on the one hand, and *Bivens* cases on the other? The most obvious answer is that *Shaw, Verizon, Hunt, Carhart*, and *Raich* were all suits for declaratory or injunctive relief. In contrast, much of the judicial discomfort in the *Bivens* line of cases has centered on the fact that *Bivens* litigants are seeking damages.

The appropriateness of particular *remedies* is a distinct question, though, from the analytically prior matter of whether a *cause of action* exists. The Court emphasized this point in its 1992 case, *Franklin v. Gwinnett County Public Schools*.[130] Even as the Court was retrenching with regard to nonexpress causes of action in statutory cases, *Franklin* held, in the context of a nonexpress damages action based on a federal statute, that where there *is* a cause of action, courts "presume the availability of all appropriate remedies unless Congress has expressly indicated otherwise."[131] *Franklin* recognized that this view "has deep roots in our jurisprudence."[132] *Bell v. Hood* rested upon this understanding as well, as did Justice Harlan's concurrence in *Bivens*.[133]

Moreover, if we suppose that, having found a cause of action, courts may provide injunctive relief but not damages, we invert the traditional understanding of equity, as *Franklin* emphasized. Any first-year law student knows that equitable relief has traditionally been available only when monetary damages cannot provide an adequate remedy.[134] In that sense, "the present juxtaposition of a hesitancy to grant damages awards with a willingness to allow injunctive relief . . . gets the traditional inter-play between law and equity exactly backwards."[135]

So why should it be that the Court has remained comfortable recog-nizing constitutional claims as arising under federal law and as giving rise to the right to prospective relief, yet has increasingly regarded the lack of congressional authorization as a ground for denying damages relief? And why has the Court not undertaken to explain this dichotomy in either the *Bivens* line of cases or in the cases providing prospective relief for con-stitutional violations under the Supremacy Clause, under the dormant Commerce Clause, and against federal officers?

The answer to the first question may be that, as Richard Fallon and Daniel Meltzer have written, when courts engage in constitutional adju-dication, they are serving one of "two basic functions in the constitutional scheme. The first is to redress individual violations. . . . The second . . . [is] to reinforce structural values, including those underlying the separation of powers and the rule of law."[136] The Court's greater hospitality to plain-tiffs seeking prospective relief for constitutional violations than to plain-tiffs seeking compensation for past wrongs may result from its deeper commitment to the second adjudicative function than to the first. Today's Court views its duty of policing the inter- and intragovernmental balance as central to what the judicial power is all about—more central, in many respects, than the duty to ensure remedies for individuals' injuries.

To be sure, the current Court has been cautious in the realm of injunc-tive suits as well. But that caution has concerned the fashioning of lim-ited remedies and the policing of the case or controversy requirement, not the closing of the courthouse doors altogether to prospective plain-tiffs alleging constitutional violations. So, while the Court has cut back on structural injunctions (the kind of detailed, institutional injunctions devised in the school desegregation cases from *Brown* onward, as well as in the later prison and mental institution class actions)[137] and on facial constitutional challenges to statutes,[138] it has never as a Court—the mus-ings of some individual justices notwithstanding[139]—repudiated the bed-rock proposition that the federal courts are open to plaintiffs who seek to assure that state and federal officials comply with the Constitution in the future even if those officials have not done so in the past.

Still, for all the reasons I have surveyed, I do not see how a doctrine imposing an inflexible dichotomy between prospective and retrospective direct constitutional suits can be justified. Justice Harlan's perception in

Bivens still holds: Once one generally accepts that private litigants have access to federal court to enforce constitutional requirements prospectively without express congressional authorization—as I have shown they do in many instances—one must also accept that the judicial provision of *retrospective* remedies is possible and proper in at least some cases, whether or not Congress has expressly provided for them. Our country's traditional common-law understanding that courts have the authority to fashion effective and appropriate remedies in cases properly before them, the wording of the Constitution ("all Cases, in Law and Equity, arising under this Constitution"), and, perhaps most importantly, the backstopping role of the judiciary in a constitutional regime as the institution with "a particular responsibility to assure the vindication of constitutional interests"[140] all lead me to this conclusion.

So how to determine the cases in which such retrospective relief is appropriate? Here are a few propositions. First, as the case law makes clear, the choice of what remedy is appropriate is one to which the judicial power applies more appropriately than the legislative power. So we judges should not look to Congress's failure to provide a constitutional damages remedy as in any way determinative. Moreover, except for its enactment of the post–Civil War statutes enforcing the Reconstruction Amendments, Congress mostly has been silent about who may enforce particular constitutional standards, and how. This reticence has continued despite many attempts in Congress over the years to enact a counterpart to § 1983 for actions against federal, as opposed to state, officers.[141] Congress's failure to act in this area even after *Bivens* is best understood, in my view, as Congress's acquiescence in the understanding that the judicial power includes deciding when damages remedies are necessary to enforce constitutional requirements.

Second, to return to the prescient Justice Harlan, a retrospective damages remedy is of particular importance where the constitutional norm itself is one that is protective of individuals—basically, a norm embodied in the Bill of Rights—rather than a structural norm. Where an individual's constitutional rights are violated, the judicial role in "vindicat[ing] the interests of the individual in the face of the popular will" may include make-whole, retrospective relief, as Justice Harlan recognized in *Bivens*.[142] In contrast, with regard to purely structural constitutional norms, the primary judicial concern is likely to be righting any constitutional dislocation for the future, so that the structure of government runs along its intended course.

Third, there are circumstances—such as in *Bivens* itself—where prospective relief is simply unavailable for practical reasons. In *Bivens*, there was no prosecution in which Bivens would enjoy the protection of the exclusionary rule, and there was also no credible basis for Bivens to claim that he would be faced with a similar search in the future and was thus entitled to equitable relief.[143] Courts should be alert to providing retrospective relief in such circumstances.

Fourth, and relatedly, as federal courts cut back on the availability of injunctive relief because of concerns over judicial competence, the case or controversy requirement, and separation of powers, it becomes more likely that retrospective relief will be the only viable means of vindicating individuals' constitutional rights in certain circumstances. For example, the recent tendency to limit facial challenges to statutes in favor of as-applied challenges necessarily entails a preference for cases in which the facts are fully developed and the need for relief for the individual plaintiff is clear. In many instances, those criteria will be fully met only after the harm has occurred, or there will not be time as a practical matter to seek judicial relief once those criteria are met. Examples are situations in which matters of life and death are at stake—such as restrictions on abortion that could affect the mother's health, as Justice Ginsburg's dissent in *Carhart* warned[144]—or circumstances in which it cannot be known in advance who will be affected by a certain restriction, as in challenges to voting identification requirements.

Finally, there is a connected consideration that matters a great deal to me as a judge: Despite the many disadvantages to retrospective damages actions as a means of enforcing constitutional principles, retrospective actions—which most often mean damages actions, or at least actions for monetary relief—do have the advantage that they are in many ways better suited to effective judicial decisionmaking. We know what happened, who was harmed, and how they were harmed, and the relief to be granted need not be created out of whole cloth, as there are centuries of jurisprudence concerning the adjudication of damages. The courts' constitutional rulings in such cases are likely to be narrowly drawn and case-specific, affecting others as judicial opinions normally do: through stare decisis.

We tend to think of constitutional damages actions as more intrusive on legislative and executive prerogatives, and therefore as a less appropriate use of Article III "judicial Power" than claims seeking prospective relief, but that is not necessarily so. Particularly in the context of suits against federal officers, where federalism concerns are not an issue, it sometimes may make more sense for courts to fashion damages remedies than injunctive remedies.

At the same time, I am sensitive to—and in large measure share—the unarticulated consideration that probably best explains the reluctance of courts in recent years to recognize the availability of monetary damages directly under the Constitution: namely, the notion that that the bedrock role of the judiciary in our tripartite federal governmental system is not individual recompense but preserving the rule of law by assuring that constitutional norms are respected in cases otherwise properly before the federal judiciary.[145] Given that priority, it makes sense to limit the availability of damages actions to circumstances in which prospective relief is for one reason or another unavailable or impractical. Conversely, there will be cases in which some form of equitable relief will be the only meaningful remedy for a given injury.

Conclusion

What is the upshot of all this? Most importantly, that we cannot sensibly decide whether constitutional enforcement actions and remedies are available in federal courts by using the same standards we use to decide the scope of enforcement actions and remedies under congressionally enacted statutes—and that, for the most part, we have not. Instead, the tradition exemplified by *Ex Parte Young* of recognizing appropriately structured prospective causes of action directly under the Constitution has continued. And, although there has been a tendency in recent years to regard direct constitutional *damages* actions as unauthorized renegades, that tendency runs counter to historical practice, the language of the Constitution, and the requirements of an effective constitutional regime. Instead, the question of appropriate remedies *is* properly committed to the "judicial Power," to be exercised carefully and with due regard for considerations of separation of powers and federalism, as well as for judicial competence. As I hope I have shown, the recognition of direct constitutional causes of action, for equitable relief and in some circumstances for damages, is an essential means by which the judiciary fulfills its responsibility to safeguard both the Constitution's structural principles and individual liberties.

Twenty-two years ago, in his second Madison Lecture, Justice Brennan proclaimed that "[o]ur founders and framers . . . took it as an article of faith that this nation prized the independence of its judiciary and that

an independent judiciary could be counted upon to enforce the individual rights and liberties of our citizens against infringement by governmental power."[146] I hope that my reflections have promoted the accom-
plishment of that "article of faith" by explaining why the federal courts
have remained, and should remain, in Madison's words, the "impenetrable bulwark against every assumption of power in the Legislature or
Executive."[147]

NOTES

1. William J. Brennan, Jr., *The Bill of Rights and the States*, 36 N.Y.U. L. REV. 761
(1961).
2. William J. Brennan, Jr., *The Bill of Rights and the States: The Revival of State Constitutions as Guardians of Individual Rights*, 61 N.Y.U. L. REV. 535 (1986).
3. Brennan, *supra* note 1, at 761–69.
4. Brennan, *supra* note 2, at 539–40, 546–48.
5. *Id.* at 550.
6. *Id.* at 552.
7. *See, e.g.*, Williams v. Taylor, 529 U.S. 420 (2000) (considering the availability of
habeas corpus in light of the Antiterrorism and Effective Death Penalty Act of
1996, Pub. L. 104-132, 110 Stat. 1214); Gonzaga Univ. v. Doe, 536 U.S. 273 (2002)
(considering the standards for determining whether a federal statute creates
"rights" within the meaning of 42 U.S.C. § 1983); Seminole Tribe v. Florida,
517 U.S. 44 (1996) (considering whether Congress has the power under the
Indian Commerce Clause, U.S. CONST. art. I, § 8, cl. 3, to abrogate the states'
Eleventh Amendment immunity from suit); Hein v. Freedom from Religion, 127
S. Ct. 2553 (2007) (considering taxpayer standing to challenge executive branch
expenditures).
8. U.S. CONST. art. III, § 1.
9. U.S. CONST. amends. I–X, XIII–XV.
10. Two exceptions are the writ of habeas corpus, U.S. CONST. art. I, § 9, cl. 2, and
the just compensation requirement, U.S. CONST. amend. V.
11. Affirmative suits to enforce *statutory* rights are another story, one I will address
only tangentially in this lecture.
12. A note on terminology is in order: We tend to use the term "implied" cause
of action not only in the context of suits to enforce statutory law but also with
regard to suits to enforce constitutional norms. As sometimes happens, the
now-accepted terminology has gotten in the way of clear thinking. As we all
learned in grammar school, a speaker "implies" and a listener "infers." The term
"implied" cause of action therefore suggests that the proper focus of judicial
inquiry is to determine what the *speakers*—that is, the drafters of a statute or of
the Constitution—intends. But as we shall see, to frame the matter that way is
to beg the hard questions about the role of the judiciary in shaping affirmative
constitutional litigation. So I am for the most part not going to use the phrase

"implied cause of action"; I shall write of "direct constitutional causes of action" and "nonexpress statutory causes of action" instead.

13. 347 U.S. 483 (1954) (*Brown I*); 349 U.S. 294 (1955) (*Brown II*).

14. 347 U.S. 497 (1954).

15. 403 U.S. 388 (1971).

16. At least two of the plaintiffs' complaints invoked 8 U.S.C. § 43, the predecessor to § 1983. *See, e.g.*, Complaint at ¶ 1, Davis v. County Sch. Bd., 103 F. Supp. 337 (E.D. Va. 1952) (Civ. A. No. 1333); Amended Complaint at ¶ 1, Brown v. Bd. of Educ., 98 F. Supp. 797 (D. Kan. 1951) (Civ. No. T-316). But the plaintiffs' filings at the Supreme Court, once the cases had been consolidated, make no mention of § 43 as the basis for suit. *See, e.g.*, Statement as to Jurisdiction at 3, Brown v. Bd. of Educ., 347 U.S. 483 (1954) (No. 1), 1951 WL 82600 ("The asserted right to injunctive relief is based upon the unconstitutionality of Chapter 72-1724 [of the General Statutes of Kansas], in that the Fourteenth Amendment to the United States Constitution strips the state of power to either authorize or require the maintenance of racially segregated public schools.").

17. *See* Harry A. Blackmun, *Section 1983 and Federal Protection of Individual Rights—Will the Statute Remain Alive or Fade Away?*, 60 N.Y.U. L. REV. 1, 19 (1985) (characterizing *Brown* as a § 1983 case—"[p]robably the most significant pre-*Monroe* case"—but noting that "[i]nterestingly, in the Court's opinion there is no citation of either § 1983 or of the [related] jurisdictional statute"). The federal district courts reversed in *Brown* similarly bypassed any inquiry into whether the plaintiffs had a cause of action under the Fourteenth Amendment or a statute in ruling against the plaintiffs' claims on the merits. Briggs v. Elliott, 103 F. Supp. 920 (E.D.S.C. 1952); Davis v. County Sch. Bd., 103 F. Supp. 337 (E.D. Va. 1952); Brown v. Bd. of Educ., 98 F. Supp. 797 (D. Kan. 1951).

18. 42 U.S.C. § 1983 (2000). Today, § 1983 reads:

> Every person who, under color of any statute, ordinance, regula-tion, custom, or usage, of any State or Territory or the District of Columbia, subjects, or causes to be subjected, any citizen of the United States or other person within the jurisdiction thereof to the deprivation of any rights, privileges, or immunities secured by the Constitution and laws, shall be liable to the party injured in an action at law, suit in equity, or other proper proceeding for redress, except that in any action brought against a judicial officer for an act or omission taken in such officer's judicial capacity, injunctive relief shall not be granted unless a declaratory decree was violated or declaratory relief was unavailable.

19. At the beginning of the *Brown* litigation, § 1983's predecessor, 8 U.S.C. § 43, read:

> Every person who, under color of any statute, ordinance, regulation, custom, or usage, of any State or Territory, subjects, or causes to be subjected, any citizen of the United States or other person within the jurisdiction thereof to the deprivation of any rights, privileges, or

immunities secured by the Constitution and laws, shall be liable to
the party injured in an action at law, suit in equity, or other proper
proceeding for redress.

8 U.S.C. § 43 (1946); *see also* 42 U.S.C. § 1983 (1952) (same text). The statute
had been relegated to near-uselessness not long after its passage by a series of
Supreme Court cases, beginning with the *Slaughter-House Cases*, that cabined
the meaning of the Fourteenth Amendment's phrase "privileges or immunities
of citizens of the United States" and adopted a similarly constricted interpretation of the concept of "state action." *See* The Slaughter-House Cases, 83 U.S. (16
Wall.) 36, 75–80 (1873); The Civil Rights Cases, 109 U.S. 3, 17 (1883). It was not
revived until 1961, when the Court reconsidered the meaning of "under color
of law" in *Monroe v. Pape*, opening up the possibility of suing state actors for
unconstitutional acts. 365 U.S. 167 (1961). This sequence explains why § 1983
was almost never used to sue state actors between 1871 and 1961. *See* Blackmun,
supra note 17, at 8–11 (1985); Eugene Gressman, *The Unhappy History of Civil
Rights Legislation*, 50 MICH. L. REV. 1323, 1357 (1952).

20. Whether an official acting "under color of" District of Columbia law could be
liable under 8 U.S.C. § 43—the predecessor to the current § 1983—was an open
question at the time of *Bolling*. The *Bolling* plaintiffs' briefs did allege what they
called "violations" of § 43 in conjunction with violations of the Fifth Amendment. *See* Brief for Petitioners on Reargument at 4, Bolling v. Sharpe, 347
U.S. 497 (1954) (No. 8), 1953 WL 48705. They also argued that the phrase "any
State or Territory" in § 43 included the District of Columbia. *Id.* at 80–81. The
Supreme Court did not decide this question in *Bolling*, but later, in *District of
Columbia v. Carter*, it concluded that the District of Columbia was not a "State
or Territory" for § 1983 purposes. 409 U.S. 418 (1973). It was not until 1979 that
Congress revised what is now § 1983 to clarify that it applies to suits for actions
taken "under color of [law] . . . of any State or Territory *or the District of Columbia*." Act of Dec. 29, 1979, Pub. L. No. 96-170, § 1, 93 Stat. 1284 (1979) (emphasis
added). In any event, the *Bolling* Court never mentioned the Civil Rights Act.
The Court's very short opinion instead appears to have assumed that general
federal question jurisdiction under § 1331 was all the congressional authorization needed. Bolling v. Sharpe, 347 U.S. 497 (1954).

21. Later, in *Davis v. Passman*, the Supreme Court explained that the *Bolling* "[p]lain-
tiffs were clearly the appropriate parties to bring such a suit . . . [for] equitable
relief," seemingly assuming that the *Bolling* plaintiffs indeed had a cause of action
directly under the Constitution. 442 U.S. 228, 243 (1979).

22. Of course, courts in those years did not always use the phrase "cause of action"
to explain what they were doing. That term has floated around for a long time,
but it did not always have the relatively fixed meaning that it does today. Sometimes courts used the term "jurisdiction" in place of what we would today call
a "cause of action" when speaking of a particular plaintiff's entitlement to sue
for relief, and sometimes courts bypassed the modern cause-of-action inquiry
altogether.

23. Judiciary Act of 1875, ch. 137, § 1, 18 Stat. 470, 470.

24. *See, e.g.*, Osborn v. Bank of the United States, 22 U.S. (9 Wheat.) 738, 817–18 (1824) (holding that federal courts' jurisdiction over cases in which the Bank of the United States was a party had been conferred by statute).

25. 28 U.S.C. § 1331 (2006).

26. 22 U.S. (9 Wheat.) 738.

27. *Id.* at 844. Ultimately, *Osborn* held the tax unconstitutional on the basis of *McCulloch v. Maryland*, 17 U.S. (4 Wheat.) 316 (1819), which rested on the Supremacy Clause. *Osborn*, 22 U.S. at 867–68.

28. The decidedly corporate profile of the early litigants in equity is due to a number of factors. *See* Michael G. Collins, *"Economic Rights," Implied Constitutional Actions, and the Scope of Section 1983*, 77 G E O. L. J. 1493, 1530–32 (1989) (discussing reasons for the prevalence of corporate litigants in federal courts).

29. Scott v. Donald, 165 U.S. 107, 108–09, 112 (1897).

30. Allen v. Balt. & Ohio R.R., 114 U.S. 311, 311–13 (1884).

31. Am. Sch. of Magnetic Healing v. MacAnnulty, 187 U.S. 94, 96, 98–99, 102 (1902).

32. *Am. Sch. of Magnetic Healing*, 187 U.S. at 108, 110; *Scott*, 165 U.S. at 114–15; *Allen*, 114 U.S. at 316–17; *see* Bell v. Hood, 327 U.S. 678, 684 & n.4 (1946) (citing nineteenth-century cases and stating that "it is established practice for this Court to sustain the jurisdiction of federal courts to issue injunctions to protect rights safeguarded by the Constitution and to restrain individual state officers from doing what the 14th Amendment forbids the State to do" (footnote and citations omitted)); Walter E. Dellinger, *Of Rights and Remedies: The Constitution as a Sword*, 85 H A R V. L. R E V. 1532, 1541 (1972) (noting a "settled practice of granting injunctive relief premised directly upon the Constitution").

33. 209 U.S. 123 (1908).

34. Because the primary focus of my writing—direct constitutional causes of action against government officials in their private capacity—does not directly implicate Eleventh Amendment or sovereign immunity concerns, discussion of those complex subjects would be a distraction. I therefore do not address them.

35. John Harrison, Ex Parte Young, 60 S T A N. L. R E V. 989, 993 (2008).

36. *Id.* at 992–93.

37. *Young*, 209 U.S. at 143–45.

38. *Id.* at 148.

39. *Id.* at 168.

40. *See* Louisville & Nashville R.R. v. Mottley, 211 U.S. 149, 152–53 (1908) (explaining that for § 1331 jurisdiction to apply, it must be clear from the face of the plaintiff's complaint that the action involves a federal question; it is not enough for the federal question to arise as a response to an anticipated defense).

41. In cases at law, claims, defenses, and answers to defenses were traditionally broken out into a series of responsive filings, which were submitted consecutively to the court. *See* Alfred Hill, *Constitutional Remedies*, 69 C O L U M. L. R E V. 1109, 1128 (1969). In equity, the pleading rules were different: The plaintiff's initial filing—called the "bill"—had to "tell the entire story" of why the defendant's action was unlawful and why an equitable remedy was needed. *Id.* at 1129. Thus, in some, but not all, circumstances, a plaintiff in equity would be able to state

his constitutional issue on the face of his initial filing even though he could not have done so had the action been one at law. *See* Collins, *supra* note 28, at 1517. This difference in pleading conventions muffled to some extent the impact of the well-pleaded complaint rule on cases in equity before equity was merged with law.

42. In the nineteenth and early twentieth centuries, if a government officer injured an individual, that injury was understood in terms of one of the familiar common law forms of action like trespass and thus was viewed primarily as a creation of state law, with federal issues arising as a response to a defense of immunity. *See* Collins, *supra* note 28, at 1510–11. The notion was that if an official acted unconstitutionally, he could not take advantage of the defense of official justification. *Id.* Over time, courts gradually came to view cases involving claims about the unconstitutionality of an official's action as grounded in *federal*, not just state, law. *See* Henry M. Hart, Jr., *The Relations Between State and Federal Law*, 54 COLUM. L. REV. 489, 523–24 (1954) (discussing the "almost imperceptible steps" by which courts came to think of the source of law of a plaintiff's suit against a federal officer as federal law, rather than state law). By the time of *Bivens*, the right to be free from unreasonable searches and seizures was seen not as derived from and limited by the scope of state trespass and battery law, but as having an independent source in the Constitution itself. *See Bivens*, 403 U.S. at 392; *id.* at 400 & n.3 (Harlan, J., concurring).

43. *See* Tennessee v. Union & Planters' Bank, 152 U.S. 454, 464 (1894) (precluding removal based on a federal defense or reply).

44. *See* Hill, *supra* note 41, at 1130.

45. 114 U.S. 307, 308 (1885).

46. *Id.*

47. *Id.*

48. 290 U.S. 13 (1933).

49. In *Jacobs*, the Court held that the Tucker Act provided jurisdiction over the United States by providing the sovereign's consent to be sued, but it did not provide the cause of action. Instead, "the right to recover just compensation for property taken by the United States for public use in the exercise of its power of eminent domain . . . rested upon the Fifth Amendment. Statutory recognition was not necessary." *Jacobs*, 290 U.S. at 16.

50. *Id.*

51. 179 U.S. 58 (1900).

52. *Id.* at 62.

53. 327 U.S. 678 (1946).

54. On the meaning of the phrase "cause of action," see note 95, *infra*.

55. 327 U.S. at 684.

56. 403 U.S. 388 (1971).

57. 403 U.S. at 410 (Harlan, J., concurring); *see also* Susan Bandes, *Reinventing Bivens: The Self-Executing Constitution*, 68 S. CAL. L. REV. 289, 295 (1995) (discussing the factual background of *Bivens*).

58. *Bivens*, 403 U.S. at 392 (emphasis added).

59. *Id.* at 397; *see* Marbury v. Madison, 5 U.S. (1 Cranch) 137, 163 (1803) ("[W]
   here there is a legal right, there is also a legal remedy. . . ." (quoting WILLIAM
   BLACKSTONE, 3 COMMENTARIES ON THE LAWS OF ENGLAND 23
   (Oxford, Clarendon Press 1768)).

60. *Bivens*, 403 U.S. at 396 (alteration in original) (citation omitted) (quoting *Bell*,
   327 U.S. at 684).

61. *Id.* (first ellipsis in original) (emphasis added) (quoting *Bell*, 327 U.S. at 684).

62. 327 U.S. 678 (1946).

63. *See* Bd. of Comm'rs of Jackson County v. United States, 308 U.S. 343, 349–53
   (1939); Dooley v. United States, 182 U.S. 222, 224–25 (1901).

64. *Bivens*, 403 U.S. at 397 (citing J.I. Case Co. v. Borak, 377 U.S. 426, 433 (1964),
   which held that a stockholder harmed by an unlawful merger had a federal
   cause of action for rescission or damages under the Securities Exchange Act
   even though the Act did not so specify).

65. *Borak*, 377 U.S. at 433.

66. The earliest appellate court usage of the phrase "implied cause of action" of
   which I am aware was in *Petition of Kinsman Transit Co.*, 338 F.2d 708, 718 (2d
   Cir. 1964), which considered but declined to decide whether a federal regulation governing the operation of drawbridges on navigable waterways "creat[ed]
   by implication a cause of action" for a party whose ship was damaged by
   negligent operation. The Supreme Court did not use the term until *Blue Chip
   Stamps v. Manor Drug Stores*, 421 U.S. 723, 734 n.6 (1975), a case in which the
   Court "express[ed] . . . no opinion" on whether section 17(a) of the Securities
   Exchange Act "gives rise to an implied cause of action."

67. *See supra* note 12.

68. 441 U.S. 677 (1979).

69. *Cannon*, 441 U.S. at 730–49 (Powell, J., dissenting) (arguing against finding
   implied causes of action in federal statutes "absent the most compelling evidence that Congress in fact intended such an action to exist").

70. 532 U.S. 275 (2001) (holding that there is no implied cause of action to enforce
   regulations enacted pursuant to Title VI of the Civil Rights Act of 1964).

71. *Id.* at 286–93 (looking only to the "text and structure of Title VI" to "determine
   whether it displays an intent to create not just a private right but also a private
   remedy").

72. *See supra* Part I.B.

73. Bivens v. Six Unknown Named Agents of the Fed. Bureau of Narcotics, 403 U.S.
   388, 402–03 (1971) (Harlan, J., concurring).

74. *Id.* at 404 (emphasis added).

75. *Id.* at 405.

76. *Id.* at 399 (explaining that damages are a "traditional judicial remedy"); *see also
   id.* at 395–96 (majority opinion) (discussing damages as an "ordinary remedy").

77. *Id.* at 407 (Harlan, J., concurring).

78. 442 U.S. 228 (1979).

79. *Id.* at 241–42.

80. *Id.* at 242, 246–47 (emphasis omitted) (quoting *Bivens*, 403 U.S. at 397).

81. Schweiker v. Chilicky, 487 U.S. 412, 421 (1988).
82. *See* Hartman v. Moore, 547 U.S. 250 (2006) (allowing a manufacturer to sue a federal prosecutor and postal inspectors for prosecuting him in retaliation for his lobbying efforts, in violation of the First Amendment); Carlson v. Green, 446 U.S. 14 (1980) (allowing suits by prisoners against federal prison officials for the denial of medical care in violation of the Eighth Amendment); *Davis*, 442 U.S. 228.
83. *See, e.g, Schweiker*, 487 U.S. 412 (1988) (refusing to permit damages action under the Fifth Amendment's Due Process Clause by recipients of disability benefits against Social Security Administration officials); United States v. Stanley, 483 U.S. 669 (1987) (refusing to permit damages action by members of the armed forces against superiors for non-consensual medical experimentation); Bush v. Lucas, 462 U.S. 367 (1983) (refusing to permit damages action by a federal civil servant under the First Amendment); Chappell v. Wallace, 462 U.S. 296 (1983) (refusing to permit damages action by members of the armed forces against their superiors for racial discrimination).
84. *Schweiker*, 487 U.S. 412.
85. *Id.* at 425–26.
86. *Id.* at 423.
87. Corr. Servs. Corp. v. Malesko, 534 U.S. 61, 75 (2001) (Scalia, J., concurring).
88. *Malesko*, 534 U.S. 61.
89. *Id.* at 67 n.3 (majority opinion); *id.* at 75 (Scalia, J., concurring).
90. *Id.* at 75 (emphasis added).
91. Although the diversity of interests and concerns in Congress may lead to a carefully balanced agreement as to what specific remedies should be available for a statutory violation, that diversity can lead just as easily to intentionally vague statutory language, leaving courts to work out the details. *See, e.g.*, Rosado v. Wyman, 397 U.S. 397, 412 (1970) (Harlan, J., concurring) ("Congress, as it frequently does, has voiced its wishes in muted strains and left it to the courts to discern the theme in the cacophony of political understanding.").
92. Bivens v. Six Unknown Named Agents of the Fed. Bureau of Narcotics, 403 U.S. 388, 430 (1971) (Blackmun, J., dissenting); *see also id.* at 428 (Black, J., dissenting); *id.* at 412, 422 (Burger, C.J., dissenting).
93. *See* JOHN NORTON POMEROY, CODE REMEDIES §§ 347–49, at 460–66 (4th ed. 1904).
94. FED. R. CIV. P. 8(a)(2).
95. *See, e.g.*, Davis v. Passman, 442 U.S. 228, 237–38 (1979) (quoting Larson v. Domestic & Foreign Commerce Corp., 337 U.S. 682, 693 (1949)); *see Larson*, 337 U.S. at 693 ("It is a prerequisite to the maintenance of any action for specific relief that the plaintiff claim an invasion of his legal rights, either past or threatened. He must, therefore, allege conduct which is 'illegal.' . . . If he does not, he has not stated a cause of action.").
96. 304 U.S. 64, 78 (1938).
97. United States v. Standard Oil Co. of Cal., 332 U.S. 301, 307 (1947).
98. 446 U.S. 14 (1980).

99. *Id.* at 38 (Rehnquist, J., dissenting).

100. Corr. Servs. Corp. v. Malesko, 534 U.S. 61, 75 (2001) (Scalia, J., concurring).

101. *See Erie*, 304 U.S. at 78 ("Except in matters governed by the Federal Constitution or by Acts of Congress, the law to be applied in any case is the law of the State.").

102. In other words, the concepts of "federal common law" and of "federal general common law" differ, and *Erie* abolished only the latter. *See, e.g.*, Martha A. Field, *Sources of Law: The Federal Common Law*, 99 HARV. L. REV. 881, 908 (1986); William A. Fletcher, *The General Common Law and Section 34 of the Judiciary Act of 1789: The Example of Marine Insurance*, 97 HARV. L. REV. 1513, 1521–25 (1984).

103. *Erie*, 304 U.S. at 74.

104. 451 U.S. 77 (1981).

105. *Id.* at 95 (internal quotations omitted).

106. *Northwest Airlines*, 451 U.S. at 97.

107. Parallel to its trend of restricting federal courts' ability to provide damages remedies, the Supreme Court has also made some less dramatic, though still significant, restrictions on the federal courts' powers in equity. *See, e.g.*, John H. Langbein, *What ERISA Means by "Equitable": The Supreme Court's Trail of Error in* Russell, Mertens, *and* Great-West, 103 COLUM. L. REV. 1317 (2003); Judith Resnik, *Constricting Remedies: The Rehnquist Judiciary, Congress, and Federal Power*, 78 IND. L.J. 223, 252–53 (2003).

108. *See* Dellinger, *supra* note 32, at 1557 ("'[T]here can be no legal right against the authority that makes the law upon which the right depends.' But in a constitutional case, the right involved does not 'depend' upon the government, but rather arises from the basic law which created and seeks to control that government." (quoting Kawananakoa v. Polyblank, 205 U.S. 349, 353 (1907))).

109. 1 ANNALS OF CONG. 439 (Joseph Gales ed., 1834); Letter from James Madison to Edmund Randolph (May 31, 1789), *in* 5 THE WRITINGS OF JAMES MADISON, 1787–1790, at 385 (Gaillard Hunt ed., 1904).

110. Cannon v. Univ. of Chi., 441 U.S. 677, 733 n.3 (Powell, J., dissenting).

111. Richard H. Fallon, Jr. & Daniel J. Meltzer, *New Law, Non-Retroactivity, and Constitutional Remedies*, 104 HARV. L. REV. 1731, 1779 (1991).

112. *See, e.g.*, Lujan v. Defenders of Wildlife, 504 U.S. 555, 560–61 (1992) (spelling out modern constitutional standing doctrine).

113. *See* Resnik, *supra* note 107, at 240 ("The constitutional charter for 'courts' with jurisdiction 'in law and equity' can thus be read to authorize institutions that . . . have the capacity to respond to changing demands, so long as federal courts work within the boundaries of their subject matter authority.").

114. *See, e.g.*, Gade v. Nat'l Solid Wastes Mgmt. Ass'n, 505 U.S. 88 (1992) (exercising jurisdiction over a business association's claim that Illinois's licensing requirements for hazardous waste handlers were preempted by the federal Occupational Safety and Health Act); Pac. Gas & Elec. Co. v. State Energy Res. Conservation & Dev. Comm'n, 461 U.S. 190 (1983) (exercising jurisdiction over a utility's claim that California's disposal requirements for nuclear power plants were preempted by the federal Atomic Energy Act); Ray v. Atl. Richfield Co.,

435 U.S. 151 (1978) (exercising jurisdiction over a claim that a Washington state law regulating the design, size, and movement of oil tankers in Puget Sound was preempted by the federal Ports and Waterways Safety Act); Fla. Lime & Avocado Growers, Inc. v. Paul, 373 U.S. 132 (1963) (exercising jurisdiction over Florida avocado growers' claim that a California statute gauging avocado maturity was preempted by applicable federal regulations); *see also* RICHARD H. FALLON, JR. ET AL., HART & WECHSLER'S THE FEDERAL COURTS & THE FEDERAL SYSTEM 903 (5th ed. 2003) (describing "the rule that there is an implied right of action to enjoin state or local regulation that is preempted by a federal statutory or constitutional provision" as "well-established").

115. 463 U.S. 85 (1983).

116. *Id.* at 96 n.14.

117. *See supra* Part I.B.

118. 535 U.S. 635 (2002).

119. *Id.* at 642.

120. *Verizon*, 535 U.S. at 642 (quoting Shaw v. Delta Air Lines, Inc., 463 U.S. 85, 96 n.14 (1983)).

121. *See also* David Sloss, *Constitutional Remedies for Statutory Violations*, 89 IOWA L. REV. 355, 392 (2004) ("As is typical in *Shaw* preemption cases, the courts simply assumed the availability of a private cause of action, without questioning the source of that right of action.").

122. *See* sources cited *supra* note 114; *see also* Lawrence County v. Lead-Deadwood Sch. Dist. No. 40-1, 469 U.S. 256, 259 n.6 (1985) (describing *Shaw* as "reaffirming the general rule" that a plaintiff claiming that a state law is preempted under the Supremacy Clause has stated a federal claim for injunctive relief).

123. 498 U.S. 439, 451 (1991).

124. 432 U.S. 333, 352–53 (1977).

125. 467 U.S. 82, 87 (1984) (emphasis added).

126. 496 U.S. 18, 51 (1990).

127. 550 U.S. 124, 168 (2007).

128. 545 U.S. 1, 7–9 (2005) (rejecting the claim that a ban on home-grown marijuana is violative of the Commerce Clause).

129. For example, in *Hein v. Freedom from Religion Foundation, Inc.*, 127 S. Ct. 2553 (2007), the Court recognized that the Establishment Clause creates a cause of action permitting a taxpayer to sue for injunctive relief but emphasized that plaintiffs must still satisfy the requirements of Article III standing.

130. 503 U.S. 60, 65–66 (1992).

131. *Franklin*, 503 U.S. at 66.

132. *Id.*

133. Bivens v. Six Unknown Named Agents of the Fed. Bureau of Narcotics, 403 U.S. 388, 402–03 (1971) (Harlan, J., concurring); Bell v. Hood, 327 U.S. 678 (1946).

134. *See Bivens*, 403 U.S. at 395 ("Historically, damages have been regarded as the ordinary remedy for an invasion of personal interests in liberty."); Osborn v. Bank of the United States, 22 U.S. (9 Wheat.) 738, 749 (1824) ("All the cases where injunctions have been granted, to protect parties in the enjoyment of a

franchise, proceed upon the principle, that the injury was consequential, not direct, and that it would be difficult, if not impossible, to estimate the damages."); 1 JOSEPH STORY, COMMENTARIES ON EQUITY JURISPRUDENCE AS ADMINISTERED IN ENGLAND AND AMERICA §§ 26–30, 44 (Boston, Little, Brown, 1861) (explaining that equitable relief was available to litigants who faced a threat of irreparable harm but who, because of the common-law writ system's rigidity, could not obtain relief in courts at law).

135. Gene R. Nichol, Bivens, Chilicky, and Constitutional Damages Claims, 75 VA. L. REV. 1117, 1135 (1989).

136. Fallon & Meltzer, supra note 111, at 1787.

137. See generally William A. Fletcher, The Discretionary Constitution: Institutional Remedies and Judicial Legitimacy, 91 YALE L.J. 635 (1982) (discussing institutional suits and injunctions).

138. See, e.g., Gonzales v. Carhart, 550 U.S. 124, 167–68 (2007) ("The latitude given facial challenges in the First Amendment context is inapplicable [in the context of a challenge to a federal abortion statute]. Broad challenges of this type impose a heavy burden upon the parties maintaining the suit[, requiring at the least that] the Act would be unconstitutional in a large fraction of relevant cases."); see also Pamela S. Karlan, The Law of Small Numbers: Gonzales v. Carhart, Parents Involved in Community Schools, and Some Themes from the First Full Term of the Roberts Court, 86 N.C. L. REV. 1369, 1373–74 (2008) (discussing the Supreme Court's resistance to facial challenges).

139. See supra notes 87–90 and accompanying text.

140. Bivens v. Six Unknown Named Agents of the Fed. Bureau of Narcotics, 403 U.S. 388, 407 (1971) (Harlan, J., concurring).

141. See FDIC v. Meyer, 510 U.S. 471, 486 n.11 (1994) (noting that "Congress has considered several proposals that would have created a Bivens-type remedy directly against the Federal Government" and collecting proposed bills from the 1970s and 1980s).

142. Bivens, 403 U.S. at 407–08 (Harlan, J., concurring).

143. See City of Los Angeles v. Lyons, 461 U.S. 95 (1983).

144. 550 U.S. 124, 189 (Ginsburg, J., dissenting) ("Surely the Court cannot mean that no suit may be brought until a woman's health is immediately jeopardized. . . . A woman suffering from medical complications needs access to the medical procedure at once and cannot wait for the judicial process to unfold.") (internal quotations and citations omitted).

145. See Fallon & Meltzer, supra note 111, at 1789–90.

146. Brennan, supra note 2, at 552.

147. 1 ANNALS OF CONG. 439 (Joseph Gales ed., 1834) (quoting James Madison in 1789).

9

Reading the Fourth Amendment

Guidance from the Mischief That Gave It Birth

M. BLANE MICHAEL

It is a special privilege for me, as a graduate of the New York University School of Law, to have been invited to deliver the James Madison Lecture. A chief purpose of this lecture series is "to enhance the appreciation of civil liberty."[1] Upon recalling this purpose, I thought immediately that the Fourth Amendment—the bulwark of our privacy protection—merits renewed attention and appreciation.

The Fourth Amendment consists of two connected clauses. The first guarantees "[t]he right of the people to be secure in their persons, houses, papers, and effects, against unreasonable searches and seizures."[2] The second specifies that "no Warrants shall issue, but upon probable cause, supported by Oath or affirmation, and particularly describing the place to be searched, and the persons or things to be seized."[3] These sound like powerful words, but their vitality is in question today. The digital age is placing our privacy in jeopardy. Technological advances in the way we communicate and store information make us increasingly vulnerable to intrusive searches and seizures. As Chief Judge Kozinski recently observed in an en banc Ninth Circuit decision: "[P]eople now have personal data that are stored [electronically] with that of innumerable strangers. [The government's] [s]eizure of, for example, Google's email servers to look for a few incriminating messages could jeopardize the privacy of millions."[4] So, my question is this: Can the Fourth Amendment—designed in the

This lecture was delivered on October 20, 2009, and appeared in *85 N.Y.U. L. Rev.* 905 (2010).

musty age of paper—offer any meaningful privacy protection today for personal electronic data?

Justice Brandeis, in his venerable dissent in *Olmstead v. United States*, said that a constitutional provision such as the Fourth Amendment must have the "capacity of adaptation to a changing world."[5] Using borrowed language, Justice Brandeis emphasized that for a constitutional "principle to be vital[,] [it] must be capable of wider application than the mischief which gave it birth."[6]

The pre-revolutionary mischief that gave birth to the Fourth Amendment can provide critical guidance in interpreting the Amendment and ensuring its vitality in a digital world. The early mischief—the British Crown's unbridled power of search—is at the center of the rich history that led to the adoption of the Fourth Amendment. This formative history illustrates the broader purpose of the Amendment: to circumscribe government discretion.

In recent years the Supreme Court has often used an interpretive methodology, championed by Justice Scalia, that fails to take account of the Fourth Amendment's animating history. Under Justice Scalia's approach, the specific common law rules of the founding era determine whether a search or seizure is unreasonable today. This approach, as I will respectfully discuss, is both impractical and cramped, and should be abandoned. We should return to the use of formative history as one of the primary sources in interpreting the Fourth Amendment. This would mean a return to a more traditional analysis that highlights the Amendment's enduring purpose. I will also address how history can guide us in applying the Amendment to novel questions arising in our ever more interconnected world.

I.

I begin by reviewing some of the history behind the Fourth Amendment's inclusion in the Bill of Rights. The Fourth Amendment owes its existence to furious opposition in the American colonies to British search and seizure practices, particularly in the area of customs enforcement. Under English law, customs officials had "almost unlimited authority to search for and seize goods [that were] imported" illegally.[7] The Act of Frauds of 1662 empowered customs officers in England to enter "any house, shop, cellar, warehouse or room, or other place" and to "break open doors, chests, trunks and other package[s]" for the purpose of seizing any "pro-hibited and uncustomed" goods.[8]

The Act of Frauds of 1696 extended the broad enforcement pow-ers in the 1662 Act to customs officers in the colonies, authorizing the officers to conduct warrantless searches at their discretion.[9] The 1662 Act also authorized the use of writs of assistance in customs searches.[10] These court-issued writs empowered customs officers to commandeer anyone—constables and ordinary citizens alike—to help in executing searches and seizures.[11] A writ of assistance, though not technically a war-rant, prominently repeated the language of both Acts of Frauds, which empowered a customs officer to search any place on nothing more than his own (subjective) suspicion.[12] Writs of assistance were especially perni-cious because they remained in effect for the life of the king or queen.[13]

In the early 1750s the growing threat of war with France[14] "prompted stricter [customs] enforcement" in the colonies as the Crown sought to increase its revenues.[15] To facilitate tougher enforcement, customs offi-cers began obtaining writs of assistance from colonial courts.[16] The use of these writs was controversial, particularly in Boston, where much of the economy depended on trade in smuggled goods.[17] The controversy intensified when King George II died in late 1760, and colonial customs officers had to reapply for writs of assistance to be issued in the name of the new king, George III.[18] In 1761 a group of Boston merchants and citizens represented by James Otis, a highly regarded Massachusetts law-yer, challenged writ applications filed by several customs collectors in the Massachusetts Superior Court.[19] Otis's advocacy in this case, later called *The Writs of Assistance Case*,[20] galvanized support for what became the Fourth Amendment.

Otis argued passionately that the writ of assistance was illegal, calling it an "instrument[ ] of slavery on the one hand, and villainy on the other."[21] This writ, he declared, "place[d] the liberty of every man in the hands of every petty officer";[22] it was thus "the worst instrument of arbitrary power, the most destructive of English liberty . . . that ever was found in an English law-book."[23] Otis's argument against the writ of assistance pressed two overarching themes that would become the bedrock of the movement against excessive search and seizure power: first, in his words, the "fundamental . . . Privilege of House"[24]—the principle that a person's home is especially private and must be protected from arbitrary govern-ment intrusion; and second, the inevitability of abuse when government officials have the sort of unlimited discretion sanctioned by the writ of assistance.

Otis's vigorous argument did not persuade the five-member Superior Court, which voted unanimously to issue the challenged writs,[25] but it nonetheless proved a powerful influence. Otis's presentation inspired future president John Adams, then a young lawyer of twenty-five, who attended the hearings[26] and was moved to action. Years later, reflecting on the impact of the case, Adams wrote:

> Otis was a flame of fire! . . . Every man of a crowded audience appeared to me to go away, as I did, ready to take up arms against writs of assistance. Then and there was the first scene of the first act of opposition to the arbitrary claims of Great Britain. Then and there the child Independence was born.[27]

Further inspiration for the Fourth Amendment came later in the 1760s from a set of highly publicized English cases arising out of the king's use of general warrants against his political enemies. The general warrant, which authorized an officer to search unspecified places or to seize unspecified persons, was in common use in both England and the colonies.[28] Typical examples permitted discretionary searches for stolen property or fugitives,[29] but in England the Crown turned to the use of general warrants as a means of silencing its critics. Specifically, general warrants were used to gather evidence for seditious libel prosecutions against the king's detractors. This practice led to other celebrated cases that helped spawn the Fourth Amendment.

The first cases, which I call *The North Briton Cases*, stemmed from the publication of *The North Briton No. 45*, an anonymous pamphlet satirizing the king and his policies.[30] Lord Halifax, the secretary of state, issued a general warrant authorizing government agents, called "messengers[,]" to make strict and diligent search for the authors, printers and publishers" of *The North Briton No. 45* and, when they were found, to seize them "together with their papers."[31] The messengers ransacked houses and printing shops in their searches, arrested forty-nine persons (including the pamphlet's author, Parliament member John Wilkes), and seized incriminating papers—all under a single general warrant.[32]

Wilkes and his associates fought back in the civil courts, filing trespass suits against Lord Halifax and the messengers who executed the warrant. Wilkes and the other plaintiffs argued that the general warrant—which was offered as a defense to the trespass claims—was invalid at common law because it failed to name suspects and because it gave "messengers [the discretionary power] to search wherever their [personal] suspicions may chance to fall."[33] The plaintiffs persuaded the courts to submit the trespass claims to juries, and one jury awarded damages to Wilkes of £4000 against Lord Halifax.[34] This was a substantial sum; £4,000 in 1763 is roughly equivalent to £500,000 today.[35] Other targets of the searches received verdicts against the messengers in the range of £200 to £400.[36]

More important than the damages awards, however, were the strong judicial pronouncements in *The North Briton Cases* against the validity of the general warrant, which echoed Otis's denunciation of the writ of assistance. Chief Justice Charles Pratt (later Lord Camden) of the Court of Common Pleas declared: "To enter a man's house by virtue of a nameless warrant, in order to procure evidence, is worse than the Spanish Inquisition; a law under which no Englishman would wish to live an hour; it was a most daring public attack made upon the liberty of the subject."[37] In a 1765 appeal in one *North Briton* case, Lord Mansfield emphasized that "[i]t is not fit, that the receiving or judging of the information should be left to the discretion of the officer. The magistrate ought to judge; and should give certain directions to the officer."[38]

In the remaining case the Crown targeted John Entick for his publication of *The Monitor*, a pamphlet alleged to contain seditious libel.[39] Lord Halifax issued a warrant for Entick's arrest, which gave messengers authority to make a general search of Entick's house and to seize any and all papers at their discretion. Like Wilkes, Entick sued the messengers in trespass and won a jury verdict of £300.[40] In upholding the verdict, Lord Camden held that the search was illegal because no law allowed "such a [general] search [as] a means of detecting offenders."[41] Otherwise, Camden warned, "the secret cabinets and bureaus of every subject in this kingdom [would] be thrown open to the search and inspection of a messenger, whenever the secretary of state shall think fit to charge, or even to suspect, a person . . . of a seditious libel."[42] In short, as Camden put it, "Papers are the owner's goods and chattels: they are his dearest property; and are so far from enduring a seizure, that they will hardly bear an inspection."[43]

The value of the *North Briton* and *Entick* opinions in the colonies came from their articulation and support of the same privacy and liberty interests advanced by James Otis in *The Writs of Assistance Case*. The cases, however, did not end the use of general warrants or writs of assistance, either in England or in the colonies.[44] Thus, a full-throated controversy about the customs writ of assistance, which was regarded as equivalent to a general warrant,[45] persisted until the first shots of the Revolution.[46] Indeed, the First Continental Congress in 1774 included customs searches under general writs of assistance in its list of grievances against Parliament.[47]

This controversy left citizens of the new American states with a deep-dyed fear of discretionary searches permitted by general warrants and writs of assistance.[48] By 1789, when James Madison submitted his proposed Bill of Rights to Congress, seven of the thirteen state constitutions already contained provisions with search and seizure protection bearing some resemblance to the Fourth Amendment.[49] Among the most influential was the provision from Massachusetts, which was the first to use the full phrase "unreasonable searches and seizures," the phrase that is the heart of the Fourth Amendment.[50] The Massachusetts provision had been drafted by none other than John Adams, who remained indelibly impressed by James Otis's argument against the writ of assistance.[51] Thus, the principles that Otis expounded—the fundamental "Privilege of House" and private papers, and the right to be free from discretionary search at "the hands of every petty officer"—profoundly influenced how the Fourth Amendment was understood at the time of its adoption. As I will discuss in more detail, these same history-tested principles should inform our understanding of the Amendment today.

II.

The immediate aim of the Fourth Amendment was to ban general warrants and writs of assistance. To this end, the Amendment's Warrant Clause requires that a warrant "particularly describ[e] the place to be searched, and the persons or things to be seized."[52] The Supreme Court, however, has never read the Fourth Amendment as simply a prohibition on general warrants.[53] Rather, the Court has consistently given substance to the Amendment's first clause, which guarantees "[t]he right of the people to be secure in their persons, houses, papers, and effects, against *unreasonable searches and seizures.*"[54] In judging whether a search or seizure is unreasonable, the Supreme Court has often looked to the formative history just discussed to inform its interpretation.[55] This practice, I believe, is sound. In recent years, however, Justice Scalia has led the Court to use a more rigid historical methodology—a methodology that fails to take heed of the core principles underlying the Fourth Amendment.

Justice Scalia set forth his methodology most clearly in his 1999 majority opinion in *Wyoming v. Houghton*.[56] As he explained, "In determining whether a particular governmental action violates [the Fourth Amendment's unreasonableness] provision, we inquire first whether the action was regarded as an unlawful search or seizure under the common law when the Amendment was framed."[57] Under this approach, if the common law or statutes of the founding era permitted a particular search or seizure, then the analysis is complete; a court is required to hold that the action is reasonable under the Fourth Amendment today.[58] Only when this historical inquiry "yields no answer" is a court permitted to consider what Justice Scalia refers to as "traditional standards of reasonableness."[59] That is, a court may balance the degree to which the search or seizure intrudes upon an individual's privacy against the degree to which the intrusion is needed to promote legitimate governmental interests.[60]

On its face the idea of looking to framing-era common law to determine the scope of Fourth Amendment protections might seem sensible. After all, the heralded search and seizure opinions in the *North Briton* and *Entick* cases were English common law decisions that reflected the principles underlying the Fourth Amendment. The problem with Justice Scalia's approach is not its consideration of the common law. The problem is that it gives dispositive weight to the substantive rules that existed in 1791 instead of applying the underlying principles of the Fourth Amendment to modern circumstances. In essence, Justice Scalia freezes in place eighteenth-century rules without considering whether this method is practical or whether these old rules still make sense more than 200 years later.[61] I will offer several reasons why we should reject Justice Scalia's frozen-common-law approach.

To begin with, the Fourth Amendment, unlike the Seventh Amendment, makes no reference to the common law anywhere in its text. The Seventh Amendment expressly guarantees a right to civil jury trial "*according to the rules of the common law*."[62] The Fourth Amendment, by contrast, affords protection against "*unreasonable* searches and seizures,"[63] a standard not inherently dictated by 1791 common law rules regarding *unlawful* searches and seizures.

Moreover, any interpretive approach that seeks to arrest the development of the common law and freeze it at a single point in time clashes with the fluid and evolutionary nature of common law.[64] The presumption of continual adaptation and improvement is one of the common law's defining features.[65] As Justice Story, the early American jurist, observed in 1837, the common law is "a system of elementary principles and of general juridical truths, which are continually expanding with the progress of society, and adapting themselves to the gradual changes of trade, and commerce, and the mechanic arts, and the exigencies and usages of the country."[66] While "certain fundamental maxims . . . are never departed from," he explained, "others . . . are . . . susceptible of modifications and exceptions, to prevent them from doing manifest wrong and injury."[67] Freezing the common law of search and seizure as it existed in 1791 in the face of dramatically changed conditions risks precisely this "manifest wrong and injury."

Further, the common law of 1791, which Justice Scalia casually refers to as though it were a single, clearly defined body of rules, was actually derived from a variety of authorities[68] and differed from jurisdiction to jurisdiction.[69] This variation in common law rules among jurisdictions could have a dramatic effect on the resulting search and seizure doctrine. To give just one example, in 1773 the King's Bench in England held an excise officer liable for trespass after he swore out a valid warrant to search a house but found no taxable goods there.[70] Twelve years later the same court reversed course and limited an officer's liability to situations in which he obtained or executed the warrant "maliciously from corrupt motives."[71] Although the later decision predated the Fourth Amendment by six years, the American legal system was slow to adopt the new rule, with treatises as late as 1824 citing the earlier decision as controlling precedent.[72] Thus, as of 1791 there were two very different liability rules for warranted excise searches that yielded no goods. Justice Scalia's approach does not make clear which one should apply.

Even when common law rules from 1791 are uniform and readily ascertainable, Justice Scalia's approach has another limitation: It provides little guidance about when and how to analogize from these 1791 rules to searches involving later-developed technologies. While I recognize that drawing analogies is often a feature of interpretation, Justice Scalia's use of analogy is particularly troublesome because it sets the stakes so high. When he deems current and historical practices sufficiently close, he imports the 1791 common law rule wholesale, and that alone determines the reasonableness of the search. Consider, for example, the practice of wiretapping. Justice Black in his dissent in *Katz v. United States* contended that "wiretapping is nothing more than eavesdropping by telephone."[73]

But is Justice Black's assessment self-evident? The common law imposed general nuisance liability for private individuals who engaged in eavesdropping,[74] but appeared to have no rule when the government sanctioned the eavesdropping. If we view the common law's silence as tacit approval for government-sanctioned *eavesdropping*, is this necessarily the appropriate rule to apply to government-sanctioned *wiretapping*?

Or consider the 1921 automobile search in *Carroll v. United States*.[75] *Carroll* upheld a Prohibition-era warrantless search of a private automobile suspected of transporting bootlegged liquor. In resolving the case, Chief Justice Taft employed a historical approach closely akin to Justice Scalia's. He observed that early Congresses distinguished between searches of "dwelling house[s] or similar place[s]" and searches for goods "concealed in a movable vessel" or ship.[76]

Congressional acts from the 1780s and 1790s afforded broader discretion to officers in the latter category, authorizing them to conduct warrantless searches of vessels "in which they [had] reason to suspect" goods "subject to duty" were hidden.[77] Chief Justice Taft reasoned that because an automobile—like a seagoing vessel—permitted the ready movement of contraband, the two "vehicles" would have been treated the same for Fourth Amendment purposes in the founding era.[78] While Justice Taft is surely correct that ships and cars present certain common concerns about the movability of evidence, is it necessarily true that the expectation of privacy is analogous in the two cases? I am not suggesting that *Carroll* should have come out differently. But *Carroll* highlights the difficulty in determining when to analogize 1791 search and seizure practices to modern-day ones, and Justice Scalia's approach offers little guidance in this respect.

Not only is the frozen-common-law approach impractical; it is also imprudent. Common law search and seizure rules from the founding era were designed to address a very different law enforcement reality than we face today. Because these differences are sufficiently stark, we should not apply founding era rules without considering whether they still make sense. For example, during the framing era there were no professional police forces, and the government's involvement in policing was much more limited than it is today. In the realm of criminal investigation, private parties or the broader community assumed responsibility for the bulk of investigation. Ordinarily, peace officers did not get involved until arrest was imminent.[79] The peace officers were mainly constables who served part-time and frequently called upon private citizens to assist in making arrests.[80] In fact, at common law, private citizens had the same powers of arrest as constables.[81] Today, the organization and reach of official law enforcement is vastly greater. Full-time professional police forces at all levels of government now control criminal investigation and engage in extensive efforts to prevent and reduce crime—activities that were basically unheard of at the time of the framing. Moreover, these highly professionalized forces are equipped with technology that enables searches unimaginable in 1791.

Unsurprisingly, the dramatic differences in law enforcement practices during the framing era led to a fundamentally different set of rules governing the relationship between citizens and law enforcement. Our present concept of official immunity—that an officer is protected from civil liability unless the officer violates a "clearly established" constitutional right—bears little resemblance to framing era notions of official immunity.[82] At the time of the framing, a court absolved an officer of liability only when he was fulfilling a ministerial duty such as executing a valid search warrant sworn out by someone else.[83] A court could hold the officer liable in trespass if he acted pursuant to his own initiative, for example by swearing out a warrant himself and conducting a search that turned out to be fruitless.[84] The substantial trespass damages assessed against the Crown's agents in the *North Briton* and *Entick* cases are clear examples of the risk faced by everyday peace officers in conducting discretionary searches.

The common law gradually evolved to address the significant changes that have occurred in law enforcement practices since the framing era. Remedies for abusive searches are no longer pressed under the law of trespass, but rather under a new body of constitutional tort law. Qualified immunity affords greater protection to officers when they conduct searches.[85] And the exclusionary rule limits the ability of the prosecution to introduce evidence obtained during searches conducted in violation of the Fourth Amendment.[86]

Resetting the clock to 1791 and ignoring these changes, as the frozen-common-law approach requires, makes little sense. We should acknowledge that dramatic changes have occurred in the structure and purpose of law enforcement and in the structure and organization of society more broadly. In confronting Fourth Amendment challenges arising from these changes, we should return to an analysis that takes into account the Amendment's formative history and principles.

Before pressing this point further, I will briefly consider Justice Scalia's fall-back position when the common law of 1791 "yields no answer."[87]

In that instance Justice Scalia requires courts to balance "the degree to which [a search or seizure] intrudes upon an individual's privacy" against "the degree to which it is needed for the promotion of legitimate governmental interests."[88] My concern here is this: Unmoored from the formative history that led to the Fourth Amendment's adoption, such analyses will give too much weight to the government's legitimate interest in fighting crime or promoting national security and too little weight to the liberty and privacy interests protected by the Amendment. When the government stands before a court and argues—either explicitly or implicitly—that a particular search practice is necessary to guard against terrorist attack, the pressure builds to declare that practice consistent with the Fourth Amendment. To the extent that new threats compel courts to engage in difficult balancing acts, Justice Scalia's approach fails to ensure that courts will give the Amendment's animating principles due weight.

III.

We should return to the tradition of using the Fourth Amendment's formative history as a basic source in interpreting the Amendment. Supreme Court decisions dating back to *Boyd v. United States* in 1886 have looked to formative history as a guide.[89] In *Boyd* Justice Bradley emphasized that to interpret the Fourth Amendment, it is "necessary to recall the contemporary or then-recent history of the controversies on the subject, both in this country and in England."[90] This rich history sheds a powerful light on the purposes that the Amendment was designed to serve.

   Perhaps the most famous use of formative history to interpret the Amendment is Justice Brandeis's dissent in the 1928 wiretapping case of *Olmstead v. United States.*[91] In a 5–4 decision the *Olmstead* majority held that a wiretapping scheme undertaken by federal agents in violation of state law did not qualify as a search or seizure under the Fourth Amendment.[92] In dissent Justice Brandeis drew heavily from the history of the Fourth Amendment's adoption to determine its purpose. Quoting James Otis's argument in *The Writs of Assistance Case*, Brandeis insisted that the unrestricted use of wiretaps, like writs of assistance of old, "places the liberty of every man in the hands of every petty officer."[93] Inspired by Otis, Brandeis added words with similar punch: "As a means of espionage," Brandeis wrote, "writs of assistance and general warrants are but puny instruments of tyranny and oppression when compared with wire-tapping."[94] Justice Brandeis thus looked to historical principles and examples to conclude that the Fourth Amendment required strict limitations on official discretion in the search and seizure arena. The 1967 decision in *Katz v. United States*, which overruled *Olmstead* and held that wiretapping is a search subject to Fourth Amendment regulation, vindicated Brandeis's conclusion in his *Olmstead* dissent.[95] *Katz* emphasized that the place or scope of a search cannot be left to the discretion of a government agent. Rather, it must be determined by a neutral and detached magistrate.[96]

In addition to Bradley and Brandeis, several other Justices have relied on the formative history of the Fourth Amendment in determining its meaning. One of the most prominent was Justice Frankfurter, who served on the Court from 1939 until 1962. Justice Frankfurter regularly recalled that "[t]he vivid memory by the newly independent Americans of the [Crown's abusive discretionary searches] produced the Fourth Amendment."[97] Other former Justices who have used the Amendment's formative history as an interpretive guide include Justice Jackson,[98] Justice Stewart,[99] and Chief Justice Burger.[100] Notably, these Justices do not fit into any particular ideological group.

More recently, Justice Stevens appeared to be the most receptive to the use of formative history in interpreting the Fourth Amendment. In the 2008 term, Justice Stevens wrote the Court's opinion in *Arizona v. Gant*,[101] a 5–4 decision that restricts the authority of police to conduct a warrantless vehicle search incident to the arrest of the driver. Justice Stevens wrote:

> A rule that gives police the power to conduct such a search whenever an individual is caught committing a traffic offense, when there is no basis for believing evidence of the offense might be found in the vehicle, creates a serious and recurring threat to the privacy of countless individuals.[102]

Justice Stevens drew on formative history to explain why the Fourth Amendment protected against this threat to privacy. "[T]he character of th[e] threat," he said, "implicates the central concern underlying the Fourth Amendment—the concern about giving police officers unbridled discretion to rummage at will among a person's private effects."[103] Justice Stevens supported his reference to history by citing *Boyd*,[104] the landmark case for using the Amendment's formative history as a guide.

Justice Scalia joined the *Gant* majority, but he wrote a separate concurrence, reiterating his frozen-common-law approach as the method for determining "what is an 'unreasonable' search within the meaning of the Fourth Amendment. . . ."[105] With Justice Scalia in *Gant's* bare majority, the decision does not suggest that the Supreme Court is making a committed return to the use of the Fourth Amendment's historical background as a source to elucidate its meaning. But *Gant* at least sends a signal that courts can use formative history in interpreting the amendment. I urge us to go further. We should return to the regular use of formative history as a guide.

As we have seen, the mischief that gave birth to the Fourth Amendment was the oppressive general search, executed through the use of writs of assistance and general warrants. The lesson from this mischief is that granting unlimited discretion to customs agents and constables inevitably leads to incursions on privacy and liberty—a lesson ably drawn by Otis in *The Writs of Assistance Case* and expressed by the English judges in the *North Briton* and *Entick* cases. The Fourth Amendment was thus adopted for the purpose of checking discretionary police authority, and that historical purpose should be kept in mind.

I do not suggest that this history should be the only guide in interpreting the Fourth Amendment. Rather, it should retake its place among other interpretive sources, including text, structure, purpose, and precedent. The Amendment's vivid history can be particularly useful in applying the Amendment to today's challenges and in measuring the consequences of a particular application. As Chief Justice Burger once wrote, the Framers "intended the Fourth Amendment to safeguard fundamental values which would far outlast the specific abuses which give it birth."[106]

IV.

Next, I will discuss how history can guide us in analyzing a new generation of Fourth Amendment issues that arise in our increasingly interconnected world. I will consider questions about privacy expectations in personal files stored online, computer search warrants that present the risk of being executed as general warrants, and potential threats to privacy from government data mining programs.

A.

Today we rely on electronic storage instead of "secret cabinets and bureaus" to file much of our private communications and information.

Our digital files include correspondence (even love letters), diaries, and personal records of all sorts, from financial to medical. A growing trend is to store files online rather than on the hard drives of personal computers.[107] For example, users of webmail programs, such as Gmail, Yahoo!, and Hotmail, store e-mail messages on their provider's remote server without any permanent storage on a home computer.[108] Online storage allows Internet users to access files from any computer connected to the Internet.[109] But online storage also raises questions about whether we retain any Fourth Amendment privacy interest in files once we store them remotely because they are then in theory accessible to the Internet service provider.

Whether the Fourth Amendment protects against a police search of a user's online files depends on whether the search would invade the user's reasonable expectation of privacy.[110] If it would, a search warrant based on probable cause is required, subject to limited exceptions.[111] It might seem indisputable that there is a reasonable expectation of privacy in personal files stored online. This assumption, however, runs up against what is sometimes called the third-party doctrine. The Supreme Court has said that "a person has no legitimate expectation of privacy in information he voluntarily turns over to third parties."[112] For example, bank customers have no reasonable expectation of privacy in deposit slips or financial statements provided to a bank, and telephone users have no expectation of privacy in the numbers dialed on a telephone.[113] If strictly applied, the third-party doctrine would foreclose any expectation of privacy in files stored on a provider's server. The doctrine, however, does not appear to be absolute. For example, the Supreme Court has declined to apply it to the results of nonconsensual drug tests performed by a hospital and handed over to the police.[114] And, in *United States v. Miller*, the case denying Fourth Amendment protection to bank records, the Court drew a distinction between those records and a person's "private papers."[115] Thus, in evaluating whether there is a privacy interest in personal files stored online, the current framework leaves room for considering other sources of interpretation, including the Fourth Amendment's formative history and contemporary norms and circumstances.[116]

Courts have already begun to consider the Fourth Amendment's application in the context of remotely stored e-mails. In *Warshak v. United States* a Sixth Circuit panel considered whether users who store their e-mails on a provider's server have a reasonable expectation of privacy in the content of their messages.[117] Although the *Warshak* panel opinion was vacated by an en banc court that ultimately dismissed for want of ripeness, the case underscores the possible tension between the Fourth Amendment's formative history and the third-party doctrine. *Warshak* was a civil action for injunctive relief arising out of a federal investigation of the plaintiff for mail fraud and related crimes. The government, without any showing of probable cause, obtained a court order directing the plaintiff's Internet service provider to turn over certain of the plaintiff's e-mails that were not protected by the warrant provision of the Electronic Communications Privacy Act.[118] In opposing a preliminary injunction prohibiting the disclosure, the government invoked the third-party doctrine.[119] It argued that because the provider maintaining the server had access to the content of the e-mails, the plaintiff no longer had a reasonable expectation of privacy.[120] Without this expectation of privacy, the government's collection of the e-mails would not constitute a "seizure" within the meaning of the Fourth Amendment. The Sixth Circuit panel disagreed. It upheld a preliminary injunction prohibiting any compelled disclosure by the provider, concluding that the plaintiff retained a reasonable expectation of privacy in the content of his e-mails stored with his service provider.[121] In reaching that conclusion, the panel emphasized that the provider did not inspect or monitor e-mail content in the ordinary course of business.[122] The panel appeared to rest its holding on the analogy it drew between e-mails and telephone conversations, noting that the latter have privacy protection under existing Fourth Amendment doctrine.[123]

Interestingly, the district court in *Warshak* had concluded that an e-mail was more like a letter sent through the U.S. Postal Service, which also has Fourth Amendment protection.[124] This view is consistent with a major function of e-mail: It is a high-speed alternative to regular mail.[125]

This analogy to traditional letters implicates the Fourth Amendment's formative history. A remote server holding private files arguably fulfills the same function as the "secret cabinets and bureaus" that Lord Camden protected from promiscuous search in the *Entick* case in 1765. The e-mails within these files can be equated with the private papers of Lord Camden's day. "Papers," as he said, "are the owner's . . . dearest property."[126] And today's e-mails and electronic documents are no less dear because they are stored on electronic servers rather than in the secret cabinets and bureaus they have replaced. As these parallels illustrate, the history of the Fourth Amendment can assist in measuring privacy expectations in today's digital world.

B.

The Fourth Amendment's formative history is also relevant in evaluating the threat to individual privacy posed by some computer searches, even when executed under a warrant.[127] As history reminds us, a central purpose of the Fourth Amendment is to ban general warrants—warrants that do not specify the place or sphere of a search, thereby granting unrestricted discretion to executing officers. One challenge is to find ways to limit the scope of computer searches under "warrants that are particular on their face" but that turn into "general warrants in practice."[128] Computer searches can easily turn into "highly invasive search[es] that uncover[ ] a great deal of information beyond the scope of the warrant."[129] Two factors drive this threat to privacy. The first is the enormous capacity of electronic storage. Today the average hard drive in a personal computer has a storage capacity of about 150 gigabytes,[130] which is roughly equivalent to 75,000,000 pages of text or 250,000 books averaging 300 pages.[131] Second, the information stored on computers is increasingly personal and records detailed accounts of our activities and interests.

Courts are grappling with the permissible scope of computer searches. In the search for evidence specified in a warrant, is it reasonable to allow police to search everywhere on a computer, or are limitations required? Some courts have been reluctant to limit police discretion.[132] These courts are concerned that suspects will "tamper [with], hid[e], or destr[oy]" damning computer files.[133] A clever suspect, for example, does not store child pornography in a file labeled "kiddyporn." As one court noted, it is easy to rename a "sexy-teenyboppersxxx.jpg" file as "sundayschoolesson.doc" and to otherwise change the names and extensions on computer files.[134] Sensitive to the potential for camouflage, some judges seem to throw up their hands and give police broad discretion to search computers so long as there is a warrant based on probable cause to search for a single category of evidence.[135]

In contrast, the Ninth Circuit, in a recent en banc decision, set forth rules to protect against what it found to be "a serious risk that every warrant for electronic information will become, in effect, a general warrant, rendering the Fourth Amendment irrelevant."[136] In that case, federal agents used a warrant authorizing the search of a laboratory's computerized drug-testing records on ten professional baseball players to conduct an unlawful general search of the records of hundreds of players.[137] The Ninth Circuit assumed that the ability of wrongdoers to hide, encrypt, or compress electronic data makes overly broad seizure "an inherent [and sometimes necessary] part of the electronic search process."[138] But instead of throwing up its hands, the court determined that the following privacy safeguards are required for issuing and administering search warrants for computer information. First, magistrate judges should insist that the government waive reliance on the plain view exception in electronic search cases.[139] Second, a "warrant application should normally include" a search protocol "designed to uncover only the information for which [the government] has probable cause."[140] Finally, seized information that the government has no probable cause to collect must be segregated and quarantined by government personnel not involved in the investigation or by an independent third party.[141]

The Tenth Circuit has also attempted to prevent general searches of computers, apparently concluding that overly broad searches and seizures are not inevitable. Unlike the Ninth Circuit, the Tenth Circuit focuses on the Fourth Amendment's particularity requirement, holding that a warrant must affirmatively limit the scope of a computer search by particularly describing either specific files or specific file formats that contain evidence of the federal crime suspected to have been committed.[142] Should the police *knowingly* exceed the warrant's scope—for example, by searching for images when the warrant is for written information—any unspecified evidence found must be suppressed.[143]

The Ninth and Tenth Circuit decisions, which protect against general searches of computers in different ways, are ultimately consistent with the Fourth Amendment's formative history. They illustrate that while history does not dictate any particular solution, it does suggest that there are constitutional limits on police discretion in the scope and execution of warrants for computer searches.

C.

Finally, there are government data mining programs that create electronic databases of personal information about U.S. citizens—information that the government then analyzes to identify suspicious patterns of behavior.[144] Data mining technologies threaten the privacy once afforded by "the inherent inefficiency of government agencies [that] analyz[ed widely dispersed] paper, rather than aggregated, computer records."[145] The government has used agency data mining programs to help detect waste and for various law enforcement purposes since at least the 1990s.[146]

Following the attacks of September 11, 2001, the government expanded efforts to acquire information and explored ways to combine all of the available information into "a single massive database."[147] One notorious example is the never-implemented Total Information Awareness (TIA) program conceived at the Department of Defense.[148] The program's Orwellian implications were captured by its original logo: "an 'all-seeing' eye atop of a pyramid looking down over the globe, accompanied by the Latin phrase *scientia est potentia* (knowledge is power)."[149]

TIA sought to compile and link vast amounts of electronic information, including credit card transactions, travel information, telephone records, and video feeds from airport surveillance cameras. This information would then have been filtered through software that constantly monitored for suspicious patterns.[150] The program's managers represented that the program would amass only transactional data that the government could access under existing law.[151] But the government can claim lawful access to enormous quantities of information simply by invoking the third-party doctrine.[152] We disclose "a vast amount of personal information to a vast array of [third-party] demanders."[153] And technology companies routinely "record the Websites [we] visit, the ads [we] click on, [and] even the words [we] enter in search engines."[154] Compiling this information into one huge database could provide government agents with access to a reasonably complete profile of any person who is singled out.[155]

Congress withdrew funding for TIA because of concerns about the privacy of U.S. citizens.[156] It is nevertheless instructive to consider the privacy implications of a TIA-type program. Suppose a government agency compiles and constantly updates a massive database of transactional information on U.S. citizens that includes records of consumer activity, subject headers on domestic e-mails, Web site visits, and real-time information about where cell phones are located. The program stipulates that assigned agents may use the data to investigate potential criminal- or terrorism-related activity. Suppose further that an agent, purely on the basis of subjective suspicion, targets a particular individual and pores through all data relating to that individual for evidence of a crime or suspicious activity.

If there was a Fourth Amendment challenge to the breadth of agent discretion to access and use the data, the government could argue that there is no reasonable expectation of privacy in transactional information collected from third parties, and that it is free to use the database for any investigative or strategic purpose.[157] But does the history of the Fourth Amendment offer any guidance here? I believe history suggests that we ought to ask whether the data mining program has the character of a general warrant because of the agent's unbridled discretion to choose his or her target and to rummage through large quantities of personal information about that target. We should ask the question James Otis would ask if he were here today: Does the agent's unchecked authority to scour the data place "the liberty [or privacy rights] of every [person] in the hands of every petty officer[?]"[158]

* * *

In concluding, I recognize that I have not provided ready answers to the challenging new questions that test the reach of the Fourth Amendment. But that was not my purpose. I have simply attempted to make the case that the mischief—the threat to liberty and privacy—that led to the inclusion of the Fourth Amendment in the Bill of Rights has not disappeared; it has only changed in form. Thus, in confronting contemporary questions, it is more important than ever to use the Fourth Amendment's formative history, which confirms the Amendment's broader purpose of limiting government discretion. This is no time for outdated common law rules from the founding era to control and restrict the contemporary meaning of the Fourth Amendment. As Justice Black firmly declared in the first Madison Lecture nearly fifty years ago: "I cannot agree with those who think of the Bill of Rights as an 18th Century straightjacket, unsuited for this age. It is old but not all old things are bad."[159]

NOTES

1. Norman Dorsen, *Introduction* to THE UNPREDICTABLE CONSTITUTION 4 (Norman Dorsen ed. 2002).
2. U.S. CONST. amend. IV.
3. *Id.*
4. United States v. Comprehensive Drug Testing, Inc., 579 F.3d 989, 1005 (9th Cir. 2009) (en banc).
5. 277 U.S. 438, 472 (1928) (Brandeis, J., dissenting).
6. *Id.* at 473 (quoting Weems v. United States, 217 U.S. 349, 373 (1910)).
7. William J. Stuntz, *The Substantive Origins of Criminal Procedure*, 105 YALE L.J. 393, 404 (1995).
8. Act of Frauds of 1662, 12 Car. 2, c. 11 § V(2) (Eng.), *reprinted in* 8 DANBY PICKERING, THE STATUTES AT LARGE 78, at 81 (London, Bentham 1763).

9. *See* Act of Frauds of 1696, 5 W. & M., c. 22 § VI (Eng.), *reprinted in* 9 DANBY PICKERING, THE STATUTES AT LARGE 428, at 430 (London, Bentham 1764); *see also* William Cuddihy & B. Carmon Hardy, *A Man's House Was Not His Castle: Origins of the Fourth Amendment to the United States Constitution*, 37 WM. & MARY Q. 371, 380–81 (1980); Stuntz, *supra* note 7, at 404–05.

10. Act of Frauds of 1662, 12 Car. 2, c. 11 § V, *reprinted in*, PICKERING, *supra* note 8, at 80–81.

11. M. H. SMITH, THE WRITS OF ASSISTANCE CASE 29 (1978); Stuntz, *supra* note 7, at 405.

12. *See* Stuntz, *supra* note 7, at 405 (describing broad scope of authority under writs of assistance); *see also* SMITH, *supra* note 11, at 375, 559–61 (providing examples of Massachusetts writs of assistance from this period).

13. Stuntz, *supra* note 7, at 405.

14. The Seven Years War began in 1756. THE COLUMBIA ENCYCLOPEDIA 2484 (5th ed. 1993).

15. Stuntz, *supra* note 7, at 405.

16. *Id.*

17. *See id.* (noting that because actions to enforce "trade rules" were infrequent, "rampant and blatant [violations]" created economy "grounded on an illegal trade").

18. *See id.* at 406; SMITH, *supra* note 11, at 130, 142–43.

19. *See* SMITH, *supra* note 11, at 131–32, 232, 316 (noting that Otis was first to challenge writ of assistance even though court had been issuing such writs for years).

20. *See id.* at 6.

21. *Id.* app. J at 552.

22. *Id.* app. J at 553.

23. *Id.* app. J at 552.

24. *Id.* app. I at 544.

25. Tracey Maclin, *The Complexity of the Fourth Amendment: A Historical Review*, 77 B.U. L. REV. 925, 946–47 (1997).

26. SMITH, *supra* note 11, at 234.

27. Letter from John Adams to William Tudor (March 29, 1817) *in* 10 THE WORKS OF JOHN ADAMS 247–48 (Boston, Little Brown & Co. 1856).

28. *See* Cuddihy & Hardy, *supra* note 9, at 387 (explaining that many "English methods of search and seizure," including general warrants, were "as common in the colonies as in the mother country").

29. While general warrants to search for fugitives and stolen property were among the most common, these warrants were used for a variety of searches and seizures. *See* WILLIAM J. CUDDIHY, THE FOURTH AMENDMENT: ORIGINS AND ORIGINAL MEANING 602-1791 at 232 (2009) (listing examples of general warrants); Cuddihy & Hardy, *supra* note 9, at 387 n.78 (same).

30. Thomas Y. Davies, *Recovering the Original Fourth Amendment*, 98 MICH. L. REV. 547, 563 n.21 (1999).

31. Stuntz, *supra* note 7, at 398.

32. Cuddihy & Hardy, *supra* note 9, at 385.
33. Wilkes v. Wood, (1763) 98 Eng. Rep. 489, 498 (K.B.).
34. Stuntz, *supra* note 7, at 399.
35. Today's sum is calculated according to relative purchasing power. *See* Measuring Worth, Purchasing Power of British Pounds from 1264 to Present, http:// www. measuringworth.com/ppoweruk.
36. Nelson B. Lasson, *The History and Development of the Fourth Amendment to the United States Constitution, in* 55 THE JOHNS HOPKINS UNIVERSITY STUDIES IN HISTORICAL AND POLITICAL SCIENCE 211, 254–55 (1937).
37. Huckle v. Money, (1763) 95 Eng. Rep. 768, 769 (K.B.); *see also* Davies, *supra* note 30, at 563 n.21 (providing summary of cases dealing with general warrants from this period).
38. Money v. Leach, (1765) 97 Eng. Rep. 1075, 1088 (K.B.).
39. *See* Davies, *supra* note 30, at 563 n.21.
40. Entick v. Carrington, (1765) 19 How. St. Tr. 1029 (C.P.) (Eng.).
41. *Id.* at 1073.
42. *Id.* at 1063.
43. *Id.* at 1066.
44. *See* Davies, *supra* note 30, at 566–67 (discussing Parliament's passage of Townshend Act of 1767, which reauthorized writs of assistance for customs searches in colonies).
45. *Id.* at 561.
46. *See id.* at 566–67 & nn.26–27 (discussing public controversy over general writs and noting increasing frequency of colonial judges' refusal to issue such writs to customs officials notwithstanding statutory authorization).
47. *Id.* at 567, 603–04.
48. *See* George C. Thomas, III, *Time Travel, Hovercrafts, and the Framers: James Madison Sees the Future and Rewrites the Fourth Amendment,* 80 NOTRE DAME L. REV. 1451, 1463 (2005) ("[T]he experience with British rule left the Framers terrified of general searches.").
49. *Id.* at 1465 & n.63.
50. Davies, *supra* note 30, at 684 (quoting MASS. CONST. OF 1780, pt. 1, art. XIV).
51. *Id.* at 685.
52. U.S. CONST. amend. IV.
53. *See, e.g.,* Boyd v. United States, 116 U.S. 616, 633–35 (1886) (applying Fourth Amendment's unreasonable search and seizure clause to invalidate court-ordered production of documents).
54. U.S. CONST. amend. IV (emphasis added).
55. *See infra* Part III.
56. 526 U.S. 295 (1999). For an excellent summary of how Justice Scalia gradually developed and adopted this approach, see David A. Sklansky, *The Fourth Amendment and Common Law,* 100 COLUM. L. REV. 1739, 1745–61 (2000).
57. *Houghton,* 526 U.S. at 299; *see also* Virginia v. Moore, 128 S. Ct. 1598, 1602 (2008) (opinion of Scalia, J.) ("We look to the statutes and common law of the

founding era to determine the norms that the Fourth Amendment was meant to preserve.").

58. *Houghton*, 526 U.S. at 299–300.

59. *Id.* In other cases Justice Scalia has said that the reasonableness balancing test applies "where there was no clear practice, either approving or disapproving the type of search at issue, at the time the constitutional provision was enacted." Vernonia Sch. Dist. 47J v. Acton, 515 U.S. 646, 652–53 (1995) (opinion of Scalia, J.).

60. *Houghton*, 526 U.S. at 300.

61. The "freezes in place" characterization is drawn from *Payton v. New York.* 445 U.S. 573, 591 n.33 (1980) ("[T]his Court has not simply frozen into constitutional law those law enforcement practices that existed at the time of the Fourth Amendment's passage.").

62. U.S. CONST. amend. VII (emphasis added).

63. U.S. CONST. amend. IV (emphasis added).

64. Joseph Story explained that "the common law is not in its nature and character an absolutely fixed, inflexible system, like the statute law, providing only for cases of a determinate form, which fall within the letter of the language, in which a particular doctrine or legal proposition is expressed." Joseph Story, *Codification of the Common Law, in* THE MISCELLANEOUS WRITINGS OF JOSEPH STORY 698, 702 (Lawbook Exchange 2000) (1852) [hereinafter Story, *Codification of the Common Law*].

65. *Id.* at 702–04 (providing examples of common law judges revising historic rules to comport with "principles of natural justice").

66. Story, *Codification of the Common Law, supra* note 64, at 702.

67. *Id.*

68. *See* Sklansky, *supra* note 56, at 1794–95 (describing common law of eighteenth century as "an amalgam of cases, statutes, commentary, custom, and fundamental principles").

69. The degree of variation between the common law of the different states in 1791 was sufficient to lead Justice Story to conclude that the "common law" explicitly incorporated into the Seventh Amendment must be English common law and "not the common law of any individual state." United States v. Wonson, 28 F. Cas. 745, 750 (C.C.D. Mass. 1812) (No. 16,750) (Story, Circuit J.).

70. Bostock v. Saunders, (1773) 95 Eng. Rep. 1141 (K.B.).

71. Cooper v. Boot, (1785) 99 Eng. Rep. 911, 916 (K.B.) (Lord Mansfield, J.).

72. *E.g.,* 7 NATHAN DANE, A GENERAL ABRIDGMENT AND DIGEST OF AMERICAN LAW § 2, at 244–46 (Boston, Cummings, Hilliard & Co. 1824); *see also* Fabio Arcila, Jr., *In the Trenches: Searches and the Misunderstood Common-Law History of Suspicion and Probable Cause*, 10 U. PA. J. CONST. L. 1, 46–48 & nn.165 & 176 (2007) (citing 5 NATHAN DANE, A GENERAL ABRIDGMENT AND DIGEST OF AMERICAN LAW § 11, at 559 (Boston, Cummings, Hilliard & Co. 1824)).

73. Katz v. United States, 389 U.S. 347, 366 (1967) (Black, J., dissenting).

74. "*Eaves-droppers*, or such as listen under walls or windows, or the eaves of a house, to hearken after discourse, and thereupon to frame slanderous and

mischievous tales, are a common nuisance, and presentable at the court-leet: or are indictable at the sessions, and punishable by fine and finding sureties for the good behaviour." 4 WILLIAM BLACKSTONE, COMMENTARIES *169.

75. 267 U.S. 132 (1925) (opinion of Taft, C.J.).

76. *Id.* at 151.

77. *Id.* at 150–51 (quoting Act of July 31, 1789, ch. 5, 1 Stat. 29, 43 (1789)).

78. *Id.* at 153.

79. Stuntz, *supra* note 7, at 407–08 & n.59. Indeed, peace officers had few responsibilities apart from responding to private complaints. Davies, *supra* note 30, at 620. A limited number of what Davies calls "complainantless crimes" did exist, but Davies contends that these crimes were regarded as less serious than the drug offenses that constitute the bulk of today's complainantless crimes. *Id.*

80. Davies, *supra* note 30, at 620–21.

81. *Id.* at 629. An eighteenth-century treatise confirmed that official authority was limited, stating that "it seems difficult to find any Case, wherein a Constable is impowered to arrest a Man for a Felony committed or attempted, in which a private Person might not as well be justified in doing it. . . ." *Id.* (quoting 2 WILLIAM HAWKINS, A TREATISE OF THE PLEAS OF THE CROWN 80 (Arno Press 1972) (1726)). Indeed, according to Davies, the common law in 1791 recognized only three justifications for a warrantless arrest, and all three could be invoked either by officers or by private persons making what we would now call a "citizen's arrest." Davies, *supra* note 30, at 629. Notably, the warrantless arrest standard at common law differs from today's arrest standard primarily in that today's standard requires only "probable cause" that a crime has been committed, whereas the common law standard required a "felony in fact." *Id.* at 632–33. This "felony in fact" requirement was also incorporated into the warrant standards at common law. Before an arrest warrant could be issued, a complainant was required to make a sworn accusation that a crime had "in fact" been committed. *Id.* at 651–52.

82. Davies notes that "because the common-law understanding was that an officer ceased to have any official status if he exceeded his lawful authority, the Framers conceived of unlawful acts by officers as *personal* trespasses, not as government illegality (which is why they never considered an exclusionary rule)." Thomas Y. Davies, *The Fictional Character of Law-and-Order Originalism: A Case Study of the Distortions and Evasions of Framing-Era Arrest Doctrine in* Atwater v. Lago Vista, 37 WAKE FOREST L. REV. 239, 403 (2002).

83. Davies, *supra* note 30, at 652.

84. *Id.*

85. *See* Maciariello v. Sumner, 973 F.2d 295, 298 (4th Cir. 1992) ("Officials are not liable for bad guesses in gray areas; they are liable for transgressing bright lines.").

86. 1 WAYNE R. LAFAVE, SEARCH AND SEIZURE § 1.6, at 186 (4th ed. 2004) ("In the typical case, the impact of the exclusionary rule is to bar from use *at trial* evidence obtained by an unreasonable search and seizure.").

87. Wyoming v. Houghton, 526 U.S. 295, 299–300 (1999).

88. *Id.* at 300.
89. 116 U.S. 616 (1886).
90. *Id.* at 624–25.
91. 277 U.S. 438 (1928).
92. *Id.* at 466.
93. *Id.* at 474 (Brandeis, J., dissenting).
94. *Id.* at 476.
95. 389 U.S. 347, 359 (1967).
96. *Id.* at 356–57.
97. Frank v. Maryland, 359 U.S. 360, 363 (1959).
98. United States v. Di Re, 332 U.S. 581, 595 (1948) ("[T]he forefathers, after consulting the lessons of history, designed our Constitution to place obstacles in the way of a too permeating police surveillance, which they seemed to think was a greater danger to a free people than the escape of some criminals from punishment.").
99. Chimel v. California, 395 U.S. 752, 760–61 (1969) ("[T]he [Fourth] Amendment's proscription of 'unreasonable searches and seizures' must be read in light of 'the history that gave rise to the words'—a history of 'abuses so deeply felt by the Colonies as to be one of the potent causes of the Revolution . . . .'" (quoting *Rabinowitz*, 339 U.S. at 69)); Stanford v. Texas, 379 U.S. 476, 480–85 (1965) (discussing at length history of Fourth Amendment and framers' goal of eliminating "arbitrary power" granted by general warrants and "[t]he hated writs of assistance").
100. United States v. Chadwick, 433 U.S. 1, 7–8 (1977) ("It cannot be doubted that the Fourth Amendment's commands grew in large measure out of the colonists' experience with the writs of assistance and their memories of the general warrants formerly in use in England.").
101. 129 S. Ct. 1710 (2009).
102. *Id.* at 1720.
103. *Id.*
104. *Id.* at 1720 n.5 (citing *Boyd v. United States*, 116 U.S. 616 (1886)).
105. *Id.* at 1724 (Scalia, J., concurring).
106. United States v. Chadwick, 433 U.S. 1, 9 (1977).
107. Brett Burney, *Storing Your Firm's Data 'In the Cloud,'* LAW TECH. NEWS, Apr. 2, 2009, *available at* http://www.law.com/jsp/lawtechnologynews/PubArticleLTN.jsp?id=1202429581722.
108. Achal Oza, *Amend the ECPA: Fourth Amendment Protection Erodes as E-Mails Get Dusty*, 88 B.U. L. REV. 1043, 1050–54 (2008).
109. Burney, *supra* note 107.
110. *See* Smith v. Maryland, 442 U.S. 735, 740 (1979) ("Consistently with *Katz*, this Court uniformly has held that the application of the Fourth Amendment depends on whether the person invoking its protection can claim a 'justifiable,' a 'reasonable,' or a 'legitimate expectation of privacy' that has been invaded by government action.").

111. *See* Arizona v. Gant, 129 S. Ct. 1710, 1716 (2009) (noting "basic rule" that warrantless searches "are *per se* unreasonable under the Fourth Amendment—subject only to a few specifically established and well-delineated exceptions" (internal quotation marks omitted)).

112. *Smith*, 442 U.S. at 743–44.

113. *Id.* (upholding use of pen register to record telephone numbers dialed), *superseded by statute*, Electronic Communications Privacy Act of 1986, Pub. L. No. 99-508, § 3121, 100 Stat. 1848, 1868 (1986) (current version at 18 U.S.C. § 3121 (2006)); United States v. Miller, 425 U.S. 435, 443 (1976) (upholding subpoena to bank to turn over documents to police), *superseded by statute*, Financial Institutions Regulatory and Interest Rate Control Act of 1978, Pub. L. No. 95-630, § 1110, 92 Stat. 3641, 3703 (codified as amended at 12 U.S.C. § 3410 (2006)).

114. *See* Ferguson v. City of Charleston, 532 U.S. 67, 78 (2001) (holding that Fourth Amendment was violated when state hospital ran drug test on pregnant patient without consent and gave results to law enforcement).

115. 425 U.S. at 440 (citing Boyd v. United States, 116 U.S. 616, 622 (1886)).

116. California v. Greenwood, 486 U.S. 35, 51 & n.3 (1988) (Brennan, J., dissenting) (noting that courts look at "understandings that are recognized and permitted by society" and "general social norms" (internal citations omitted)).

117. 490 F.3d 455 (6th Cir. 2007), *vacated*, Warshak v. United States, 532 F.3d 521 (6th Cir. 2008) (en banc).

118. *Id.* at 460.

119. *Warshak*, 490 F.3d at 468–69.

120. *Id.*

121. *Id.* at 471.

122. *Id.* at 475.

123. *Id.* at 469–71.

124. Warshak v. United States, No. 1:06-CV-357, 2006 WL 5230332, at *4–5 (S.D. Ohio July 21, 2006).

125. *See* Brigid Schulte, *So Long, Snail Shells; Mail Volume Expected to Decline; U.S. Postal Service Adapts by Pulling Collection Boxes*, WASH. POST, July 25, 2009, at A1 ("Snail mail is a dying enterprise because Americans increasingly pay bills online, send Evites for parties [and otherwise communicate electronically].").

126. Entick v. Carrington, (1765) 19 How. St. Tr. 1029, 1066 (C.P.) (Eng.).

127. Police generally need a warrant to search a personal computer or, as often occurs, a mirror image of the computer's hard drive. *See* United States v. Payton, 573 F.3d 859, 861–62 (9th Cir. 2009) (holding that absent special circumstances, search of computer not expressly authorized by warrant is not reasonable search).

128. Orin S. Kerr, *Searches and Seizures in a Digital World*, 119 HARV. L. REV. 531, 565 (2005).

129. *Id.* at 566.

130. John Seal, *Computers Need Maintenance To Avoid Problems*, JUPITER COURIER (Jupiter, Fl.), Feb. 15, 2009, at A11.

131. *See* Kerr, *supra* note 128, at 542 (observing that 80 gigabytes can store approximately 40,000,000 pages of text).

132. *See, e.g.*, United States v. Williams, 592 F.3d 511, 521–22 (4th Cir. 2010) (upholding seizure of child pornography during computer search for evidence of harassment because officer had lawful right to view each file momentarily to determine whether or not it was within warrant's scope); United States v. Miranda, 325 F. App'x 858, 860 (11th Cir. 2009) (same when warrant was for evidence of counterfeiting).

133. United States v. Hunter, 13 F. Supp. 2d 574, 583 (D. Vt. 1998).

134. United States v. Hill, 322 F. Supp. 2d 1081, 1091 (C.D. Cal. 2004).

135. *See, e.g.*, *Miranda*, 325 F. App'x at 859–60 (denying suppression of child pornography files discovered pursuant to computer search for counterfeiting files); *Hill*, 322 F. Supp. 2d at 1090–91 (rejecting alternate search methodologies because possibility of camouflage would render them ineffective); Rosa v. Virginia, 628 S.E.2d 92, 94–97 (Va. Ct. App. 2006) (denying suppression of child pornography files discovered pursuant to computer search for files relating to distribution of controlled substances).

136. United States v. Comprehensive Drug Testing, Inc., 579 F.3d 989, 1004 (9th Cir. 2009) (en banc).

137. *Id.* at 993.

138. *Id.* at 1006.

139. *Id.* at 997–98, 1006. Orin Kerr would limit the plain view exception by having courts suppress any evidence discovered that is outside the scope of a warrant for the search of a computer unless such evidence is otherwise admissible. Kerr, *supra* note 128, at 571–84.

140. *Comprehensive Drug Testing*, 579 F.3d at 1000, 1006. The Tenth Circuit has indicated that in some circumstances the police must adopt a search protocol designed to limit their search to files likely to contain evidence specified in the warrant. *See* United States v. Brooks, 427 F.3d 1246, 1251–52 (10th Cir. 2005).

141. *Comprehensive Drug Testing*, 579 F.3d at 1000, 1006.

142. *See* United States v. Riccardi, 405 F.3d 852, 862 (10th Cir. 2005) ("Our case law therefore suggests that warrants for computer searches must affirmatively limit the search to evidence of specific federal crimes or specific types of material."); United States v. Carey, 172 F.3d 1268, 1272–73 (10th Cir. 1999) (holding that officers exceeded warrant's scope when warrant specified search for "documentary evidence" and officers searched image files).

143. *Carey*, 172 F.3d at 1273, 1276.

144. Daniel J. Solove, *Data Mining and the Security-Liberty Debate*, 75 U. CHI. L. REV. 343, 343 (2008) (describing data mining and its use by government to identify criminal patterns of behavior); U.S. GEN. ACCOUNTING OFFICE REPORT NO. GAO-04-548, DATA MINING: FEDERAL EFFORTS COVER A WIDE RANGE OF USES 2–3 (2004) [hereinafter DATA MINING] (same).

145. DATA MINING, *supra* note 144, at 6.

146. *See* George Cahlink, *Data Mining Taps the Trends*, GOV'T EXECUTIVE, Oct. 2000, at 85, *available at* http://www.govexec.com/tech/articles/1000managetech.

htm (describing history of data mining and increasing use by wide array of government agencies).

147. Larry Greenemeier, *Data Grab: The Feds Want Data for Security and Crime Fighting, and Businesses Have What They Need. The Trick Is Knowing What To Share and Where To Draw the Line*, INFORMATION WEEK, June 5, 2006, at 23, 26.

148. *See Data Mining: Know-Alls*, ECONOMIST, Sept. 27, 2008, at 73; Cynthia L. Webb, *Total Information Dilemma*, WASHINGTON POST.COM, May 27, 2004, http:// www.washingtonpost.com/wp-dyn/articles/A60986-2004May27.html (describing critical reaction to Total Information Awareness project).

149. JEFFREY W. SEIFERT, CONG. RESEARCH SERV., DATA MINING AND HOMELAND SECURITY: AN OVERVIEW 7 (2008), *available at* http://www.fas/org/sgp/crs/intel/RL31798.pdf.

150. Adam Clymer, *Congress Agrees To Bar Pentagon from Terror Watch of Americans*, N.Y. TIMES, Feb. 12, 2003, at A1.

151. INFO. AWARENESS OFFICE, DEF. ADVANCED RESEARCH PROJECTS AGENCY, REPORT TO CONGRESS REGARDING THE TERRORISM INFORMATION AWARENESS PROGRAM; IN RESPONSE TO CONSOLIDATED APPROPRIATIONS RESOLUTION, 2003, PUB. L. NO. 108-7, DIVISION M, § 111(B), at 14 (2003), *available at* http://epic.org/privacy/profiling/ tia/may03_report.pdf.

152. *See* LAFAVE, *supra* note 86, § 2.7(b) at 744 (noting that despite "'enormous quantity of personal information'" collected and maintained by "'banks, telephone companies, hospitals, doctors' offices, [and] credit bureaus,'" courts "have not been receptive to the assertion that the subjects of this information are at all protected by the Fourth Amendment against [its search and seizure by government]" (quoting Note, *Government Access to Bank Records*, 83 YALE L.J. 1439, 1439 (1974))).

153. Richard A. Posner, *Privacy, Surveillance, and Law*, 75 U. CHI. L. REV. 245, 248 (2008).

154. Adam Cohen, *The Already Big Thing on the Internet: Spying on Users*, N.Y. TIMES, Apr. 5, 2008, at A16.

155. *See* Greenemeier, *supra* note 147, at 26.

156. SEIFERT, *supra* note 149, at 6–7.

157. Susan W. Brenner, *The Fourth Amendment in an Era of Ubiquitous Technology*, 75 MISS. L.J. 1, 59 (2005).

158. *See* SMITH, *supra* note 11, app. J at 553 (excerpting Otis's argument that general warrants are illegal because of overbroad scope).

159. Hugo L. Black, *The Bill of Rights*, 35 N.Y.U. L. REV. 865, 879 (1960).

10

Living Our Traditions

ROBERT H. HENRY

All new laws, though penned with the greatest technical skill, and passed on the fullest and most mature deliberation, are considered as more or less obscure and equivocal, until their meaning be liquidated and ascertained by a series of particular discussions and adjudications.
—THE FEDERALIST NO. 37 (James Madison)[1]

I. Daddy's Ghost

In a book published in 1990, Bernard Schwartz bemoaned:

> Like Hamlet's father, "original intention" is a ghost that refuses to remain in repose. The notion that constitutional construction should be based solely upon the intention of the framers has, despite its utter fatuousness, never been laid to rest. For it is one of those delusively simple concepts that promises a facile solution to the most difficult of our legal problems— purporting, in the process, to eliminate the uncertainty that too frequently prevails in constitutional law and to curb the excesses of judicial activism.[2]

Today I want to talk about originalism, but through a somewhat narrow lens. I want to focus on Justice John Marshall Harlan II. Justice Harlan had a particularly interesting, and I think principled, response to originalism (at least with respect to the Fourteenth Amendment's Due Process Clause, though a case may be made that he was not an originalist in other contexts as well).[3] In a remarkable dissent in the case of *Poe v. Ullman*,[4] the good Justice took a strong stand for the idea that the Constitution must be interpreted in light of history and tradition, and famously noted "[t]hat tradition is a living thing."[5] Harlan's view has received much

This lecture was delivered on October 12, 2010, and appeared in *86 N.Y.U. L. Rev.* 673 (2011).

praise, but also some criticism.[6] It is still quoted, still influential, and an important law review article written in 2004 correctly concluded, "American law has not yet plumbed Justice Harlan's meaning in proclaiming that our 'tradition is a living thing.'"[7]

I find it interesting that the popular justification for originalism today is not that our framers were divinely inspired, or omniscient, or even exceptionally wise. I think I can make something of a case for all three of those traits. But originalism is popular today not for the merits of our framers but for the malice of their judicial successors,[8] least-dangerous-branch occupiers though they may be.[9] Originalism is touted as the only preventive for judicial activism (or perhaps for its clever conspiratorial companion, legislative history).[10] Of course, it isn't—as Judge Posner has written and demonstrated, originalism is a "clever disguise."[11] Originalism's disciples sometimes claim that it also corrects the so-called "counter-majoritarian difficulty."[12]

I want to remind you about *Poe* and Justice Harlan's famous phrase. I want to describe what I think he meant, and see if we can plumb his meaning a bit. I think there are some considerable restraints in his plan (e.g., reasoned judgment, faithfulness to precedent, attention to tradition, legal professionalism, and judicial restraint),[13] that it better explicates a republican form of government than does originalism, and that it adequately handles the counter-majoritarian difficulty. First, I will give just a bit of biography about Justice Harlan, which will help explain why he is so influential in interpretive debates. Next, I will discuss *Poe* as an example of Harlan's method. Finally, I will address Harlan's famed "living traditions" and his interpretive restraint. Whether these living traditions will give Hamlet's father's ghost some repose or not, I cannot tell.

II. Justice John Marshall Harlan II[14]

Justice John Marshall Harlan II was born in Chicago in 1899 and died in Washington, D.C., in 1971.[15] He was an Associate Justice from 1955 to 1971.[16] The fact that he was the second indicates that there was a first, and certainly there was. That was his grandfather, the first Justice Harlan.[17] His grandfather also advocated a moderate version of substantive due process.[18] The first Justice Harlan is most famous for his dissents,[19] particularly in *Plessy v. Ferguson*[20] and *Lochner v. New York*,[21] which acknowledged deferential review to state purposes but not complete abdication by the courts of their task. The father of Justice Harlan II, John Maynard

Harlan, was a lawyer and a Chicago alderman, who raised him as a "patrician."[22] Justice Harlan attended Princeton University, where he was chairman of the student newspaper and was selected as a Rhodes Scholar.[23] He was also selected for Balliol College, one of Oxford's most demanding and intellectual colleges,[24] whose men possessed the "tranquil consciousness of effortless superiority."[25] There was a poem about its master, Benjamin Jowett, the great Plato scholar:

> First come I. My name is J[o]w[e]tt.
> There's no knowledge but I know it
> I am Master of this College.
> What I don't know isn't knowledge.[26]

After completing his British education in law and jurisprudence, Harlan enrolled in New York Law School, completing a two-year program in one year.[27] A prominent New York City law firm retained him, and he eventually became the leader of the firm's litigation team.[28] He briefly served on the Court of Appeals for the Second Circuit, having been appointed by President Eisenhower, who later appointed him to succeed Justice Robert H. Jackson on the Supreme Court in 1954.[29]

Harlan has been called the "paradigm of the true conservative judge."[30] Anthony Lewis observed:

> Conservative judges . . . should respect a precedent once established, even though they opposed that result during the process of decision. For such a true conservative as Justice John Marshall Harlan, that consideration was certainly a factor; he might warn in dissent against what he foresaw as the baleful effects of a decision, but he would hesitate thereafter to subject it to constant relitigation. He valued stability over perfection.[31]

In fact, stability might have described Justice Harlan himself. As Judge Henry Friendly noted, "[T]here has never been a Justice of the Supreme Court who has so consistently maintained a high quality of performance or, despite differences in views, has enjoyed such nearly uniform respect from his colleagues, the inferior bench, the bar, and the academy."[32] Justice Harlan's paradigmatic conservatism was clearly demonstrated by the two judicial values he most often advocated: federalism and proceduralism. He valued the "experimental social laboratories" represented by the state governments.[33] His belief in federalism as a "bulwark of freedom" was so strong that he saw federalism as equivalent to the Bill of Rights and the Fourteenth Amendment as a guarantee of personal liberty.[34]

With respect to proceduralism, Justice Harlan took a narrow view of both due process and judicial power. He dissented in *Reynolds v. Sims*, the Warren Court's landmark reapportionment decision, writing that he rejected the view that "every major social ill in this country can find its cure in some constitutional 'principle,' and that this Court should 'take the lead' in promoting reform when other branches of government fail to act."[35] Elaborating, he wrote: "The Constitution is not a panacea for every blot upon the public welfare, nor should this Court, ordained as a judicial body, be thought of as a general haven for reform movements."[36]

Justice Black, who both tangled and tangoed with Justice Harlan, once observed that Justice Harlan proves that there "is such a thing as a good Republican."[37] Coming from the populist prophet, it was high praise. Harlan was truly a lawyer's lawyer and a "judge's judge."[38]

Today, Justice Harlan is remembered for his marvelously crafted opinions, his consistent and principled judicial conservatism, and his patrician traditionalism that was, at the same time, remarkably sensitive to other views.[39] Upon learning that he had terminal cancer, he delayed the announcement of his own resignation to avoid interfering with the accolades accompanying the retirement of his seriously ill confrere, Justice Black[40] (who proved there can be such a thing as a good Democrat).

Though Justice Harlan represents the best of the judicial "conservative" tradition, he did concur in some of the "liberal" activisms of the Warren Court.[41] And he dissented from illiberalisms as well. It was in his dissent in *Poe v. Ullman* where he noted that Fourteenth Amendment due process is informed by history and tradition and that "tradition is a living thing."[42] Harlan's language describing his method of construing his holy writ is perhaps the most eloquent defense of nonliteralism ever written by a conservative:

> [T]he basis of judgment as to the Constitutionality of state action must be a rational one, approaching the text [of the Constitution] which is the only commission for our power not in a literalistic way, as if we had a tax statute before us, but as the basic charter of our society, setting out in spare but meaningful terms the principles of government.[43]

He could be read in *Poe* to suggest a constitutional right of privacy[44] several years before the majority reached the same conclusion.[45]

Perhaps his former clerk, Norman Dorsen, presented the best summary of his character:

> It fell to John Marshall Harlan, by nature a patrician traditionalist, to serve on a Supreme Court which, for most of his years, was rapidly revising and liberalizing constitutional law. In these circumstances, it is not surprising that Harlan would protest the direction of the Court and the speed with which it was traveling. He did this in a remarkably forceful and principled manner, thereby providing balance to the institution and the law it generated. Despite his role, Harlan joined civil liberties rulings on the Court during his tenure to the degree that his overall jurisprudence can fairly be characterized as [moderate,] conservative primarily in the sense that it evinced caution, a fear of centralized authority, and a respect for process.[46]

In noting the departures of Justices Harlan and Black, one cannot help but wonder what effects their continued presence on the Court would have had. The once great "liberal," Black, and the "paradigmatic conservative," Harlan, might even have changed ideological positions on the most controversial case of modern times, *Roe v. Wade*.[47] Black, dissenting in *Griswold v. Connecticut*, could not see a constitutional right to privacy in a penumbra of substantive due process or anywhere else.[48] Harlan, joining *Griswold*[49] and echoing his instructive concurrence in *United States v. Katz*,[50] might very well have gone the other way, adopting the *Roe* balance.[51] Interestingly, the Justices who replaced Black and Harlan voted contrary to their predecessors' probable votes: In *Roe*, Lewis Powell voted with the majority[52] and William Rehnquist dissented.[53]

III. *Poe v. Ullman*

In *Poe*, a married couple, a married woman, and a physician challenged a Connecticut statute enacted in 1879 that forbade the use of contraceptives or even medical assistance in the use of contraceptives, even within a marriage.[54] The plaintiffs argued that for the situation each woman confronted, the best medical treatment would be advice in preventing conception.[55] But since the prosecutors claimed that giving such advice constituted an offense under Connecticut law, the physician, the married woman, and the couple sought a declaratory judgment that Connecticut law deprived them of life and liberty without due process of law.[56] The Connecticut Supreme Court had sustained demurrers in the case, in effect upholding the statute, while noting that the law had been used to prosecute only three persons since its enactment.[57]

At the Justices' conference on *Poe*, Justice Harlan let it be known where he stood on this debate. In a highly emotional statement, unusual for the refined patrician, he declared that the Court had "no business dismissing these cases"[58] and argued: "I think the statute is egregiously unconstitutional on its face. . . . The Due Process Clause has substantive content for me. The right to be let alone is embodied in due process. Despite the broad powers to legislate in the area of health, there are limits."[59] Referring to Justice Brandeis's famous phrase, he concluded his statement by asserting, "This is more offensive to the right to be let alone than anything possibly could be."[60] Justice Harlan expressed his "fear that the Court ha[d] indulged in a bit of sleight of hand to be rid of [the] case."[61]

Justice Frankfurter wrote the plurality opinion for the Court (joined by Chief Justice Warren, and Justices Clark and Whittaker), dismissing the case.[62] Frankfurter argued that the case was not justiciable because the appellants "do not clearly, and certainly do not in terms, allege that appellee Ullman threatens to prosecute them for use of, or for giving advice concerning, contraceptive devices."[63] Justice Brennan concurred in the judgment of dismissal, noting that the threat of prosecution against the individuals was not "definite and concrete."[64]

Justices Black, Douglas, Harlan, and Stewart all dissented, agreeing, for differing or unstated reasons, that the issues should be decided—that the case was justiciable.[65] But the most important dissent was the somewhat uncharacteristic one of Justice Harlan. Apologizing both for the unusual length of his dissent (he might have apologized for the unusual length of some of his sentences, too), as well as the necessity to discuss constitutional issues not mentioned in the plurality opinion, his passion continued for thirty-three pages.[66]

Here is how Professor Schwartz described it:

> In his *Poe* dissent, Justice Harlan indicated why the right to be let alone was guaranteed even though it was not mentioned in the constitutional text. First of all, said Harlan, the Court must approach "the text which is the only commission for our power not in a literalistic way, as if we had a tax statute before us, but as the basic charter of our society, setting out in

spare but meaningful terms the principles of government." For Harlan, "[I]t is not the particular enumeration of rights . . . which spells out the reach of" constitutional protection. On the contrary, the "character of Constitutional provisions . . . must be discerned from a particular provision's larger context. And . . . this context is one not of words, but of history and purposes."[67]

Nothing radical so far; the Constitution is not a tax statute. Harlan continued:

[T]he full scope of the liberty guaranteed by the Due Process Clause cannot be found in or limited by the precise terms of the specific guarantees elsewhere provided in the Constitution. This "liberty" is not a series of isolated points pricked out in terms of the taking of property; the freedom of speech, press, and religion; the right to keep and bear arms; the freedom from unreasonable searches and seizures; and so on. It is a rational continuum which, broadly speaking, includes a freedom from all substantial arbitrary impositions and purposeless restraints . . . and which also recognizes . . . that certain interests require particularly careful scrutiny of the state needs asserted to justify their abridgment.[68]

Justice Harlan saw due process as "a discrete concept which subsists as an independent guaranty of liberty and procedural fairness, more general and inclusive than the specific prohibitions."[69]

Justice Harlan articulated the idea that living traditions supply the content to the all-important constitutional concept of due process of law. Noting that due process represented a balance between individual liberty and the demands of organized society, he wrote:

The balance of which I speak is the balance struck by this country, having regard to what history teaches are the traditions from which it developed as well as the traditions from which it broke. That tradition is a living thing. A decision of this Court which radically departs from it could not long survive, while a decision which builds on what has survived is likely to be sound. No formula could serve as a substitute, in this area, for judgment and restraint.[70]

IV. Balance, History and Tradition, Living
Things, and Judgment and Restraint

Let's examine Justice Harlan's passage carefully. It seems that four matters need to be addressed. First, the Due Process Clause represents a balance—a rational continuum. It regards history, both traditions we follow
and those from which we have broken. Second, that tradition is living—
evolving. And, third, in trying to determine the scope of the continuum,
we should utilize judgment (hopefully a judicial quality) and restraint.
And, fourth, decisions contrary to that living tradition will not survive
long. What does all of this tell us about the good Justice?

A. Not an Originalist

The mentioning of traditions and utilizing them in the balancing required
to create a rational continuum of due process tells us that Justice Harlan is
not an originalist. This fact has been important for several reasons. First
of all, Justice Harlan's reputation, as indicated at the outset of this lecture,
is sterling. His tenure was marked by great and widespread respect for his
persona and his opinions. His work is influential and remains prominent
in many areas of law. When a great Justice takes sides in a debate, it lends
credibility to the cause. And when a "conservative" Justice takes a "liberal" position, it allows for what some call "[c]ross-[q]uotesmanship."[71]

Professor Schwartz strongly supported both the idea of nontextual
rights and a Constitution that, in his words, "states, not rules for the passing hour, but principles for an ever-expanding future."[72] Although Justice Harlan perhaps would not go that far, it was significant to Professor
Schwartz that Harlan—"the very model of the true conservative judge"—
was not one who looked at narrow literal meanings but examined rationality, history, purposes, and tradition.[73]

Whereas Professor Schwartz was likely to see the Ninth Amendment's
unenumerated rights, rather than the idea of due process, as support for
his flexible Constitution, he welcomed Justice Harlan's membership in
the non-originalist camp. He said:

> That Justice Harlan relied upon due process rather than the Ninth Amend-
> ment did not detract from his full acceptance of the concept of nonenu-
> merated rights. As Harlan saw it, due process "is a discrete concept which

subsists as an independent guaranty of liberty and procedural fairness, more general and inclusive than the specific prohibitions." Except for its terminology, the Harlan approach is essentially similar to the approach that relies on the Ninth Amendment. If the right is a basic right "which [is] *fundamental*; which belong[s] . . . to the citizens of all free governments," it is one retained by the people under the Ninth Amendment or, in Harlan's view, included in the "liberty" protected by due process.[74]

The idea that the literal text of the Constitution needs some content supplied to it, and further that this content might come from history and tradition, has been articulated by a good number of other famous judges, "conservative" and "liberal" alike. Chief Justice Marshall famously wrote the first principles of constitutional interpretation, noting:

A constitution, to contain an accurate detail of all the subdivisions of which its great powers will admit, and of all the means by which they may be carried into execution, would partake of the prolixity of a legal code, and could scarcely be embraced by the human mind. . . . [W]e must never forget, that it is *a constitution* we are expounding.[75]

Justice Holmes asserted that the Constitution must be flexible in the joints,[76] and Justice Felix Frankfurter reasoned that "[j]udicial exegesis is unavoidable with reference to an organic act like our Constitution, drawn in many particulars with purposed vagueness so as to leave room for the unfolding future."[77]

Additionally, Justice Frankfurter wrote, quoting Justice Cardozo:

These standards of justice are not authoritatively formulated anywhere as though they were specifics. Due process of law is a summarized constitutional guarantee of respect for those personal immunities which, as Mr. Justice Cardozo twice wrote for the Court, are "so rooted in the traditions and conscience of our people as to be ranked as fundamental," . . . or are "implicit in the concept of ordered liberty."[78]

Also, Justice Frankfurter wrote that provisions "like 'due process of law' or 'the equal protection of the laws[]' . . . do not carry contemporaneous fixity. By their very nature they imply a process of unfolding content."[79]

B. Living Traditions?

Besides consulting tradition and history, Justice Harlan termed the tradition side of the equation "living." What does that mean? Justice Rehnquist said: "At first blush it seems certain that a *living* Constitution is better than what must be its counterpart, a *dead* Constitution. It would seem that only a necrophile could disagree."[80] Well, courageously opposing necrophilia, as I often have, I have to join Harlan in supporting living traditions that animate our consequently living Constitution. That is, I think by "living," Justice Harlan means evolving. Judge Bork, who is considerably more into constitutional necrophilia, agrees with my analysis, terming Justice Harlan's view "a jurisprudential version of Darwinism."[81] Bork's point is a bit more complicated, and we will return to it below.[82]

Until recently, I don't think Harlan's view was that controversial. As one scholar wrote, "Nowadays, liberal and conservative fundamental rights theorists alike, from Laurence Tribe to Charles Fried, celebrate [the idea of living traditions]. . . ."[83] Indeed, Charles Fried, who clerked for Justice Harlan,[84] wrote a book about his tenure in a Republican administration Department of Justice, where he said that he signed on to battling *Roe v. Wade*, but not to an originalist agenda.[85] Fried, in fact, wrote the memos behind *Poe* and may have helped Justice Harlan crystallize his formulation.[86] Justice Harlan's formulation continues to be cited and to influence jurists.[87]

Again, Professor Schwartz wrote,

> Most of us today have no doubt about the proper answer. A basic document, drawn up in an age of knee-breeches and three-cornered hats, can serve the needs of an entirely different day only because our judges have recognized the truth of Marshall's celebrated reminder that it is a *constitution* they are expounding—an instrument that could hardly have been intended to endure through the ages if its provisions were fixed as irrevocably as the laws of the Medes and Persians. The constantly evolving nature of constitutional doctrine has alone enabled our system to make the transition from the eighteenth to the twentieth century.
>
> The outstanding feature of the Constitution is thus its plastic nature. Its key provisions are malleable and must be construed to meet the changing needs of different periods.[88]

What are some of these living traditions? Harlan's remarkable dissent requires considerable quoting here. We can start with the tradition of substantive due process. As Harlan notes,

> Were due process merely a procedural safeguard it would fail to reach those situations where the deprivation of life, liberty or property was accomplished by legislation which by operating in the future could, given even the fairest possible procedure in application to individuals, nevertheless destroy the enjoyment of all three. . . . Thus the guaranties of due process, though having their roots in Magna Carta's *"per legem terrae"* and considered as procedural safeguards "against executive usurpation and tyranny," have in this country "become bulwarks also against arbitrary legislation."[89]

So, our tradition includes Magna Carta, but not just as written, for that phrase, *"per legem terrae"*—the "law of the land"—had considerable substantive flesh on its bones by the time our country was founded.[90] Harlan argued that rights older than the Fourteenth Amendment were fundamental and belong to the citizens of all free governments, and it is for the purpose of securing these rights that men enter into society.[91] (Sounds like Jefferson, doesn't it?) He pointed out that the Court had "[a]gain and again . . . resisted the notion that the Fourteenth Amendment is no more than a shorthand reference" to the first eight amendments in the Bill of Rights.[92]

He argued that the character of constitutional provisions "must be discerned from a particular provision's larger context," and that that context was "one not of words, but of history and purposes," and thus "cannot be found in or limited by the precise terms of the specific guarantees. . . ."[93] The rational continuum he saw, "broadly speaking, includes a freedom from all substantial arbitrary impositions and purposeless restraints. . . ."[94] (I suspect he meant improperly purposed restraints.)

In addition, he cited cases involving the education of children where the court had used "the right of the individual to . . . establish a home and bring up children,"[95] and the principle that "[t]he fundamental theory of liberty upon which all governments in this Union repose excludes any general power of the State to standardize its children by forcing them to accept instruction from public teachers only."[96] (He noted, however, that Fourteenth Amendment incorporation of the First Amendment would probably have guided these decisions at the time he was writing.)[97] Harlan was again the purposivist: "For it is the purposes of those guarantees and not their text, the reasons for their statement by the framers and not the statement itself . . . which have led to their present status in the compendious notion of 'liberty' embraced in the Fourteenth Amendment."[98]

C. Decisions Based on Our History and Tradition Must Be Restrained

This somewhat bracing language does not sound very restrained. So, he reins it in a bit:

> Each new claim to Constitutional protection must be considered against a background of Constitutional purposes, as they have been rationally perceived and historically developed. Though we exercise limited and sharply restrained judgment, yet there is no "mechanical yard-stick," no "mechanical answer." The decision of an apparently novel claim must depend on grounds which follow closely on well-accepted principles and criteria. The new decision must take "its place in relation to what went before and further [cut] a channel for what is to come."[99]

He continues:

> The vague contours of the Due Process Clause do not leave judges at large. We may not draw on our merely personal and private notions and disregard the limits that bind judges in their judicial function. Even though the concept of due process of law is not final and fixed, these limits are derived from considerations that are fused in the whole nature of our judicial process. . . . These are considerations deeply rooted in reason and in the compelling traditions of the legal profession.[100]

Having stated the premises upon which his quest was based, Harlan turned to the particular constitutional claim in the case and pointed out the lines of battle. On the one hand, the appellants argued that the State, "without any rational, justifying purpose" deprived them of "a substantial measure of liberty in carrying on the most intimate of all personal relationships . . . ."[101] As Harlan wrote,

> The State, on the other hand, assert[ed] that it [was] acting to protect the moral welfare of its citizenry, both directly, in that it consider[ed] the practice of contraception immoral in itself, and instrumentally, in that the

availability of contraceptive materials tends to minimize "the disastrous consequence of dissolute action," that is fornication and adultery.[102]

Harlan argued that "throughout the English-speaking world," there was a tradition, and evidently one very much alive, of privacy in the home, and very specifically a tradition guarded in the Third and Fourth Amendments.[103] But he goes beyond that to invoke Brandeis's famous phrase from his *Olmstead* dissent about the right to be let alone:

> The protection guaranteed by the [Fourth and Fifth] Amendments is much broader in scope. The makers of our Constitution undertook to secure conditions favorable to the pursuit of happiness. They recognized the significance of man's spiritual nature, of his feelings and of his intellect. They knew that only a part of the pain, pleasure and satisfactions of life are to be found in material things. They sought to protect Americans in their beliefs, their thoughts, their emotions and their sensations. They conferred, as against the Government, the right to be let alone—the most comprehensive of rights and the right most valued by civilized men. To protect that right, every unjustifiable intrusion by the Government upon the privacy of the individual, whatever the means employed, must be deemed a violation of the Fourth Amendment.[104]

Quoting *Weems v. United States*,[105] Harlan argues, "A principle to be vital must be capable of wider application than the mischief which gave it birth."[106] After continuing to discuss privacy and family, and the private realm of family life, he invokes divine literary reference (he's really getting wound up after previously referencing the secular state). He perorates, "We would indeed be straining at a gnat and swallowing a camel[107] were we to show concern for the niceties of property law involved in our recent decision, under the Fourth Amendment, in *Chapman v. United States*[108] . . . and yet fail at least to see any substantial claim here."[109]

One last bit of restraint remains to be played:

> [C]onclusive, in my view, is the utter novelty of this enactment. Although the Federal Government and many States have at one time or other had on their books statutes forbidding or regulating the distribution of contraceptives, none, so far as I can find, has made the *use* of contraceptives a crime. Indeed, a diligent search has revealed that no nation, including

several which quite evidently share Connecticut's moral policy, has seen fit to effectuate that policy by the means presented here.[110]

Yup. There it is. Foreign law.
Having gone this far, Justice Harlan concludes:

> Though undoubtedly the States are and should be left free to reflect a wide variety of policies, and should be allowed broad scope in experimenting with various means of promoting those policies, I must agree with Mr. Justice Jackson that "There are limits to the extent to which a legislatively represented majority may conduct . . . experiments at the expense of the dignity and personality" of the individual. . . . In this instance these limits are, in my view, reached and passed.[111]

D. Decisions That Depart from Living Traditions Will Not Long Survive

Space does not allow detailed discussion of one final—and perhaps even the most interesting—point. And that is Harlan's final first aid in the hand of restraint: for he argues that a court decision that departs from living traditions will not long survive. But for now, I will simply note it. Professor Bruce Ledewitz wrote:

> Justice Harlan's view was that a decision that "radically departs from" tradition "could not long survive." But how, exactly, was that to happen? What agency could account for such a consequence? What phenomenon was Justice Harlan expecting to come into play? Why could a decision departing from our nation's "balance" of tradition not survive?
>
> The *Poe* language is suggestive but not clear. . . . I believe that Justice Harlan was referring to the power of public opinion—in a broad and organic sense—in a democratic society. The *Poe* dissent does not dismiss the views of the people after a judicial decision is reached. The "tradition" is not a passive and static resource for a judge to rummage through in order to reach a decision, but an ongoing force in public affairs capable of controlling constitutional interpretation in the long run.[112]

According to Ledewitz, Harlan is pointing out that although tradition may be a source of judicial decision making, "living tradition continues to determine constitutional law after judicial decisions are made."[113] This is sort of Mr. Dooley's famous point, that he did not know whether the Constitution followed the flag or not, but he did know that the Supreme Court follows the election returns.[114]

But, it is more than that. Ledewitz cites my favorite framer, Benjamin Franklin, and his reported comment upon being accosted when emerging from the final Constitutional Convention. A woman allegedly asked him what form of government he had created, a republic or a monarchy.[115] Franklin's wise reply was, "A republic . . . if you can keep it."[116] In concluding his fascinating article, Professor Ledewitz states:

> American law is plagued by doubts about the proper relationship of law to democracy. To paraphrase Robert Dahl, we lawyers both cannot deny and cannot accept that law is essentially political. Justice John Harlan was aware of this tension and considered it a central problem of American law that judges decide fundamental issues of governance without elections and without close democratic oversight. Justice Harlan resolved this problem for himself first by reference to certain lawyerly virtues: reasoned judgment, faithfulness to precedent, attention to tradition, and judicial restraint. Yet, he knew that these qualities were not guarantees of the proper use of judicial power in a democratic society.
>
> This is the framework of Justice Harlan's celebrated dissent in *Poe v. Ullman*. . . . In the living tradition quotation, Justice Harlan wrestles with the power of the judge and the authority of democratic consensus. In a short few sentences, Justice Harlan reorients our view of American law. In just a few words, Justice Harlan places democratic consensus at the center of legal activity.
>
> American law has not yet plumbed Justice Harlan's meaning in proclaiming that our "tradition is a living thing." His meaning goes beyond our current, tired debates about the proper sources of judicial constitutional decision. Justice Harlan is pointing to something outside law and judges. Something else—something vital, alive, and popular—controls. Given America's currently inflated view of law, this is a message we very much need to hear.[117]

V. Answering Harlan's Critics

Harlan's approach, of course, has its critics, including Robert Bork. Judge Bork takes aim at Justice Harlan, but because of the latter's credibility, he aims a little more moderately than usual. Stating that "many people find [Justice Harlan's method] attractive," as it both avoids the "obvious intellectual disingenuousness of some methods and, on the other [hand], the necessity of allowing a bad law to stand," Judge Bork remains unconvinced that rights that are not explicit in the Constitution should receive constitutional protection.[118]

Bork writes that Harlan "employed the [D]ue [P]rocess [C]lause of the [F]ourteenth [A]mendment since it was abundantly clear that nothing else in the Constitution could conceivably apply to the statute, and the [D]ue [P]rocess [C]lause has become the usual resort when no actual provision is available."[119] Noting that Harlan agreed with precedent that the Due Process Clause did not just protect procedural rights and that due process's substantive content did not come from incorporating just the Bill of Rights, Bork argues that Harlan arrogates too much power to judges:

> He assumed that judges possess a legitimate method of deciding when the substance of a state law, even when applied fairly, *improperly* deprives people of life, liberty, and property. Such a method is also required to justify an undefined residue of judicial power outside the provisions of the Bill of Rights.[120]

Also, Bork dismisses Harlan's idea that there has been, or should be, judicial involvement in the balance our nation strikes between liberty and the demands of organized society.[121] (Might as well, as Bernard Schwartz would suggest, bring back "cropping of ears, selling into servitude, branding, and whipping as punishments for crime.")[122] And, as to the idea that a decision departing from living traditions could not long survive, Bork interjects: "This is pure early Alexander Bickel. The primary safeguard against judicial willfulness seems to be a theory of the survival of the fittest decisions, a jurisprudential version of Darwinism."[123]

Bork suggests that the state interests offered to justify the Connecticut law (essentially that contraception is immoral) would be difficult for the Court to overcome, as "much law is based on moral precepts."[124] Bork notes that Harlan predicted some of what Douglas would write in *Griswold*, about the importance of privacy in our Constitution, but he is still not persuaded that any other privacy is guaranteed except that explicit in the Third and Fourth Amendments.[125] As to Harlan's statement that marital intimacy was part of an institution that must always be allowed and always be protected, Bork notes that the state had never really enforced the law.[126] He seems unconcerned that the state was arguing that it had a right to enforce it in the very case at bar. Bork cites Harlan's conclusion that no other state or nation had imposed such a law, but he does not raise the foreign law bugaboo.[127] And Bork admits that it was a "lunatic law," but rests his prescription for judicial inaction on the conclusion that "the Constitution has nothing whatever to do with issues of sexual morality."[128] Professor Ledewitz makes the obvious rejoinder:

> By entitling his book *The Tempting of America*, Judge Bork seemed to be acknowledging that the problem was not just that the Justices were usurping inappropriate political power, but that the American people might well have decided that this is a good, or at least occasionally necessary, thing. Justice Harlan, on the other hand, might regard this "temptation" as a deeply democratic decision about the role of the Supreme Court in the American system of government.[129]

Or, Harlan might just say that Bork loses and tradition lives. But the best answer to Bork comes from a federal judge: Richard Posner describes the fallacies of Borkian originalism. Judge Posner not only shows the fallacies of originalism; he underscores Professor Ledewitz's point. He thought that Bork misread the lessons of his Senate defeat:

> The decisive factor [in Bork's defeat] . . . was that a large number of Americans . . . do not want the Constitution to be construed as narrowly as Bork would construe it. They do not think that states should be allowed to forbid abortion . . . or to enforce racial restrictive covenants. . . . They do not think that the federal government should be free to engage in racial discrimination. . . . They do not think that states should be free to enact "savage" laws, or that a judge should practice "moral abstention." . . . They do not believe that under Chief Justice Rehnquist as under his predecessors "the political seduction of the law continues apace." . . . The people are entitled to ask what the benefits to them of originalism would be, and they will find no answers in *The Tempting of America*.[130]

Justice Harlan's jurisprudence, as exemplified in *Poe v. Ullman*, continues to illuminate how to interpret constitutional texts—issues that will animate our discussions of the law for the rest of time. Coming from our Anglo-American traditions of unwritten constitutions and evolving ones, the argument that tradition lives is a strong one. Magna Carta's "law of the land" has grown with that land, as has due process in our land.[131] Personally, I would prefer to remain in the common law camp, the camp of Holmes and Harlan, than the camp of Bork and his jurisprudential allies. Restraint exists. Tradition lives.

Conclusion

A paragraph that I wrote in 1998, closing a chapter in *The Burger Court: Counter-Revolution or Confirmation*, still describes the problem, at least as I see it (and I don't often agree with things I wrote over a decade ago):

> The moderate highly principled approach of John Harlan II seems to have few advocates, though many admirers. As Anthony Lewis has said, "[We are] all activists now . . . [Activists] for what is a different question." Perhaps the real battle of future courts will not be "dignity" versus "deference," originalism versus instrumentalism, or liberalism versus conservativism. The real battle presaged by the Burger Court—perhaps the most activist Court of our history—will be to seek a principled resolution of cases before the Court, a resolution that carefully utilizes Judge Posner's "flexibility in the joints." It must be a resolution free from political control but wary of political restraints; it must properly preserve separation of powers and federalism, and respect constitutional and even common-law restraints, while addressing Justice Harlan's living traditions and Roscoe Pound's prophecy that the "law must be stable and yet it cannot stand still."[132]

In closing, I would say that in one important sense, Justice Harlan could be thought of as an originalist. He believed his approach both faithful to the principles of the nation and more likely to lead to just decisions. He was far more confident than Judge Bork that good judges can, as they have for centuries, exercise their authority in a principled, restrained way without requiring an ahistorical, formal rule to constrain them.

Justice Harlan was living our traditions.

NOTES

1. THE FEDERALIST NO. 37, at 229 (James Madison) (Edward Mead Earle ed., 1937).
2. BERNARD SCHWARTZ, THE NEW RIGHT AND THE CONSTITUTION: TURNING BACK THE LEGAL CLOCK 7 (1990).

3. For Fourteenth Amendment due process decisions, see JOHN HART ELY, DEMOCRACY AND DISTRUST: A THEORY OF JUDICIAL REVIEW 2 & 185 n.3, 3 & 186 n.10 (1980), which advocates an interpretivist approach whereby Justices repair to express or implicit purposes in the language of the Constitution when deciding Fourteenth Amendment due process cases.

4. 367 U.S. 497, 522 (1961) (Harlan, J., dissenting).

5. *Id.* at 542.

6. *See, e.g.*, SCHWARTZ, *supra* note 2, at 67–72 (supporting Harlan's approach to substantive due process); CHARLES FRIED, ORDER AND LAW: ARGUING THE REAGAN REVOLUTION—A FIRSTHAND ACCOUNT 72–82 (1991) (supporting Harlan's *Poe* dissent, but criticizing substantive due process as applied in *Roe v. Wade*, 410 U.S. 113 (1973)); ROBERT H. BORK, THE TEMPTING OF AMERICA: THE POLITICAL SEDUCTION OF THE LAW 231–35 (1990) (criticizing Justice Harlan's approach as judicial Darwinism).

7. Bruce Ledewitz, *Justice Harlan's Law and Democracy*, 20 J.L. & POL. 373, 460 (2004) (quoting *Poe*, 367 U.S. at 542 (Harlan, J., dissenting)).

8. *See, e.g.*, Robert H. Bork, *Neutral Principles and Some First Amendment Problems*, 47 IND. L.J. 1, 2–4 (1971) (arguing that courts violate "Madisonian" democracy and thereby usurp power when unconstrained by neutral principles derived from Constitution itself, employing instead values of particular judges).

9. *See* ALEXANDER M. BICKEL, THE LEAST DANGEROUS BRANCH: THE SUPREME COURT AT THE BAR OF POLITICS (Yale Univ. Press 1986) (1962) (arguing that Supreme Court is least dangerous branch of government whose power of judicial review secures our rights, liberties, and values).

10. *See, e.g.*, BORK, *supra* note 6, at 9 (arguing that courts abandoning original intent introduce into Constitution elitist principles that otherwise could not be achieved democratically).

11. Robert Henry, *The Players and the Play*, *in* THE BURGER COURT: COUNTERREVOLUTION OR CONFIRMATION? 13, 39–40 (Bernard Schwartz ed., 1998) (citing RICHARD A. POSNER, OVERCOMING LAW 237–55 (1995)).

12. BICKEL, *supra* note 9, at 16–18 (describing "counter-majoritarian difficulty"); *see, e.g.*, BORK, *supra* note 6, at 143–60 (arguing that originalism avoids counter-majoritarian problem).

13. These "restraints," along with judicial review itself, may be among our living traditions.

14. This part of the lecture was largely adapted from my previous essay, Robert Henry, *The Players and the Play*, *in* THE BURGER COURT: COUNTER-REVOLUTION OR CONFIRMATION? 13, 17–18 (Bernard Schwartz ed., 1998), by permission of Oxford University Press.

15. TINSLEY E. YARBROUGH, JOHN MARSHALL HARLAN: GREAT DISSENTER OF THE WARREN COURT 9, 333–35 (1992).

16. *Id.* at viii.

17. *Id.* at 3.

18. *See* TINSLEY E. YARBROUGH, JUDICIAL ENIGMA: THE FIRST JUSTICE HARLAN 163–64 (1995) (describing first Justice Harlan as writing and joining substantive due process opinions).

19. LOREN P. BETH, JOHN MARSHALL HARLAN: THE LAST WHIG JUSTICE 156 (1992) (describing Justice Harlan's dissents as his "most memorable opinions" and noting that "when history has judged him to be right he was usually dissenting").

20. 163 U.S. 537, 552 (1896) (Harlan, J., dissenting), *overruled by* Brown v. Bd. of Educ., 347 U.S. 483 (1954); *see also* BETH, *supra* note 19, at 156 (describing Justice Harlan's dissent in *Plessy* as one of his most memorable opinions).

21. 198 U.S. 45, 65–74 (1905) (Harlan, J., dissenting), *abrogated by* West Coast Hotel Co. v. Parrish, 300 U.S. 379 (1937).

22. YARBROUGH, *supra* note 15, at 5, 138.

23. *Id.* at 11, 13.

24. *Id.* at 13.

25. PETER BARBERIS, LIBERAL LION: JO GRIMOND: A POLITICAL LIFE 19 (2004) (quoting H. H. Asquith's famous saying about Balliol men) (internal quotation marks omitted).

26. This poem—attributed to H. C. Beeching—was originally printed in 1881 as part of a collection of verses written by undergraduates at Balliol College and appeared under the title, "A Masque of B[a]ll[io]l." ANTHONY POWELL, UNDER REVIEW: FURTHER WRITINGS ON WRITERS, 1946–1990, at 236 (1991).

27. YARBROUGH, *supra* note 15, at 13, 15.

28. *Id.* at 13, 15, 41–42.

29. *Id.* at 82, 87.

30. BERNARD SCHWARTZ, A HISTORY OF THE SUPREME COURT 375 (1993).

31. Anthony Lewis, *Foreword* to THE BURGER COURT: THE COUNTER-REVOLUTION THAT WASN'T, at viii (Vincent Blasi ed., 1983).

32. Henry J. Friendly, *Mr. Justice Harlan, As Seen by a Friend and Judge of an Inferior Court*, 85 HARV. L. REV. 382, 384 (1971).

33. Norman Dorsen, *John Marshall Harlan, Civil Liberties, and the Warren Court*, 36 N.Y.L. SCH. L. REV. 81, 84 (1991) (quoting Roth v. United States, 354 U.S. 476, 505 (1957) (Harlan, J., dissenting)).

34. *Id.* at 83–84 (quoting John M. Harlan, *Thoughts at a Dedication: Keeping the Judicial Function in Balance*, 49 A.B.A. J. 943, 943 (1963)). Federalism may be both a bulwark and a barrier. Perhaps certain limitations that Harlan liked, especially federalism, made possible his careful use of substantive due process.

35. 377 U.S. 533, 624 (1964) (Harlan, J., dissenting).

36. *Id.* at 624–25.

37. ROGER K. NEWMAN, HUGO BLACK: A BIOGRAPHY 588 (2d ed. 1997) (internal quotation marks omitted).

38. YARBROUGH, *supra* note 15, at 337.

39. *See id.* at 337–44 (providing overview of Justice Harlan's multiple influences and multidimensional jurisprudence).

40. *Id.* at 333.

41. *See* Dorsen, *supra* note 33, at 93–97 (cataloguing cases where Justice Harlan concurred with or wrote liberal Warren Court opinions).

42. 367 U.S. 497, 542 (1961) (Harlan, J., dissenting).

43. *Id.* at 540.

44. *See id.* at 550 ("I think the sweep of the Court's decisions, under both the Fourth and Fourteenth Amendments, amply shows that the Constitution protects the privacy of the home against all unreasonable intrusion of whatever character.").

45. *See* Griswold v. Connecticut, 381 U.S. 479 (1965) (holding that zone of privacy exists, within penumbras of constitutional guarantees, that precludes states from prohibiting married couples from using contraceptives).

46. Dorsen, *supra* note 33, at 107.

47. 410 U.S. 113 (1973).

48. 381 U.S. at 507–11 (Black, J., dissenting).

49. *Id.* at 499 (Harlan, J., concurring).

50. 389 U.S. 347, 360–61 (1967) (Harlan, J., concurring) (arguing in favor of reasonable expectation of privacy test to limit government's ability to intrude upon individual's privacy right without warrant).

51. But Harlan apparently believed laws forbidding adultery and homosexuality were constitutionally allowable. *See* Poe v. Ullman, 367 U.S. 497, 553 (1961) (Harlan, J., dissenting) ("Adultery, homosexuality and the like are sexual intimacies which the State forbids altogether, but the intimacy of husband and wife is necessarily an essential and accepted feature of the institution of marriage . . . .").

52. 410 U.S. at 113.

53. *Id.* at 171 (Rehnquist, J., dissenting).

54. 367 U.S. at 498–501; *see also* Ledewitz, *supra* note 7, at 376 (explaining facts of *Poe*).

55. 367 U.S. at 499–500.

56. *Id.*

57. *Id.* at 500–02; *see also* YARBROUGH, *supra* note 15, at 310 (explaining facts and procedural history of *Poe*).

58. YARBROUGH, *supra* note 15, at 311 (internal quotation marks omitted).

59. BERNARD SCHWARTZ, SUPER CHIEF: EARL WARREN AND HIS SUPREME COURT—A JUDICIAL BIOGRAPHY 379 (1983) (internal quotation marks omitted).

60. *Id.* (internal quotation marks omitted).

61. 367 U.S. at 533 (Harlan, J., dissenting).

62. *Id.* at 498 (plurality opinion).

63. *Id.* at 501.

64. *Id.* at 509 (Brennan, J., concurring).

65. *See id.* (Black, J., dissenting) (dissenting on ground that Court ought to reach and decide merits of case); *id.* at 509–10 (Douglas, J., dissenting) (arguing that case is justiciable); *id.* at 522–23 (Harlan, J., dissenting) ("In my view the course which the Court has taken does violence to established concepts of 'justiciability,' and unjustifiably leaves these appellants under the threat of unconstitutional prosecution."); *id.* at 555 (Stewart, J., dissenting) (agreeing with dissents of Douglas and Harlan).

66. *Id.* at 522–55 (Harlan, J., dissenting).
67. SCHWARTZ, *supra* note 2, at 67 (quoting *Poe*, 367 U.S. at 541–43 (Harlan, J., dissenting)).
68. 367 U.S. at 543 (Harlan, J., dissenting).
69. *Id.* at 542.
70. *Id.*
71. JAMES C. HUMES, SPEAK LIKE CHURCHILL, STAND LIKE LINCOLN: 21 POWERFUL SECRETS OF HISTORY'S GREATEST SPEAKERS 47 (2002).
72. SCHWARTZ, *supra* note 2, at 10.
73. *Id.* at 67.
74. *Id.* at 68 (quoting *Poe*, 367 U.S. at 541 (Harlan, J., dissenting)).
75. McCulloch v. Maryland, 17 U.S. (4 Wheat.) 316, 407 (1819).
76. Dissenting in *Lochner v. New York*, 198 U.S. 45 (1905), Justice Holmes wrote:

> I think that the word liberty in the Fourteenth Amendment is perverted when it is held to prevent the natural outcome of a dominant opinion, unless it can be said . . . that the statute proposed would infringe fundamental principles as they have been understood by the traditions of our people and our law.

Id. at 76 (Holmes, J., dissenting). Holmes is clearly protean on constitutional jurisprudence. He would tell Harold Laski in a letter "that a law was constitutional unless it made him want to 'puke.'" POSNER, *supra* note 11, at 192 (quoting 2 HOLMES-LASKI LETTERS: THE CORRESPONDENCE OF MR. JUSTICE HOLMES AND HAROLD J. LASKI 1916–1935, at 888 (Mark DeWolfe Howe ed. 1953)). Yet Judge Posner exposes him for the pragmatist that he was:

> Holmes's influential conception of free speech as an open marketplace of ideas owes more to Mill and Darwin than to the values that all reasonable Americans could or can be brought to agree on. The great judges have enriched political thought and practice precisely by bringing controversial values, whether of an egalitarian, populist, or libertarian cast, into the formation of public policy. Marshall, Holmes, Brandeis, and Black, to name only a few of the most important American judges, are major figures in the history of American political liberalism because they used their judicial office to stamp the law with a personal vision.

Id. at 197.
77. Graves v. New York, 306 U.S. 466, 491 (1939) (Frankfurter, J., concurring).
78. Rochin v. California, 342 U.S. 165, 169 (1952) (quoting Snyder v. Massachusetts, 291 U.S. 97, 105 (1934) and Palko v. Connecticut, 302 U.S. 319, 325 (1937), respectively).
79. FHA v. Darlington, Inc., 358 U.S. 84, 92 (1958) (Frankfurter, J., dissenting).
80. William H. Rehnquist, *The Notion of a Living Constitution*, 54 TEX. L. REV. 693, 693 (1976); *see also* SCHWARTZ, *supra* note 2, at 264 (mentioning Justice Rehnquist's statements regarding "living Constitution").
81. BORK, *supra* note 6, at 232.
82. *See infra* notes 118–130 and accompanying text.

83. James E. Fleming, *Securing Deliberative Autonomy*, 48 STAN. L. REV. 1, 60 (1995).
84. YARBROUGH, *supra* note 15, at 310.
85. FRIED, *supra* note 6, at 72.
86. *See* YARBROUGH, *supra* note 15, at 310–11 (describing memorandum written by Fried and Justice Harlan's agreement with it).
87. *See* Ledewitz, *supra* note 7, at 375 ("Given his position as 'The Great Dissenter' on the Warren Court, Justice Harlan has emerged . . . as surprisingly influential. . . ." (quoting YARBROUGH, *supra* note 15)).
88. SCHWARTZ, *supra* note 2, at 264–65.
89. Poe v. Ullman, 367 U.S. 497, 541 (1961) (Harlan, J., dissenting) (quoting Hurtado v. California, 110 U.S. 516, 523, 532 (1884)).
90. *See* Michael W. McConnell, *Tradition and Constitutionalism Before the Constitution*, 1998 U. ILL. L. REV. 173, 192 (explaining that organic documents of United States incorporate understanding that our rights are "preconstitutional and prepolitical").
91. *Poe*, 367 U.S. at 541 (Harlan, J., dissenting).
92. *Id.*
93. *Id.* at 542–43.
94. *Id.* at 543.
95. *Id.* (quoting Meyer v. Nebraska, 262 U.S. 390, 399 (1923) (internal quotation marks omitted)).
96. *Id.* at 543–44 (quoting Pierce v. Soc'y of Sisters, 268 U.S. 510, 535 (1925) (internal quotation marks omitted)).
97. *Id.* at 544.
98. *Id.*
99. *Id.* (quoting Irvine v. California, 347 U.S. 128, 147 (1954)).
100. *Id.* at 544–45 (quoting Rochin v. California, 342 U.S. 165, 170–71 (1952)) (internal quotation marks omitted).
101. *Id.* at 545.
102. *Id.*
103. *Id.* at 548–49.
104. *Id.* at 550 (quoting Olmstead v. United States, 277 U.S. 438, 478 (1928) (Brandeis, J., dissenting)) (internal quotation marks omitted).
105. 217 U.S. 349, 373 (1910). The Court in *Weems* found that a Philippine law inflicted cruel and unusual punishment. *Id.* at 363–65. The law prohibited falsification of a public document by a public official, making it punishable by fine, twelve to twenty years of hard labor, and subsequent deprivation of political rights. *Id.* The Court held, "we cannot think that [the Cruel and Unusual Punishment Clause] was intended to prohibit only practices like the Stuarts, or to prevent only an exact repetition of history." *Id.* at 373.
106. *Poe*, 367 U.S. at 551 (Harlan, J., dissenting) (quoting *Weems*, 217 U.S. at 373) (internal quotation marks omitted).
107. Straining at a gnat and swallowing a camel is the literary reference. *Matthew* 23:24. I mention this only because I just saw a recent survey that said that eighty percent of young people believe that Sodom married Gomorrah.

108. 365 U.S. 610 (1961) (holding warrantless search of house based upon suspicion that contraband was inside violated Fourth Amendment, and that landlord could not consent to search of tenant's home).

109. *Poe*, 367 U.S. at 552 (Harlan, J., dissenting).

110. *Id.* at 554–55.

111. *Id.* at 555 (quoting Skinner v. Oklahoma, 316 U.S. 535, 546 (1942) (Jackson, J., concurring) (agreeing with majority that forced sterilization statute for habitual criminals is unconstitutional)).

112. Ledewitz, *supra* note 7, at 387 (quoting *Poe*, 367 U.S. at 542 (Harlan, J., dissenting)).

113. *Id.* at 411.

114. Finley P. Dunne, *Mr. Dooley Reviews the Supreme Court's Decision*, SUNDAY CHAT, June 9, 1901, at 6.

115. Ledewitz, *supra* note 7, at 412.

116. *Id.* (quoting 3 THE RECORDS OF THE FEDERAL CONVENTION OF 1787 app. A, at 85 (Max Farrand ed., Yale Univ. Press rev. ed. 1937)).

117. *Id.* at 460–61 (quoting Poe v. Ullman, 367 U.S. 497, 542 (1961) (Harlan, J., dissenting)).

118. BORK, *supra* note 6, at 231, 234.

119. *Id.*

120. *Id.* at 231–32.

121. *Id.* at 232.

122. SCHWARTZ, *supra* note 2, at 15.

123. BORK, *supra* note 6, at 232.

124. *Id.* at 232–33.

125. *See id.* at 234–35 (citing Poe v. Ullman, 367 U.S. 497, 541 (1961) (Harlan, J., dissenting), and Griswold v. Connecticut, 381 U.S. 479 (1965)) (arguing that judiciary usurps constitutional power when employing Harlan's approach).

126. *See id.* at 233–34 (conceding that state never possessed interest in applying law to married couples, and never did enforce it, but still rejecting Justice Harlan's formulation of constitutional right to privacy).

127. *See id.* at 233 (acknowledging without questioning Harlan's argument that "no other state or nation, though many shared Connecticut's moral policy, had imposed a criminal prohibition on the use of contraceptives").

128. *Id.* at 234.

129. Ledewitz, *supra* note 7, at 418.

130. POSNER, *supra* note 11, at 254 (quoting BORK, *supra* note 6, at 240, 259).

131. Poe v. Ullman, 367 U.S. 497, 541 (1961) (Harlan, J., dissenting) (arguing that due process is not limited to procedure, but conforms to situations that deprive individuals of life, liberty, or property).

132. Henry, *supra* note 11, at 44 (quoting Lewis, *supra* note 31, at ix, PETER IRONS, BRENNAN VS. REHNQUIST: THE BATTLE FOR THE CONSTITUTION, at xi (1994), and ROSCOE POUND, INTERPRETATIONS OF LEGAL HISTORY 1 (1923), respectively).

11

Statutes

ROBERT A. KATZMANN

Introduction

I owe much to James Madison, that diminutive giant, one of the founding architects of our constitutional structure. In my pre-bench, academic days, much of my work focused on the challenges of governance, on the ways that our institutions operate, and on the obstacles to and steps toward the more effective functioning of government. My research and writing concentrated on a range of subjects having to do with governance, including the determinants of agency discretion,[1] and how the institutions of national government—the legislative, executive, and judicial branches—affect outcomes over time.[2] I viewed lawmaking as a continuum of institutional processes, which interact with one another in complex and subtle ways. My appreciation for interbranch inquiry was heightened when my friend, collaborator, and mentor, Judge Frank Coffin, became chair of the Committee on the Judicial Branch of the Judicial Conference of the United States (a statutory group of twenty-six federal judges, as well as the Chief Justice, that makes national administrative policy for the federal courts). Judge Coffin, who represented Maine in the House of Representatives, called for a systematic examination of the full range of judicial-legislative relations—past, present, and future. Judge Coffin asked that I assist in devising and implementing the Committee's research agenda. In time, we and some colleagues created the Governance Institute as the vehicle for our work.[3] The first product of that enterprise was *Judges and Legislators: Toward Institutional Comity,*[4] a symposium that brought together scholars, judges, legislators, and others

This lecture was delivered on October 18, 2011, and appeared in *87 N.Y.U. L. Rev.* 637 (2012).

to examine relations between the first and third branches. And, two years before becoming a judge, I published *Courts and Congress*,[5] which represented my thinking to date on that subject.

Now, having been on the bench for a dozen years, I return to the subject of courts and Congress, with a focus on federal statutes—that is, the laws enacted by Congress. As a federal circuit judge, I spend a considerable amount of time interpreting federal statutes, construing what the laws of Congress mean. Indeed, a substantial majority of the Supreme Court's caseload involves statutory construction (two-thirds of its recent docket by one estimate).[6] This steady diet of statutory cases reflects the simple reality that just as Congress produces legislation, so courts are called on to interpret those laws, especially when they are vague, ambiguous, or seemingly contradictory.

In the best of all possible worlds, the language of the statute is plain on its face, pristine, and brimming with clarity. Then, the job of the judge is generally straightforward. Consider this statute, which I had to interpret: "It shall be unlawful for any person to knowingly or intentionally purchase at retail during a 30 day period more than 9 grams of . . . pseudoephedrine base . . . in a scheduled listed chemical product."[7] The appellant in the case before me purchased 24.48 grams in a thirty-day period from six different pharmacies. My task in this case was simple. Under the plain words of the statute, he violated the law.[8]

But when—as often happens—the statute is ambiguous, vague, or otherwise imprecise, the interpretative task is not obvious. Now, consider these statutes I had to construe. In one case,[9] the statute says that a court may award a prevailing party "reasonable attorneys' fees as *part of costs*."[10] The parents of a disabled child who won relief sought compensation for the costs of expert fees. Are those expert fees compensable as "costs" under the statute? Or consider this statute in another case before me: The law bars suits against the government as to "any claim arising out of the loss, miscarriage or *negligent transmission* of letters or postal matter."[11] A postal customer seeks to recover for injuries suffered when she tripped over mail left on her porch by the mail carrier.[12] The question before the panel was: What constitutes "negligent transmission" under the statute? And then there was this issue before a panel on which I sat: Under a statute, "[i]t shall be unlawful for any person[,] . . . who has been *convicted in any court* of[] a crime punishable by imprisonment for a term exceeding one year . . . [,] to . . . possess in or affecting commerce, any firearm or ammunition . . . which has been shipped or transported in interstate or foreign commerce."[13] Does the language "convicted in any court" mean any prior conviction in any court anywhere in the world, or does it only apply to convictions in courts of the United States?[14] How should I, as a judge, interpret such statutes? Should the judge confine herself to the text? Should the judge, in seeking to make sense of the ambiguity or vagueness, go behind the text of the statute to legislative materials, and if so, which ones? Should the judge seek to ascertain Congress's purposes and intentions?

These questions of statutory construction are of fundamental importance because the methodology of interpretation can affect the outcome in a case and thus whether the law has been construed consistently with Congress's meaning—to the degree that it can be divined.

Not only have these questions sparked considerable discussion within the federal judiciary itself, but also congressional hearings have been devoted to the subject.[15] Senators ask judicial nominees for their views on how they would construe statutes,[16] and law journals are filled with learned articles on statutory construction.[17] When Congress reverses a statutory decision of the Supreme Court, the mainstream media may cover it. That was the case, for example, when Congress enacted the Lily Ledbetter Fair Pay Act of 2009,[18] which states that the 180-day statute of limitations for filing an equal-pay lawsuit regarding pay discrimination resets with each new discriminatory paycheck.[19] Then Congress heeded Justice Ruth Bader Ginsburg's dissent in *Ledbetter v. Goodyear Tire & Rubber Co.*[20] and objections from many civil rights groups to the Supreme Court's ruling that pay discrimination claims under Title VII of the Civil Rights Act of 1964[21] are time-barred if the pay-setting decision was made outside of the 180-day statute of limitations period.[22]

Judicial interpretation of statutes has been part of this nation's constitutional experience from early days. In a Madison Lecture on statutory construction, I would be remiss in failing to note the famous case bearing Madison's name, *Marbury v. Madison*,[23] in which Chief Justice John Marshall interpreted section 13 of the 1789 Judiciary Act to be unconstitutional. He thus avoided the dilemma of ordering Madison to deliver William Marbury his judicial commission (which President Jefferson would have overridden) or refusing to issue the writ—either way exposing the Court's limited power.

Attention to statutes is not surprising. Statutes affect all manner of life, including the most pressing public policy issues of the day. They are the basis of much governmental activity—"the beginnings," in Charles Jones's words, "of life through law."[24] The numbers and kinds of statutes are enormous. Some statutes mandate particular actions;[25] others prohibit particular behaviors;[26] and still others give considerable discretion to agencies to implement the legislature's meaning.[27] A few statutes specifically provide for court tests.[28] Some statutes affect states directly by conditioning federal aid on local government's acceptance of particular responsibilities or agreement to implement particular policies.[29] How statutes are drafted—tightly or loosely—can give executive branch agencies more or less discretion to make policy.[30]

Statutes can address everything from the seemingly trivial to matters of fundamental significance with substantial impact.[31] Legislation is the basis for the administrative state as we know it. The Administrative Procedure Act,[32] for example, established the essential framework for the regulatory process of the past sixty-five years. The Americans with Disabilities Act of 1990,[33] in another instance, is a civil rights statute that was meant to afford broad protections to persons with disabilities. The Clean Air Act[34] and the Clean Water Act[35] have been cornerstones of the environmental movement. Title IX of the Education Amendments of 1972[36] led to major changes in education such that women and girls had new opportunities in the classroom and on the athletic field.[37]

William N. Eskridge Jr. and John Ferejohn observed in their monumental work, *A Republic of Statutes*,[38] that some statutes transform constitutional baselines, going beyond filling in gaps. Thus, the principle of *Brown v. Board of Education*[39] that de jure racial segregation violated the Constitution has been realized through a panoply of statutes, such as the Civil Rights Act of 1964,[40] which entrenched the principle that discrimination on the basis of race is unacceptable. Given the vital issues that statutes address—civil rights,[41] national security,[42] the environment,[43] the economy,[44] voting rights,[45] and gender discrimination,[46] to name a few— how courts construe legislation is a matter of great consequence and thus attention. The phenomenon of "statutorification" of the law, as my colleague Guido Calabresi put it, is common to both the federal and state levels.[47] (My topic in this lecture is federal statutes and their interpretation by federal courts, realizing, however, that state legislative and judicial activity[48] is extensive and profoundly important.)

When a court interprets a statute, it articulates the meaning of the words of the legislative branch. Although, over the years, considerable ink has been spilled about how courts should interpret statutes, there has been scant consideration given to what I think is critical as courts discharge their interpretative task—an appreciation of how Congress actually functions, how Congress signals its meaning, and what Congress expects of those interpreting its laws. Although in a formal sense the legislative process ends with legislative enactment of a law, in their interpretive role courts inescapably become participants in that process. For the judiciary, understanding that process is essential if it is to construe statutes in a manner that is faithful to legislative meaning. Hence, Part I of this lecture focuses on how Congress works and on the lawmaking process as it has evolved.

In examining that process, I look in Part II to how legislators who comprise Congress signal their legislative meaning to agencies—the first interpreters of statutes—and, another subject deserving full empirical inquiry, how agencies regard Congress's work product in interpreting and executing the law. That context should be instructive to courts as they interpret statutes. By understanding statutory interpretation as an enterprise involving other institutions, we can better address the question of how courts ought to interpret statutes. Against that background, I examine in Part III two approaches to the judicial interpretation of statutes—purposivism and textualism. I conclude in Part IV with a discussion of practical ways in which Congress may better signal its meaning, and how courts may better inform Congress of problems they perceive in the statutes they review.

By way of preview, it is my contention that in its practices, Congress intends that its work should be understood through its institutional processes and legislative history. These include, for example, committee and conference committee reports that accompany legislative text. Agencies well appreciate and are responsive to Congress's perspective that such materials are essential to construing statutes. What follows, then, reinforces my view that a purely textualist approach, which maintains that judges should restrict themselves only to the words of the statute, is inadequate when interpreting ambiguous laws.

I. Congress and the Lawmaking Process

Madison and his colleagues offered a general blueprint on the structure of government, but they provided little about the internal workings of institutions themselves. Our founders envisioned governance as a process of interaction among institutions, at the federal level—legislative, executive, and judicial branches—and between the federal and state levels. In Madison's and the other founders' design, each institution would have its own structure, purposes, and interests. The members of each branch would have the self-interest to resist the other branches' encroachments upon their prerogatives; yet, these institutions would in practice operate interdependently. And that system—characterized by both the constructive tension arising from the separation of powers, as well as institutional interdependence—would produce informed and deliberative outcomes. Although each institutional element would have its own structures, workways, interests, and purposes, together those parts would yield a balanced system. Senator Daniel Patrick Moynihan, another great mentor of mine, remarked on "the degree to which the founders of this nation thought about *government.*"[49] It was to the institutions of government, he observed, that they "looked to confine and to moderate" the political struggle they feared.[50]

Congress is the engine of statutes. The Constitution defines the powers of the legislative branch, the qualifications and terms of members, the circumstances in which legislators may be held to account for their speech and actions, the presentment of enacted bills to the President, and the requirements for overturning presidential vetoes. Madison asserted that the legislative institution should be designed so that legislators would "study . . . the comprehensive interests of their country,"[51] as well as more immediate needs. *The Federalist* argued that the legislative branch needed to develop procedures so that its members would develop specialized competence and experience devising "a succession of well-chosen and well-connected measures."[52] As envisioned, the legislative body should have a relatively stable composition with its members acquiring thorough mastery of the public business over time.[53] Madison cautioned:

> It will be of little avail to the people that the laws are made by men of their own choice, if the laws be so voluminous that they cannot be read, or so incoherent that they cannot be understood; if they be repealed or revised before they are promulged [sic], or undergo such incessant changes that no man who knows what the law is to-day can guess what it will be to-morrow.[54]

But the Constitution hardly delineated how the lawmaking process was to be organized within each chamber. It limited such instruction to a few clauses: "The House of Representatives shall chuse their Speaker and other officers";[55] "The Vice President of the United States shall be President of the Senate, but shall have no vote, unless they be equally divided";[56] "Each house may determine the rules of its proceedings, punish its members for disorderly behaviour, and, with the concurrence of two-thirds, expel a member";[57] "Each house shall keep a journal of its proceedings";[58] "Neither house, during the session of Congress, shall without the consent of the other, adjourn for more than three days, nor to any other place than that in which the two houses shall be sitting";[59] "All bills for raising revenue shall originate in the house of representatives."[60]

Beyond these words, it was up to succeeding Congresses to determine their lawmaking processes. The framers who lived through the frailties of the Articles of Confederation thought that through the institutional learning that would come with time, the branches could best craft the procedures that would enable effective governance. As Gouverneur Morris of New York wrote about the Constitution: "Nothing human can be perfect. . . . Surrounded by difficulties, we did the best we could; leaving it with those who should come after us to take counsel from experience. . . ."[61] And, in thinking about the first Congresses, which would create those initial processes, the framers might very well have felt that the task was manageable, because the legislature's universe was small and thus more conducive to deliberation—a mere sixty-five members in the House and twenty-six in the Senate in the first Congress.[62]

Congressional committees have been central to lawmaking since the early nineteenth century. Without committees, Congress could not function. By the mid-1820s, each legislative chamber had established standing committees that could expect that bills within their substantive jurisdiction would be referred to them.[63] In 1885, a young scholar, Woodrow Wilson, wrote: "Congress in session is Congress on public exhibition, whilst Congress in its committee rooms is Congress at work."[64] Richard Fenno, Jr., a contemporary observer, commented that members seek committee assignments that fit with their policy interests and constituent concerns.[65] The committee system can channel the pursuit of the individual interest of legislators to the good of Congress itself. Political scientist and Congressman David Price observed: "The committee system . . . accommodates the aspirations of disparate members but also represents a corrective of sorts to congressional individualism—a means of bringing expertise and attention to bear on the legislature's task in a more concerted fashion than the free enterprise of individual members could accomplish."[66]

Congressional staffs, on committees or in the personal offices of legislators, importantly assist members in their legislative work.[67] Today there are some 126 standing committees and subcommittees of various kinds in the House and ninety-six in the Senate.[68] Some committees are authorizing committees, charged with making substantive policy as well as recommending spending levels to fund programs in their jurisdiction. Appropriations committees, responsible for determining how much money will be allocated to those programs, can very much affect policy through the power of the purse. As part of the lawmaking function, committees examine how laws are being implemented through their oversight of the executive branch (and, to a lesser degree, oversight of the administration of the judicial branch). Because so many issues are cross-cutting, committee jurisdictional categories can make lawmaking difficult. Hence, with greater frequency, especially in the House of Representatives, alternative arrangements assist or even supplant existing committee processes—for example, multi-committee arrangements, task forces, leadership-organized panels, outside blue-ribbon commissions, and "high level 'summit' conferences between legislative leaders and the executive branch."[69]

Congressional decision making is the product of multiple decision points; it is the product of both centrifugal and centripetal forces. The latter is characterized by the decentralization of the committee system, and the former by efforts towards centralization, leadership at the top, and party discipline. Judge Coffin, a former legislator, once noted: "What complicates matters is that both movements coexist today, something like the various shiftings of the tectonic plates underlying the continents."[70] There are many reasons that account for ambiguous or vague legislation: the difficulty of foreseeing all problems; the legislature's decision to identify an issue generally and then to delegate the issue to the executive branch for resolution; and the nature of coalition politics, which, in cobbling together the necessary majority, may yield legislation that is deliberately vague and ambiguous. Congressional organization—with its many decision points—can frustrate coherent decision making, producing muddy statutory language. And political polarization further complicates deliberation.

Drawing upon the invaluable compilation of vital congressional statistics produced by Ornstein, Mann, and Malbin,[71] I offer this snapshot of the 111th Congress (2009–2010) to give a sense of the congressional institution.[72] In that Congress, 383 public bills were enacted, with a total of 7,679 pages, averaging thirteen pages per statute.[73] In the House of Representatives, 6,677 bills were introduced (including joint resolutions), and 861 passed, with a 0.129 ratio of bills passed to bills introduced.[74] In the

Senate, 4,149 bills were introduced and 454 bills passed, with a ratio of 0.109 bills passed to bills introduced.[75] Additionally, the Senate held 2,374 committee and subcommittee hearings.[76]

In recent decades, Congress has more frequently enacted legislation through large omnibus bills or resolutions, packing together a wide range of disparate issues.[77] The omnibus mechanism is a departure from the traditional approach of handling individual pieces of legislation.[78] In part, Congress uses omnibus bills to facilitate passage of overdue measures.[79] For example, in 2009 and again in 2010, Congress packaged several appropriations bills that were considerably past timely consideration into a single omnibus bill, lessening opportunities for further delay than if each bill had been individually considered. This process, in the view of some, lets legislators avoid individual hard votes on controversial issues by packaging those issues with other measures that command broad support.[80] Each chamber has its own rules of procedure for referring legislation to committees and calling up measures for floor consideration. The House's rules and procedures are far more extensive than the Senate's. The Senate, owing to its smaller membership, is more flexible in relaxing standing rules to accommodate the interests of individual senators than the House, which structures rules that encourage representatives to accede to the will of the leadership and the majority.[81]

Congressional life is marked by incredible pressure—such as the pressures of the permanent campaign for reelection,[82] raising funds, balancing work in Washington and time in the district, balancing committee and floor work in an environment of increasing polarization, and balancing work and family responsibilities. Consider these statistics: In 1955, the number of recorded votes in the House was 147;[83] in 2009, it was 991; and in 2010, it was 664.[84] In 1955, the number of recorded votes in the Senate was 88;[85] in 2009, it was 400;[86] and in 2010, it was 307.[87] At times, these votes take place in the dead of night, especially as the legislative session moves at a frenetic pace to recess or end. In the 1960s and 1970s, the average Congress was in session 323 days; from 2001 to 2006, the average was 250 days.[88] But the hours per day in session have substantially risen. In the House, the session day consisted of an average of 7.84 hours per day in 2009,[89] as compared to 4.1 hours per day in 1955–1956.[90] In the Senate, the session day consisted of 7.44 hours per day in 2009,[91] as compared to 6.1 hours per day in 1955–1956.[92] In 1955–1956, the average total of committee assignments for members of the House was 3.0;[93] in 2011, it was 5.10 (1.72 standing committee assignments, 3.27 subcommittee assignments, and

0.10 other committee assignments).[94] Similarly, in the Senate, the average number of committee assignments was 7.9 in 1955–1956;[95] in 2011, it was 13.82 (3.52 standing committee assignments, 9.59 subcommittee assignments, and 0.71 other committee assignments).[96]

The key point is that the expanding, competing demands on legislators' time reduce opportunities for reflection and deliberation.[97] In that circumstance, beyond the work of their own committees, of which legislators have direct knowledge, members operate in a system in which they rely on the work of colleagues on other committees.[98] They accept the trustworthiness of statements made by their colleagues on other committees, especially those charged with managing the bill, about what the proposed legislation means. They cannot read every word of the bills they vote upon, but they, and certainly their staffs, become educated about the bill by reading the materials produced by the committees and conference committees from which the proposed legislation emanates. These materials include, for example, committee reports, conference committee reports, and the joint statements of conferees who drafted the final bill.

Committee reports accompanying bills have long been important means of informing the whole chamber about proposed legislation; they are often the principal means by which staffs brief their principals before voting on a bill.[99] Committee reports are generally circulated at least two calendar days before legislation is considered on the floor.[100] Those reports provide members and their staffs with explanatory material about a bill's context, purposes, policy implications, details, as well as information about who the committee supporters of a particular bill are and about possible minority views.[101] Conference committee reports represent the views of legislators from both chambers who are charged with reconciling bills that have passed both the House and the Senate and presenting them for final legislative consideration.[102] Members and their staffs will also hear from interest groups about particular bills—including groups they find credible—and the executive branch.[103] The system works because committee members and their staffs will lose influence with their colleagues as to future bills if they do not accurately represent the bills under consideration within their jurisdiction.

Although any legislator can introduce a bill, it is the committee of jurisdiction that generally processes the proposed measure. In drafting bills, legislators and their staffs look to multiple sources. All but the appropriations committees are aided by professional drafters in each chamber's Office of Legislative Counsel; these drafters are trained in the nuances of statute writing.[104] Although legislators and their staffs are not required to consult with legislative counsel, doing so is prudent because a poorly drafted bill can lead to all manner of problems for agencies and courts charged with interpreting the statute. Typically, a committee staffer will contact the office for assistance in framing the bill so that it is technically correct. The legislative counsel thinks of the committees as clients.[105] Its role is not to offer views about the merits of a particular proposal; it is to determine how best to commit the bill's purposes to writing.[106]

Not all bills emanate from the committees themselves: Some originate with the executive branch, others from interest groups, lobbyists, businesses, and state and local governments. These various interests may assist in drafting bills as well, but not necessarily with the care that the Office of Legislative Counsel provides. Not all bills are drafted in the committee; bills can also be drafted, or at least substantially revised, on the floor and in conference committee.[107] In the Senate, flexible procedures allow senators to draft bills in the course of debate. When bills are drafted on the floor, for example, the pressures of time mean that legislators do not generally check with the legislative counsel, and thus there is more likely to be problematic drafting language.[108] In conference committee, the pressure to come to closure and produce a law can compromise technical precision.

A case study by Nourse and Schacter, focusing on the Senate Judiciary Committee, reveals that committee staffers are well aware that how they construct statutes will affect how agencies and courts interpret them. The staffers view their task not primarily as creating technically correct statutes, but as addressing political and policy issues through legislation.[109] Lawmaking, as legislators and staffs understand it, involves not just the text of legislation, but also legislative history—such as the reports and debates associated with the legislative text. In the view of legislators and staffs, legislative history is an essential part of Congress's work product. As I described, committee reports and conference committee reports accompanying bills can provide guidance to legislators in the enactment process.[110] As I will discuss below, they can also be helpful post-enactment by providing direction to agencies as to how to interpret and implement legislation.

II. Congress and Agencies: Interpreting and Implementing Statutes

The debate within the academy and the federal judiciary—as to whether judges should consult only the laws' text in ascertaining meaning or go beyond the text to legislative materials that accompany the text—must seem odd not only to those in Congress and their staffs, but also to agencies responsible for administering the law. Through laws and lawmaking, Congress communicates to those charged with construing and interpreting its work. Congress's immediate objects in that exercise are generally not courts, which may someday be called on to construe statutes, but agencies, which more immediately grapple with how to implement the law. Statutes may express the sense of Congress, but agencies must translate that sense into action. As Peter Strauss observed some years ago, agencies are generally the first—often the primary—interpreters of statutes.[111] And agencies are constantly looking for clues as to what particular statutes mean. Herbert Kaufman wrote in his classic text, *The Administrative Behavior of Federal Bureau Chiefs*:

> The [agency bureau] chiefs were consciously looking over their shoulders, as it were, at the elements of the legislative establishment . . . estimating reactions to contemplated decisions and actions, trying to prevent misunderstandings and avoidable conflicts, and planning responses when storm warnings appeared on the horizon. Not that cues and signals from Capitol Hill had to be ferreted out; the denizens of the Hill were not shy about issuing suggestions, requests, demands, directives, and pronouncements.[112]

Congress and agencies share an understanding as to how to discern legislative meaning that goes beyond statutory text. In communicating with agencies about legislation, Congress has a variety of tools at its disposal, such as confirmation hearings, oversight hearings and investigations, reports, floor debates at the time of legislative consideration of a bill, and a variety of non-statutory controls.[113]

The confirmation process provides senators with a venue to press nominees to commit to interpreting statutes in particular ways as a condition for affirmative votes. At confirmation hearings, nominees may be pressed to undertake specific actions or to refrain from specific actions under the statutes they are charged with enforcing.[114] The cost for the nominee of not adhering to her promise post-confirmation may be appropriations cuts or legislative changes. Committee reports and conference committee reports accompanying legislation will often require that the agency undertake or refrain from particular actions. Statements of bill managers can also provide direction in floor debate as a measure nears passage. Oversight hearings provide opportunities for legislators to monitor executive interpretation and implementation of statutes and to take corrective action if the laws are not being executed as legislators envisioned.[115] Similarly, investigations offer another kind of congressional review: In their aftermath, legislators may press the executive to interpret the law in a different way, or legislators may move to change the law itself.[116] Congress can mandate that agencies issue reports detailing compliance with the laws as a way of checking on executive performance.[117]

Nonstatutory controls include informal means to monitor executive behavior, such as letters and telephone calls.[118] Although almost three decades ago the Supreme Court declared the legislative veto unconstitutional in *INS v. Chadha*,[119] committee and subcommittee vetoes continue to exist. Louis Fisher reports that since *Chadha* there have been hundreds of such vetoes provided for in legislation or through informal and nonstatutory means, whereby Congress grants agencies considerable discretion in exchange for a system of review and control by the committees of jurisdiction.[120] Through such congressional entities—such as the Government Accountability Office (GAO), which undertakes audits and reports of governmental agencies—the legislative branch conveys its concerns about the operations of those units to the executive branch.[121]

Legislators quite clearly view these various techniques as legitimate components of the legislative process. Members expect that agencies will follow their directives, not just expressed in legislation, but also in legislative history, through a variety of statutory and non-statutory devices. And agencies recognize the importance of being sensitive to the signals and directives that members of Congress send beyond words in statutes. Agency administrators appreciate that they undertake activities pursuant to statutory authority and that having a full understanding of what Congress expects helps the agency discharge its functions consistent with statutory meaning. Agencies are charged with implementing legislation that is often unclear and the product of an often-messy legislative process. Trying to make sense of the statute with the aid of reliable legislative history is rational and prudent.

And thus, agency officials carefully monitor how the legislative branch expresses itself, not just in statutes but also through other means as well. Not surprisingly, legislative history materials can be key resources. For instance, if Congress passes energy legislation with an accompanying committee report providing detailed direction to the Department of Energy, it is unfathomable that the Secretary of Energy or any other responsible agency officials would ignore the report, let alone not read that report. Agency sensitivity to Congress's workways reflects an often-intimate involvement in the legislative process. Executive branch staffers often draft bills that Congress considers, and even assist committee staffers in drafting committee report language.

Agency responsiveness to congressional signals that go beyond statutory text makes sense from a policy and good-governance perspective of trying to interpret and implement the law consistent with legislative meaning. It also makes sense from the perspective of practical politics. Agency administrators know that their budgets and legislative goodwill could be threatened if they ignore congressional communications. And, hence, agency staffers commonly consult with committee staffers in the ordinary course of business as to what actions the agency is contemplating and as to how it is interpreting the law. Agency preparation for congressional hearings will typically involve close review of legislative directives in legislative history materials. Any administrator who ignores a directive in a committee report, or in a communication from the congressional committee, may suffer the consequences at the next congressional hearing, if not before.

Attention as to what legislators and agencies view as the work product of the legislative branch needing to be followed is instructive as we consider judicial interpretation of statutes. Supreme Court doctrine indicates that generally courts should defer to an agency's interpretation of an ambiguous statute that it administers, as long as that interpretation is reasonable or permissible.[122] Judges, I am suggesting here, would do well to understand the methodology of agency interpretation of statutes, to understand how agencies use pre-enactment legislative history accompanying proposed legislation, and to take stock of that learning when they construe legislation in the full range of cases before them, apart from those involving review of agency interpretation of statutes.[123] Although there has been some thoughtful writing on agency construction of statutes,[124] there is a dearth of empirical knowledge about the methodology of agency interpretation. I would urge a full empirical inquiry across agencies.

It is, as I noted, striking that while agencies view legislative history as essential reading, there has in recent years been a vigorous debate within the federal judiciary as to whether legislative history materials should carry weight as judges interpret statutes, and if so, the measure of that weight. This discussion has taken place in a vacuum, largely removed from the reality of how Congress actually functions. An understanding

of how Congress operates and how agencies and their respective committees interact reinforces the view that courts, when interpreting statutes,
should respect legislators' sense of their own work product. Having set
the stage with an examination of the workways of Congress, I turn now
to an examination of two differing conceptions—purposivism and textualism—of how courts should interpret statutes and the materials to be
used in interpreting statutes.[125]

III. Judicial Interpretation of Statutes

Given that I have argued that courts should respect Congress's work
product, it will not surprise you that I find legislative history, in reliable
form, useful as I interpret statutes. I start with the premise that the role
of the courts is to interpret the law in a way that is faithful to its meaning.
The role of the court is not to substitute its judgment or to alter the terms
of the statute. When statutes are unambiguous, as I have noted earlier, the
inquiry for a court generally ends with an examination of the words of
the statute.[126] At times, even when the statute is plain on its face, the judge
may find legislative history helpful in reinforcing the court's understanding of the words. If, for example, the result seems absurd, then a broader
inquiry, including consideration of legislative history, might be in order.
But if that inquiry leads to the same result, then a court cannot alter it.
    Generally, the interpretative problem arises because the statute is
ambiguous.[127] From the start, the founders understood that legislation
would often be unclear and admit of differing interpretations. Madison
wrote in *The Federalist* No. 37, describing laws in general:

All new laws, though penned with the greatest technical skill, and passed
on the fullest and most mature deliberation, are considered as more or
less obscure and equivocal, until their meaning be liquidated and ascertained by a series of particular discussions and adjudications. Besides the
obscurity arising from the complexity of objects, and the imperfection of
the human faculties, the medium through which the conceptions of men
are conveyed to each other, adds a fresh embarrassment. . . . [N]o language
is so copious as to supply words and phrases for every complex idea, or so
correct as not to include many equivocally denoting different ideas. Hence,
it must happen that however accurately objects may be discriminated in
themselves, and however accurately the discrimination may be considered,
the definition of them may be rendered inaccurate by the inaccuracy of

the terms in which it is delivered. And this unavoidable inaccuracy must be greater or less, according to the complexity and novelty of the objects defined.[128]

Scholars have debated what role the founders conceived the judiciary as having—whether it was to be a faithful agent of Congress or a co-equal partner with authority to depart from the words of a statute.[129] But how judges were to resolve ambiguities was not something that preoccupied the founders, concerned as they were with broad principles of governing. Although they understood that natural law principles and canons of statutory construction could aid judges, the framers were under no illusion that such tools necessarily dictated particular results.[130] Judges— members of the Supreme Court, other federal judges if Congress authorized them, and state judges—however, could fill the interpretative void through the exercise of sound judgment. But the framers did not set forth the precise methodology of how judges would do so.[131] It was inevitable, however, that as ambiguous statutes were crafted, the question of how to interpret them would become important.

It seems to me that at bottom, the task for the judge is to determine what Congress—in particular the bill's sponsors and others who worked to secure its approval by a majority of the members—was trying to do in passing the law. In other words, the task is to construe language in light of the statute's purpose as enacted by elected legislators.[132]

The dominant mode of statutory interpretation over the past century has been one premised on the view that legislation is a purposive act, and judges should construe statutes to execute that legislative purpose. This approach finds lineage in the sixteenth-century English decision, *Heydon's Case*, which summons judges to interpret statutes in a way "as shall suppress the mischief, and advance the remedy."[133] From this perspective, legislation is the product of a deliberative and informed process. Statutes in this conception have purposes or objectives that are discernible. The task of the judge is to make sense of legislation in a way that is faithful to Congress's purposes. When the text is ambiguous, a court, as Congress's agent, is to provide the meaning that the legislature intended. In that circumstance, the judge gleans the purpose and policy underlying the legislation and deduces the outcome most consistent with those purposes.

The classic exposition of this approach is found in *Church of the Holy Trinity v. United States.*[134] The statute in question, the Alien Contract

Labor Act, made it unlawful to "prepay the transportation, or in any way assist or encourage the importation or migration of any alien or aliens, any foreigner or foreigners, into the United States . . . to perform labor or service of any kind."[135] In arranging for an English minister to come to New York to serve as the church's rector and pastor, Holy Trinity seemingly violated the explicit language of the statutory prohibition. But the Supreme Court, in an opinion by Justice Brewer, held that Congress only sought to bar manual labor, not professional services: "[A] thing may be within the letter of the statute and yet not within the statute, because not within its spirit, nor within the intention of its makers."[136] In reaching its conclusion that the law did not apply to the minister's services, the Court went beyond the text of the statute to an inquiry into underlying purposes. Thus, the Court determined that the statute's title made reference to "labor," not professionals, and that the law was meant to remedy the problem of "great numbers of an ignorant and servile class of foreign laborers."[137] The Court looked to legislative history—to committee hearings, to the House report, which referred to workers "from the lowest social stratum," and to the Senate Labor Committee report, which, in the Court's view, understood the bill to apply only to manual labor.[138] It also reasoned that because of the role of religion in this country—"this is a Christian nation,"[139] wrote Justice Brewer—Congress could not have intended to make the hiring of a cleric illegal. With its inquiry beyond the text into the underlying purposes of the statute and with resort to legislative history,[140] *Holy Trinity* became paradigmatic of how federal courts in the twentieth century interpreted legislation.[141] It would also, in the view of its critics, such as Justice Scalia, become a prime example of supposed deficiencies in the purposive approach.[142]

Judge Learned Hand of the U.S. Court of Appeals for the Second Circuit echoed *Holy Trinity*:

> All [legislators] have done is to write down certain words which they mean to apply generally to situations of that kind. To apply these literally may either pervert what was plainly their general meaning, or leave undisposed of what there is every reason to suppose they meant to provide for. Thus it is not enough for the judge just to use a dictionary. If he should do no more, he might come out with a result which every sensible man would recognize to be quite the opposite of what was really intended; which would contradict or leave unfulfilled its plain purpose.[143]

The champions of the purposive approach, post–World War II, were two Harvard Law School professors, Henry M. Hart, Jr. and Albert M. Sacks, whose compilations of materials on the legal process influenced generations of jurists and scholars, including Norman Dorsen—the Madison Lecture's impresario who developed extensive supplemental materials to the Hart and Sacks work.[144] They wrote that a court's role is to interpret the statutes "to carry out the purpose as best it can," subject to the caveat that it does not give the words either "a meaning they will not bear, or . . . a meaning which would violate any established policy of clear statement."[145] In contrast to the legal realists of the 1930s, who believed that judges make law, the proponents of the legal process approach viewed judges as agents of the legislature with the ability to discern Congress's purposes and to interpret laws consistent with those purposes. Although the canons of construction can be "useful as reassurances about the meaning which particular configurations of words *may* have in an appropriate context," they should not be treated as rigid rules that dictate what these configurations "invariably *must* have" regardless of context.[146] This approach allows for an examination of legislative history so as to better understand the legislation under review. Understanding the underlying purposes of the legislation allows for the laws to be applied in situations not necessarily anticipated by the enacting Congress. I agree with Justice Breyer that, if courts are faithful to the statute's objectives, Congress will view the third branch as a cooperating partner—a perspective that can only promote the fair and effective administration of justice.[147]

Critics of the purposive approach argue that because the laws of Congress are often ambiguous, it is not possible to say with any certainty what the purposes of the legislature were. There may be many purposes, with ambiguity permitting legislators of differing views to vote for a bill, each interpreting it in ways to support their differing conceptions. In the words of Kenneth Shepsle, "Congress [i]s a '[t]hey,' [n]ot an '[i]t,'" and legislative intent is an oxymoron.[148] Legislation—particularly large omnibus bills passed with great speed at the end of a legislative session—may at points be contradictory. As to these large omnibus measures that contain a hodgepodge of unrelated measures, a legislator may vote for the whole bill because she supports certain parts, even though she would vote against other parts if considered separately. In these circumstances, critics of the purposive approach contend that it blinks reality to assert that legislation has knowable purposes that courts can identify.

That legislation is the institutional product of a collection of individuals with a variety of motives and perspectives should not foreclose the effort to discern purposes. Just as intentions are attributed to other large entities—such as local governments, trade associations, and businesses—so too do linguistic protocols, everyday mores, and context facilitate an inquiry into what Congress intended to do when statutory text is vague or ambiguous. At times, it is difficult to ascertain purposes, and the search for purpose as to particular statutes may be elusive. But to jettison the inquiry altogether, because of the difficulty in particular cases, means that judges will interpret statutes unmoored from the reality of the legislative process and what the legislators were seeking to do.

Most judges, in my experience, are neither wholly textualists nor purposivists (that is, seekers of purpose). Purposivists tend not to go beyond the words of an unambiguous statute; at times, textualists look to purposes and extratextual sources such as dictionaries. What sets them apart is a difference in emphasis and the tools they employ to find meaning.

In approaching the interpretative task, I have, as a judge, several tools I can use, including: text, statutory structure, history, word usage in other relevant statutes, common law usages, agency interpretations, dictionary definitions, technical and scientific usages, lay usages, canons, common practices, and purpose.[149] The judge's work takes place not on the lofty plane of grand, unified theory, but on the ground of practical, common-sense inquiry.[150] The judge pulls from the toolbox those instruments that can help extract "[u]seful [k]nowledge,"[151] as Benjamin Franklin termed it, about what the statute means in light of congressional purposes. The toolbox can help the judge, for example, appreciate the institutional context that can serve as a guide to understanding a statute's meaning. Statutes vary in design and substance,[152] and so, the interpretative task may change and the tools used may vary depending on the particular statutory issue at hand.

Thus, as I have noted, some statutes are precise, specific, and closed-ended, such that the text itself provides definitive direction. Justice Souter said: "The language is straightforward, and with a straightforward application ready to hand, statutory interpretation has no business getting metaphysical."[153] Some statutes deal with subjects where words have specialized meanings. Tax law is an example, as its subtleties are not necessarily obvious in the text itself. Still other statutes are more open-ended in construction, such that agencies and courts must go beyond the text in the interpretative process. For instance, it is not self-evident as to what constitutes "unfair methods of competition in or affecting commerce, and unfair or deceptive acts or practices in or affecting commerce."[154] Nor is it self-evident as to what constitutes a "reasonable accommodation" under the Americans with Disabilities Act.[155] In deciphering statutes, we would do well to remember, as Justice Frankfurter wrote: "Unhappily, there is no table of logarithms for statutory construction. . . . One or another [item of evidence] may be decisive in one set of circumstances, while of little value elsewhere."[156] If judges exclude legislative history they will eliminate a useful source of information about the law's meaning. Legislative history is not the law, but can help us understand what the law means. Depriving judges of what appeared to animate legislators risks having courts interpret the legislation in ways that the legislators did not intend. The danger, as Justice Breyer observed, is that a court will "divorce[] law from life."[157] Textualists have argued that it is difficult to discern the purposes of 535 legislators, but by eliminating authoritative materials such as committee reports and conference committee reports as interpretative tools—which can provide valuable guides in understanding purpose—they make their interpretative task not only that much harder, but also more prone to incorrect outcomes. Earlier, I explained how those who deal most frequently with statutes—that is, agencies—look to legislative history so as to be faithful to Congress's meaning. Courts should be no different in examining pre-enactment legislative sources that assist the interpretative task.

Legislative history can help provide meaning when a statute is silent or unclear about a contested issue. I have found this to be true in a number of cases on which I have worked on the Second Circuit, including some I discussed at the outset of this lecture.[158] Legislative history can be especially valuable when a judge is construing a specialized term or phrase in statutes dealing with complex matters beyond the ordinary ken of the judge. In that circumstance, it can aid the judge in understanding how the legislation's congressional proponents wanted the statute to work, what problems they sought to address, what purposes they sought to achieve, and what methods they employed to secure those purposes.[159] Legislative history can be helpful, Justice Stevens commented, "when an exclusive focus on text seems to convey an incoherent message, but other reliable evidence clarifies the statute and avoids the apparent incoherence."[160] And, at times, as I indicated earlier, authoritative legislative history can be useful, even when the meaning can be discerned from the statute's language, to reinforce or to confirm a court's sense of the text.[161]

When courts construe statutes in ways that respect what legislators consider their work product, the judiciary promotes comity with the first branch of government. It is a bipartisan institutional perspective within Congress that courts should consider reliable legislative history and failing to do so impugns Congress's workways. Several years ago, then-Congressman Robert W. Kastenmeier (D-WI), the longtime chair of the House Judiciary Subcommittee on Courts, put it this way: Disregarding legislative history "is an assault on the integrity of the legislative process."[162] Senators Orrin Hatch (R-UT), Charles E. Grassley (R-IA), and Arlen Specter (as R-PA), as Republican chairs or ranking members, and Senators Joseph Biden (D-DE) and Patrick Leahy (D-VT), as Democratic chairs or ranking members have consistently supported judicial resort to legislative history; indeed, senators often press that view on judicial nominees at confirmation hearings.

Senator Grassley, currently ranking member of the Judiciary Committee, has long defended legislative history. In 1986, at the confirmation hearing of Antonin Scalia for Supreme Court Justice, he expressed concern about the then–D.C. Circuit judge's "pretty doggone strong language" in his opposition to legislative history: "[A]s one who has served in Congress for 12 years, legislative history is very important to those of us here who want further detailed expression of that legislative intent."[163] Nearly two decades later, Senator Grassley pressed nominee John G. Roberts, Jr., with a series of questions about legislative history, noting:

> Justice Scalia is of the opinion that most expressions of legislative history, like Committee reports or statements by the Senators on the floor, or in the House, are not entitled to great weight because they are unreliable indicators of legislative intent. Presumably, Justice Scalia believes that if the members don't actually write a report or don't actually vote on a report, then there is no need to defer to this expression of congressional intent.
>
> Now, obviously, I have great regard for Justice Scalia, his intellect and legal reasoning. But, of course, as I told you in my office, I don't really agree with his position.[164]

Senator Hatch, who for many years was chair or ranking member of the Senate Judiciary Committee, commented that "[t]ext without context often invites confusion and judicial adventurism."[165] As an example of how legislative history might be useful, he pointed to a bail law that did not incorporate a reference to the Speedy Trial Act, but where "[t]he legislative history . . . imparted the additional information necessary to preserve the basic goal of pretrial detention."[166] Then-Senator Specter of Pennsylvania stated: "I think when justices disregard that kind of material [legislative history], it is just another way to write their own law. . . ."[167]

The approach I advocate has not gone unchallenged. Indeed, within the judiciary, a sustained attack on the use of legislative history began in the 1980s, largely led by Antonin Scalia, first as a D.C. Circuit judge and then as a Supreme Court Justice. In a 1993 Supreme Court opinion, he wrote: "We are governed by laws, not by the intentions of legislators. . . . 'The law as it passed is the will of the majority of both houses, and the only mode in which that will is spoken is in the act itself. . . .'"[168] Justice Scalia agrees with the view that because legislation often consists of a brew of deals, compromises, and inconsistencies, the search for coherent purpose is elusive. Thus, it is the statute's final wording that must prevail; he has argued over "unenacted legislative intent."[169] Textualism, as Justice Scalia championed it, involves an assault on the dependence of any extratextual source in determining statutory meaning. Legislative history became a central target. "We are a Government of laws, not of committee reports," he asserted.[170] In another case, he explained:

I am confident that only a small proportion of the Members of Congress read either one of the Committee Reports in question . . . [and] that very few of those who did read them set off for the nearest law library to check out what was actually said in the four cases at issue (or in the more than 50 other cases cited by the House and Senate Reports). . . . As anyone familiar with modern-day drafting of congressional committee reports is well aware, the references to the cases were inserted, at best by a committee staff member on his or her own initiative, and at worst by a committee staff member at the suggestion of a lawyer-lobbyist; and the purpose of those references was not primarily to inform the Members of Congress what the bill meant . . . but rather to influence judicial construction. What a heady feeling it must be for a young staffer, to know that his or her citation of obscure district court cases can transform them into the law of the land, thereafter dutifully to be observed by the Supreme Court itself.[171]

This textualist critique of legislative history has at least four parts. The first, which is premised on the Constitution, is the idea that the only legitimate law is text that both chambers and the President have approved (or passed by a two-thirds vote of Congress over the President's veto). This view looks in part for support from *INS v. Chadha*, in which the Supreme Court held legislative vetoes unconstitutional because they evaded procedures of bicameralism and presentment. Because (so the narrative goes) legislators do not review legislative history, that history lacks authority. Legislative history materials, Justice Scalia stated, are "frail substitutes for bicameral vote upon the text of a law and its presentment to the President. It is at best dangerous to assume that all the necessary participants in the law-enactment process are acting upon the same unexpressed assumptions."[172] A system that relies on committee reports delegates power to unelected staff at the expense of the whole chamber, so textualists claim.[173] The use of legislative history, the argument continues, violates the constitutional rule prohibiting congressional self-delegation.[174] Committee reports should not be looked to when the statute is interpreted, and neither should materials such as floor debates and statements in the Congressional Record. In the view of legislative history critics, apart from the fact that statements in the Congressional Record are not the laws themselves, the Congressional Record is suspect as a guide to legislative meaning because it does not differentiate between remarks made by those who were involved in crafting the legislation—such as bill managers—and those who were not; it can include statements inserted by legislators who were not present on the floor; and legislators can revise for publication statements that colleagues heard them make on the floor.

Second, critics of legislative history argue that its use impermissibly increases the discretion of judges to roam through the wide range of often-inconsistent materials and rely on those that suit their position.[175] By so choosing, critics charge judges with substituting their policy preferences for those of elected officials, with whom such a choice properly resides.

A third component of the assault on legislative history is grounded in the idea that legislators will be compelled to write statutes with more precision if they know that courts cannot consult such materials.

Fourth, underlying the criticism of legislative history is a decidedly negative conception of the legislative process, based on the "public choice" school, which employs principles of market economics to explain decision making.[176] Like many schools, its scholars are not all of one mind and cannot be simply characterized.[177] Generally, though, it characterizes the legislative process as fueled by rational, egoistic, utility-maximizing legislators whose primary objective is to be reelected. From this perspective, legislators enact laws that tend to transfer wealth and reduce efficiency at the expense of the public good to special interest groups that lobby the legislature. Evading responsibility—the narrative continues—members of Congress pass unclear statutes, leaving it to administrators and courts to resolve unsettled issues.[178] Laws benefiting society will be few and far between because of a collective action problem. As Mancur Olson put it, "rational, self-interested individuals will not act to achieve their common . . . interests"[179] by lobbying for legislation that benefits the general public because the benefits being sought are collective to the group as a whole; thus the rational individual is content to be a free rider. It is thus by no means obvious that interest groups will arise to press legislators to enact "public interest" legislation, echoing in part Madison's concern in *The Federalist* No. 10.

Sharply different from the "public interest" conception, this vision of the legislature is grim.[180] On this conception, legislators—motivated by the goal of reelection—evade choices on critical issues that could provoke opposition from well-organized groups. They do not develop well-conceived legislation, preferring instead to satisfy interest groups through ad hoc bargaining. This view is manifested in Justice Scalia's lament about committee report language written by lawyer-lobbyists, at the behest of client groups, and about committees that serve client interests rather than Congress itself.[181]

Over time, the textualist critique has become more nuanced. John Manning, who has contributed many distinguished writings in the field, observed that textualists have focused more on formal constitutional arguments such as bicameralism, presentment, and nondelegation. While they continue to look askance at legislative history, they are less inclined to draw upon public choice theory. Rather, they emphasize the importance of judges' "respect[ing] the terms of an enacted text *when its semantic meaning is clear,* even if it seems contrary to the statute's apparent *overall purpose.*"[182] They take as given the bargaining of the legislative process—whatever the motivations of legislators—and argue that adherence to text is appropriate in part because of legislative compromises, which may make the search for coherent purpose a fool's errand. In interpreting statutes, textualists seek to understand language in context, looking to dictionary definitions,[183] colloquial meanings, the technical definitions of terms of art, and background conventions associated with certain phrases or types of legislation.[184]

Although I agree that dictionaries can be helpful—especially when dealing with a specialized term or a term of art, or a word usage at the time of the law's enactment—more often than not, the interpretative challenge comes from the ambiguity of the word as situated in a sentence. In that situation, resort to dictionaries can hardly be definitive. In any event, if it is appropriate to look to dictionaries as an extraneous source, it is not at all clear why legislative history—in its reliable forms—should be excluded.

That textualists have moved away from public choice theory is understandable, given the inability of that theory to capture the complexity of the decision-making process. There is a substantial literature, to which I have offered some writings, that questions the underlying factual assertions for its sweeping propositions.[185] The calculus of Congress cannot be reduced only to the idea that interest groups dictate the behavior, votes, and agenda of legislators eager for the financial support necessary for reelection.[186] A variety of case studies track the passage of legislation where interest group involvement was not decisive.[187] And where groups have had a role, their interests, as James Q. Wilson has written, have not necessarily been economic.[188] Moreover, some legislation predated interest groups' activity and, indeed, led to the creation of particular interest groups. One example is section 504 of the Rehabilitation Act of 1973, outlawing discrimination against those with disabilities in programs receiving federal aid or assistance.[189] Certainly Congress has enacted a variety of legislation in spite of the opposition of large, powerful economic interests. Examples include laws having to do with airline and trucking deregulation and measures that address health, environmental, and safety concerns.[190] Surely, legislators are concerned about reelection,[191] and public choice theory quite usefully draws attention to how incentives can affect behavior. It would be naive to think that legislators would not well consider how interest groups can affect, positively or negatively, their hopes to return to office. But legislators also have policy objectives that cannot simply be understood as interest group driven. Even where interest groups have a substantial impact on the legislative process, it does not follow that their goals are against the public interest.[192] Legislation that benefits the personal interests of an interest group may, depending on the measure, also benefit the wider public.

Textualists have appropriately identified misuses and manipulation of legislative history. Without doubt, language is on occasion put into committee reports unnoticed by the whole legislative chamber or even by members of relevant committees. Martin Ginsburg, for example, pointed to such excesses in the area of tax legislation,[193] and Senator Moynihan once expressed concern over how report language in one particular piece of legislation was not reviewed by the legislators on the relevant committee.[194] By putting a spotlight on legislative history, the textualist critique has had some effect on individual legislators. Representative Barney Frank (D-MA) reportedly warded off an effort to insert compromise language in a committee report rather than in the bill itself.[195] He did so with two words: "Justice Scalia."[196] Although among Supreme Court Justices, pure textualists can claim only Antonin Scalia and Clarence Thomas as faithful supporters,[197] the textualist critique has had an undeniable impact. Today, it is commonplace for a statutory opinion of a federal court to state: "where the statutory language provides a clear answer, it ends there as well."[198]

Gone are the days when a Supreme Court opinion would declare, as it did in 1971:

> The legislative history of both § 4(f) of the Department of Transportation Act, 49 U.S.C. § 1653(f) (1964 ed., Supp. V), and § 138 of the Federal-Aid Highway Act, 23 U.S.C. § 138 (1964 ed., Supp. V), is ambiguous. . . . Because of this ambiguity, it is clear that we must look primarily to the statutes themselves to find the legislative intent.[199]

By 2005, Justice Kennedy, in an opinion of the Court, to which Justices Stevens, O'Connor, Ginsburg, and Breyer dissented, would exclaim:

> Extrinsic materials have a role in statutory interpretation only to the extent they shed a reliable light on the enacting Legislature's understanding of otherwise ambiguous terms. Not all extrinsic materials are reliable sources of insight into legislative understandings . . . and legislative history in particular is vulnerable to two serious criticisms. First, [it is] often murky, ambiguous, and contradictory. . . . [It often becomes, in] Judge Leventhal's memorable phrase, an exercise in "looking over a crowd and picking out your friends." . . . Second, judicial reliance on legislative materials like committee reports, which are not themselves subject to the requirements of Article I, may give unrepresentative committee members—or, worse yet, unelected staffers and lobbyists—both the power and the incentive to attempt strategic manipulations of legislative history to secure results they were unable to achieve through the statutory text.[200]

While judges still use legislative history,[201] they tend to give it more of a supporting rather than a leading role in statutory interpretation.[202] Courts tend to approach legislative history with what Justice Ginsburg termed "hopeful skepticism."[203]

Although textualists have helpfully shown some of the pitfalls of legislative history, I do not think they have made the case for its exclusion. I question their view that restricting interpretation to the text will lead to more responsible legislating and more clearly drafted laws. Certainly, textual ambiguity may be a consequence of carelessly drafted laws. And sometimes rather than confront difficult problems in text, legislative drafters may address them in committee reports. But ambiguity is often the product of the simple fact that the issues are difficult and Congress, having identified the general problem, leaves it to an agency or court to determine how best to address the problem.[204] As Richard Stewart observed: "The demands on Congress' agenda far exceed its capacity to make collective decisions."[205] Given policy complexities, it is unreasonable to expect Congress to anticipate all interpretive questions that may present themselves in the future.[206] Inadvertence as a result of time pressures may be the explanation, especially when fast-moving amendments are added to larger bills. In other circumstances, it may be that the sponsors were unable or deliberately chose not to craft legislation that was both precise and enactable. The language may be imprecise to facilitate the bill's passage, such that even competing interests can find language in the bill that supports their positions. Ambiguity, as Herbert Kaufman remarked, can be the solvent of disagreement, at least temporarily.[207] In these circumstances, textualists should be under no illusions that decrying ambiguity will change legislative behavior.[208]

As to constraining judicial preferences, it seems to me that excluding legislative history when interpreting ambiguous statutes will just as likely expand a judge's discretion as reduce it. When a statute is unambiguous, resorting to legislative history is generally not necessary; in that circumstance, the inquiry ordinarily ends. But when a statute is ambiguous, barring legislative history leaves a judge only with words that could be interpreted in a variety of ways without contextual guidance as to what legislators may have thought. Lacking such guidance increases the probability that a judge will construe a law in a manner that the legislators did not intend. It is seemingly inconsistent that textualists, who look to such extratextual materials as the records of the Constitutional Convention and *The Federalist* in interpreting the Constitution, would look askance at the use of legislative history sources when interpreting legislation.[209]

The contention that the use of legislative history violates the constitutional proscription against self-delegation is premised on a mistaken view of the legislative process. Legislative history accompanying proposed legislation precedes legislative enactment. When Congress passes a law, it can be said to incorporate the materials that it or at least the law's principal sponsors (and others who worked to secure enactment) deem useful in interpreting the law.[210] After all, Article I of the Constitution gives each chamber the authority to set its own procedures for the introduction, consideration, and approval of bills. And each chamber has established its own rules and practices[211] governing lawmaking—some favoring certain proceedings over others—establishing "a resultant hierarchy of internal communications."[212] Those rules and procedures give particular legislators—such as committee chairs, floor managers, and party leaders—substantial control over the process by which legislation is enacted. Communications from such members as to the meaning of proposed statutes can provide reliable signals to the whole chamber. And, as I noted above, members and their staffs have every incentive to accurately represent the meaning of proposed statutes to colleagues, as written and discussed in legislative history.

Chief Justice Roberts, who makes use of legislative history, stated at his confirmation hearing that "[a]ll legislative history is not created equal. There's a difference between the weight that you give a conference report and the weight you give a statement of one legislator on the floor. You have to, I think, have some degree of sensitivity in understanding exactly what you're looking at. . . ."[213] I concur. The task, as Senator Hatch commented, is to draw upon legislative history "properly applied" in "reliable forms,"[214] and to separate the wheat from the chaff among legislative materials. For courts, that means in part having a better understanding of the legislative process and appreciating the internal hierarchy of communications. Conference committee reports and committee reports should sit at the top, followed by statements of the bill's managers, with ersatz statements of legislators on the floor—who had heretofore not been involved in consideration of the bill—at the bottom of reliable authority. For Congress, the challenge is to communicate its meaning in ways that assure that the "[d]ignity of [l]egislation,"[215] in Jeremy Waldron's felicitous phrase, is preserved and respected.

IV. Promoting Understanding

At some basic level, each institution—that is, the courts and the legislature—could benefit from a deeper appreciation of how the other operates.
Congress, which writes the laws, might find it useful to learn more about
how the judiciary interprets its laws. The judiciary, for its part, could find
it useful to learn more about the legislative process. The lineage of jurists
with legislative experience stretches back across the centuries, including
the English Lord Mansfield in the eighteenth century.[216] Today—in contrast to a generation ago—only two federal judges have served as members of Congress.[217] And in the Congress, there is only one former federal
judge and one state supreme court justice, though some federal legislators clerked for judges.[218] To aid the judiciary in understanding Congress, it might be worthwhile if some entity such as the Congressional
Research Service of the Library of Congress, perhaps in conjunction with
the legislative counsels' offices in both legislative chambers, sponsored
periodic seminars for judges and law clerks about the legislative process,
even developing a manual and videos about lawmaking in Congress. (A
start on this task is a pamphlet for judges on legislative drafting conventions by M. Douglas Belliss, long-time member of the House legislative
counsel's office.)[219] Similarly, to assist Congress in understanding how the
courts work, the Federal Judicial Center and the Administrative Office
of the U.S. Courts might develop programs for legislators and their staffs
about how the judiciary functions. Optimally, such activities for legislators, judges, and staffs could be incorporated into orientation programs
for new judges, legislators, and staffs.

　　While mutual appreciation and deeper knowledge are always desirable, it would, of course, be fanciful to think that Congress would—or
even could—do away with ambiguity in its laws. As I noted earlier, ambiguity may be a deliberate strategy to secure the necessary votes, or it
may be a product of the policy and political challenges surrounding the
problem at hand.[220] Nevertheless, there may be ways for Congress to help
clarify legislative meaning, through both the drafting and the statutory
revision processes, as well as the development of more reliable legislative
histories.

A. Drafting and Statutory Revision

Ideally, legislators and their staffs should make greater use of the offices of legislative counsel, trained and skilled legislative drafters. If all legislative drafting were funneled through those offices, which apply accepted linguistic conventions and standards, then courts would have an easier time interpreting statutes. But that is not the reality of the legislative process. For those who do not avail themselves of the legislative drafting services, a checklist of common issues might be prepared—for example, dealing with such matters as attorneys' fees, private rights of action, preemption, and exhaustion of administrative remedies. There have already been several proposals for such a checklist.[221] When not addressed in the law, such issues are resolved in court. While such a checklist would not prevent strategic, deliberate omissions, it could be useful in avoiding drafting oversights, clarifying legislative intent, and reducing burdens on the courts.

Similarly, the offices of legislative counsel could prepare a drafting guidebook for members and staffs. Seminars with legislative counsel and judges could be useful. Law school courses and continuing legal education programs on drafting would also be helpful, not only for those who work in Congress, but also for those in interest groups and organizations urging legislators and staffs to introduce bills for which they have crafted language.

Finally, as a way to provide more precision, Congress might resort more to default positions, which would become effective when Congress has not dealt with the particular issue in a specific substantive statute. For example, as to civil statutes, Congress has declared: "Except as otherwise provided by law, a civil action arising under an Act of Congress enacted after the date of the enactment of this section may not be commenced later than 4 years after the cause of action accrues."[222] Hence, the default position is triggered if a particular statute has not addressed the time limitations on the commencement of civil actions arising under it.

The flip side of drafting before bills are enacted is the statutory revision process. Interbranch understanding of statutes can also be enhanced through the process of statutory revision. Supreme Court justices will from time to time identify an opinion meriting further congressional attention, as Justice Ginsburg did, to prominent effect, in the Lilly Ledbetter case.[223] Congress is generally aware of Supreme Court decisions, as evidenced by legislative reversals of decisions of our highest tribunal.[224]

But the first branch tends to give little attention to the large number of statutory opinions of the lower courts. This lack of attention—while understandable given Congress's workload—is curious in view of the role that courts play in construing statutes.

"Most of the work currently done by the federal courts, including the Supreme Court," commented Justice Ginsburg, "involves not grand constitutional principle, but the interpretation and application of laws passed by Congress, laws that are sometimes ambiguous or obscure."[225] She further observed:

When Congress is not clear, courts often invite, and are glad to receive, legislative correction. The law Congress declares, as the Chief Justice recently stated, is by and large the law federal courts apply. When Congress has been delphic or dense, or simply imprecise, legislative clarification can ward off further confusion.[226]

Nearly five decades ago, Judge Henry J. Friendly of the Second Circuit, writing about the importance of statutory law, lamented "the problems posed by defective draftsmanship," especially in uncontroversial legislation.[227] He wrote about "the occasional statute in which the legislature has succeeded in literally saying something it probably did not mean,"[228] observed that "even the best draftsman is likely to have experienced the occasional shock of finding that what he wrote was not at all what he meant,"[229] and commented on the legislative time pressures that result in "neglect of the undramatic type of legislative activity."[230] Three decades later, another circuit judge, James Buckley of the D.C. Circuit and also a former senator, remembered that in Congress, "[w]ith time often the enemy, mistakes—problems of grammar, syntax, and punctuation—are made in the drafting of statutes and affect the meaning of legislation."[231]

Over the years, several proposals have been made to facilitate statutory revision.[232] Justice Ginsburg and her coauthor Peter Huber recommended that a "second look at laws" committee be created, and that the Office of Law Revision Counsel, which has had a ministerial role of correcting citations, assist in "statutory housekeeping."[233] Judge Frank M. Coffin urged that a unit within the judiciary collate and sift judicial opinions with suggestions for the legislative branch and send them to Congress.[234] Then–Chief Judge James L. Oakes of the U.S. Court of Appeals for the Second Circuit seconded the proposal.[235] Judge Wilfred Feinberg called for the Judicial Conference to "designate a handful of law professors working on a part-time basis as a committee to call attention to . . . conflicts [among the circuits]."[236] Justice John Paul Stevens suggested that Congress create a legislative mechanism to resolve intercircuit conflicts.[237]

These thoughts have a distinguished lineage. In 1921, Benjamin Cardozo, then an associate judge on the New York Court of Appeals, drawing upon Roscoe Pound and Jeremy Bentham, recommended the creation of ministries of justice to facilitate law revision.[238] In the early 1960s, Judge Friendly stated that "[i]t would seem elementary that an agency whose task is to [help] formulate legislation . . . should be attached to the legislature."[239]

An approach that promotes improved drafting and may also lead to statutory revision is a practical effort, designed over twenty years ago by the Governance Institute.[240] Through this project of "statutory housekeeping"[241]—in Justice Ginsburg's apt phrase—courts of appeals send opinions that identify possible technical problems in statutes to Congress for its information and whatever action it wishes to take.[242] The effort informs those who draft bills of the technical problems that judges identify in opinions applying statutes.

The project began in 1988 when some judges of the U.S. Court of Appeals for the D.C. Circuit invited Judge Frank Coffin, then chair of the Judicial Conference's Judicial Branch Committee, and me,[243] to analyze what happened in Congress after the courts issued statutory decisions that referred to problems in grammar, apparent "glitches," ambiguous terminology, and omissions of key details, such as effective dates.[244] After identifying a small body of relevant opinions, with the aid of the D.C. Circuit judges, we assessed legislative awareness of these opinions. We discovered that committee staff did not know about judicial opinions concerning technical aspects of the statutes under the committee's jurisdiction, although they knew about decisions on broad, policy-oriented issues of statutory interpretation or decisions that a losing party with influence had asked Congress to reverse.[245]

Working with legislators and their staffs, we—along with the counsel of Governance Institute Distinguished Fellow and former House member Robert W. Kastenmeier—conceived of a pilot project, whereby the D.C. Circuit Court of Appeals would transmit its relevant statutory opinions to the House of Representatives.[246] Chief Justice Rehnquist backed the pilot project in 1993,[247] and two years later the Judicial Conference recommended that all courts of appeals participate.[248]

In the early 2000s, more than half of the courts of appeals had transmitted opinions to Congress. Participation declined, however, because the project had not been fully institutionalized within the judiciary. In May 2006, the legislative counsel in both houses of Congress asked the Governance Institute, led by Russell Wheeler, to revitalize the project.[249] The result was a June 2007 memorandum from the Director of the Administrative Office of the U.S. Courts, James Duff, and from the leadership of the U.S. Judicial Conference Committee on the Judicial Branch, to all circuit judges, along with letters from the bipartisan leadership of both Judiciary Committees, asking all courts of appeals to participate.[250] Statutory opinions that are appropriate for transmission include those where the court has identified possible grammatical problems that affect meaning and where the statute requires courts to fill in a gap (for example, whether Congress intended the statute to be retroactive). They also include statutes that may present ambiguities in language or ambiguities arising from having to interpret related statutes, or statutes with a perceived problem, about which a judicial opinion suggests the possibility of legislative action.

The questions raised in the opinions[251] have been far-ranging. For instance, one opinion confronted the question of whether the Immigration and Nationality Act's (INA) requirement that an individual "lawfully resided continuously" for seven years, necessary for a waiver of inadmissibility, begins when an alien applies for adjustment of status or when that status is actually granted.[252] Another case examined whether, pursuant to chapter 13 of the U.S. Bankruptcy Code, debtors, who own rather than lease a vehicle, may deduct ownership costs from repayment plans.[253] In still another example, the Seventh Circuit considered whether the Sex Offender Registration and Notification Act's registration requirement applies to travel by offenders that occurred before the Act's passage[254] (a gap that the Supreme Court resolved in *Carr v. United States*)[255] and whether conviction for failure to register requires evidence that the defendant "knowingly" violated the registration provision.[256] Grappling with a provision in the Class Action Fairness Act of 2005,[257] appellate courts split as to the meaning of "not less than 7 days after the entry of the order" where a court of appeals "may accept an appeal from an order of a district court granting or denying a motion to remand a class action . . . if application is made to the court of appeals not less than 7 days after entry of the order."[258] The Third Circuit read the statute as meaning "not more than,"[259] while the Seventh Circuit read the statute literally.[260] Ultimately, Congress amended the section to read "not more than 10 days" after entry of the order.[261]

Under protocols worked out with legislative personnel, clerks of the courts of appeals send opinions identified by the clerk, staff attorney, or the three-judge panel, to the House Speaker and Senate President Pro Tempore. The letter, which is in the nature of an executive communication, does not comment on the opinion, saying only: "Enclosed please find an opinion of the United States Court of Appeals for the [X] Circuit, which may be of interest to the Congress."[262] At the same time, the clerk sends electronic copies of the letters and opinions to the respective House and Senate Legislative Counsels (and to Governance Institute President Russell Wheeler and to Brett Saxe in the Office of the General Counsel in the Administrative Office of the U.S. Courts).[263] The legislative counsel uses the opinions as teaching tools about how the courts of appeals deal with drafting problems.[264] The counsel offices also transmit the opinions to the House and Senate committees with jurisdiction over the legislation in question for any action those committees may wish to take.[265]

Legislative support has been vital to this project throughout its history. Both legislative counsels had participated enthusiastically in the pilot project.[266] Legislators themselves have been consistently positive.[267] Most recently, in September 2010, in remarks to the Judicial Conference, Senator Jeff Sessions, then–ranking member of the Senate Judiciary Committee, urged the participation of all circuits as a good government project.[268]

The strongest indicator of the project's value is the legislative testimonials calling for all courts of appeals to participate. Legislators and their staffs, including the Offices of Legislative Counsel, have much to do. That they would call for all circuits to participate suggests that the transmitted opinions benefit the drafting process.

A second measure of the project's worth derives from the ways that the Legislative Counsel uses the transmissions. Having examined how courts apply statutory language in specific contexts, the Legislative Counsel can be more sensitive to drafting issues that result in litigation. Frank Burk, head of the Senate Office of Legislative Counsel in the 1990s, reported that the project "helped stimulate a comprehensive two-year review of the basic rules of legislative drafting"[269] by his office. He further stated that the office "developed a drafting manual that compiles the drafting rules and conventions identified during the review," and that the office used transmitted opinions as teaching devices for "beginning staff attorneys."[270] James Fransen, Burk's successor, has been similarly support-ive.[271] House Legislative Counsel M. Pope Barrow concurred, observing that "[t]he opinions of judges would be especially useful if they can iden-tify persistent patterns in drafting errors."[272] Deputy Legislative Coun-sel M. Douglass Bellis, who has overseen the project in the House for many years, has said that "[t]he greater the communication between the judicial and legislative branches of government, the more the courts and Congress will grow to understand each other and the more the public can examine what its agents are doing on its behalf."[273] Both Bellis and Fran-sen circulate transmitted opinions to their respective staffs because of the opinions' instructive value.[274]

At first glance, one might think that the most important metric of the project's effectiveness would be the number of statutes passed to remedy problems identified in the opinions. From the outset, however, the proj-ect's creators cautioned that its principal purpose was not to produce leg-islative change, but rather to inform busy legislators and their staffs of possible technical problems in statutes. And, as Bellis noted, Congress may do nothing because it may determine that the relevant court "is making good decisions in hard cases,"[275] thereby creating no reason for Congress to intervene. The goal of the project "is not to find 'mistakes' that Congress made and should correct . . . [but] to open communication so that Congress can learn how the courts are reacting to and interpret-ing statutes."[276] He observed that the feedback is invaluable: "[I]t calls our attention to drafting situations that are capable of repetition," suggesting that the referrals may "have a greater ultimate influence on the language of statutes than when (and to the extent) they lead to an amendment of the particular law."[277]

In sum, the mechanism for transmitting opinions has the following virtues: (1) it is a neutral mechanism of communication, merely a trans-mission belt of communication; (2) it does not require the creation of a body or committee; (3) Congress has encouraged it; and (4) it promotes good government. In the words of the chair and ranking members of the House and Senate Judiciary Committees: "These modest efforts have supplied pertinent and timely information to Congress that it might not otherwise receive," including information about "possible technical prob-lems in statutes that may be susceptible to technical amendment; and, in any case, how statutes might be drafted to reflect legislative intent most accurately."[278] Although it is inherent in the system that there will be occasional tensions between courts and Congress, this effort promotes inter-branch comity and dialogue in a way that reduces conflict. Indeed, it may well be worth considering whether it might be useful to develop a parallel transmission process between the executive branch and Congress, whereby agency general counsels sifting through judicial opinions identify issues of relevance to Congress, perhaps with suggestions for Congress to consider. The Administrative Conference of the United States[279] might play a useful role in examining the feasibility of this idea and its implementation.

B. Making Legislative History More Reliable

To better signal its meaning, legislative leadership could also more clearly identify legislative history that courts should take into account. For instance, the floor managers of a bill could indicate what constitutes the definitive legislative history, including floor statements and colloquies. Such signaling would simplify a court's task in reviewing the Congressional Record.

Moreover, as Stephen Ross proposed several years ago, having committee members sign committee reports, with signature sheets attached to the document, could effectively meet the charge that those reports are not endorsed by a majority of the committee. This could address the concern that committee members are not aware of the reports, or just do not read them.[280] Now, generally, only those offering additional views sign the reports.

Identifying authoritative legislative history, moreover, will make it easier for courts to assess amicus briefs of legislators that are filed to persuade the courts about what Congress meant in passing the statute. For legislators to try to achieve through such briefs what they could not in Congress itself is something Representative Kastenmeier deemed "a questionable procedure."[281] The more authoritative the legislative history is, the more likely that courts can review amicus briefs and interpret statutes in ways, as Senator Hatch put it, that do not result in "'slippage' from agreements reached in Congress."[282]

Conclusion

In conclusion, my points are simply these. In our constitutional system in which Congress is charged with enacting laws, how Congress makes its purposes known—through text and reliable accompanying materials—should be respected, lest the integrity of legislation be undermined. The experience of the executive branch in interpreting statutes can be helpful to courts. And practical ways should be pursued to further the objective of promoting statutory understanding. With greater sensitivity to the workings of the branches in the lawmaking process, we will be closer to realizing Publius's—most likely Madison's—vision in *The Federalist* No. 62: "A good government implies two things: first, fidelity to the object of government, which is the happiness of the people[;] secondly, a knowledge of the means by which the object can be best attained."[283]

NOTES

1. *See generally* ROBERT A. KATZMANN, REGULATORY BUREAUCRACY: THE FEDERAL TRADE COMMISSION AND ANTITRUST POLICY (1980).
2. *See generally* ROBERT A. KATZMANN, INSTITUTIONAL DISABILITY: THE SAGA OF TRANSPORTATION POLICY FOR THE DISABLED (1986) [hereinafter KATZMANN, INSTITUTIONAL DISABILITY] (examining how legislative, administrative, and judicial processes have dealt with problems of mobility for the disabled).
3. Created in 1986, the Governance Institute is a small nonprofit organization in Washington, D.C., concerned with exploring, explaining, and easing problems associated with both the separation and the division of powers in the American federal system. The Institute's focus is on institutional process—a nexus linking law, institutions, and policy. Products of the Governance Institute's program on judicial-legislative relations include: ROBERT A. KATZMANN, COURTS AND CONGRESS (1997) [hereinafter KATZMANN, COURTS AND CONGRESS]; JUDGES AND LEGISLATORS: TOWARD INSTITUTIONAL COMITY (Robert A. Katzmann ed., 1988) [hereinafter JUDGES AND LEGISLATORS]; Frank M. Coffin, *Communication Among the Three Branches: Can the Bar Serve as Catalyst?* 75 JUDICATURE 125 (1991); Frank M. Coffin & Robert A. Katzmann, *Steps Towards Optimal Judicial Workways: Perspectives from the Federal Bench*, 59 N.Y.U. ANN. SURV. AM. L. 377 (2003); Robert A. Katzmann & Russell R. Wheeler, *A Mechanism for "Statutory Housekeeping": Appellate Courts Working with Congress*, 9 J. APP. PRAC. & PROCESS 131 (2007) [hereinafter Katzmann & Wheeler, *A Mechanism for "Statutory Housekeeping"*]; Robert A. Katzmann & Russell R. Wheeler, *A Primer on Interbranch Relations*, 95 GEO. L.J. 1155 (2007). Russell Wheeler is currently the president of the Governance Institute. Katzmann & Wheeler, *A Mechanism for "Statutory Housekeeping," supra*, at 131.
4. JUDGES AND LEGISLATORS, *supra* note 3, at vii.
5. KATZMANN, COURTS AND CONGRESS, *supra* note 3 (examining "key aspects of the relationship between the courts and Congress," including "the confirmation process, communications, statutory interpretation, and statutory revision").
6. William Eskridge, Jr. estimates that in 2008, two-thirds of the Supreme Court's caseload consisted of pure statutory cases, and just one-fourth consisted of pure

constitutional cases. E-mail from Prof. William N. Eskridge, Jr., John A. Garver Prof. of Jurisprudence, Yale Law Sch., to author (Aug. 8, 2011, 10:12 EST) (on file with the *New York University Law Review*).

7. 21 U.S.C. § 844 (2006).

8. *See* United States v. Morgan, 412 F. App'x 357, 359–60 (2d Cir. 2011) (rejecting appellant's claim that his purchase of pseudoephedrine for personal consumption did not violate the statute because Congress's purpose, on his argument, was to prevent the manufacture of methamphetamine).

9. Murphy v. Arlington Cent. Sch. Dist. Bd. of Educ., 402 F.3d 332, 333 (2d Cir. 2005) (holding that expert fees are compensable costs under the statute), *rev'd*, 548 U.S. 291 (2006).

10. 20 U.S.C. § 1415(i)(3)(B) (2006) (emphasis added).

11. 28 U.S.C. § 2680(b) (2006) (emphasis added).

12. *See* Raila v. United States, 355 F.3d 118 (2d Cir. 2004) (holding that the plaintiff's claims under the Federal Tort Claims Act were not barred by the statute's postal matter exception); Dolan v. USPS, 546 U.S. 481 (2006) (upholding *Raila*).

13. 18 U.S.C. § 922 (emphasis added).

14. *See* United States v. Gayle, 342 F.3d 89, 90 (2d Cir. 2003) (holding that convictions in foreign courts did not satisfy the "convicted in any court" element of the statute (quoting 18 U.S.C. § 922 (2006)); United States v. Small, 544 U.S. 385 (2004) (upholding *Gayle*).

15. *See Statutory Interpretation and the Uses of Legislative History: Hearing Before the Subcomm. on Courts, Intellectual Prop., and the Admin. of Justice of the H. Comm. on the Judiciary*, 101st Cong. (1990); *Interbranch Relations: Hearings Before the Joint Comm. on the Org. of Cong.*, 103d Cong. 76, 298 (1993) [hereinafter *Interbranch Relations*].

16. *See infra* text accompanying notes 165–70 (discussing various theories of congressional intent).

17. *See* Robert A. Katzmann, *Statutes*, 187 N.Y.U. L. REV. 637, 698-703 (2012) (noting publications on statutory interpretation over the last fifteen years).

18. Lilly Ledbetter Fair Pay Act of 2009, Pub. L. No. 111-2, 123 Stat. 5 (to be codified at 42 U.S.C. § 2000e-5).

19. *See, e.g.*, Gail Collins, *Lilly' Big Day*, N.Y. TIMES, Jan. 29, 2009, at A27; Sheryl Gay Stolberg, *Obama Signs Equal-Pay Legislation*, N.Y. TIMES (Jan. 30, 2009), http://www.nytimes.com/2009/01/30/us/politics/30ledbetter-web.html.

20. 500 U.S. 618, 667 (2007) (Ginsburg, J., dissenting) ("As in 1991, the Legislature may act to correct this Court's parsimonious reading of Title VII.").

21. 42 U.S.C. § 2000e-2(a) (2006).

22. 500 U.S. at 618–19.

23. 5 U.S. (1 Cranch) 137 (1803); *see* MARK TUSHNET, ARGUING MARBURY V. MADISON (2005) (presenting historical background and analysis of *Marbury* scholarship); William Michael Treanor, *The Story of* Marbury v. Madison: *Judicial Autonomy and Political Struggle*, *in* FEDERAL COURTS STORIES 29–56 (Vicki C. Jackson & Judith Resnik eds., 2010).

24. Charles O. Jones, *A Way of Life and Law*, 89 AM. POL. SCI. REV. 1, 8 (1995).

25. *See, e.g.*, Federal Trade Commission Act of 1914, 15 U.S.C. § 45(a)(1) (2006) (establishing requirements designed to "prevent unfair or deceptive acts or practices in or affecting commerce").

26. *See, e.g.*, 42 U.S.C. § 2000e (proscribing discrimination on the basis of race, color, religion, sex, or national origin); Americans with Disabilities Act of 1990, 42 U.S.C. § 12112 (2006) (proscribing discrimination on the basis of disability).

27. *See, e.g.*, Clean Water Act of 1972, 33 U.S.C. § 1362(7) (2006) (prohibiting the discharge of any pollutant into "navigable waters," defined without further elaboration as "the waters of the United States, including the territorial seas").

28. *See, e.g.*, Gramm-Rudman-Hollings Balanced Budget and Emergency Deficit Control Act of 1985, 2 U.S.C. § 922 (2006) (authorizing members of Congress to file a suit challenging the constitutionality of the Act and providing for challenge to be heard by a special three-judge federal court with direct appeal to the Supreme Court).

29. *See, e.g.*, 23 U.S.C. § 158 (2006) (directing the Secretary of Transportation to withhold a percentage of federal highway funds otherwise allocable from States "in which the purchase or public possession . . . of any alcoholic beverage by a person who is less than twenty-one years of age is lawful"); South Dakota v. Dole, 483 U.S. 203, 211–12 (1987) (holding that 23 U.S.C. § 158 was a valid exercise of Congress's spending power).

30. *See* Robert A. Katzmann, *The American Legislative Process as a Signal*, 9 J. PUB. POL'Y 287, 292 (1989) ("As a signal of government, legislation affects both the substance and process of policymaking.").

31. On the impact of statutes on the administrative state in the twentieth century, see JAMES WILLARD HURST, THE GROWTH OF AMERICAN LAW 419–23 (1950), where the author explains that the "sheer bulk" of legislation and the need for expertise drove the creation of specialized agencies in the years after 1910. *See also* JAMES WILLARD HURST, DEALING WITH STATUTES (1982); CASS R. SUNSTEIN, AFTER THE RIGHTS REVOLUTION: RECONCEIVING THE REGULATORY STATE (1990). Grant Gilmore famously described the "orgy of statute making" in GRANT GILMORE, THE AGES OF AMERICAN LAW 95 (1977).

32. Pub. L. No. 79-404, 60 Stat. 237 (1946) (current version at 5 U.S.C. §§ 500–59 (2006)).

33. Pub. L. No. 101-336, 104 Stat. 327 (1990) (codified at 42 U.S.C. §§ 12, 101–213 (2006)).

34. Pub. L. No. 88-206, 77 Stat. 392 (1963) (current version at 42 U.S.C. §§ 7401–8146 (2006))

35. The Clean Water Act of 1977 was at first called the Federal Water Pollution Control Act Amendments, Pub. L. No. 92-500, 86 Stat. 816 (1972) (codified as amended at 33 U.S.C. §§ 1251–376 (2006)).

36. 20 U.S.C. § 1681 (2006).

37. Barbara Winslow, *The Impact of Title IX*, THE GILLER LEHRMAN INST. OF AM. HISTORY, http://www.gilderlehrman.org/history-by-era/seventies/essays/impact-title-ix (last visited Apr. 26, 2012) (noting that Title IX is "[o]ne of the great achievements of the women's movement" and that its impact extends

beyond sports to higher education, employment, learning environment, math and science, sexual harassment, standardized testing, and technology).

38. WILLIAM N. ESKRIDGE JR. & JOHN FEREJOHN, A REPUBLIC OF STATUTES: THE NEW AMERICAN CONSTITUTION (2010).

39. 347 U.S. 483 (1954).

40. Pub. L. No. 88-352, 78 Stat. 241 (1964) (codified as amended at 42 U.S.C. § 2000e (2006)).

41. See, e.g., Thompson v. N. Am. Stainless, LP, 131 S. Ct. 863, 870 (2011) (holding that an employee who claims he was terminated because his fiancée had filed a discrimination charge against their mutual employer may pursue a retaliation claim under Title VII); Jones v. Alfred H. Mayer Co., 392 U.S. 409, 438–39 (1968) (holding that 42 U.S.C. § 1982 (1964) prohibits racial discrimination in housing by private, as well as governmental, housing providers).

42. See, e.g., Wilner v. Nat'l Sec. Agency, 592 F.3d 60, 74–75 (2d Cir. 2009) (upholding, under section 6 of the National Security Agency Act of 1959, 50 U.S.C. § 402 (2006), a denial of a request under the Freedom of Information Act, 5 U.S.C. § 552 (2006), for information gathered under the Terrorist Surveillance Program because the requested information would reveal activities of the National Security Agency).

43. See, e.g., Massachusetts v. EPA, 549 U.S. 497, 532 (2007) (holding that section 202(a)(1) of the Clean Air Act, 42 U.S.C. § 7521(a)(1) (2006), gives the Environmental Protection Agency authority to regulate emissions of greenhouse gases from new motor vehicles).

44. See, e.g., Morrison v. Nat'l Austl. Bank Ltd., 130 S. Ct. 2869, 2888 (2010) (holding that section 10(b) of the Securities Exchange Act of 1934, 15 U.S.C. § 78j(b) (2006), does not provide a cause of action to foreign plaintiffs suing foreign and American defendants for misconduct in connection with securities traded on foreign exchanges).

45. See, e.g., Bartlett v. Strickland, 556 U.S. 1, 14–15 (2009) (holding that a racial minority group that constitutes less than fifty percent of a proposed district's population cannot state a vote dilution claim under section 2 of the Voting Rights Act of 1965, 42 U.S.C. § 1973 (2006)).

46. See, e.g., Meritor Sav. Bank v. Vinson, 477 U.S. 57, 66 (1986) (holding that a plaintiff could establish a violation of Title VII "by proving that discrimination based on sex has created a hostile or abusive work environment").

47. GUIDO CALABRESI, A COMMON LAW FOR THE AGE OF STATUTES 1 (1982) (arguing that "many disparate current legal-political phenomena are reactions" to the fundamental change of American law from a legal system once dominated by common law to a system dominated by statutes).

48. State court cases interpreting statutes are numerous. See, e.g., Commonwealth v. Gomez, 940 N.E.2d 488, 492–93 (Mass. App. Ct. 2011) (explaining that statutes on the same subject matter should be read as a whole to produce internal consistency); Gordon v. Registry of Motor Vehicles, 912 N.E.2d 9, 13 (Mass. App. Ct. 2009) (determining that whether a statute is criminal or civil depends on the legislature's intent, which is a matter of statutory construction); Kramer v.

Zoning Bd. of Appeals of Somerville, 837 N.E.2d 1147, 1152 (Mass. App. Ct. 2005) ("[S]tatutes are to be interpreted in a common-sense way which is consistent with the statutory scheme, and in a way which avoids constitutional issues.").

49. DANIEL PATRICK MOYNIHAN, CAME THE REVOLUTION: ARGUMENT IN THE REAGAN ERA 66 (1988).

50. *Id.*

51. THE FEDERALIST NO. 62, at 445 (James Madison) (Pocket Books ed., 2004).

52. THE FEDERALIST NO. 63, *supra* note 51, at 451 (James Madison).

53. *See* THE FEDERALIST NO. 53, *supra* note 51, at 388 (James Madison) ("The greater the proportion of new members, and the less the information of the bulk of the members, the more apt will they be to fall into the snares that may be laid for them.").

54. THE FEDERALIST NO. 62, *supra* note 51, at 447 (James Madison).

55. U.S. CONST. art. I, § 2, cl. 6.

56. *Id.* § 3, cl. 4.

57. *Id.* § 5, cl. 2.

58. *Id.* § 5, cl. 3.

59. *Id.* § 5, cl. 4.

60. *Id.* § 7, cl. 1.

61. JAMES L. SUNDQUIST, CONSTITUTIONAL REFORM AND EFFECTIVE GOVERNMENT 1 (1986) (quoting Letter from Gouverneur Morris to W. H. Wells (Feb. 24, 1815), *in* 3 THE RECORDS OF THE FEDERAL CONVENTION OF 1787, at 421–22 (Max Farrand ed., rev. ed., 1937)).

62. *House History: 1st Congress (1789–1791)*, OFF. CLERK U.S. HOUSE REPRE-SENTATIVES, http://artandhistory.house.gov/house_history/index.aspx (last visited Apr. 26, 2012) (noting the number of members in the first House of Representatives); *The Senate Moves to Philadelphia*, U.S. SENATE, http://www.senate.gov/artandhistory/history/minute/The_Senate_Moves_To_Philidelphia.htm (last visited Apr. 26, 2012) (noting the number of members in the first Senate).

63. *See* JOSEPH COOPER, THE ORIGINS OF THE STANDING COMMITTEES AND THE DEVELOPMENT OF THE MODERN HOUSE (1971) (analyzing the impact of the standing committee system in the House of Representatives); David T. Canon & Charles Stewart III, *The Evolution of the Committee System in Congress, in* CONGRESS RECONSIDERED 163 (Lawrence C. Dodd & Bruce I. Oppenheimer eds., 2001) (presenting evidence on the influence of select commit-tees in the nineteenth century); Jeffery A. Jenkins & Charles H. Stewart III, *Order from Chaos: The Transformation of the Committee System in the House, 1816–1922, in* PARTY, PROCESS, AND POLITICAL CHANGE IN CONGRESS 195 (David W. Brady & Mathew D. McCubbins eds., 2002) (examining the social choice prob-lems that contributed to the rise of the early nineteenth-century committee sys-tem); Eric Schickler, *Institutional Development of Congress, in* THE LEGISLATIVE BRANCH 35, 37–41 (Paul J. Quirk & Sarah A. Binder eds., 2005) (explaining the rise of the standing committee system in both the House of Representatives and the Senate); Gerald Gamm & Kenneth Shepsle, *Emergence of Legislative Institu-tions: Standing Committees in the House and Senate, 1810–1825*, 14 LEGIS. STUD.

Q. 39, 39 (1989) (discussing and applying institutional development theories to the development of standing committees in Congress). On the study of the modern committee system and changes in modern scholarship on committees, see C. Lawrence Evans, *Congressional Committees, in* THE OXFORD HANDBOOK OF THE AMERICAN CONGRESS 396 (Eric Schickler & Frances E. Lee eds., 2011).

64. WOODROW WILSON, CONGRESSIONAL GOVERNMENT 79 (15th prtg. 1901).

65. *See* RICHARD F. FENNO, JR., CONGRESSMEN IN COMMITTEES xiv–xv (1973).

66. DAVID E. PRICE, THE CONGRESSIONAL EXPERIENCE: A VIEW FROM THE HILL 152 (1992).

67. NORMAN J. ORNSTEIN, THOMAS E. MANN & MICHAEL J. MALBIN, VITAL STATISTICS ON CONGRESS 2008, at 109–21 (2008); *see also* ROGER H. DAVIDSON, WALTER J. OLESZEK & FRANCES E. LEE, CONGRESS AND ITS MEMBERS 204–05 (13th ed. 2012) (discussing the influence and importance of committee staff in drafting, negotiating, and shaping legislation).

68. ORNSTEIN ET AL., *supra* note 67, at 102. Here, "committees" include standing committees, subcommittees of standing committees, select and special committees, subcommittees of select and special committees, joint committees, and subcommittees of joint committees. *Id.*

69. Roger H. Davidson, *The House of Representatives: Managing Legislative Complexity, in* WORKWAYS OF GOVERNANCE: MONITORING OUR GOVERNMENT'S HEALTH 24, 33 (Roger H. Davidson ed., 2003).

70. Frank M. Coffin, *Working with the Congress of the Future, in* THE FEDERAL APPELLATE JUDICIARY IN THE TWENTY-FIRST CENTURY 199, 201–13 (Cynthia Harrison & Russell R. Wheeler eds., 1989).

71. ORNSTEIN ET AL., *supra* note 67. For compiling these data, I am grateful to Andrew Rugg, who works as a researcher for Norman J. Ornstein, Thomas E. Mann, and Michael J. Malbin, on *Vital Statistics on Congress. Id.*

72. E-mail from Andrew Rugg, Research Assistant, Am. Enter. Inst., to author (July 12, 2011, 11:06 EST) (on file with the *New York University Law Review*).

73. *Id.*

74. E-mail from Andrew Rugg, Research Assistant, Am. Enter. Inst., to author (Jan. 24, 2012, 16:38 EST) (on file with the *New York University Law Review*).

75. E-mail from Andrew Rugg, Research Assistant, Am. Enter. Inst., to author (Aug. 12, 2011, 11:06 EST) (on file with the *New York University Law Review*).

76. *Id.*

77. DAVIDSON ET AL., *supra* note 67, at 172.

78. *See id.* at 219 (noting that omnibus bills "contain an array of issues that were once handled as separate pieces of legislation").

79. *See id.* at 221 (noting that omnibus bills "minimize the opportunities for further delay").

80. *See* ROGER H. DAVIDSON, WALTER J. OLESZEK & FRANCES E. LEE, CONGRESS AND ITS MEMBERS 241 (12th ed. 2010) (quoting a former chair of the House Budget Committee as saying that "[l]arge bills can be used to hide legislation that otherwise might be controversial").

81. *See generally* WALTER J. OLESZEK, CONGRESSIONAL PROCEDURES AND THE POLICY PROCESS 28 (8th ed. 2011) (discussing the congressional law-making process and how Congress's rules and procedures affect policy).

82. David Brady & Morris Fiorina, *Congress in the Era of the Permanent Campaign*, *in* THE PERMANENT CAMPAIGN AND ITS FUTURE 134 (Norman J. Ornstein & Thomas E. Mann eds., 2000).

83. ORNSTEIN ET AL., *supra* note 67, at 126 tbl.6-3.

84. E-mail from Andrew Rugg (Jan. 24, 2012, 16:38 EST), *supra* note 74.

85. ORNSTEIN ET AL., *supra* note 67, at 126 tbl.6-3; E-mail from Andrew Rugg (July 12, 2011, 11:06 EST), *supra* note 72.

86. E-mail from Andrew Rugg (Aug. 12, 2011, 11:06 EST), *supra* note 75.

87. *Id.*

88. ORNSTEIN ET AL., *supra* note 67, at 18.

89. E-mail from Andrew Rugg (Aug. 12, 2011, 11:06 EST), *supra* note 75.

90. ORNSTEIN ET AL., *supra* note 67, at 124 tbl.6-1.

91. E-mail from Andrew Rugg (Aug. 12, 2011, 11:06 EST), *supra* note 75.

92. ORNSTEIN ET AL., *supra* note 67, at 125 tbl.6-2.

93. *Id.* at 104 tbl.4-4.

94. E-mail from Andrew Rugg (Aug. 12, 2011, 11:06 EST), *supra* note 75.

95. ORNSTEIN ET AL., *supra* note 67, at 104 tbl.4-5.

96. E-mail from Andrew Rugg (Aug. 12, 2011, 11:06 EST), *supra* note 75.

97. For a discussion on the challenges of deliberation, see generally SARAH A. BINDER, STALEMATE: CAUSES AND CONSEQUENCES OF LEGIS-LATIVE GRIDLOCK (2003); PAUL J. QUIRK & GARY MUCCIARONI, DELIBERATIVE CHOICES: DEBATING PUBLIC POLICY IN CONGRESS (2006).

98. For theoretical analyses of the congressional committee system, see for example KEITH KREHBIEL, INFORMATION AND LEGISLATIVE ORGANIZATION (1991); David P. Baron, *Legislative Organization with Informational Committees*, 44 AM. J. POL. SCI. 485 (2000); Thomas W. Gilligan & Keith Krehbiel, *Organization of Informative Committees by a Rational Legislature*, 34 AM. J. POL. SCI. 531 (1990); Forrest Maltzman, *Meeting Competing Demands: Committee Performance in the Post-reform House*, 39 AM. J. POL. SCI. 653 (1995).

99. James L. Buckley, a former senator from New York and judge on the D.C. Circuit, remarked as senator that "[m]y understanding of most of the legislation I voted on was based entirely on my reading of its language and, where necessary, on explanations contained in the accompanying report." *Statutory Interpretation and the Uses of Legislative History: Hearing Before the Subcomm. on Courts, Intellectual Prop., and the Admin. of Justice of the H. Comm. on the Judiciary*, 101st Cong. 21 (1990) (statement of James L. Buckley, J., D.C. Cir.). In the words of another former legislator and judge, Abner Mikva, a committee report is "the most useful document in the legislative history." JUDGES AND LEGISLATORS, *supra* note 3, at 171.

100. ANDREA LARUE, SENATE MANUAL CONTAINING THE STANDING RULES, ORDERS, LAWS, AND RESOLUTIONS AFFECTING THE

BUSINESS OF THE UNITED STATES SENATE, S. DOC. NO. 107-1, at 17 (1st Sess. 2001). This period of two days does not include Sundays and legal holidays. *Id.*

101. *See, e.g.,* GEORGE MILLER, LILLY LEDBETTER FAIR PAY ACT OF 2007, H.R. REP. NO. 110-237.

102. *See, e.g.,* DON YOUNG, SAFE, ACCOUNTABLE, FLEXIBLE, EFFICIENT TRANSPORTATION ACT: A LEGACY FOR USERS, H.R. REP. NO. 109-105 (2005) (Conf. Rep.).

103. Clyde Wilcox, *The Dynamics of Lobbying the Hill, in* 1 THE INTEREST GROUP CONNECTION: ELECTIONEERING, LOBBYING, AND POLICYMAKING IN WASHINGTON 89 (Paul S. Herrnson, Ronald G. Shaiko & Clyde Wilcox eds., 1998) (noting that members of Congress are interested in obtaining views of interest groups on proposed legislation).

104. TOBIAS A. DORSEY, LEGISLATIVE DRAFTER'S DESKBOOK: A PRAC-TICAL GUIDE § 2.16 (2006); M. Douglass Bellis, *Drafting in the U.S. Congress,* 22 STATUTE L. REV. 38 (2001). For examples of drafting manuals created by thoffices of legislative counsel, see OFFICE OF THE LEGISLATIVE COUN-SEL, UNITED STATES SENATE, LEGISLATIVE DRAFTING MANUAL (1997), *available at* http://www.law.yale.edu/documents/pdf/Faculty/SenateOf-ficeoftheLegislativeCounsel_LegislativeDraftingManual(1997).pdf; OFFICE OF THE LEGISLATIVE COUNSEL, HOUSE LEGISLATIVE COUNSEL'S MANUAL ON DRAFTING STYLE, H.L.C. DOC. NO. 104-1 (1995), *available at* www.house.gov/legcoun/pdf/draftstyle.pdf; BJ Ard, Comment, *Interpreting by the Book: Legislative Drafting Manuals and Statutory Interpretation,* 120 YALE L.J. 185, 187–93 (2010) (describing how the manuals recommend formatting legislation and incorporating canons of construction). The Supreme Court has from time to time made reference to the drafting manuals in its decisions. *See, e.g.,* Carr v. United States, 130 S. Ct. 2229, 2244–46 (2010) (Alito, J., dissenting) (discussing widely accepted legislative drafting conventions); Koons Buick Pon-tiac GMC, Inc. v. Nigh, 543 U.S. 50, 60–61 (2004) (citing the House and Senate drafting manuals in differentiating between a subparagraph and a clause).

105. Victoria F. Nourse & Jane S. Schacter, *The Politics of Legislative Drafting: A Con-gressional Case Study,* 77 N.Y.U. L. REV. 575, 588 (2002) (noting that legislative counsel view their involvement as "'strictly up to the client' (i.e., the senator or the committee)").

106. Katzmann, *supra* note 30, at 288–89.

107. Nourse & Schacter, *supra* note 105, at 592–93 (2002). ·

108. *See, e.g.,* Jonathan R. Siegel, *What Statutory Drafting Errors Teach Us About Statu-tory Interpretation,* 69 GEO. WASH. L. REV. 309, 309, 311–19 (2001) (pointing out an error in the federal venue statute).

109. Nourse & Schacter, *supra* note 105, at 600, 615.

110. *See supra* notes 97–100 and accompanying text.

111. Peter L. Strauss, *When the Judge Is Not the Primary Official with Responsibility To Read: Agency Interpretation and the Problem of Legislative History,* 66 CHI.-KENT L. REV. 321, 321 (1990). *See also* Jerry L. Mashaw, *Agency-Centered or Court-Centered Administrative Law? A Dialogue with Richard Pierce on Agency Statutory Interpretation,*

59 ADMIN. L. REV. 889, 903 (2007) [hereinafter Mashaw, *Agency-Centered or Court-Centered*] (rejecting the idea that the focus of administrative law should be "even more judicio-centric than it currently is"); Henry P. Monaghan, Marbury *and the Administrative State*, 83 COLUM. L. REV. 1, 25–26 (1983) (noting pre-*Chevron* judicial deference to agency interpretation of law); Trevor W. Morrison, *Constitutional Avoidance in the Executive Branch*, 106 COLUM. L. REV. 1189, 1190 (2006) ("Statutory interpretation is not the exclusive province of the courts; it is a core function of the executive branch as well."); Cass R. Sunstein, *Beyond* Marbury: *The Executive's Power To Say What the Law Is*, 115 YALE L.J. 2580, 2583 (2006) (stating that the executive branch is initially responsible for statutory interpretation); Cass R. Sunstein, Is *Tobacco a Drug? Administrative Agencies as Common Law Courts*, 47 DUKE L.J. 1013, 1068 (1998) ("[A]dministrative agencies have become America's common law courts."); Cass R. Sunstein & Adrian Vermeule, *Interpretation and Institutions*, 101 MICH. L. REV. 885, 926–27 (2003) (describing Strauss's defense of *Chevron*); Edward L. Rubin, *Law and Legislation in the Administrative State*, 89 COLUM. L. REV. 369, 373 (1989) (noting that statutes vest agencies with implementation authority). *But see* Richard J. Pierce, Jr., *How Agencies Should Give Meaning to the Statutes They Administer: A Response to Mashaw and Strauss*, 59 ADMIN. L. REV. 197, 204 (2007) (disagreeing with Strauss and Mashaw that agencies are "'the primary official interpreters of federal statutes'" (quoting Jerry L. Mashaw, *Norms, Practices, and the Paradox of Deference: A Preliminary Inquiry into Agency Statutory Interpretation*, 57 ADMIN. L. REV. 501, 501–02 (2005) [hereinafter Mashaw, *Norms, Practices, and the Paradox of Deference*])).

112. HERBERT KAUFMAN, THE ADMINISTRATIVE BEHAVIOR OF FEDERAL BUREAU CHIEFS 47 (1981).

113. For more background on how Congress exercises influence over agencies, see generally LAWRENCE C. DODD & RICHARD L. SCHOTT, CONGRESS AND THE ADMINISTRATIVE STATE 155–211 (2d ed. 1986); JOSEPH P. HARRIS, CONGRESSIONAL CONTROL OF ADMINISTRATION (1964); Charles R. Shipan, *Congress and the Bureaucracy, in* THE LEGISLATIVE BRANCH 432, 438–46 (Paul J. Quirk & Sarah A. Binder eds., 2005).

114. *See* ARTHUR MAASS, CONGRESS AND THE COMMON GOOD 183–88 (1983) ("[T]he committees require nominees, as a condition of confirmation, to make policy-related promises during confirmation hearings."); Steven V. Roberts, *A Lesson in Advising and Consenting*, N.Y. TIMES, Apr. 14, 1983, at B10 (quoting Senator Carl Levin as saying that "[w]e all ask questions at confirmation hearings, hoping to obtain answers that affect future actions").

115. *See generally* JOEL D. ABERBACH, KEEPING A WATCHFUL EYE: THE POLITICS OF CONGRESSIONAL OVERSIGHT (1990) (discussing trends in congressional oversight as well as the politics and processes underlying such oversight); DANIEL CARPENTER, REPUTATION AND POWER 333–34 (2010) (explaining that congressional hearings play a critical role in determining a federal agency's reputation due to the adversarial nature of the hearings and the public testimony presented in them); CHRISTOPHER H. FOREMAN, JR., SIGNALS FROM THE HILL: CONGRESSIONAL OVERSIGHT AND THE

CHALLENGE OF SOCIAL REGULATION 2 (1988) (exploring "the formal tools that Congress employs to oversee administration"); WILLIAM T. GORMLEY, JR. & STEVEN J. BALLA, BUREAUCRACY AND DEMOCRACY: ACCOUNT-ABILITY AND PERFORMANCE 83 (2d ed. 2008) (noting that oversight as a percentage of total committee activity increased from 9.1% in 1971 to 25.2% in 1983).

116. PAUL C. LIGHT, GOVERNMENT'S GREATEST INVESTIGATIONS: CON-GRESS, THE PRESIDENT, AND THE SEARCH FOR ANSWERS, 1945-2012 (forthcoming 2013) (on file with the *New York University Law Review*).

117. DAVIDSON ET AL., *supra* note 67, at 338.

118. *Id.*

119. 462 U.S. 919 (1983).

120. LOUIS FISHER, CONG. RESEARCH SERV., RS22132, LEGISLATIVE VETOES AFTER CHADHA 3-6 (2005). *See also* JESSICA KORN, THE POWER OF SEPARATION: AMERICAN CONSTITUTIONALISM AND THE MYTH OF THE LEGISLATIVE VETO 13 (1996) (arguing that "the legislative veto shortcut was inconsequential to congressional control of the policy making process").

121. *See* WILLIAM T. GORMLEY, JR., TAMING THE BUREAUCRACY 159-64 (1989) (describing the effect of the Government Accountability Office (GAO) reports on agencies).

122. *See, e.g.*, Chevron U.S.A., Inc. v. Natural Res. Def. Council, Inc., 467 U.S. 837, 843-44 (1984) ("[I]f the statute is silent or ambiguous with respect to the spe-cific issue, the question for the court is whether the agency's answer is based on a permissible construction of the statute.").

123. In arguing that courts can learn from agencies, I emphasize that I focus on pre-enactment legislative history accompanying legislation. While a court's inquiry into legislative history is essentially limited to pre-enactment materials, I note that agencies are also sensitive to post-enactment signals of legislators in the current and succeeding Congresses.

124. *See, e.g.*, Mashaw, *Agency-Centered or Court-Centered, supra* note 111; Pierce, *supra* note 111; Strauss, *supra* note 111.

125. *See generally* WILLIAM D. POPKIN, STATUTES IN COURT: THE HISTORY AND THEORY OF STATUTORY INTERPRETATION 2-3 (1999) (detailing the evolution of statutory interpretation in the United States and recommending the adoption of a "discretionary judicial role" in statutory interpretation); William S. Blatt, *The History of Statutory Interpretation: A Study in Form and Substance*, 6 CARDOZO L. REV. 799 (1985) (chronicling the history of statutory intrepration in the United States and noting the shifting emphasis that courts have placed on form over substance). There are, of course, other theories of statutory construc-tion, apart from those discussed in the succeeding pages, advanced by prominent law professors. *See, e.g.*, WILLIAM N. ESKRIDGE, JR., DYNAMIC STATU-TORY INTERPRETATION 9 (1994) (endorsing dynamic statutory interpreta-tion, which holds that "the meaning of a statute is not fixed until it is applied to concrete circumstances, and [that] it is neither uncommon nor illegitimate for the meaning of a provision to change over time"); RONALD DWORKIN, LAW'S

EMPIRE 313–54 (1986) (advocating an approach to statutory interpretation that accounts for questions of fit, integrity, and political morality).
126. Judge Henry J. Friendly observed:

Illogical though it was to hold that a "plain meaning" shut off access to the very materials that might show it not to have been plain at all, it was equally wrong to deny the natural meaning of language its proper primacy; like Cardozo's "Method of Philosophy," it "is the heir presumptive. A pretender to the title will have to fight his way."

Henry J. Friendly, *Mr. Justice Frankfurter and the Reading of Statutes, in* Benchmarks 206 (1967) (quoting BENJAMIN N. CARDOZO, THE NATURE OF THE JUDICIAL PROCESS 9, 32 (1921)).
127. *See, e.g.*, Graham Cnty. Soil & Water Conservation Dist. v. United States *ex rel.* Wilson, 130 S. Ct. 1396, 1411 (2010) (Sotomayor, J., dissenting) ("In my view, the Court misreads the statutory text and gives insufficient weight to contextual and historical evidence of Congress' purpose. . . ."); Barnhart v. Sigmon Coal Co., 534 U.S. 438, 472 (2002) (Stevens, J., dissenting) ("There are occasions when an exclusive focus on text seems to convey an incoherent message. . . .").
128. THE FEDERALIST NO. 37, at 255 (James Madison) (Cynthia Brantley Johnson ed., 2004).
129. *See, e.g.*, William N. Eskridge, Jr., *All About Words: Early Understandings of the "Judicial Power" in Statutory Interpretation, 1776–1806,* 101 COLUM. L. REV. 990, 990–98 (2001) (providing an historical overview of statutory interpretation at the founding and arguing that judges are agents of as well as partners with Congress, with interpretative authority not confined to the text); John F. Manning, *Deriving Rules of Statutory Interpretation from the Constitution,* 101 COLUM. L. REV. 1648, 1648–53 (2001) (contending that although the founders did not definitively resolve the judiciary's relationship with Congress, they developed a constitutional structure that fits better with the faithful agent theory and textualism than the co-equal partner model).
130. *See* Philip A. Hamburger, *Natural Rights, Natural Law, and American Constitutions,* 102 YALE L.J. 907, 954 (1993) ("[F]ar from being a practicable measure for determining which laws accorded with a constitution and which did not, natural law tended to be a theoretical explanation of limitations on natural rights.").
131. *See* Adrian Vermeule, *The Cycles of Statutory Interpretation,* 68 U. CHI. L. REV. 149 (2001) (arguing that courts have changed their interpretative practices with some frequency).
132. As Justice Breyer stated: "Only by seeking that purpose can we avoid the substitution of judicial for legislative will. Only by reading language in its light can we maintain the democratic link between voters, legislators, statutes, and ultimate implementation, upon which the legitimacy of our constitutional system rests." Arlington Cent. Sch. Dist. Bd. of Educ. v. Murphy, 548 U.S. 291, 323–24 (2006) (Breyer, J., dissenting). Justice Breyer has written that he finds "purposes and consequences . . . most helpful most often . . . to help unlock the meaning of a statutory text." STEPHEN BREYER, MAKING OUR DEMOCRACY WORK:

A JUDGE'S VIEW 88 (2010). As to consequences, he writes: "The judge also examines the likely consequences of a proposed interpretation, asking whether they are more likely to further than to hinder achievement of the provision's purpose." *Id.* at 92.

133. Heydon's Case, (1584) 76 Eng. Rep. 637 (K.B.) 638; 3 Co. Rep. 7a, 7b.

134. 143 U.S. 457 (1892).

135. Alien Contract Labor Act of 1885, ch. 164, § 1, 23 Stat. 332, 332 (amended 1888).

136. 143 U.S. at 459.

137. *Id.* at 462.

138. *Id.* at 464–65.

139. *Id.* at 471.

140. *See* William S. Blatt, *Missing the Mark: An Overlooked Statute Redefines the Debate over Statutory Interpretation,* 104 NW. U. L. REV. COLLOQUY 147, 150 (2009), http://www.law.northwestern.edu/lawreview/colloquy/2009/36/ ("Long after it was decided, *Holy Trinity* was regarded as an important case, both for its willingness to depart from text, and for its reliance on legislative history.").

141. *See, e.g.,* William N. Eskridge, Jr., *"Fetch Some Soupmeat,"* 16 CARDOZO L. REV. 2209, 2217 n.38 (1995) ("*Church of the Holy Trinity* has . . . been the focal point of the debate between the Supreme Court's 'new textualists' and more purpose-based interpreters."); Frederick Schauer, *Constitutional Invocations,* 65 FORDHAM L. REV. 1295, 1307 (1997) ("*Church of the Holy Trinity v. United States* is not only a case, but is the marker for an entire legal tradition, . . . [one that emphasizes that] there is far more to law than the plain meaning of authoritative legal texts. . . .").

142. *See* Antonin Scalia, *Common-Law Courts in a Civil-Law System: The Role of United States Federal Courts in Interpreting the Constitution and Laws, in* A MATTER OF INTERPRETATION: FEDERAL COURTS AND THE FEDERAL LAW 3, 22 (Amy Gutmann ed., 1997) (criticizing *Holy Trinity* and its inquiry beyond the text into legislative intent).

143. Learned Hand, *How Far Is a Judge Free in Rendering a Decision?, in* NAT'L ADVISORY COUNCIL ON RADIO IN EDUC., LAW SERIES I 1 (1935), *reprinted in* THE SPIRIT OF LIBERTY 103, 106 (Irving Dilliard ed., 1952).

144. *See* HENRY M. HART, JR. & ALBERT M. SACKS, THE LEGAL PROCESS: BASIC PROBLEMS IN THE MAKING AND APPLICATION OF LAW (William N. Eskridge, Jr. & Philip P. Frickey eds., 1994).

145. HART & SACKS, *supra* note 144, at 1374.

146. *Id.* at 1376. For a discussion of the legal process school, see Robert Post, *Theorizing Disagreement: Reconceiving the Relationship Between Law and Politics,* 98 CALIF. L. REV. 1319, 1332–36 (2010).

147. *See* BREYER, *supra* note 132, at 88 (linking "whether [the Court's] interpretations will effectively carry out the statute's objectives" to "whether its relationship with Congress will tend more toward the cooperative or the confrontational"); Linda Greenhouse, *Making Congress All It Can Be,* N.Y. TIMES OPINIONATOR BLOG (Oct. 7, 2010, 9:38 PM), http://opinionator.blogs.

nytimes.com/2010/10/07/making-congress-all-it-can-be/ (noting that Justice Breyer views the Supreme Court as helping Congress).

148. Kenneth A. Shepsle, *Congress Is a "They," Not an "It": Legislative Intent as Oxymoron*, 12 INT'L REV. L. & ECON. 239, 239 (1992). For a similar view, see Diarmuid F. O'Scannlain, *Lawmaking and Interpretation: The Role of a Federal Judge in Our Constitutional Framework*, 91 MARQ. L. REV. 895, 907 (2008) (each legislator has own reasons for voting for a bill).

149. For a thoughtful discussion recognizing the legitimacy of multiple approaches and factors, see Todd D. Rakoff, *Statutory Interpretation as a Multifarious Enterprise*, 104 NW. U. L. REV. 1559, 1569, 1570–86 (2010).

150. Commenting on the challenge of developing a "grand theory" of judicial decision making, Judge Frank Coffin wrote: "I suspect that any such attempt is about as likely to succeed as trying to shoehorn an elephant's foot into a ballet slipper." Frank M. Coffin, U.S. Senior Circuit Judge, My Judicial Key Ring: Remarks upon Receipt of the Morton A. Brody 2006 Award for Distinguished Judicial Service at Colby College 4 (Mar. 19, 2006) (transcript on file with the *New York University Law Review*).

151. BENJAMIN FRANKLIN, A PROPOSAL TO PROMOTE USEFUL KNOWLEDGE AMONG THE BRITISH PLANTATIONS IN AMERICA 1 (1743), *available at* http://nationalhumanitiescenter.org/pds/becomingamer/ideas/text4/amerphilsociety.pdf.

152. *See, e.g.*, FRIENDLY, *supra* note 126, at 203–04 (1967) (emphasizing that statutes come in varying levels of specificity and open-endedness); Pierre N. Leval, *Trademark: Champion of Free Speech*, 27 COLUM. J.L. & ARTS 187, 195–98 (2004) (describing "micromanager" statutes and delegating statutes that adopt common law or make "new policy").

153. Lexecon, Inc. v. Milberg Weiss Bershad Hynes & Lerach, 523 U.S. 26, 37 (1998).

154. 15 U.S.C. § 45(a)(1) (2006).

155. Americans with Disabilities Act of 1990, 42 U.S.C. § 12111(9) (2006).

156. Felix Frankfurter, *Some Reflections on the Reading of Statutes*, 47 COLUM. L. REV. 542, 543 (1947), *reprinted in* JUDGES ON JUDGING: VIEWS FROM THE BENCH 221, 229 (David M. O'Brien ed., 1997).

157. Arlington Cent. Sch. Dist. Bd. of Educ. v. Murphy, 548 U.S. 291, 324 (2006) (Breyer, J., dissenting).

158. *See supra* notes 9–14 and accompanying text. In another case, I found legislative history useful in assessing whether the jurisdictional bar of the False Claims Act, 31 U.S.C. § 3730(e)(4)(A) (2006), applies when the plaintiff's allegations are based on materials produced in response to a Freedom of Information Act, 5 U.S.C. § 552 (2006), request. United States *ex rel.* Kirk v. Schindler Elevator Corp., 601 F.3d 94, 108–10 (2d Cir. 2010).

159. *See* A. Raymond Randolph, *Dictionaries, Plain Meaning, and Context in Statutory Interpretation*, 17 HARV. J.L. & PUB. POL'Y 71, 77 (1994) (explaining how analysis of legislative history supplements rigorous textual analysis by enabling a judge to "test[] his tentative construction of the statutory language").

160. Barnhart v. Sigmon Coal Co., 534 U.S. 438, 472 (2002) (Stevens, J., dissenting).

161. See, for example, Justice Sotomayor's opinion in *Carr v. United States*, 130 S. Ct. 2229, 2241–42 (2010), where the Court used legislative history to supplement textual analysis in determining whether a provision of the Sex Offender Registration and Notification Act that criminalized interstate travel of unregistered sex offenders was intended to apply to sex offenders who traveled before the passage of the Act, and Justice Kagan's opinion in *Tapia v. United States*, 131 S. Ct. 2382, 2391 (2011), where the Court observed that the legislative history provided further confirmation of the use of textual analysis in determining whether the Sentencing Reform Act precludes federal courts from lengthening a prison term to promote rehabilitation.

162. *Interbranch Relations*, supra note 15, at 277 (statement of Robert W. Kastenmeier, Fellow, Governance Inst.).

163. *Nomination of Judge Antonin Scalia: Hearings Before the S. Comm. on the Judiciary on the Nomination of Antonin Scalia, To Be Associate Justice of the Supreme Court of the United States*, 99th Cong. 65–66 (1986) (statement of Sen. Charles E. Grassley).

164. *Confirmation Hearing on the Nomination of John G. Roberts, Jr. To Be Chief Justice of the United States: Hearing Before the S. Comm. on the Judiciary*, 109th Cong. 318–19 (2005) (statement of Sen. Charles E. Grassley). A few months later, Senator Grassley would question Judge Samuel Alito on his views of legislative history. *See Confirmation Hearing on the Nomination of Judge Samuel A. Alito, Jr. To Be an Associate Justice of the Supreme Court of the United States: Hearing Before the S. Comm. on the Judiciary*, 109th Cong. 503 (2006) (statement of Sen. Charles E. Grassley).

165. Orrin Hatch, *Legislative History: Tool of Construction or Destruction*, 11 HARV. J.L. & PUB. POL'Y 43, 43 (1988).

166. *Id.* at 47.

167. Joan Biskupic, *Scalia Takes a Narrow View in Seeking Congress' Will*, 48 CONG. Q. WKLY. REP. 913, 917 (1990) (alteration in original). At the most recent Supreme Court confirmation hearing, that of Elena Kagan, Senator Al Franken (D-MN), criticized a Supreme Court decision for not looking into legislative history, and urged the nominee to consider such history, observing that "we spend a lot of time in hearings and on the floor debating legislation." *The Nomination of Elena Kagan To Be an Associate Justice of the United States: Hearing Before the S. Comm. on the Judiciary*, 111th Cong. 219 (2010) (statement of Sen. Al Franken).

168. Conroy v. Aniskoff, 507 U.S. 511, 519 (1993) (Scalia, J., concurring) (emphasis omitted) (quoting Aldridge v. Williams, 44 U.S. (3 How.) 9, 24 (1845)).

169. INS v. Cardoza-Fonseca, 480 U.S. 421, 453 (1987) (Scalia, J., concurring).

170. Wisconsin Public Intervenor v. Mortier, 501 U.S. 597, 620 (1991) (Scalia, J., concurring in the judgment).

171. Blanchard v. Bergeron, 489 U.S. 87, 98–99 (1989) (Scalia, J., concurring in part and concurring in the judgment).

172. Thompson v. Thompson, 484 U.S. 174, 192 (1988) (Scalia, J., concurring) (citation omitted).

173. As then–D.C. Circuit Judge Scalia wrote: "[R]outine deference to the detail of committee reports . . . [is] converting a system of judicial construction into a system of committee-staff prescription." Hirschey v. Fed. Energy Regulatory Comm'n, 777 F.2d 1, 8 (D.C. Cir. 1985) (Scalia, J., concurring).

174. See John F. Manning, *Textualism as a Nondelegation Doctrine*, 97 COLUM. L. REV. 673, 698 (1997) ("[T]extualists have opened a second front in pressing their constitutional objections to the authority of legislative history—Lockean nondelegation principles.").

175. Scalia, *supra* note 142, at 36 ("In any major piece of legislation, the legislative history is extensive, and there is something for everybody. . . . The variety and specificity of result that legislative history can achieve is unparalleled.").

176. See generally DANIEL A. FARBER & PHILIP P. FRICKEY, LAW AND PUBLIC CHOICE: A CRITICAL INTRODUCTION 21–33 (1991) (outlining principles of public choice theory); William C. Mitchell & Michael C. Munger, *Economic Models of Interest Groups: An Introductory Survey*, 35 AM. J. POL. SCI. 512 (1991) (reviewing several scholars' earlier models of how interest groups influence policies); Susan Rose-Ackerman, Comment, *Progressive Law and Economics—and the New Administrative Law*, 98 YALE L.J. 341, 344–47 (1988) (outlining public choice theory).

177. See, e.g., Frank H. Easterbrook, *The Supreme Court, 1983 Term—Foreword: The Court and the Economic System*, 98 HARV. L. REV. 4, 45–51 (1984) (observing that the Supreme Court has, through its opinions, become more sympathetic to the public choice/interest group approach toward legislation); Richard A. Epstein, *Toward a Revitalization of the Contract Clause*, 51 U. CHI. L. REV. 703, 704 (1984) (noting that an interest group's ability to influence legislation has been used as a justification for very limited constitutional protection of economic liberties); Jonathan R. Macey, *Promoting Public-Regarding Legislation Through Statutory Inter-pretation: An Interest Group Model*, 86 COLUM. L. REV. 223, 226 (1986) (arguing that the judiciary, through its interpretation of statutes, serves as a critical check on the ability of private interest groups to advance their particular interests at the expense of the public); Geoffrey P. Miller, *Public Choice at the Dawn of the Special Interest State: The Story of Butter and Margarine*, 77 CALIF. L. REV. 83 (1989) (applying public choice principles to examine the history of the American dairy industry's efforts to pass laws discriminating against margarine).

178. See, e.g., Peter H. Aronson, Ernest Gellhorn & Glen O. Robinson, *A Theory of Legislation Delegation*, 68 CORNELL L. REV. 1, 37–62 (1982) (describing responsibility-shifting and lottery models). *But see* Jerry L. Mashaw, *Prodelega-tion: Why Administrators Should Make Political Decisions*, 1 J.L. ECON. & ORG. 81, 85–91 (1985) (critiquing opponents of the delegation doctrine).

179. MANCUR OLSON, THE LOGIC OF COLLECTIVE ACTION: PUBLIC GOODS AND THE THEORY OF GROUPS 2 (1971) (emphasis omitted).

180. See, e.g., MORRIS P. FIORINA, CONGRESS: KEYSTONE OF THE WASH-INGTON ESTABLISHMENT 39–49 (1977) (describing a self-interested con-gressional establishment concerned primarily with its own reelection).

181. Blanchard v. Bergeron, 489 U.S. 87, 98–99 (1989) (Scalia, J., concurring in part and concurring in the judgment).

182. John F. Manning, *Second Generation Textualism*, 98 CALIF. L. REV. 1287, 1309–10 (2010).

183. *See* Adam Liptak, *Justices Turning More Frequently to Dictionary, and Not Just for Big Words*, N.Y. TIMES, June 14, 2011, at A11 (noting that Supreme Court justices have increased their use and citation of dictionaries to aid in interpreting statutory language).

184. In earlier writings, Professor Manning did leave open a narrow window for the use of legislative history when it supplies "an objective unmanufactured history of a statute's context." Manning, *supra* note 174, at 731. He wrote:

> If such legislative history *persuasively* describes that objective context (rather than merely offering the committee's or sponsor's own idiosyncratic expression of intent), a court may consider that history for "'the thoroughness evident in its consideration, the validity of its reasoning, its consistency with earlier and later pronouncements, and all those factors [sic] which give it power to persuade, if lacking power to control.'"

John F. Manning, *Putting Legislative History to a Vote: A Response to Professor Siegel*, 53 VAND. L. REV. 1529, 1529 n.2 (2000) (quoting John F. Manning, *Textualism as a Nondelegation Doctrine*, 97 COLUM. L. REV. 673, 733 n.252 (1997) (quoting Skidmore v. Swift & Co., 323 U.S. 134, 140 (1944))).

185. *See, e.g.*, FARBER & FRICKEY, *supra* note 176, at 116–17 (discussing the limitations of public choice theory); KATZMANN, COURTS AND CONGRESS, *supra* note 3, at 52–53 (criticizing the public choice view as oversimplified and noting that Congress sometimes acts without interest group support or despite powerful opposition); THE POLITICS OF REGULATION (James Q. Wilson ed., 1980); Robert A. Katzmann, *Comments on Levine and Forrence, "Regulatory Capture, Public Interest, and the Public Agenda: Toward a Synthesis,"* 6 J.L. ECON. & ORG. 199 (1990) (discussing several possible reasons for legislative and regulatory outcomes outside of the paradigmatic public choice analysis).

186. On agenda setting, see BRIAN D. JONES & FRANK R. BAUMGARTNER, THE POLITICS OF ATTENTION (2005), where the author examines how policymakers obtain and use information to set the agenda, and JOHN W. KINGDON, AGENDAS, ALTERNATIVES, AND PUBLIC POLICIES (2d ed. 2011), where the author explores how issues become part of the public agenda.

187. R. Shep Melnick found little interest group involvement in his studies of the food stamp program, aid to families with dependent children, and special education. *See* R. SHEP MELNICK, BETWEEN THE LINES: INTERPRETING WELFARE RIGHTS 259–60 (1994) (noting that legislators' desires to advance what they believed to be good public policy were driving forces in the development of these policies as well as broader public opinion).

188. *See* James Q. Wilson, *The Politics of Regulation*, *in* THE POLITICS OF REGULATION, *supra* note 185, at 357, 357–72 (assessing non-economic reasons driving the politics of regulation).

189. *See* KATZMANN, INSTITUTIONAL DISABILITY, *supra* note 2, at 189 n.1 (arguing that in the case of the disability rights movement, "policy origination owe[d] little to 'interest group liberalism'").

190. *See* MARTHA DERTHICK & PAUL J. QUIRK, THE POLITICS OF DEREGULATION 16–19 (1985) (noting that industry interests were vehemently opposed to the deregulation of the air transport, trucking, and wireline telephone industries); Wilson, *supra* note 188, at 357–72 (reviewing various regulatory proposals and analyzing their sources of political support).

191. DAVID R. MAYHEW, CONGRESS: THE ELECTORAL CONNECTION 13 (1974).

192. *See, e.g.,* MELNICK, *supra* note 187, at 260 (noting that legislators' desires to advance what they believed to be good public policy were driving forces in the development of these policies as well as broader public opinion).

193. Martin D. Ginsburg, Luncheon Speech at the New York State Bar Association Tax Section Annual Meeting Luncheon (Jan. 24, 1991), *in Interbranch Relations, supra* note 15, at 293–95 (noting that in the area of tax legislation, many provisions in the committee reports are not read by members of Congress).

194. Observing that he was "considerably involved in writing" the "uniform capitalization rules" on authors, Senator Moynihan contended that the rules—designed to provide a better matching of income and expenses of manufacturing property—did not apply to books. Daniel Patrick Moynihan, Letter to the Editor, *How To Tell a Manufacturer from a Writer,* N.Y. TIMES, Sept. 6, 1987, at E14. However, a footnote in a conference committee report that later became law did appear to encompass books. Senator Moynihan was moved to write:

> I was a member of the conference committee. I do not ever recall the subject's having been raised, nor does any senator or representative with whom I've talked. My best guess is that staff members wrote it into the report thinking it was *already* law. . . . It is not law, and must not be construed as law.

Id.

195. Joan Biskupic, *Congress Keeps Eye on Justices as Court Watches Hill's Words,* 49 CONG. Q. WKLY. REP. 2863, 2863 (1991).

196. *Id.*

197. When Justice Scalia rebuked Justice Alito's use of legislative history in *Zedner v. United States,* 547 U.S. 489, 509–11 (Scalia, J., concurring in part and concurring in the judgment), the mainstream media took notice. *See* Tony Mauro, *Alito the Latest To Feel Scalia's Sting,* LEGAL TIMES, June 12, 2006, at 8.

198. Hughes Aircraft Co. v. Jacobson, 525 U.S. 432, 438 (1999); *see also* United States v. Gayle, 342 F.3d 89, 92 (2d Cir. 2003) ("Statutory construction begins with the plain text and, if that text is unambiguous, it usually ends there as well.").

199. Citizens to Preserve Overton Park v. Volpe, 401 U.S. 402, 412 n.29 (1971) (emphasis added).

200. Exxon Mobil Corp. v. Allapattah Servs., Inc., 545 U.S. 546, 568 (2005) (quoting Patricia M. Wald, *Some Observations on the Use of Legislative History in the 1981 Supreme Court Term,* 68 IOWA L. REV. 195, 214 (1983)).

201. *See, e.g.*, William N. Eskridge, Jr. & Lauren E. Baer, *The Continuum of Defer-ence: Supreme Court Treatment of Agency Statutory Interpretation from* Chevron *to* Hamdan, 97 GEO. L.J. 1083, 1135–36 (2008) (noting that the Supreme Court uses legislative history in the *Chevron* inquiry).

202. *See generally* FRANK B. CROSS, THE THEORY AND PRACTICE OF STAT-UTORY INTERPRETATION 59 (2009) (noting that even proponents of legisla-tive history acknowledge that its use must be grounded first in the text, for they "do not disregard the text, they seek to illuminate it"); James J. Brudney, *Confir-matory Legislative History*, 76 BROOK. L. REV. 901 (2011) (discussing the use of legislative history as a tool for judges to confirm and complete conclusions they have already reached); James J. Brudney & Corey Ditslear, *The Decline and Fall of Legislative History? Patterns of Supreme Court Reliance in the Berger and Rehnquist Eras*, 89 JUDICATURE 220 (2006) (noting the sharp decline in the Court's interest in legislative history over time); James J. Brudney & Corey Ditslear, *The Warp and Woof of Statutory Interpretation: Comparing Supreme Court Approaches in Tax Law and Workplace Law*, 58 DUKE L.J. 1231 (2009) (identifying an overall decline in the use of legislative history, but pointing out that the Court continues to use legislative history to identify congressional bargains or to borrow expertise from a more knowledgeable branch, depending on the substantive area of law); Michael H. Koby, *The Supreme Court's Declining Reliance on Legislative History: The Impact of Justice Scalia's Critique*, 36 HARV. J. ON LEGIS. 369, 369 (1999) (positing that Justice Scalia has "contributed signifi-cantly to a sharp reduction in the Court's use of legislative history").

203. *Nomination of Ruth Bader Ginsburg, To Be Associate Justice of the Supreme Court of the United States: Hearings Before the S. Comm. on the Judiciary*, 103d Cong. 224 (1993).

204. *See* Elena Kagan, *Presidential Administration*, 114 HARV. L. REV. 2245, 2255 (2001) (discussing the inability or unwillingness of Congress to legislate specific solutions to problems and noting its preference for general delegations of power); Rubin, *supra* note 111, at 411 (expressing a preference for goal-oriented statutes that leave the precise implementation to agencies, given the complexity of the issues that face Congress).

205. Richard B. Stewart, *Beyond Delegation Doctrine*, 36 AM. U. L. REV. 323, 331 (1987).

206. *See* Daniel J. Meltzer, *The Supreme Court's Judicial Passivity*, 2002 SUP. CT. REV. 343, 387 ("An absence of textual specification may equally reflect the incapacity of legislators, no matter how willing to try to resolve statutory uncertainties, to anticipate all of the uncertainties that will arise, as well as the difficulties of crafting language that, in the myriad context to which it is applied, will avoid ambiguity.").

207. HERBERT KAUFMAN, TIME, CHANCE AND ORGANIZATIONS: NATU-RAL SELECTION IN A PERILOUS ENVIRONMENT 52 (1985).

208. *See* Elizabeth Garrett, *Legal Scholarship in the Age of Legislation*, 34 TULSA L.J. 679, 688 (1999) (calling for more empirical scholarship on how Congress func-tions to test theories such as textualism).

209. As scholars have pointed out, the records of the Constitutional Convention consulted by textualists are incomplete. *See, e.g.,* James H. Hutson, *The Creation of the Constitution: The Integrity of the Documentary Record,* 63 TEX. L. REV. 1 (1986).

210. James J. Brudney, *Intentionalism's Revival,* 44 SAN DIEGO L. REV. 1001, 1009–10 (2007); Jonathan R. Siegel, *The Use of Legislative History in a System of Separated Powers,* 53 VAND. L. REV. 1457, 1480 (2000). *But see* Manning, *supra* note 174, at 706–25 (arguing that interpretative reliance on legislative history creates an opportunity for legislative self-delegation, contrary to the clear assumption of constitutional structure).

211. *See supra* note 104 and accompanying text (noting established drafting rules and practices in the Senate and House). For an interesting view suggesting that Congress could legislate doctrines of statutory construction, see Nicholas Quinn Rosenkranz, *Federal Rules of Statutory Interpretation,* 115 HARV. L. REV. 2085 (2002).

212. Brudney, *supra* note 202, at 1010.

213. *Confirmation Hearing on the Nomination of John G. Roberts, Jr. To Be Chief Justice of the United States: Hearing Before the S. Comm. on the Judiciary,* 109th Cong. 319 (2005) (statement of Sen. Charles E. Grassley).

214. Hatch, *supra* note 165, at 43.

215. JEREMY WALDRON, THE DIGNITY OF LEGISLATION 5 (1999).

216. *See* JAMES OLDHAM, ENGLISH COMMON LAW IN THE AGE OF MANSFIELD 31–32 (2004) (discussing Mansfield's legislative and judicial experience). For this reference, I am grateful to Professor Bernadette Meyler of Cornell Law School.

217. Magistrate Judge Edward G. Bryant of Tennessee was a member of the House of Representatives from Tennessee, and Judge Gregory Carman of the Court of International Trade was a member of the House of Representatives from New York. In the 1980s, judges who had been members of Congress included Frank M. Coffin, Abner Mikva, Thomas Meskill, James L. Buckley, Donald Russell, Oren Harris, Charles Wiggins, William Hungate, and Gregory Carman.

Several federal judges have had substantial legislative experience as congressional staffers, including Justice Breyer, but they comprise a small percentage of judges as a whole. On this point, I am grateful to Daniel Holt of the Federal Judicial Center's History Office, see E-mail from Richard Jaffe to author (Oct. 12, 2011, 17:50 EST) (on file with the *New York University Law Review*), as well as to Judge Richard Eaton of the Court of International Trade, himself a former congressional chief of staff, and to Richard Jaffe of the Administrative Office of the U.S. Courts, for their insights.

218. Representative Alcee Hastings of Florida was a federal district court judge, and Senator John Cornyn of Texas was a Texas Supreme Court justice. Legislators who clerked for federal judges include Senator Richard Blumenthal of Connecticut, Senator Kirsten Gillibrand of New York, Senator Mike Lee of Utah, and Representative Judy Biggert of Illinois.

219. M. DOUGLASS BELLIS, FED. JUDICIAL CTR., STATUTORY STRUC-
TURE AND LEGISLATIVE DRAFTING CONVENTIONS: A PRIMER FOR
JUDGES (2008), *available at* http://www.fjc.gov/public/pdf.nsf/lookup/draftcon.
pdf/$file/draftcon.pdf.
220. *See supra* notes 185–91 and accompanying text.
221. *See* JUDICIAL CONFERENCE OF THE U.S., LONG RANGE PLAN FOR
THE FEDERAL COURTS 126 (1995), *available at* http://www.uscourts.gov/
uscourts/FederalCourts/Publications/FederalCourtsLongRangePlan.pdf (pro-
posing a checklist of potential technical problems for use by legislative staff);
JOSEPH F. WEIS, JR. ET AL., REPORT OF THE FEDERAL COURTS
STUDY COMMITTEE 91–92 (1990), *available at* http://www.fjc.gov/public/pdf.
nsf/lookup/repfcsc.pdf/$file/repfcsc.pdf (same); Peter H. Schuck, *Trimming Liti-
gation*, AM. LAW., Dec. 2008, at 79 (discussing the cost savings and other benefits
of a checklist aimed at common, inadvertent problems with legislative drafting).
222. 28 U.S.C. § 1658(a) (2006).
223. Ledbetter v. Goodyear Tire & Rubber Co., 500 U.S. 618, 643, 667 (2007) (Ginsburg, J., dissenting) ("As in 1991, the Legislature may act to correct this Court's
parsimonious reading of Title VII.").
224. *See* William N. Eskridge, Jr., *Overriding Supreme Court Statutory Interpretation
Decisions*, 101 YALE L.J. 331, 334 (1991) ("Congress and its committees are aware
of the Court's statutory decisions, devote significant efforts toward analyzing their
policy implications, and override those decisions with a frequency heretofore
unreported."); Michael E. Solimine & James L. Walker, *The Next Word: Congressional
Response to Supreme Court Statutory Decisions*, 65 TEMP. L. REV. 425, 425 (1992)
(noting Congress's willingness to override Supreme Court decisions with which it
disagrees).
225. Ruth Bader Ginsburg, *Communicating and Commenting on the Court's Work*, 83
GEO. L.J. 2119, 2125 (1995).
226. *Id.* (footnote omitted).
227. HENRY J. FRIENDLY, *The Gap in Lawmaking—Judges Who Can't and Legislators Who Won't, in* BENCHMARKS 41, 49 (1967).
228. *Id.* at 47.
229. *Id.* at 47–48.
230. *Id.* at 58.
231. James L. Buckley, Commentary, *The Perspective of a Judge and Former Legislator*,
85 GEO. L.J. 2223, 2224 (1997).
232. For a review of such mechanisms, especially in the states, see Shirley S.
Abrahmson & Robert L. Hughes, *Shall We Dance? Steps For Legislators and
Judges in Statutory Interpretation*, 75 MINN. L. REV. 1045, 1059–81 (1991), where
the author discusses mechanisms for legislative monitoring of judicial opinions
interpreting statutes.
233. Ruth Bader Ginsburg & Peter W. Huber, *The Intercircuit Committee*, 100 HARV.
L. REV. 1417, 1428, 1432 (1987) (internal quotation marks omitted).
234. *Interview with Chief Judge Frank M. Coffin*, THE THIRD BRANCH (Admin.
Office of the U.S. Courts, Washington, D.C.), June 1982, at 1, 6.

235. James L. Oakes, *Grace Notes on "Grace Under Pressure,"* 50 OHIO ST. L.J. 701, 714–15 (1989).

236. Wilfred Feinberg, *A National Court of Appeals?*, 42 BROOK. L. REV. 611, 627 (1976) (recognizing that if conflicts among the circuits can be brought to Congress's attention, then they may be easily resolved by a "formal expression of legislative intent").

237. *See* John Paul Stevens, *Some Thoughts on Judicial Restraint*, 66 JUDICATURE 177, 183 (1982) (discussing the efficiency and appropriateness of a congressional role in the resolution of intercircuit conflicts on questions of statutory construction).

238. Benjamin N. Cardozo, *A Ministry of Justice*, 35 HARV. L. REV. 113, 114 (1921) (citing Roscoe Pound, *Juristic Problems of National Progress*, 22 AM. J. SOC. 721, 729, 731 (1917)); 9 THE WORKS OF JEREMY BENTHAM 597–612 (John Bowring ed., 1843)); *see also* Larry Kramer, *"The One-Eyed Are Kings": Improving Congress's Ability To Regulate the Use of Judicial Resources*, 54 LAW & CONTEMP. PROBS. 73, 90–97 (1991) (discussing the need for an interbranch agency to reconcile discrepancies between Congress and the judiciary).

239. FRIENDLY, *supra* note 227, at 62.

240. *See supra* note 3 and accompanying text (discussing the work of the Governance Institute).

241. Ginsburg & Huber, *supra* note 233, at 1428.

242. Here, I draw upon Katzmann & Wheeler, *A Mechanism for "Statutory Housekeeping,"* *supra* note 3 (arguing that Congress finds helpful the courts of appeals' program, which serves to alert Congress of potential drafting problems).

243. At the time, I was president of the Governance Institute and a Brookings Institution fellow, and taught at Georgetown.

244. Proceedings of the Forty-Ninth Judiciary Conf. of the D.C. Cir., 124 F.R.D. 241, 312–36 (1988).

245. KATZMANN, COURTS AND CONGRESS, *supra* note 3, at 73–74.

246. *Id.* at 76–77 (noting the meeting between congressional members and D.C. Circuit Judges Wald, Buckley, Ginsburg, and Mikva).

247. *See* William H. Rehnquist, *Chief Justice Issues 1992 Year-End Report*, 25 THIRD BRANCH 1, 5–6 (Jan. 1993) (noting that the Supreme Court decided in 1993 to make the pilot project permanent).

248. *See* JUDICIAL CONFERENCE OF THE U.S., *supra* note 221, at 127 (setting out Implementation Strategy 91e). The early days of the project were the subject of a special report in the *Georgetown Law Journal. See* Robert A. Katzmann & Stephanie M. Herseth, Special Report, *An Experiment in Statutory Communication Between Courts and Congress: A Progress Report*, 85 GEO. L.J. 2189 (1997). The issue included individual commentaries by M. Douglass Bellis, Frank Burk, Mark J. Langer, and Judge James L. Buckley. *See* M. Douglass Bellis, Commentary, *A View from the House of Representatives*, 85 GEO. L.J. 2209 (1997); Frank Burk, Commentary, *Statutory Housekeeping: A Senate Perspective*, 85 GEO. L.J. 2217 (1997); Mark J. Langer, Commentary, *Implementing the Project: A Court Administrator's Role*, 85 GEO. L.J. 2219

(1997); James L. Buckley, Commentary, *The Perspective of a Judge and Former Legislator*, 85 GEO. L.J. 2223 (1997).

249. The Offices of Legislative Counsel in the House and the Senate are nonpartisan units that provide confidential drafting services requested by individual legislators and legislative committees. *See* OFFICE OF LEGISLATIVE COUNSEL, U.S. HOUSE OF REPRESENTATIVES, http://www.house.gov/legcoun/; OFFICE OF LEGISLATIVE COUNSEL, U.S. SENATE, http://slc.senate.gov/index.htm. Background of the legislative counsels' interest in the project is set forth in Memorandum from James C. Duff, Dir., Admin. Office of U.S. Courts, D. Brock Hornby, J., U.S. Dist. Court for Dist. of Me., & Robert A. Katzmann, J., U.S. Court of Appeals for the Second Circuit, to Judges, U.S. Courts of Appeal, and Clerks of Court, U.S. Courts of Appeal, Project To Provide Congress with Appellate Opinions Bearing on Technical Matters of Statutory Construction 1, 2 (July 19, 2007) [hereinafter Memorandum from Duff, Hornby & Katzmann] (on file with the *New York University Law Review*).

250. The Memorandum also announced that the Administrative Office's Assistant General Counsel would help institutionalize the project by tracking the number of opinions sent and consulting periodically with the legislative counsels and the appellate courts as to whether the project needed adjustment. Memorandum from Duff, Hornby & Katzmann, *supra* note 249, at 2.

251. *See* Memorandum from Russell R. Wheeler, President, Governance Institute, on Statutory Housekeeping Project 5–28 (Aug. 1, 2011) (on file with the *New York University Law Review*) (providing a list and description of cases).

252. Rotimi v. Holder, 577 F.3d 133, 134 (2d Cir. 2009) (upholding a Board of Immigration Appeals decision that held that an applicant for a waiver of inadmissibility had not "lawfully resided continuously" in the United States as required by the statute during the period in which his visitor visa had expired, and noting that the fact that the applicant had applied for asylum and for adjustment of status had no bearing).

253. *See* Ross-Tousey v. Neary (*In re* Ross-Tousey), 549 F.3d 1148, 1150 (7th Cir. 2008) (holding that "an above-median-income debtor who has no monthly vehicle loan or lease payment can claim a vehicle ownership expense deduction when calculating . . . disposable income"). *But see* Ransom v. MBNA, Am. Bank, N.A. (*In re* Ransom), 577 F.3d 1026, 1031–32 (9th Cir. 2009) (holding that a debtor is not entitled to a vehicle ownership expense deduction for a vehicle that he owned free and clear of liens). In January 2011, the Supreme Court held that car owners are not entitled to the deduction. *See* Ransom v. FIA Card Servs., N.A., 131 S. Ct. 716, 730 (2011) (holding that a debtor who does not make loan or lease payments may not take the car ownership deduction).

254. *See* United States v. Dixon, 551 F.3d 578, 582–83 (7th Cir. 2008) (holding that section 2250 of the Act does not require that the defendant's travel postdate the Act), *rev'd*, 130 S. Ct. 2229 (2010).

255. *See* Carr v. United States, 130 S. Ct. 2229, 2242 (2010) (holding that section 2250 does not apply to sex offenders whose interstate travel occurred before the Sex Offender Registration and Notification Act's effective date).

256. *See* United States v. Vasquez, 611 F.3d 325, 328 (7th Cir. 2010) (holding that the government was not required to prove that the defendant had specific knowledge that he was required to register under the Sex Offender Registration and Notification Act).

257. Class Action Fairness Act of 2005, Pub. L. No. 109-2, 119 Stat. 4 (codified as amended in scattered sections of 28 U.S.C.).

258. 28 U.S.C. § 1453(c)(1) (2006) (effective Feb. 18, 2005).

259. Morgan v. Gay, 466 F.3d 276, 277 (3d Cir. 2006).

260. *See* Spivey v. Vertrue, Inc., 528 F.3d 982, 983–84 (7th Cir. 2008) (noting that an imprecisely stated deadline in the statute does not constitute a sufficient basis for courts to simply disregard the language of the actual statute).

261. Statutory Time-Periods Technical Amendments Act of 2009, Pub. L. No. 111-16, 123 Stat. 1607, 1608 (to be codified at 28 U.S.C. § 1453(c)(1)).

262. Memorandum from Duff, Hornby & Katzmann, *supra* note 249, at 3 attach.1.

263. *Id.*

264. *See id.* at 2 ("[T]he opinions help Congress understand how statutes may be drafted to make legislative intent as clear as possible. . . . The House and Senate legislative counsel . . . are principally responsible for analyzing the drafting issues identified in each opinion. . . .").

265. *Id.*

266. *See* Bellis, *supra* note 248, at 2209 (noting that the House Office of Legislative Counsel has been "involved with the project since its inception"); Burk, *supra* note 248, at 2217 (noting that the Senate Office of Legislative Counsel's participation in the project "has been a success").

267. *See, e.g.*, Letter from Rep. Thomas S. Foley, U.S.H.R. Speaker, Richard A. Gephardt, U.S. Sen. Majority Leader, & Sen. Robert H. Michel, U.S. Sen. Republican Leader, to David Meade, Legis. Couns. (Sept. 28, 1992), *in Interbranch Relations*, *supra* note 15, at 309 (1993); Letter from George J. Mitchell, U.S. Sen. Majority Leader, Robert Dole, U.S. Sen. Republican Leader, & Robert C. Byrd, U.S. Sen. President Pro Tempore, to Frank L. Burk, Jr., Legis. Couns., U.S. Sen., *in Interbranch Relations*, *supra* note 15, at 310; H.R. Rep. No. 103-413(I), at 25 (1993) (encouraging "the appropriate committees of jurisdiction in the House and Senate to monitor regularly and systematically Federal court decisions and to report periodically to their respective Chambers on the significant issues that merit review in this relationship"); S. Rep. 103-215(I) (1993); Letter from John Conyers, Jr., U.S.H.R. Chairman of Judiciary Comm. & Lamar S. Smith, U.S.H.R. Ranking Member, to M. Pope Barrow, Legis. Couns., U.S.H.R. 2 (May 23, 2007) (on file with the *New York University Law Review*) (recommending that the Office of Legislative Counsel "continue its participation in the project") [hereinafter Conyers & Smith Letter]; Letter from Orrin Hatch, Chairman, U.S. Sen. Comm. on the Judiciary, & Patrick Leahy, Ranking Democratic Member, U.S. Sen. Comm. on the Judiciary, to James Fransen, Legis. Couns., U.S. Sen. (Mar. 21, 2001) (on file with the *New York University Law Review*); Letter from Patrick Leahy, Chairman, U.S. Sen. Comm. on the Judiciary, and Arlen Specter, Ranking Republican Member, U.S. Sen. Comm. on the Judiciary, to James

Fransen, Legis. Couns., U.S. Sen. (Feb. 14, 2007) [hereinafter Leahy & Specter Letter] (on file with the *New York University Law Review*) (recommending that the Office of Legislative Counsel "continue its participation in the project").

268. Email from Danielle Cutrona, Chief Nominations Counsel for Senator Jeff Sessions, Senate Judiciary Comm., to author (Sept. 14, 2010, 10:41 EST) (indicating Senator Jeff Sessions's remarks to the Judiciary).

269. Burk, *supra* note 248, at 2217.

270. *Id.*

271. *See Feedback Requested on Technical Aspects of Law,* 39 THIRD BRANCH 7, 9 (Aug. 2007), *available at* http://www.uscourts.gov/News/TheThird-Branch/07-08-01/Feedback_Requested_on_Technical_Aspects_of_Laws.aspx (discussing how Fransen believes in the usefulness of the project).

272. *Id.*

273. Bellis, *supra* note 248, at 2215.

274. Katzmann & Wheeler, *A Mechanism for "Statutory Housekeeping," supra* note 3, at 140.

275. Bellis, *supra* note 248, at 2213.

276. *Id.*

277. Robert Katzmann & Russell Wheeler, *More About the "Statutory Housekeeping Project,"* IN CAMERA, FED. JUDGES ASS'N (Fed. Judges Ass'n), Aug. 31, 2010, *available at* http://www.federaljudgesassoc.org/egov/docs/newsletters/38_167_716.asp; *Feedback on Technical Matters Aids Legislation,* 42 THE THIRD BRANCH 4 (Admin. Office of the U.S. Courts, Washington, D.C.), Feb. 2010, at 4, *available at* http://www.uscourts.gov/News/TheThirdBranch/TTB-Viewer.aspx?doc=/uscourts/news/ttb/archive/2010-02%20Feb.pdf.

278. Conyers & Smith Letter, *supra* note 267; Leahy & Specter Letter, *supra* note 267.

279. The Administrative Conference of the United States, currently chaired by the well-known legal scholar and administrator, Paul Verkuil, is an independent federal agency dedicated to improving the administrative process. ADMIN. CONFERENCE OF THE U.S., http://www.acus.gov/ (last visited Apr. 26, 2012).

280. *See* Stephen F. Ross, *Where Have You Gone Karl Llewellyn? Should Congress Turn Its Lonely Eyes to You?* 45 VAND. L. REV. 561, 575–76 (1992) (noting that conference committee reports are signed by members).

281. Robert A. Katzmann, *Summary of Proceedings, in* JUDGES AND LEGISLATORS, *supra* note 3, at 167.

282. Hatch, *supra* note 165, at 48.

283. THE FEDERALIST NO. 62, *supra* note 51, at 445 (James Madison).

Marsha S. Berzon is a judge of the U.S. Court of Appeals for the Ninth Circuit.

Michael Boudin is a judge and former chief judge of the U.S. Court of Appeals for the First Circuit.

Stephen Breyer is a Justice of the U.S. Supreme Court and former chief judge of the U.S. Court of Appeals for the First Circuit.

Guido Calabresi is a senior judge and former chief judge of the U.S. Court of Appeals for the Second Circuit.

Robert H. Henry is president of Oklahoma City University and former chief judge of the U.S. Court of Appeals for the Tenth Circuit.

Robert A. Katzmann is a judge of the U.S. Court of Appeals for the Second Circuit and shortly will become chief judge of the circuit.

Pierre N. Leval is a senior judge of the U.S. Court of Appeals for the Second Circuit.

M. Blane Michael was a judge of the U.S. Court of Appeals for the Fourth Circuit.

David S. Tatel is a judge of the U.S. Court of Appeals for the District of Columbia Circuit.

J. Harvie Wilkinson III is a senior judge and former chief judge of the U.S. Court of Appeals for the Fourth Circuit.

Diane P. Wood is a judge of the U.S. Court of Appeals for the Seventh Circuit and shortly will become chief judge of the circuit.

Norman Dorsen is Stokes Professor of Law and Codirector of the Arthur Garfield Hays Civil Liberties Program at New York University School of Law. He is also counselor to the president of New York University. He has directed the James Madison lecture series since 1977. Professor Dorsen was the founding president of the Society of American Law Teachers 1971-1973 and president of the American Civil Liberties Union 1976-1991.

Catharine DeJulio is an associate in the law firm of Sidley Austin LLP. She received her J.D. from New York University School of Law in 2011. During law school, she served as editor-in-chief of the *New York University Law Review.*

INDEX

Abortion, 39, 229. See also *Roe v. Wade*

Active liberty: campaign finance reform and, 13–14; consequential approach and, 17; democratic self-government and, 8–9, 13–14, 16–17; emphasis on, 8–10; federalism and, 17–21; free speech and, 13–14, 16; positive liberty and, 31n9; protection of, 13; statutory drafting and, 25–28. *See also* Ancient liberty

Act of Frauds of 1662, 246–47

Act of Frauds of 1696, 247

Adams, John: citizen participation and, 8, 31; Otis inspiring, 248, 250

The Administrative Behavior of Federal Bureau Chiefs (Kaufman), 308

Administrative Conference of the United States, 332, 356n279

Administrative Office of the U.S. Courts, 325, 354n250

Administrative Procedure Act, 58, 300

Affirmative constitutional adjudication, in federal courts: aversion to retrospective relief and, 230–34; *Bell v. Hood*, 216, 218–19, 230; *Bivens v. Six Unknown Named Agents of the Federal Bureau of Narcotics*, 209–10, 216–24, 226–27, 230–33; *Bolling v. Sharpe*, 209–11, 214, 226, 237nn20–21; Brennan and, 207, 234–35; *Brown v. Board of Education*, 209–11, 214, 226, 231;

cause of action and, 208, 210–12, 214, 216, 218–19, 222–28; constitutional text and, 222–27; direct constitutional cases at law, 214–16, 238n41; direct constitutional cases in equity, 212–14, 238n41, 242n107; dormant Commerce Clause and, 228–31; early claims under Constitution, 211–16; *Ex Parte Young*, 212–14, 226, 234; historical foundations of, 209–16; introduction to, 207–9; mid-century cases, 209–11; modern cases, 216–30; separation of powers and, 222–27; suits against federal officers, unconstitutional law and, 229–30, 239n42; Supremacy Clause and, 199, 227–28, 231

Affordable Care Act, 3

Agencies: Congress and, 111, 307–11; separation of powers strained by, 110–12; statutes interpreted by, 307–11; Supreme Court and, 310

Agnew, Spiro, 93n101

Agostini v. Felton, 85

Agriculture laws, 15

Alden v. Maine, 114

Alexander v. Holmes County Board of Education, 63, 66

Alexander v. Sandoval, 218, 220–21

Alien Contract Labor Act, 312–13

Alito, Samuel, 346n164, 349n197

>> 361

Amendment process, 128–29
Americans with Disabilities Act of 1990, 300, 316
Ancient liberty: Constant and, 5, 7, 9, 11, 13, 18; defined, 7; emphasis on, 8–10; judicial modesty and, 10–11; modern liberty and, 5–6, 9
Antidiscrimination laws, 15
Appeal, lack of, 147
Appellate federal judges, Madison lectures delivered by, 6n4
Appropriations committees, 304
"Arising under" test, 175
Arizonans for Official English v. Arizona, 46
Arizona v. Gant, 256–57
Arkansas, school desegregation in, 62, 90n51, 91n54
Article I: Contracts Clause in, 212; democratic self-government and, 8–9; individual rights in, 114, 215; separation of powers and, 109, 113, 198, 324
Article II, 109
Article III: Case or Controversy Clause of, 229; individual rights in, 114; separation of powers and, 109, 145, 208, 214, 222, 225–26, 233
Article IV: democratic self-government and, 8; guarantees of, 110; individual rights in, 114
Article VI: guarantees of, 110; Supremacy Clause of, 199
Articles of Confederation, 303
Atkins v. Georgia, 124
Authoritative legislative history, 316, 332

Bailyn, Bernard, 29
Baker, Howard, 69
Balance, of federal and state courts: certification and, 42–44, 46, 50n23, 50n26, 50n30; criminal law in, 38–41, 47; federal claims in, 38, 47; history of, 37–38; pillars of, 38–47; private law in, 38, 41–44, 47; restoration of, 4, 47–48; state action in, 38, 44–47
Balliol College, 275
Bankruptcy, 329
Barapind v. Enomoto, 140, 153

Barrow, M. Pope, 331
Beale, Joseph, 170
Bellis, M. Douglass, 325, 331
Bell v. Hood, 216, 218–19, 230
Bentham, Jeremy, 328
Berlin, Isaiah, 31n9
Better law, 28
Biden, Joseph, 317
Biggert, Judy, 351n218
Bill of Rights: individual rights in, 114–15, 276; Madison and, 225, 250; usefulness of, 263. *See also specific amendments*
The Bill of Rights as a Code of Criminal Procedure (Friendly), 176
Bills, making of, 305–7
Bivens v. Six Unknown Named Agents of the Federal Bureau of Narcotics: affirmative constitutional adjudication in, 209–10, 216–24, 226–27, 230–33; Brennan and, 217–20, 222; Harlan, John Marshall, II, and, 217, 219–20, 222, 231–32; scope of, 4–5
Black, Hugo: dual sovereignty-double jeopardy and, 49n20; first Madison lecture by, 2, 263; Friendly and, 184; on Harlan, John Marshall, II, 275; liberalism of, 6n3, 276–77, 294n76; *Poe v. Ullman* and, 278; *Roe v. Wade* and, 277; on wiretapping, 252–53
Blackmun, Harry, 70
Blackstone, William, 123
Blumenthal, Richard, 351n218
Board of Education v. Dowell: fundamental problem with, 59, 87; lack of explanation in, 84–87; school desegregation and, 56, 58–60, 72–78, 81, 83–87, 104n267
Bolling v. Sharpe: affirmative constitutional adjudication and, 209–11, 214, 226, 237nn20–21; Fifth Amendment and, 209–11, 237n20
Book of Common Prayer, 181
Bork, Robert, 282, 287–90
Bowers v. Hardwick, 2
Boyd v. United States, 255–56
Boykin v. Alabama, 153–55, 164nn56–57, 164nn66–68
Bradley, Joseph, 255–56

Bradwell v. Illinois, 128
Brady Act, 40
Brandeis, Louis: constitutional formalism
overthrown by, 1; Friendly and, 170, 182–
83, 187n47; on lawmaking, 146; liberalism
of, 294n76; *Olmstead v. United States*
and, 246, 285; on wiretapping, 255–56
Brennan, William: affirmative constitutional adjudication and, 207, 234–35;
*Bivens v. Six Unknown Named Agents
of the Federal Bureau of Narcotics* and,
217–20, 222; civil liberties reexamined
by, 2; *Davis v. Passman* and, 219–20; habeas corpus and, 178; liberalism of, 6n3;
liberty and, 2, 118, 178; *Moore v. City of
East Cleveland* and, 118; *Poe v. Ullman*
and, 278; *Wright v. City of Emporia* and,
97n142
Brewer, David Josiah, 313
Breyer, Stephen, 314, 322, 343n132; legislative
experience of, 351n217; *Saucier* rule and,
168n91
Briefing, absence of, 147
Brown v. Board of Education: affirmative
constitutional adjudication and, 209–11,
214, 226, 231; candor and, 179; Fourteenth
Amendment and, 210; Friendly and, 183;
interposition doctrine and, 61, 90n44;
Plessy v. Ferguson and, 60–61, 85, 128;
school desegregation and, 5, 56, 60–66,
68–74, 83–85, 91nn55–56, 97n142, 231,
300; second decision, 61, 63, 83; statutes
and, 300
Bryant, Edward G., 351n217
Buckley, James, 327, 339n99, 351n217
Buckley v. Valeo, 110–11
Buckner, Emory, 171
Burger, Warren: Fourth Amendment and,
256–57; individual rights and, 118, 130n37,
199; judicial activism and, 290; school
desegregation and, 67, 69–70, 83, 97n132
Burk, Frank, 330–31
Bush, George H. W., 55, 72
Bush v. Gore, 3, 56, 193
Busing: decreased miles of, 91n64; in school
desegregation, 59, 64–70, 74, 77, 85,
91n64, 94n105, 99n184

Cable subscribers, caps on, 57
Cahn, Edmond, 2
Calabresi, Guido, 300
Camden, Lord, 249, 259
Campaign finance reform: active liberty and,
13–14; free speech and, 11–15; judicial
modesty and, 14
Campbell v. Acuff-Rose Music, Inc., 151
Canadian courts, 37
Candor, 178–80
Cannon v. University of Chicago, 218, 220–21,
225–26
Cardozo, Benjamin N., 139, 153, 180, 184,
281, 328
Carlson v. Greene, 223
Carman, Gregory, 351n217
Carroll v. United States, 253
Carr v. United States, 346n161
Carswell, G. Harrold, 68
Case, question beyond, 149–50
Case or Controversy Clause, 229
Cause of action: affirmative constitutional
adjudication and, 208, 210–12, 214, 216,
218–19, 222–29; *Erie R.R. Co. v. Tompkins*
and, 223–24; origin of, 222–23, 237n22,
240n66; terminology, 235n12
Certification, 42–44, 46, 50n23, 50n26,
50n30
Certiorari jurisdiction, 38, 44, 102n234
Chafee, Zechariah, 170
Chapman v. United States, 285
*Chevron v. Natural Resources Defense
Council*, 26–27
Church of the Holy Trinity v. United States,
312–13
*Church of the Lukumi Babalu Aye, Inc. v. City
of Hialeah*, 121
Citizen participation, in government, 8,
30 31
Civil liberties: lower federal courts and, 45;
new phase of, 1; reexamination of, 1–2
Civil Rights Act of 1871, 210
Civil Rights Act of 1964, 65, 299–300
Civil Rights Cases, 60
Civil statutes, 326
Civil War Amendments, 9, 115, 126
Clark, Charles E., 50n26, 187n47

Clark, Tom C., 278

Class Action Fairness Act of 2005, 329–30

Clean Air Act, 300

Clean Water Act, 300

Cleary, Gottlieb, Friendly & Cox, 171

Coffin, Frank, 297, 304, 327–28, 345n150, 351n217

Cohens v. Virginia, 161n16

Coker v. Georgia, 123

Commandeering decisions, of Congress, 17, 19

Commerce Clause: Affordable Care Act and, 3; Congress's power under, 3, 17, 19, 39, 125–26, 198, 205n14, 229; direct constitutional cases in equity and, 212–13; dormant, 20–21, 198–99, 228–31; Marshall, John, and, 125–26; Rehnquist Court and, 205n14

Committee on the Judicial Branch of the Judicial Conference of the United States, 297

Committee system, 303–7

Common law: evolution of, 251–52, 266n64; Fourth Amendment and, 251–55, 267n81; frozen, 251–55; Seventh Amendment and, 251, 266n69; tradition, 173, 290

Communications laws, 15

Community, Constitution and, 199–200

Complainantless crimes, 267n79

Computer searches, 260–61, 269n127, 270n140

Concreteness, 147

Confirmation process, 201, 308–9, 317, 346n164, 346n167

Congress: agencies and, 111, 307–11; commandeering decisions of, 17, 19; Commerce Clause and, 3, 17, 19, 39, 125–26, 198, 205n14, 229; committee system of, 303–7; Constitution creating and limiting, 224–25, 302; default positions, 326; flexibility in, 20; House of Representatives, 304–5; hypothetical desire of, 26–28; lawmaking process and, 301–7, 326–32; legislative history and, 310–11, 313, 316; legislative veto, 110–12, 309; 111th, 304–5; polarization of, 304; spending power of, 198; state legislatures

and, 17, 19; statutes and, 298–333; war powers of, 112–13, 125. See also Senate

Congressional Budget and Impoundment Control Act of 1974, 112

Congressional Record, 319

Congressional Research Service, 325

Consent requirement, 22

Consequential approach: active liberty and, 17; federalism and, 20; literalists and, 29–30; objectivity and, 29; virtue of, 8, 10

Constant, Benjamin, 5, 7, 9, 11, 13, 18

Constitution, of Texas, 123, 127, 136n145

Constitution, U.S.: amendment process, 128–29; broader concept of, 1–2; community and, 199–200; Congress created and limited by, 224–25, 302; democratic self-government and, 8–9, 11–17, 28–31; dicta and, 145–46; dynamic approach to, 107–8, 113, 119–20, 127–29; early claims under, 211–16; embattled, 4; evolution of, 2–3, 107–8, 128; expectations of, 108–22; federal courts and, 37–38; formalism, 1; general objectives of, 8–9, 11, 13, 16–17, 28, 122; Holmes and, 1, 58; individual rights in, 114–22; interpretation of, 8, 29, 281; literalists and, 10, 29–30, 107, 113, 119, 125–27; as living tradition, 273–90; nationalism in, 197–99; originalist approach to, 4, 107–8, 125–27; as practical document, 24; structural rules, 109–14; in twenty-first century, 107–29; unity and, 196–200; unwritten, 108, 112, 122–24, 126–27. See also Affirmative constitutional adjudication; Bill of Rights; specific articles

Constitutional Convention, 287, 323, 351n209

Constitutional law: Friendly and, 4, 169–85; new phase of, 1; realism in, 170; rights and, 199; temperance in making, 182

Constitutional rulings, unnecessary, 157–58

Consumer protection laws, 15

Contextual deviation, 202

Contraceptives, 276–79

Contracts Clause, 212

Cooperative federalism, 18–19

Cooper v. Aaron, 62, 83, 91n55, 97n142

Copyright, 150–51

Cornyn, John, 351n218
Correctional Services Corp. v. Malesko, 221, 223
Counterfactual hypothesis, 150–51
Counter-majoritarian difficulty, 274
Courts: Canadian, 37; English, 226; European constitutional, 46–47, 52n46; experts appointed by, 162n27; in federalism, 37; law made by, 145–48, 156; role of, 55; state, 4; statutes and, 298–333; witnesses called by, 162n26. *See also specific courts*
Cox, Hugh, 171
Criminal law: in balance of federal and state courts, 38–41, 47; central objectives of, 177
Crowell v. Benson, 111
Customs: *Chevron v. Natural Resources Defense Council* and, 26–27; enforcement of, 246–47, 250, 257

Damages cases, 214–17, 230–34
Dartmouth Holmes Lecture, 180–81, 184
Data mining, 261–63
Davis v. Passman, 219–20
Dayton Board of Education v. Brinkman, 80, 104n267
D.C. Circuit, 57
Death penalty, 123–24
Decision making, market economics explaining, 319–20
Declarations and Understandings, of U.S., 121
Democracy, law's relationship to, 287
Democratic self-government: active liberty and, 8–9, 13–14, 16–17; Article I and, 8–9; Article IV and, 8; citizen participation in, 8, 30–31; Constitution and, 8–9, 11, 28–31; equal protection and, 24–25; federalism and, 17–21; Fifteenth Amendment and, 9; free speech in, 11–17; importance of, 30–31; Nineteenth Amendment and, 9; privacy in, 21–24; statutory drafting and, 25–28; Twenty-Fourth Amendment and, 9; Twenty-Sixth Amendment and, 9; voting rights in, 24–25
Dennis v. Higgins, 229

Dent, Harry, 97n132
Department of Health, Education, and Welfare (HEW), 65–66, 93n94
Desegregation. *See* School desegregation
Dewey, John, 179
Dicta: acceptance of, 152–55; appeals lacking in, 147; *Barapind v. Enomoto* and, 140, 153; *Boykin v. Alabama* and, 153–55, 164nn56–57, 164nn66–68; briefing absent in, 147; careful use of, 141, 159; common abuses of, 148–52; concreteness and, 147; Constitution and, 145–46; counterfactual hypothesis and, 150–51; defined, 142–44; erudite opinions and, 151–52; Friendly and, 139, 143; good faith immunity and, 156–59, 165n77; gratuitous statement of standards and, 151–52; holding distinguished from, 139–44, 153, 159, 161n18, 161n20; implications of, 4, 139–60; importance of, 141–42, 144, 159; lawmaking and, 145–48, 156; *McDonnell Douglas Corp. v. Green* and, 149–50, 163n38; *Myers v. Loudoun County Public Schools* and, 140–41, 160n14; non-dispositive determinations and, 152; question beyond case and, 149–50; stare decisis and, 142, 144; structural limitations of, 146–48; Supreme Court, 155–56, 160n14, 163n38
Disability Benefits Law, 227
Discrimination: Fifteenth Amendment and, 24–25; Fourteenth Amendment and, 24–25, 60, 82–83, 202; invidious, 24–25; laws against, 15; positive, 24–25
Diversity jurisdiction, 41–43
Dormant Commerce Clause, 21, 198–99; affirmative constitutional adjudication and, 228–31; judicial modesty and, 20; Supreme Court and, 228–29
Dorsen, Norman, 277, 314
Douglas, William O.: civil liberties reexamined by, 2; *Griswold v. Connecticut* and, 288; liberalism of, 6n3; *Poe v. Ullman* and, 278; *Wright v. City of Emporia* and, 97n142
Drafting, of statutes, 25–28, 326–32
Dred Scott v. Sandford, 60
Dual sovereignty-double jeopardy, 49n20

Due process: clause, 118, 124, 209, 212, 273, 278–80, 284, 288; Fifth Amendment and, 124, 209, 220; Fourteenth Amendment and, 118, 124, 212–13, 273–74, 276; Harlan, John Marshall, II, and, 273–74, 276–81, 283–84, 288, 292n34; individual rights and, 279; as living tradition, 283; *Poe v. Ullman* and, 278–79; *Reynolds v. Sim* and, 276
Duff, James, 329
Dynamic approach, to Constitution, 107–8, 113, 119–20, 127–29

Economic protectionism, 20
Education Amendments of 1972, 300
Ehrlichman, John, 67
Eighth Amendment, 123–24
Eighth Circuit, 80
Eisenhower, Dwight, 171, 275
Electronic Communications Privacy Act, 259
Electronic data: computer searches and, 260–61, 269n127, 270n140; Fourth Amendment and, 245–46, 257–63; government mining, 261–63
Eleventh Amendment, 17, 19, 110, 113–14, 116
Elk Grove v. Newdow, 140
Ellsworth, Oliver, 38
English courts, 226
Entick case, 249, 251, 254, 257, 259
Equal protection, 24–25
Equal Rights Amendment, 197
Equity, cases in, 212–14, 238n41, 242n107
Erie R.R. Co. v. Tompkins, 38, 41, 171, 174–75, 223–24
ERISA, 227
Erudite opinions, dicta and, 151–52
Eskridge, William N., Jr., 300, 333n6
Ethnicity, neutrality toward, 201–3
EU. *See* European Union
European constitutional courts, 46–47, 52n46
European Union (EU), 125
The Evolving Constitution, 2–3
Excessive fines, 123, 134n123
Ex Parte Young, 212–14, 226, 234
Experts, courts appointing, 162n27

Fallon, Richard, 226, 231
Faubus, Orval, 62, 90n51, 91n54
Federal authority, established, 9
Federal claims, in balance of federal and state courts, 38, 47
Federal courts: certification and, 42–43; Constitution and, 37–38; history of, 37–38; lower, civil liberties and, 45; Madison and, 37–38, 48, 208, 235; role of, 207–8, 222–27. *See also* Affirmative constitutional adjudication, in federal courts; Balance, of federal and state courts
The Federal Courts and the Federal System (Hart and Wechsler), 172
Federalism: active liberty and, 17–21; consequential approach and, 20; cooperative, 18–19; court system, 37; democratic self-government and, 17–21; Harlan, John Marshall, II, and, 276–77, 292n34; *Milliken II* and, 82; O'Connor and, 17; September 11 and, 19; toxic chemical regulation and, 18–20
Federalist Papers: constitutional standards and, 127; Madison and, 114, 273, 302, 311–12, 320; statutes and, 302, 311–12, 320, 324, 333
Federal Judicial Center, 325
Federal jurisdiction: "arising under" test for, 175; state courts and, 4
Federal Maritime Commission v. South Carolina State Ports Authority, 114
Federal officers, suits against, 229–30, 239n42
Federal Rules of Civil Procedure, 222–23
Federal Rules of Criminal Procedure, 155, 164n66, 164n68
Federal Trade Commission (FTC), 111
Feinberg, Wilfred, 41–42, 327–28
Felony in fact, 267n81
Fenno, Richard, Jr., 303
Ferejohn, John, 300
Fifteenth Amendment: democratic self-government and, 9; discrimination and, 24–25; passage of, 60
Fifth Amendment: *Bell v. Hood* and, 216; *Bolling v. Sharpe* and, 209–11, 237n20; due process and, 124, 209, 220; *Jacobs v.*

United States and, 215; liberty recognized in, 116; *Olmstead v. United States* and, 285

Fines, excessive, 123, 134n123

First Amendment, 57, 133n101, 183; campaign finance reform and, 12–14; democratic self-government and, 12–17; Fourteenth Amendment and, 283; individual rights in, 114–15; privacy and, 23; religion and, 121; role of, 13–15. *See also* Free speech

First Continental Congress, 250

Fisher, Louis, 309

Foreign law, 285–86

Formative history, 255–57, 259–61

Fourteenth Amendment, 17, 195, 237n19; *Brown v. Board of Education* and, 210; discrimination and, 24–25, 60, 82–83, 202; due process and, 118, 124, 212–13, 273–74, 276; First Amendment and, 283; liberty recognized in, 116, 132n81, 276; passage of, 60; Privileges or Immunities Clause, 55; structural rules, 109

Fourth Amendment: Burger and, 256–57; common law and, 251–55, 267n81; computer searches and, 260–61, 269n127, 270n140; electronic data and, 245–46, 257–63; formative history of, 246–50, 255–57, 259–61; Frankfurter and, 256; government data mining and, 261–63; immediate aim of, 250; *Mapp v. Ohio* and, 180; mischief giving birth to, 246, 257, 263; privacy and, 5, 24, 210, 216–17, 245–63, 285; protection of, 58; third-party doctrine and, 258–59; unreasonable searches and seizures in, 217, 239n42, 245, 250; warrants and, 245–50, 252–61, 263

Framers: judicial power and, 225–26; unwritten Constitution and, 122–23, 126–27

Frank, Barney, 322

Franken, Al, 346n167

Frankfurter, Felix, 152–53, 170, 182, 281; Fourth Amendment and, 256; on interpretation of statutes, 316; *Poe v. Ullman* and, 278

Franklin, Benjamin, 287, 315

Franklin v. Gwinnett County Public Schools, 230

Fransen, James, 331

Freedom-of-choice, in school desegregation, 62–63, 66, 68

Freeman v. Pitts, 86

Free speech, 133n101; active liberty and, 13–14, 16; campaign finance reform and, 11–15; defined, 12; democratic self-government and, 11–17; Holmes and, 294n76; money as, 12–13; of mushroom growers, 14–15; negative, 13, 15–16

Freund, Paul, 169, 181, 183

Fried, Charles, 282

Friendly, Henry: *The Bill of Rights as a Code of Criminal Procedure* by, 176; Black and, 184; Brandeis and, 170, 182–83, 187n47; *Brown v. Board of Education* and, 183; candor of, 178–80; at Cleary, Gottlieb, Friendly & Cox, 171; clerkship of, 170; constitutional law and, 4, 169–85; constraints and, 173–74; Dartmouth Holmes Lecture of, 180–81, 184; depth of, 178–80; dicta and, 139, 143; *The Gap in Lawmaking—Judges Who Can't and Legislators Who Won't* by, 183; Hand and, 169–72, 174, 178–79, 182–83, 185; on Harlan, John Marshall, II, 275; at Harvard Law School, 170, 179; holding and, 139, 143; Holmes and, 170, 172, 175, 184–85; influence of, 169, 184–85; *Is Innocence Irrelevant?* by, 177; practical judgment and, 175–76; precedent and, 174–75; rigor of, 178–80; *Roe v. Wade* and, 183–84; at Root, Clark, Buckner & Ballantine, 170–71; on Second Circuit, 169; *Some Kind of Hearing* by, 177–78; statutes and, 327–28, 343n126; writing by, 169, 171–78, 180–84

FTC. *See* Federal Trade Commission

Fuller, Thomas, 181

GAO. *See* Government Accountability Office

The Gap in Lawmaking—Judges Who Can't and Legislators Who Won't (Friendly), 183

Garcia v. San Antonio Metropolitan Authority, 85

Garment, Leonard, 95nn115–16

General warrants, 248–50, 257, 260, 264n29

George II (king), 247

George III (king), 247–48

Gillibrand, Kirsten, 351n218

Gilmore, Grant, 185

Ginsburg, Martin, 321

Ginsburg, Ruth Bader: *Gonzales v. Carhart* and, 233; *Ledbetter v. Goodyear Tire & Rubber Co.* and, 299, 326; legislative history and, 322–23; *Saucier* rule and, 168n91; school desegregation and, 84; statutes and, 299, 322–23, 326–28

Goesaert v. Cleary, 128

Goldberg, Arthur, 178

Gonzales v. Carhart, 229–30, 233

Gonzales v. Raich, 229–30

Good faith: immunity, dicta and, 156–59, 165n77; in school desegregation, 64, 66–67, 78, 91n54, 95n108, 100n211, 101n214, 104n269

Governance Institute, 297, 328–30, 333n3

Government Accountability Office (GAO), 309

Government data mining, 261–63

Grassley, Charles E., 317, 346n164

The Great Rights, 1–2

Green v. County School Board of New Kent County: principles established by, 64–65, 75, 85; school desegregation and, 58–59, 63–73, 75, 77–79, 83–85, 100n211

Griffin v. County School Board, 63, 68

Griswold v. Connecticut, 2, 277, 288

Guilty plea, 153–55, 164n66, 164n68

Gun-Free School Zones Act, 205n14

Gunther, Gerald, 112, 172

Habeas corpus, 27, 114, 177–78

Halifax, Lord, 248–49

Hamdi v. Rumsfeld, 128

Hand, Learned, 11, 41; *Church of the Holy Trinity v. United States* and, 313; Friendly and, 169–72, 174, 178–79, 182–83, 185; writing by, 172

Harlan, John Marshall, 274

Harlan, John Marshall, II: biography of, 274–77; *Bivens v. Six Unknown Named Agents of the Federal Bureau of Narcotics* and, 217, 219–20, 222, 231–32; Black on, 275; critics of, 287–90; due process and,

273–74, 276–81, 283–84, 288, 292n34; education of, 171, 275; federalism and, 276–77, 292n34; Friendly on, 275; influence of, 280; judicial restraint and, 264–87, 290; originalism and, 273–90; *Poe v. Ullman* and, 273–74, 276–79, 289, 293n51; Posner and, 274, 289–90, 294n76; proceduralism and, 276–77; *Roe v. Wade* and, 277

Harlan, John Maynard, 274–75

Harmless error rule, 3

Harris v. McRae, 128

Hart, Henry M., Jr., 172, 179, 189n81, 314

Harvard Law School, 170, 179

Hastings, Alcee, 351n218

Hatch, Orrin, 317, 324, 332

Haynsworth, Clement, 67–68

Health laws, 15

Hein v. Freedom from Religion Foundation, Inc., 243n129

HEW. *See* Department of Health, Education, and Welfare

Higher-education cases, Michigan, 202

High school civics education, 30

Hill, Alfred, 214

Hills v. Gautreaux, 81–82

Hobbs Act, 39

Holding: defined, 143; dicta distinguished from, 139–44, 153, 159, 161n18, 161n20; Friendly and, 139, 143

Holmes, Oliver Wendell, Jr., 117, 290; Constitution and, 1, 58; free speech and, 294n76; Friendly and, 170, 172, 175, 184–85; Posner and, 294n76

House of Representatives, 304–5

Howe, Mark de Wolfe, 172

Huber, Peter, 327

Human rights, 120–22, 126, 227

Human Rights Law, 227

Humphrey's Executor v. United States, 111

Hunt v. Washington State Apple Advertising Commission, 229–30

Hurst, Willard, 173

Illiberalisms, 276

Immigration and Nationality Act (INA), 329

Immunity: good faith, 156–59, 165n77;

official, 254, 267n82; Privileges or
Immunities Clause and, 55; sovereign,
212–14
Impeachment, 189n68
Impoundment, 112
INA. *See* Immigration and Nationality Act
Incorporation doctrine, 124
Individual rights: in Article I, 114, 215; in
Article III, 114; in Article IV, 114; in Bill
of Rights, 114–15, 276; Burger and, 118,
130n37, 199; in Constitution, 114–22; due
process and, 279; in First Amendment,
114–15; on international stage, 120–22;
Madison on, 114; in Nineteenth
Amendment, 115; in Ninth Amendment,
115, 281; Rehnquist and, 118, 130n37, 199;
in Second Amendment, 115, 119; in Tenth
Amendment, 115; in Twenty-Fourth
Amendment, 115; in Twenty-Sixth
Amendment, 115; Warren Court and, 2,
199; White and, 118, 130n37
Information-based workplace, 15
INS v. Chadha, 110–11, 309, 319
International Covenant on Civil and
Political Rights, 120–21
International stage, individual rights on,
120–22
Interposition doctrine, 61, 90n44
Interstate effects, 19–20
Invidious discrimination, 24–25
Irvine, Alexander, 6n4
Is Innocence Irrelevant? (Friendly), 177

Jackson, Robert H., 176–77, 189n68, 256, 275
Jacobs, Dennis, 39
Jacobs v. United States, 215, 239n49
James Madison lectures: appellate federal
judges delivering, 6n4; first, 2, 263; new
phase marked by, 1; volumes of, 1–4
Jefferson, Thomas, 8, 283, 299
J.I. Case Co. v. Borak, 218, 220
Jones, Charles, 299
Jowett, Benjamin, 275
Judges: appellate federal, Madison lectures
delivered by, 6n4; clearly established
rights and, 167n81; in common law tradi-
tion, 173; confirmation process of, 201,

308–9, 317, 346n164, 346n167; as Platonic
Guardians, 183; role of, 142, 201, 208–9,
225, 232, 312; ruling class of, 196; statutes interpreted by, 4, 298–301, 311–24;
Supreme Court Justices, 4, 6n3. *See also
specific judges*
*Judges and Legislators: Toward Institutional
Comity*, 297
Judgment, practical, 175–76
Judicial activism: Burger and, 290; defined,
56–57; divisiveness of, 195–96; legitimacy
and, 86–87; originalism preventing, 274;
perception of, 59; reactions to, 55–56,
87n6; Rehnquist and, 55–56, 195; *Roe v.
Wade as*, 55, 195; school desegregation
and, 55–87; stare decisis and, 56, 58, 86,
88n16, 89n24; by Warren Court, 55–56,
59, 69, 86, 178–79
Judicial Branch Committee, 328
Judicial Conference, 328–30
Judicial modesty: ancient liberty and, 10–11;
campaign finance reform and, 14; dormant Commerce Clause and, 20; judicial
restraint and, 11; privacy and, 23–24
Judicial power, 214, 233–34; defined, 208;
framers and, 225–26; *Reynolds v. Sim*
and, 276
Judicial restraint: defined, 195; Harlan, John
Marshall, II, and, 264–87, 290; Harvard
Law School and, 170; judicial modesty
and, 11; principles, 57–59; special factors
and, 220; unity and, 195–96
Judiciary Act, 38, 174, 188n48, 222, 299
Judiciary Committee, Senate, 307, 317
Justices, Supreme Court: liberal, 6n3; swing,
4. *See also specific justices*

Kagan, Elena, 346n161, 346n167
Kansas City, descgregation in, 78–86,
101n224, 102n228
Kastenmeier, Robert W., 317, 328, 332
Katz v. United States, 252–53, 256, 277
Kaufman, Herbert, 308, 323
Kelo v. City of New London, 119
Kennedy, Anthony: *Alden v. Maine* and, 114;
legislative history and, 322; school deseg-
regation and, 73; as swing Justice, 4

Kennedy, John F., 200
Kerr, Orin, 270n139
Keyes v. School District Number 1, 71–72, 85
Kluger, Richard, 60
Korematsu v. United States, 128
Kozinski, Alex, 245

Labor Committee, Senate, 313
Law: agriculture, 15; antidiscrimination, 15; better, 28; communications, 15; consumer protection, 15; courts making, 145–48, 156; criminal, 38–41, 47, 177; democracy's relationship to, 287; direct constitutional cases at, 214–16, 238n41; enforcement, professional, 253–54; foreign, 285–86; health, 15; local, 41; private, 38, 41–44, 47; purposes of, 204; rule of, 55–87; securities, 15; statutorification of, 300; tort, 41; unconstitutional, 229–31, 233–34; unifying role of, 5, 193–204; warranty, 15. *See also* Constitutional law; Criminal law; Statutes; *specific laws*
Lawmaking: Brandeis on, 146; dicta and, 145–48, 156; process, Congress and, 301–7, 326–32
Lawrence v. Texas, 85, 121
Leahy, Patrick, 317
Ledbetter v. Goodyear Tire & Rubber Co., 299, 326
Ledewitz, Bruce, 286–87, 289
Lee, Mike, 351n218
The Legal Process (Hart and Sacks), 179, 189n81
Legislative history: authoritative, 316, 332; Congress and, 310–11, 313, 316; Ginsburg, Ruth Bader, and, 322–23; Kennedy, Anthony, and, 322; reliability of, 332; Roberts and, 317, 324; Scalia and, 317–20, 322, 349n197; statutes and, 310–11, 313, 316–19, 321–24, 332, 346n167; Stevens on, 316
Legislative veto, 110–12, 309
Letters, traditional, 259
Leval, Pierre, 41–42
Lewis, Anthony, 275, 290
Liberalism: of Black, 6n3, 276–77, 294n76; of Brandeis, 294n76; of Justices, 6n3; of

Warren Court, 6n3, 183, 276
Liberty: civil, 1–2, 45; clauses, 116, 118–19; Constant and, 5, 7; in Fifth Amendment, 116; in Fourteenth Amendment, 116, 132n81, 276; positive, 16, 31n9; principles of, 7. *See also* Active liberty; Ancient liberty; Modern liberty
Lily Ledbetter Fair Pay Act of 2009, 299, 326
Linguistic approach, 26
Literalism: consequential approach and, 29–30; Constitution and, 10, 29–30, 107, 113, 119, 125–27; problems with, 107, 125–27; subjectivity of, 29–30
Little Rock, school desegregation in, 62, 90n51, 91n54
Local law, 41
Lochner v. New York, 9, 16, 116–17, 195, 274
Longshoremen's and Harbor Worker's Compensation Act, 111
Loving v. Virginia, 121, 132n81
Lower federal courts, 45

Madison, James: Bill of Rights and, 225, 250; federal courts and, 37–38, 48, 208, 235; *Federalist Papers* and, 114, 273, 302, 311–12, 320; on individual rights, 114; statutes and, 297, 299, 301–2, 311–12, 320, 333; words chosen by, 122
Madison lectures. *See* James Madison lectures
Magna Carta, 283, 290
Maher v. Roe, 128
Manning, John, 320, 348n184
Mansfield, Lord, 249, 325
Mapp v. Ohio, 180
Marbury, William, 299
Marbury v. Madison, 55, 62, 91n55, 217, 299
Marshall, John: Commerce Clause and, 125–26; on courts' role, 55; *Marbury v. Madison* and, 55, 299; principles of constitutional interpretation by, 281; school desegregation and, 78, 84, 97n142, 100n196, 101n215; *Wright v. City of Emporia* and, 97n142
Marshall, Thurgood, 118
McDonnell Douglas Corp. v. Green, 149–50, 163n38

McGill, Ralph, 63
McIlwain, Charles, 169
McKesson Corp. v. Division of Alcoholic Beverages & Tobacco, 229
McReynolds, James Clark, 117
Melnick, R. Shep, 348n187
Meltzer, Daniel, 226, 231
Menand, Louis, 185
Metropolitan Washington Airports Authority v. Citizens for the Abatement of Aircraft Noise, 112
Meyer v. Nebraska, 117–18, 121, 132n81
Michigan higher-education cases, 202
Mid-century cases, of affirmative constitutional adjudication, 209–11
Milliken II, 82, 104n261, 104n267
Milliken v. Bradley, 73, 79–81, 104n262
Miranda v. Arizona, 176
Missouri v. Holland, 121–22
Missouri v. Jenkins: fundamental problem with, 59, 87; lack of explanation in, 84–87; school desegregation and, 56, 59–60, 72–73, 78–87, 104n267
Mistretta v. United States, 111
Mitchell, John, 68–69, 93n88
Modern cases, of affirmative constitutional adjudication, 216–30
Modern liberty: ancient liberty and, 5–6, 9; Constant and, 5, 7, 9, 11, 13, 18; defined, 7
Money, free speech and, 12–13
The Monitor, 249
Moore, Inez, 118
Moore v. City of East Cleveland, 118, 121
Morris, Gouverneur, 303
Moynihan, Daniel Patrick, 302, 321–22, 349n194
Murphy, Frank, 6n3
Mushroom growers, 14–15
Myers v. Loudoun County Public Schools, 140–41, 160n14

Nationalism, in Constitution, 197–99
National unity. *See* Unity
Negative freedom, 13, 15–19
Neutrality, unity and, 201–3
New Deal Court, 9
Newman, Jon O., 40–42

New York: Court of Appeals, 43–44, 46; tort law, 41
Nineteenth Amendment: democratic self-government and, 9; individual rights in, 115
Ninth Amendment, 115, 281
Ninth Circuit, 45, 245, 260–61
Nixon, Richard, 87n6, 97n132; school desegregation and, 55, 65–69, 87, 93n101, 94n105, 95nn115–16, 96n117, 96n122; Southern Strategy of, 65, 93n88
Non-dispositive determinations, 152
The North Briton Cases, 248–49, 251, 254, 257
Northwest Airlines v. Transport Workers Union, 224

Oakes, James L., 327
Oberdorfer, Louis, 59
Obiter dictum. *See* Dicta
Objectivity, safeguards of, 29–30
O'Connor, Sandra Day, 29, 322; death penalty and, 124; federalism and, 17; school desegregation and, 73; as swing Justice, 4
Office of Law Revision Counsel, 327
Offices of Legislative Counsel, 306–7, 330, 354n249
Official immunity, 254, 267n82
Oklahoma, desegregation in, 73–78, 83–85
Olmstead v. United States, 246, 255–56, 285
Olson, Mancur, 320
Omnibus bills, 305, 314
111th Congress, 304–5
Online storage, 258–59
Open-ended statutes, 315–16
Originalism: approach of, 4, 107–8, 125–27; Bork's, 289; Harlan, John Marshall, II, and, 273–90; judicial activism prevented by, 274; Posner and, 274, 289–90
Osborn, Ralph, 212
Osborn v. Bank of the United States, 212
Otis, James, 247–50, 255, 257, 263

Palko v. Connecticut, 118
Panetta, Leon, 93n94
Partial-birth abortions, 39, 229
Partisanship, 201
Peace officers, 253–54, 267n79

Pericles, 31
Phillips, Kevin, 93n88
Pierce v. Society of Sisters, 117–18
Plain view exception, 261, 270n139
Planned Parenthood v. Casey, 128
Platonic Guardians, 183
Pledge of Allegiance, 140–41, 160n14
Plessy v. Ferguson, 60–61, 85, 128, 274
Poe v. Ullman: due process and, 278–79;
    Harlan, John Marshall, II, and, 273–74,
    276–79, 289, 293n51
Poker, 143
Polarization: of Congress, 304; partisanship
    and, 201; of Supreme Court, 1, 4; of U.S.,
    1, 4, 193–95, 201
Positive discrimination, 24–25
Positive liberty, 16, 31n9
Posner, Richard: Harlan, John Marshall, II,
    and, 274, 289–90, 294n76; Holmes and,
    294n76; originalism and, 274, 289–90
Pound, Roscoe, 170, 328
Powell, Lewis, 69–70, 118, 130n37, 181;
    Cannon v. University of Chicago and, 218,
    225–26; *Roe v. Wade* and, 277
Powell, Thomas Reed, 170, 179
Practical judgment, 175–76
Pratt, Charles, 249
Pratt, John, 66
Precedent, Friendly and, 174–75
President: 2000 election of, 3, 56, 193; war
    powers of, 112–13, 125
Price, David, 303
Prima facie case, 150, 162n33
Privacy: complexity of, 21–23; defined, 21;
    democratic self-government and, 21–24;
    Electronic Communications Privacy
    Act and, 259; First Amendment and,
    23; Fourth Amendment and, 5, 24, 210,
    216–17, 245–63, 285; judicial modesty
    and, 23–24; liberty clauses protecting,
    118–19; September 11 and, 21; sexual, 2,
    118; technological advances influencing,
    22; tradition of, 285
Private law, 38, 41–44, 47
Privileges or Immunities Clause, 55
Proceduralism, 276–77
Process, unity and, 203–4

Property rights, 9
Public choice theory, 319–21
Publius, 333
Pupil assignment plans, 202
Pure-speech/mixed-speech distinction, 15
Purposivism, 283–84, 301, 311–15

Quinn v. Robinson, 140, 160n5, 160n7

Race, neutrality toward, 201–3
Randolph, A. Raymond, 183
Rasul v. Bush, 128
Reagan, Ronald, 55, 72, 87n6
Realism, in constitutional law, 170
Reasonable contracting party, 26
Reasonable doubt, 3
Reasonableness balancing test, 251, 266n59
Rehabilitation Act of 1973, 321
Rehnquist, William: appointment of, 55–56;
    Carlson v. Greene and, 223; Commerce
    Clause and, 205n14; *Correctional Services
    Corp. v. Malesko* and, 221; death penalty
    and, 124; individual rights and, 118, 130n37,
    199; judicial activism and, 55–56, 195; *Roe v.
    Wade* and, 277; school desegregation and,
    70–73, 85–86; statutory drafting and, 328
Religion, First Amendment and, 121
A Republic of Statutes (Eskridge and
    Ferejohn), 300
retrospective relief, aversion to, 230–34
Revision, of statutes, 326–32
Reynolds v. Sim, 276
Richardson, Elliott, 95n116
Rights: clearly established, 167n81; constitu-
    tional law and, 199; evolution of, 29; hu-
    man, 120–22, 126, 227; property, 9; trial,
    153–55, 164n66, 164n68; voting, 24–25,
    215. *See also* Individual rights
Rigor, 178–80
Roberts, John G., Jr., 317, 324
Roe v. Wade: Black and, 277; current re-
    gime compared with, 128; Fried and,
    282; Friendly and, 183–84; Harlan, John
    Marshall, II, and, 277; as judicial activ-
    ism, 55, 195; Powell, Lewis, and, 277;
    Rehnquist and, 277; sexual privacy and,
    2, 118

Roosevelt, Eleanor, 120
Roosevelt, Franklin, 9, 128
Root, Clark, Buckner & Ballantine, 170–71
Roper v. Simmons, 124
Ross, Stephen, 332
Rutledge, Wiley, 6n3

Sacks, Albert M., 179, 189n81, 314
Same-sex marriage amendments, 197, 200
Saucier rule, 156, 158, 167n84, 168n85, 168n91
Saxe, Brett, 330
Scalia, Antonin: Arizona v. Gant and, 256–
57; Church of the Holy Trinity v. United
States and, 313; Correctional Services
Corp. v. Malesko and, 221, 223; death
penalty and, 124; historical methodology of, 250–55; legislative history and,
317–20, 322, 349n197; reasonableness
balancing test of, 251, 266n59; Saucier
rule and, 168n91; school desegregation
and, 73, 86; statutes and, 317–20, 322,
347n173, 349n197; Verizon Maryland Inc.
v. Public Service Commission of Maryland
and, 228
Schiavo, Theresa Marie, 132n82
School desegregation: Alexander v. Holmes
County Board of Education and, 63,
66; Board of Education v. Dowell and,
56, 58–60, 72–78, 81, 83–87, 104n267;
Brown v. Board of Education and, 5,
56, 60–66, 68–74, 83–85, 91nn55–56,
97n142, 231, 300; Burger and, 67, 69–70,
83, 97n132; busing in, 59, 64–70, 74,
77, 85, 91n64, 94n105, 99n184; Dayton
Board of Education v. Brinkman and, 80;
effectiveness of, 105n286; freedom-of-
choice in, 62–63, 66, 68; Ginsburg, Ruth
Bader, and, 84; good faith in, 64, 66–67,
78, 91n54, 95n108, 100n211, 101n214,
104n269; Green v. County School Board
of New Kent County and, 58–59, 63–73,
75, 77–79, 83–85, 100n211; Griffin v.
County School Board and, 63, 68; judicial methodology and, 55–87; in Kansas
City, 78–86, 101n224, 102n228; Kennedy,
Anthony, and, 73; Keyes v. School District
Number 1 and, 71–72, 85; in Little Rock,

62, 90n51, 91n54; Marshall, John, and, 78,
84, 97n142, 100n196, 101n215; Milliken
II and, 82, 104n261, 104n267; Milliken
v. Bradley and, 73, 79–81, 104n262;
Missouri v. Jenkins and, 56, 59–60, 72–73,
78–87, 104n267; Nixon and, 55, 65–69,
87, 93n101, 94n105, 95nn115–16, 96n117,
96n122; O'Connor and, 73; in Oklahoma,
73–78, 83–85; path of, 5; Rehnquist and,
70–73, 85–86; resistance to, 55, 61–62,
65–69, 90n51; rule of law and, 55–87;
Scalia and, 73, 86; Swann v. Charlotte-
Mecklenburg Board of Education and,
58–59, 63–65, 67, 69–73, 75, 77–79, 83–85,
104n261; Tenth Circuit and, 75–76,
99n192, 100n203; Thomas and, 73; United
States v. Scotland Neck City Board of
Education and, 63, 92n67; Wright v. City
of Emporia and, 70–71, 83, 97n142
Schwartz, Bernard, 273, 278–82, 288
Schweiker v. Chilicky, 220
Search and seizure: British practices of, 246,
250; computer searches, 260–61, 269n127,
270n140; Fourth Amendment and, 217,
239n42, 245, 250; unreasonable, 217,
239n42, 245, 250–56, 259; wiretapping
and, 252–53, 255–56
Second Amendment, 115, 119, 197
Second Circuit, 40–41, 46, 145, 169, 275, 316
Securities, 15, 41, 218
Securities Exchange Act, 218
Segregation. See School desegregation
Self-government. See Democratic self-
government
Senate, 305–6, 308, 313; Judiciary
Committee, 307, 317; Labor Committee,
313
Seneca, 151
Sentencing Commission, U.S., 111
Separation of powers: affirmative constitu-
tional adjudication and, 222–27; agencies
straining, 110–12; Article I and, 109, 113,
198, 324; Article III and, 109, 145, 208,
214, 222, 225–26, 233
September 11: data mining and, 262; federal-
ism and, 19; privacy and, 21
Sessions, Jeff, 330

Seventeenth Amendment, 109

Seventh Amendment, 251, 266n69

Seventh Circuit, 330

Sex Offender Registration and Notification Act, 329, 346n161

Sexual privacy, 2, 118

Shapiro v. Thompson, 121

Shaw v. Delta Air Lines, 227–28, 230

Shelley v. Kraemer, 183

Shepsle, Kenneth, 314

Sherman Act, 173

Simple Justice (Kluger), 60

Single-house legislative veto, 110–12

Sixteenth Amendment, 109

Sixth Amendment, 154

Sixth Circuit, 259

Skinner v. Oklahoma, 132n81

Social Security Act, 220

Socrates, 10

Soft money, 12

Some Kind of Hearing (Friendly), 177–78

Sony Corp. of America v. Universal City Studios, Inc., 150–51

Sotomayor, Sonia, 346n161

Souter, David, 315

South-Central Timber Development, Inc. v. Wunnicke, 229

Southern Manifesto, 61

Southern Strategy, 65, 93n88

Sovereign immunity, 212–14

Special factors, judicial restraint and, 220

Specter, Arlen, 317

Speech: kinds of, 15; opportunities, 13. See also Free speech

Speedy Trial Act, 317

Spending power, of Congress, 198

Stare decisis: defined, 144; dicta and, 142, 144; judicial activism and, 56, 58, 86, 88n16, 89n24

State action: in balance of federal and state courts, 38, 44–47; doctrine, 180

State courts, 4. See also Balance, of federal and state courts

State legislatures, 17, 19

State statutes, 300, 336n48

Statutes: agencies interpreting, 307–11; Brown v. Board of Education and, 300;

Church of the Holy Trinity v. United States and, 312–13; civil, 326; Congress and, 298–333; construction of, 298–99, 342n125; courts and, 298–333; drafting of, 25–28, 326–32; Federalist Papers and, 302, 311–12, 320, 324, 333; Friendly and, 327–28, 343n126; Ginsburg, Ruth Bader, and, 299, 322–23, 326–28; implementation of, 307–11; judicial interpretation of, 4, 298–301, 311–24; lawmaking process and, 301–7, 326–32; legislative history of, 310–11, 313, 316–19, 321–24, 332, 346n167; Madison and, 297, 299, 301–2, 311–12, 320, 333; open-ended, 315–16; promoting understanding of, 325–33; purposivism and, 301, 311–15; revision of, 326–32; Scalia and, 317–20, 322, 347n173, 349n197; state, 300, 336n48; Stevens and, 224, 316, 322, 328; textualism and, 311, 315, 318–23

Statutorification, of law, 300

Statutory decisions, Congress reversing, 299

Stevens, John Paul, 19, 118, 193; Arizona v. Gant and, 256; on legislative history, 316; statutes and, 224, 316, 322, 328

Stewart, Potter, 57, 70, 118, 256; Poe v. Ullman and, 278; Wright v. City of Emporia and, 97n142

Stewart, Richard, 323

Stone, Harlan, 1

Story, Joseph, 252, 266n64

Strauss, Peter, 308

Structural rules, 109–14

Subjectivity, 29–30

Sunshine Anthracite Coal Co. v. Adkins, 111

Supremacy Clause, 199, 227–28, 231

Supreme Court: agencies and, 310; aversion to retrospective relief and, 230–34; Case Selections Act, 131n72; cases taken by, 47, 131n72; certiorari jurisdiction, 38, 44, 102n234; constitutional objectives emphasized by, 9; dicta, 155–56, 160n14, 163n38; dormant Commerce Clause and, 228–29; errors by, 124–25, 190n96; polarized, 1, 4; state action doctrine of, 180; statutory decisions, Congress reversing, 299; suits against federal officers, unconstitutional laws and, 229–30; Supremacy

Clause and, 199, 227–28, 231; third-party
doctrine of, 258–59; turnover, 128; unaccountability of, 58; unnecessary constitutional rulings and, 157–58. *See also*
Justices, Supreme Court; *specific cases*
Sutherland, George, 117
*Swann v. Charlotte-Mecklenburg Board of
Education*: internal deliberations over,
69; principles established by, 64–65, 75,
85; school desegregation and, 58–59, 63–
65, 67, 69–73, 75, 77–79, 83–85, 104n261
Swift v. Tyson, 174, 181
Swing Justices, 4

Taft, William Howard, 178, 253
Tapia v. United States, 346n161
T.B. Harms Co. v. Eliscu, 175
Telecommunications Act, 228
Tenth Amendment, 82, 113, 115
Tenth Circuit: computer searches and, 261,
270n140; school desegregation and,
75–76, 99n192, 100n203
Texas Constitution, 123, 127, 136n145
Textualism, 311, 315, 318–23
Thayer, James Bradley, 170, 179, 182–83
Thermal imaging, 23–24
Third Circuit, 329–30
Third-party doctrine, 258–59
Thirteenth Amendment, 60
Thomas, Clarence: death penalty and, 124;
*Federal Maritime Commission v. South
Carolina State Ports Authority* and, 114;
school desegregation and, 73; as textual-
ist, 322
Thucydides, 31
Thurmond, Strom, 61, 65, 67
TIA. *See* Total Information Awareness
Title IX, 300, 335n37
Title VI, 65
Title VII, 149–50, 299
Tort law, 41
Total Information Awareness (TIA), 262
Tower, John, 65, 67
Toxic chemical regulation, 18–20
Transfer procedures, convoluted, 90n47
Traynor, Roger, 184
Trent, Stanley, 62–63

Trial rights, 153–55, 164n66, 164n68
Trop v. Dulles, 123
Tucker Act, 239n49
Twelfth Amendment, 109–10
Twentieth Amendment, 109
Twenty-Fifth Amendment, 109
Twenty-Fourth Amendment, 9, 115
Twenty-Second Amendment, 109
Twenty-Seventh Amendment, 109
Twenty-Sixth Amendment: democratic
self-government and, 9; individual rights
in, 115
2000 presidential election, 3, 56, 193

Unconstitutional laws, 229–31, 233–34
United Nations, 120, 126
United States (U.S.): Administrative
Conference of, 332, 356n279;
Administrative Office of the U.S.
Courts in, 325, 354n250; Committee
on the Judicial Branch of the Judicial
Conference of, 297; Declarations and
Understandings of, 121; Department of
Health, Education, and Welfare, 65–66,
93n94; human rights and, 120–22, 126,
227; law unifying, 5, 193–204; polarized,
1, 4, 193–95, 201; population, 108, 129n1;
Sentencing Commission, 111. *See also*
Congress; Constitution, U.S.; Supreme
Court
United States v. Booker, 130n36
United States v. Lopez, 39, 125
United States v. Miller, 258
United States v. Morrison, 121, 125
United States v. Printz, 19
United States v. Rubin, 139
*United States v. Scotland Neck City Board of
Education*, 63, 92n67
United States v. Virginia, 121
Unity: community and, 199–200;
Constitution and, 196–200; judicial re-
straint and, 195–96; law and, 5, 193–204;
nationalism and, 197–99; need for, 204;
neutrality and, 201–3; partisanship and,
201; polarization and, 1, 4, 193–95, 201;
process and, 203–4
Universal Declaration of Human Rights, 120

The Unpredictable Constitution, 3
Unwritten Constitution, 108, 112, 122–24, 126–27
U.S. *See* United States

Verizon Maryland Inc. v. Public Service Commission of Maryland, 228, 230
Verkuil, Paul, 356n279
Violence Against Women Act, 205n14
Vives v. City of New York, 166n80
Voting rights: damages cases and, 215; democratic self-government and, 24–25

Waldron, Jeremy, 324
Wallace, George, 61, 65
War powers, 112–13, 125
Warrants: computer searches and, 260–61, 269n127, 270n140; felony in fact and, 267n81; in Fourth Amendment, 245–50, 252–61, 263; general, 248–50, 257, 260, 264n29
Warranty laws, 15
Warren, Charles, 174
Warren, Earl, 2, 6n3, 55, 278
Warren Court: habeas corpus and, 177; individual rights and, 2, 199; judicial activism by, 55–56, 59, 69, 86, 178–79;

liberalism of, 6n3, 183, 276; *Reynolds v. Sim* and, 276
Warshak v. United States, 258–59
Wechsler, Herbert, 172
Weems v. United States, 123, 285, 295n105
Whalen v. Roe, 121
Wheeler, Russell, 329–30
White, Byron, 73, 97n142; individual rights and, 118, 130n37; on structural doctrines, 110–11
White flight, 79, 81, 101n224, 102n228
White v. Greenhow, 215
Whittaker, Charles E., 278
Wiley v. Sinkler, 215
Wilkes, John, 248–49
Williston, Samuel, 170
Wilson, James Q., 321
Wilson, Woodrow, 303
Wiretapping, 252–53, 255–56
Wisconsin v. Yoder, 121
Witnesses, 162n26
Wright v. City of Emporia, 70–71, 83, 97n142
The Writs of Assistance Case, 247–50, 255, 257
Wyoming v. Houghton, 251

Young, Edward, 213